ESSAYS IN THE PHILOSOPHY OF RELIGION

Essays in the Philosophy of Religion

PHILIP L. QUINN

Edited by
CHRISTIAN B. MILLER

CLARENDON PRESS · OXFORD

OXFORD

UNIVERSITY PRESS

Great Clarendon Street, Oxford OX2 6DP

Oxford University Press is a department of the University of Oxford.
It furthers the University's objective of excellence in research, scholarship,
and education by publishing worldwide in

Oxford New York

Auckland Cape Town Dar es Salaam Hong Kong Karachi
Kuala Lumpur Madrid Melbourne Mexico City Nairobi
New Delhi Shanghai Taipei Toronto

With offices in

Argentina Austria Brazil Chile Czech Republic France Greece
Guatemala Hungary Italy Japan Poland Portugal Singapore
South Korea Switzerland Thailand Turkey Ukraine Vietnam

Oxford is a registered trade mark of Oxford University Press
in the UK and in certain other countries

Published in the United States
by Oxford University Press Inc., New York

British Library Cataloguing in Publication Data

Data available

Library of Congress Cataloging in Publication Data

Data available

Typeset by Laserwords Private Limited, Chennai, India
Printed in Great Britain
on acid-free paper by
Biddles Ltd, King's Lynn, Norfolk

ISBN 0–19–929703–7 978–0–19–929703–0
ISBN 0–19–929704–5 (Pbk.) 978–0–19–929704–7 (Pbk.)

1 3 5 7 9 10 8 6 4 2

Dedicated to Charles and Joyous Miller

Foreword

It is hard to sketch a complicated person in a few lines, to make a picture of him in words; but I want to try here, to honor Phil Quinn by remembering him.

The first year he came to my house for Thanksgiving dinner was when I was at Notre Dame as a Fellow in the Center for Philosophy of Religion. I enticed him to come by telling him that the turkey would be dry, the mashed potatoes would be lumpy, and the children would be all over the place. You had to know how perverse he was to know why that was the right way to ask him to dinner. Once when we were all together at a restaurant at some conference, he ordered trout; and I made the mistake of asking prissily whether he was going to have the head and tail removed in the kitchen. He not only had the fish brought to the table entirely intact, but he began eating it by sticking his fork in its head. He was a formidable opponent when he wanted to be, and I am sure that there are administrators of more than one organization who remember his powerful principled stands with some vividness and considerable rue.

He gave a lot of his life to politics and administration. He was Ombudsman for the APA for some years, and he held various other administrative positions in the APA as well. He was Chairman of the National Board during a difficult time for the National Office. And he was heavily involved in politics at Notre Dame, where he held the John A. O'Brien Chair for many years until the time of his death in the Fall of 2004. He cared greatly about democracy in university governance structure and elsewhere, and he was willing to spend time and effort fighting for it. He also minded intensely when he thought he saw injustice. He withdrew from consideration for the Chairmanship of the Notre Dame Philosophy Department because he could not get the Notre Dame administration to listen to his concerns about gay issues at Notre Dame. And he was vitriolic about the Presidential election before his death. When his own illness should have been the thing uppermost on his mind, he was furious and despondent about the re-election of the President. As the time of the election drew near, he said to me, "Nothing could be worse than the re-election of George Bush!" "Nonsense," I said to him. "Didn't Caligula get his horse elected to political office?" "No, that wouldn't be worse," he rejoined obstinately, enjoying his own contrariness, "a horse would at least bring a certain innocence to the office."

His principled obstinacy also made him enviably courageous and steadfast. It was easy to see these virtues in him when it came to religion. He was and he wanted to be not just a Christian but a Catholic. In practice, it was hard for him to be a Catholic because there were so many things he found hard to stand about the Church. He was allergic to anything which struck him as hypocritical, as pretending to a love of truth or a love of goodness which were in fact rejected. Whatever his differences with the Church, however, he identified himself as a Catholic, and he was stalwart in defense of central Christian doctrines. I saw him defend the doctrine of the atonement, for example, in hostile environments where a lesser person would have been afraid and would have found something safe and mealy-mouthed to say. It was just typical of him that he went to mass daily in the last weeks of his life and then complained because the priest at those masses never gave a homily—as if there was any chance that that priest might have given a homily Phil would have liked.

The boyishness in him was utterly disarming just because he was in other ways so tough. He had a boyish taste for mischief. Once I took a picture of him sitting at my breakfast table next to the pretty red-headed wife of a couple who were also staying at my house for Thanksgiving. He was in an old tweed jacket with a cigarette in his hand, and she was in her nightgown with a cup of coffee and the newspaper. He put that picture up on the bulletin board next to his office door at Notre Dame and let people make of it what they would. And he could be irresistibly endearing in a boyish way. He had an educated palate for absurdity, maybe because he was an unathletic intellectual raised in Texas; and when he laughed, which was often, the laughter was infectious. One of the last pictures of him was taken by Lisette Bolduc, who was among those in the Notre Dame community who cared unstintingly for him in his last weeks. The picture shows him ravaged by chemo and filled with laughter all the same. The Notre Dame community never looked more admirable to me than they did in their care for him while he was sick. He found as much laughter and peace as he did in his dying weeks because the Notre Dame community surrounded him with love.

I realize that I have so far said nothing about his philosophical gifts or accomplishments and that there is something perverse about proceeding in this way in this context. I do it in honor of him. He would have enjoyed this idiosyncratic contravening of customary expectations. It is in any event true that, even after death, he needs no introduction as far as philosophy is concerned. He received many honors in his lifetime, including his election to the Presidency of the Central Division of the APA, and his work is widely known and used in the profession. He himself was a much prized, much feared regular at philosophy conferences across the nation. He had such a piercingly clear mind. When you saw his hand up in the audience after you gave a paper, you knew you were going to have to be on your mettle. He wasn't always right, but he was always smart, and he was meticulous when it came to detail. He was an analytic philosopher's analytic philosopher, with a great care for precision and accuracy. What is surprising is that he managed to combine those lapidary skills with great sensitivity and insightfulness for those things in the world not susceptible of precision. His work on philosophy of religion, philosophy of science, ethics, and politics is superb; it has been very influential, and it will continue to be. But he also did wonderful work in the area of philosophy and literature. His philosophical work on the rich, messy, nuances of literary texts is as moving and deep as it is excellent. He was one of the best in our profession, and he is sadly missed.

And so this volume is designed to remember and honor a superb philosopher to whom the profession owes a great debt, for his administrative work at the highest levels of our organization, for his political fights on behalf of all of us, for his exemplary philosophical work, and above all for his inestimable enriching of our lives by the person he was.

Eleonore Stump
Robert J. Henle Professor of Philosophy, St Louis University

Acknowledgements

"Religious Obedience and Moral Autonomy," *Religious Studies*, 11 (1975), 265–81. Reprinted with permission of Peter Byrne and Cambridge University Press.

"Divine Command Ethics: A Causal Theory," in J. M. Idziak (ed.), *Divine Command Morality: Historical and Contemporary Readings* (Edwin Mellen Press, 1980), 305–25. Reprinted with permission of Edwin Mellen Press.

"The Primacy of God's Will in Christian Ethics," in J. E. Tomberlin (ed.), *Philosophical Perspectives*, vi. *Ethics* (Ridgeview Publishing Company, 1992), 493–513. Reprinted with permission of Ridgeview Publishing Company.

"Moral Obligation, Religious Demand, and Practical Conflict," in Robert Audi and William Wainwright (eds.), *Rationality, Religious Belief, and Moral Commitment* (Ithaca: Cornell University Press, 1986), 195–212. Reprinted with permission of Robert Audi and William Wainwright.

"Tragic Dilemmas, Suffering Love, and Christian Life," *Journal of Religious Ethics*, 17 (1989), 151–84. Reprinted with permission of Blackwell Publishers.

"In Search of the Foundations of Theism," *Faith and Philosophy*, 2 (1985), 469–86. Reprinted with permission of Michael Peterson and *Faith and Philosophy*.

"The Foundations of Theism Again: A Rejoinder to Plantinga," in L. Zagzebski (ed.), *Rational Faith* (Notre Dame: University of Notre Dame Press, 1993), 14–47. Reprinted with permission of the University of Notre Dame Press.

"Political Liberalisms and Their Exclusions of the Religious," *Proceedings and Addresses of the American Philosophical Association*, 69/2 (1995), 35–56. Reprinted with permission of the American Philosophical Association.

"Religious Citizens within the Limits of Public Reason," *Modern Schoolman* (2001), 105–24. Reprinted with permission of William Charron and *Modern Schoolman*.

" 'In Adam's Fall, We Sinned All'," *Philosophical Topics*, 16/2 (1988), 89–118. Reprinted with permission of Edward Minar and *Philosophical Topics*.

"Christian Atonement and Kantian Justification," *Faith and Philosophy*, 3 (1986), 440–62. Reprinted with permission of Michael Peterson and *Faith and Philosophy*.

"Kantian Philosophical Ecclesiology," *Faith and Philosophy* (2000), 512–34. Reprinted with permission of Michael Peterson and *Faith and Philosophy*.

"Toward Thinner Theologies: Hick and Alston on Religious Diversity," *International Journal for Philosophy of Religion*, 38 (1995), 145–64. Reprinted with permission of Springer.

"On Religious Diversity & Tolerance," *Daedalus* (2005), 136–139. Reprinted with permission of MIT Press.

Contents

RELIGIOUS DIVERSITY

Introduction

Christian B. Miller

The publication of these selected papers by Philip L. Quinn is intended to honor one of the leading philosophers of religion in the twentieth century. Philip Quinn died on November 15, 2004 at the age of 64, leaving behind an immensely impressive legacy of publication, service, and intellectual achievement.

My goal in this brief introduction is twofold: first, to sketch briefly some of the life of this remarkable man; and second, to provide an overview of the papers that make up this collection. The papers themselves have been organized around the following central topics in Quinn's research: Religious Ethics, Religion and Tragic Dilemmas, Religious Epistemology, Religion and Political Liberalism, Christian Philosophy, and Religious Diversity.

A BRIEF SKETCH OF QUINN'S LIFE

Many who know Quinn's work may be surprised to learn that his philosophy training was actually in the philosophy of science. He graduated with a BA in philosophy from Georgetown University in 1962, and then studied at the University of Delaware, where he earned an MS in physics. The combination of his philosophy and science backgrounds led him to enroll at the University of Pittsburgh, where he earned an MA and then a Ph.D. in philosophy in 1969.

The first half of Quinn's professional career was spent at Brown University, where he rose from assistant professor to the William Herbert Perry Faunce Professorship in the span of only thirteen years. Perhaps surprisingly again, all of his early publications were in the philosophy of science, and ranged from such topics as continuous spatial manifolds to how best to interpret Duhem's work. It wasn't until 1975 that his first paper in the philosophy of religion appeared, an essay on religious obedience that is reprinted in this collection (Chapter 1). In 1985, Quinn's career took a major turn as he moved from Brown to the University of Notre Dame, where he would remain for the rest of his life. At Notre Dame he became the John A. O'Brien Professor of Philosophy, a title he would hold for the next nineteen years.

During his thirty-five years of active research, Quinn published over 200 papers and reviews in many areas of philosophy, including metaphysics, epistemology, literature, aesthetics, history, and ethics, as well as the philosophy of religion and science. He published *Divine Commands and Moral Requirements* with Oxford University Press in 1978, and also edited *A Companion to the Philosophy of Religion* (with Charles Taliaferro) and *The Philosophical Challenges of Religious Diversity* (with Kevin Meeker). As a side pursuit, Quinn authored 193 review papers for the journal *Mathematical Reviews*, which required him to be well versed in the latest technical work in central areas of physics and mathematics.

Quinn was also renowned for his service to his home universities, to the American Philosophical Association, and to the discipline of philosophy as a whole. In his nineteen years at Notre Dame, he served on a total of fifty-three separate committees, reviews, or councils. Similarly, his work for the APA is well known; there he served in fifty-five different official capacities, including most notably as president of the Central Division from 1994 to 1995 and as chair of the National-al Board of Officers from 1996 to 1999. And it almost goes without saying that Quinn was extremely dedicated to the profession of philosophy in general. He refereed multiple times for over twenty journals, twenty-six book publishers, and seventeen grant providers. He was on the editorial board of several journals, and was the editor for five years of *Faith and Philosophy*, the leading journal in philosophy of religion.

While I knew him only during his time at Notre Dame, Quinn always struck me as the epitome of a traditional academic. He refused to use e-mail, and indeed avoided computers of any kind. As a result, each of his 200 published papers was first written out in long hand and was finally sent to a typist only after multiple revisions. Quinn had not owned a car for many years and walked to campus every day from a nearby apartment complex. Although I never visited his apartment, it allegedly was filled from floor to ceiling with books.

This last fact would not come as a surprise to anyone who knew him. In many ways Phil Quinn's life was all about books. A shy and somewhat reclusive person, he spent most of his time each day reading. He was greatly helped in this regard by his speed-reading ability, and could easily finish a dense philosophy book or several novels in a single day. His office was filled with his philosophy collection; he even had additional bookshelves installed in the middle of the room to help organize the thousands of volumes he wanted to have around him, which left very little room for seating visitors. And his reading interests extended well beyond philosophy—he was extremely well versed in history, literature, religion, and science. Most intriguing, perhaps, was his love for mysteries; Phil subscribed to all the mystery book clubs, and every night he would read one or two brand new novels.

Despite his knowledge of the medical risks, Quinn was a heavy smoker for much of his life. His smoking finally caught up with him in the summer of 2004, when he was diagnosed with cancer of the esophagus. After a three-month struggle, Phil Quinn passed away in the company of friends and caretakers. He died a year before his planned retirement, when he had hoped to move to a warmer climate and try his hand at writing mystery novels of his own.

OVERVIEW OF THE PAPERS IN THIS COLLECTION

This section provides some background on each of the papers in this collection. In some cases, I supplement the presentation of a position to which Quinn was directly responding. In other cases, I try to note instances where Quinn's own view evolved over time in ways that may not be readily apparent from the papers reprinted here. At no place in what follows, however, do I attempt critically to evaluate Quinn's views or arguments, a task which in my opinion is best left for another occasion.

Religious Ethics

Perhaps Quinn's most significant contribution to philosophy is his attempt to revitalize divine command theory as a legitimate position in meta-ethics and normative theory. Along with Robert Adams, Quinn can be considered one of the two foremost philosophical proponents of divine command theory in the twentieth century. He made important contributions to the theory's formulation, to its justification, and to its defense. Let us take each of these in turn.

Formulating Divine Command Theory. The central idea behind divine command theory is that morality, or at least certain central aspects of morality, depend on God. Given this basic starting point, however, divine command theories can be developed in a number of different ways depending on how the following schema is fleshed out:

> (1) Moral status M stands in dependency relation D to divine act A.[1]

In most of his work, Quinn construes M as deontological moral status, i.e. moral requirement (obligation), moral permission (rightness), and moral prohibition (wrongness). The one exception is his 1978 book, *Divine Commands and Moral Requirements*, where he also attempts to account for moral axiology (goodness, badness, and indifference) in such a framework.[2]

Quinn seems to have changed his mind several times when it came to construing the dependency relation D. In his early work, divine commands and moral requirements were treated as necessarily coextensive. Such a view allows for *being commanded by God* and *being morally required* to be distinct properties, while still mandating that they necessarily co-vary as do other properties

[1] See Quinn, "Divine Command Theory," in H. LaFollette (ed.), *The Blackwell Guide to Ethical Theory* (Oxford: Blackwell, 1999), 53.

[2] Quinn, *Divine Commands and Moral Requirements* (Oxford: Clarendon Press, 1978), 67–73.

such as a triangle's being equilateral and equiangular.[3] But in the paper reprinted here entitled "Divine Command Ethics: A Causal Account" (Chapter 2), Quinn offered a second proposal according to which divine commands are asymmetrically related to moral requirements in virtue of the latter's being causally related to the former. Finally, in his most recent work Quinn argued that the dependence relation should best be construed as one of 'bringing about.'[4]

When it comes to divine act A, Quinn initially held that moral status is related to divine *commands*. However, due in part to recent work by Mark Murphy,[5] Quinn came to adopt a divine *will* theory according to which, at least roughly, it is God's divine will and in particular his intentions that ground the deontological status of actions. The commands themselves, in turn, serve merely as expressions of the divine will.[6]

Supporting Divine Command Theory. When Quinn first started publishing on divine command ethics, he took his main task to be that of responding to extant objections to the view given its almost uniformly perceived implausibility at the time. Eventually, however, he began to address the need for positive arguments in favor of a divine command approach. At first he tried his hand at constructing a logically deductive argument from theistic premises for his preferred divine command theory.[7] Later, though, he switched strategies and attempted to offer a cumulative case argument using a variety of considerations which theists in general, and Christians in particular, would be inclined to accept. A nice example of this more recent approach can be found in the paper, "The Primacy of God's Will in Christian Ethics" (Chapter 3 in this volume). Here Quinn offers three independent arguments from assumptions widely shared by Christians—an argument from divine sovereignty, an argument from the immoralities of the patriarchs, and an argument from the biblical commands to love God and to love our neighbors.[8]

Defending Divine Command Theory. As mentioned already, Quinn viewed much of the challenge involved in revitalizing divine command theory to be responding systematically to the leading objections in print at the time. In his book he carefully addresses ten such objections, and considers four more in the paper "Divine Command Ethics: A Causal Theory."[9] But it is in his first publication on divine

---

[3] This is the proposal in *Divine Commands and Moral Requirements*.

[4] See his "Divine Command Theory," 54–5.

[5] Mark Murphy, "Divine Command, Divine Will, and Moral Obligation," *Faith and Philosophy*, 15 (1998), 3–27.

[6] See e.g. Quinn, "Divine Command Theory," 55.

[7] See his "An Argument for Divine Command Ethics," in Michael Beaty (ed.), *Christian Theism and the Problems of Philosophy* (Notre Dame: University of Notre Dame Press, 1990), 289–302.

[8] Quinn also employs the cumulative case method on behalf of divine command theory in "Divine Command Theory" and in "The Recent Revival of Divine Command Ethics," *Philosophy and Phenomenological Research*, 50 (1990), 345–65.

[9] For additional discussion of objections, see also his "Divine Command Theory" and "The Recent Revival of Divine Command Ethics."

command theory, and indeed his first publication in philosophy of religion in general, that we find Quinn at his best in carrying out this task, as he slowly and carefully tries to undermine an objection offered by James Rachels. The paper, "Religious Obedience and Moral Autonomy," is also reprinted here (Chapter 1), and centers on the following argument by Rachels:

   (i)   If any being is God, he must be a fitting object of worship.
   (ii) No being could possibly be a fitting object of worship, since worship requires the abandonment of one's role as an autonomous moral agent.
   (iii) Therefore, there cannot be any being who is God.[10]

Quinn's paper is significant not only for his critical discussion of this argument, but also because it contains his first published treatment of the story of Abraham and Isaac, a story with which he would spend a great deal of time and effort trying to come to grips in the remainder of his career.

Religion and Tragic Dilemmas

We read in the Old Testament book of Genesis that:

Some time later God tested Abraham. He said to him, "Abraham!"
   "Here I am," he replied.
Then God said, "Take your son, your only son, Isaac, whom you love, and go to the region of Moriah. Sacrifice him there as a burnt offering on one of the mountains I will tell you about."[11]

While God would eventually intervene and command Abraham not to kill his son, it should be clear enough why this story, if accurate, poses a problem for divine command theorists. Robert Adams has formulated the problem nicely as three logically inconsistent propositions:

   (2) If God commands me to do something, it is not morally wrong for me to do it.
   (3) God commands me to kill my son.
   (4) It is morally wrong for me to kill my son.[12]

A number of attempts have been made to resist the inconsistency here by rejecting one of the propositions; Adams himself, in the course of helpfully summarizing and evaluating the most prominent such attempts, argues that we should reject (3).[13] Quinn's own discussion of the case of Abraham and Isaac in his paper "Moral Obligation, Religious Demand, and Practical Conflict" (Chapter 4

---

[10] Quinn, "Religious Obedience and Moral Autonomy," 21, below. The argument is from James Rachels, "God and Human Attitudes," *Religious Studies*, 7 (1971), 325.

[11] Genesis 22: 1–2. New International Version.

[12] Robert Adams, *Finite and Infinite Goods: A Framework for Ethics* (Oxford: Oxford University Press, 1999), 284.

[13] See ibid. ch. 12.

in this volume) is original and intriguing; he accepts the *possibility* of cases like Abraham's, but rejects the actuality of this particular case. Let us separate these two claims.

Quinn argues for the possibility of what he elsewhere calls 'tragic dilemmas,' namely situations with the following structure:

(i) There are requirements for an agent to adopt two alternatives.

(ii) It is wrong to violate either requirement.

(iii) The agent cannot adopt both alternatives together.

(iv) The agent can adopt each alternative separately.[14]

For Quinn tragic dilemmas need not be limited to moral dilemmas—in the abovementioned paper, he argues that moral values do not exhaust the normative realm and can conflict with other realms of value. More specifically, he claims that possible cases such as Abraham's can be understood as tragic dilemmas in which a moral requirement has come into conflict with a religious requirement. How does this help with the original puzzle that was raised by the Genesis story and is represented in (2) through (4)? Quinn wants to argue that since this case would be an instance of a tragic dilemma, the moral requirement not to kill an innocent child would still be in place and would not be overridden by the religious requirement to obey God's commands. Thus it *would* be morally wrong for Abraham to do the thing which God has commanded him to do. Hence proposition (2) is false.

Recall, though, that Quinn is only arguing for possibility claims here. He maintains that it is possible for tragic dilemmas to obtain, and furthermore that it is even possible for a person to be justified in believing that he or she is in such a dilemma.[15] But what about actuality? In other words, have there ever actually been any such situations? Concerning the Genesis story of Abraham, Quinn denies "the scriptural literalist's claim that the narrative of Genesis 22 is in all details sober historical truth. It is a price I am willing to pay."[16] And in general, he voices a deep-seated skepticism that we will ever be justified in thinking ourselves in actual tragic dilemmas in which one of the conflicting requirements is religious.[17] Quinn's struggle to reconcile the apparent tension between his views about the possibility and actuality of tragic dilemmas forms the basis of the final paragraphs of the paper.

The story of Abraham and Isaac is not the only example of a possible tragic dilemma that Quinn discusses in his published work; another notable case is the

---

[14] Quoted from "Agamemnon and Abraham: The Tragic Dilemma of Kierkegaard's Knight of Faith," *Journal of Literature and Theology*, 4/2 (1990), 183. Tragic dilemmas are similar in structure to what Quinn calls 'Kierkegaardian conflicts' in "Moral Obligation, Religious Demand, and Practical Conflict," reprinted here.

[15] See "Agamemnon and Abraham" and esp. "Moral Obligation, Religious Demand, and Practical Conflict."

[16] "Agamemnon and Abraham," 192.

[17] See esp. the final paragraphs of "Moral Obligation, Religious Demand, and Practical Conflict."

Greek story of the gods' command that Agamemnon kill his daughter.[18] And yet a third concerns the main character of Shusaku Endo's famous novel *Silence*. In his paper "Tragic Dilemmas, Suffering Love, and Christian Life" (Chapter 5 in this volume), Quinn provides a moving discussion of the apparent conflict that this character confronts at the very heart of his Christian faith between manifesting love for God and love for his fellow human beings. Those who have not read Endo's book should not be deterred from Quinn's paper as he first provides a long and careful summary of the central plot elements. And this paper is not to be passed over lightly; in my view, it is the deepest, the most stimulating, and indeed the best piece that Quinn ever wrote.

Religious Epistemology

The next two reprinted papers present Quinn's well-known critique of Alvin Plantinga's 'Reformed Epistemology.' Ideally, they should be read together with Plantinga's work in the following order:

Plantinga, "Reason and Belief in God," in A. Plantinga and N. Wolterstorff (eds.), *Faith and Rationality: Reason and Belief in God* (Notre Dame: University of Notre Dame Press, 1983), 16–93.

Quinn, "In Search of the Foundations of Theism" (Chapter 6 in this volume).

Plantinga, "The Foundations of Theism: A Reply," *Faith and Philosophy*, 3/3 (1986), 298–313.

Quinn, "The Foundations of Theism Again: A Rejoinder to Plantinga" (Chapter 7 in this volume).

Plantinga, *Warranted Christian Belief* (Oxford: Oxford University Press, 2000), esp. pp. 358, 366–7, 369–73.

Here I briefly summarize Plantinga's original position and Quinn's four central objections.[19]

In his 1983 paper, Plantinga is concerned with the question of whether belief in the existence of God can be properly basic. A belief is *basic* if, at least roughly, it is a belief which is not based on any other beliefs or evidence.[20] Familiar examples of basic beliefs might include a person's beliefs that $2 + 2 = 4$, that he is identical to himself, that there is a computer in front of him, and that he ate cereal for breakfast, all of which may be beliefs he typically forms immediately and not as a result of making inferences or weighing evidence in their favor.

Some basic beliefs, however, might be formed improperly. While under the influence of a hallucinogen, the person might come to believe that there is a ghost

---

[18] See "Agamemnon and Abraham."

[19] For an excellent evaluation, see William Hasker, "The Foundations of Theism: Scoring the Quinn-Plantinga Debate," *Faith and Philosophy*, 15/1 (1998), 52–67. For what it's worth, I agree with Hasker's scorekeeping.

[20] Plantinga, "Reason and Belief in God," 46.

in front of him, but such a belief would be epistemically defective. *Properly* basic beliefs, then, are basic beliefs that satisfy the relevant epistemic norms governing belief formation. For Plantinga's purposes in his paper, the norms are those of 'rational acceptability.'[21]

Plantinga's question, then, is whether belief in the existence of God can be both basic and rational. According to those philosophers whom he labels 'evidentialists,' the answer is a decided no. The central claim of evidentialism that interests Plantinga is the following:

> (5) It is irrational or unreasonable to accept theistic belief in the absence of sufficient evidence or reasons.[22]

Thus the evidentialist is making an evaluative claim about the epistemic propriety of forming basic theistic beliefs.

Plantinga's strategy for rejecting evidentialism is to argue that the view depends upon a more general normative position in epistemology that he calls 'classical foundationalism.' On this view:

> (6) A proposition *p* is properly basic for a person *S* if and only if *p* is either self-evident to *S* or incorrigible for *S* or evident to the senses for *S*.[23]

Since belief in God allegedly does not meet any of these requirements, it cannot be rational to hold it in the basic way.

In response, Plantinga raises two objections to classical foundationalism. First, it would render a tremendous number of our beliefs irrational, such as our beliefs about the past, about material objects, and about other minds. Second, and more importantly for the subsequent exchange with Quinn, Plantinga argues that classical foundationalism is self-refuting since the view itself does not meet any of the above criteria, nor does it seem that there are any basic beliefs meeting one of the criteria in (6) that could be used in an evidential pathway to classical foundationalism.[24]

For Plantinga, then, it can be perfectly rational for someone to start with belief in God and use that belief itself as a premise in various religious arguments.[25] Yet Plantinga in this paper does not provide his own account of proper basicality; instead he claims that we should proceed inductively by starting with what we take to be central examples of basic beliefs, and then try to infer from them general criteria of rationality. The 'we' here will be important—Christians, for example, will include belief in God among their central examples of basic beliefs, while atheists will not. But this is entirely appropriate since "[t]he Christian community is responsible to *its* set of examples, not to theirs."[26]

---

[21] Plantinga, "Reason and Belief in God," 19, 55.   [22] Ibid. 27.

[23] Ibid. 59. Classical foundationalism itself is the disjunction of ancient or medieval foundationalism on the one hand (proper basicality = self-evidence or being evident to the senses) and modern foundationalism on the other (proper basicality = incorrigibility or self-evidence).

[24] Ibid. 59–63.   [25] Ibid. 72.   [26] Ibid. 77. Emphasis his.

To Plantinga's claims in his 1983 paper, Quinn raises four main objections. Let us briefly take them each in turn:

Justifying Epistemic Criteria. The first objection is directed at Plantinga's inductive method for arriving at epistemic criteria for proper basicality, and specifically at the passage just quoted about the Christian community's appeal to its own examples. According to Quinn, the "difficulty is, of course, that this is a game any number can play. Followers of Muhammad, followers of Buddha, and even followers of the Reverend Moon can join in the fun. Even the modern foundationalist can play."[27]

Classical Foundationalism. Quinn is also not convinced that classical foundationalism has been refuted. While he agrees that (6) is neither self-evident nor incorrigible nor evident to the senses, Quinn argues that Plantinga has not shown that (6) cannot be derived from other propositions it countenances as properly basic. In fact, the classical foundationalist might use Plantinga's own inductive method against him by starting with examples such as:

(7) The belief that I am being appeared to redly is properly basic in conditions optimal for visual experience in which I am being appeared to redly.

And:

(8) The belief that Jove is expressing disapproval is not properly basic in conditions optimal for auditory experience in which I am being appeared to thunderously.[28]

Both (7) and (8), or suitably revised versions of them, can plausibly be regarded as self-evident, and thus along with other such examples can be used as the building blocks for an inductive procedure which could yield and thereby justify (6).

The (Un)importance of Proper Basicality. According to Plantinga, the beliefs that a theist is likely to arrive at in the properly basic way will not typically be beliefs like *God exists* or *theism is true*, but rather beliefs like the following:

(9) God is speaking to me.
(10) God disapproves of what I have done.
(11) God forgives me for what I have done.[29]

Quinn, however, notes that what might instead happen is that a belief in a proposition like (9) is arrived at indirectly as a result of first believing that:

(12) It seems to me that God is speaking to me.[30]

But such an indirect belief in (9), Quinn claims, can be justified to the same degree that it would be if it were arrived at directly by way of an experience of

---

27 Quinn, "In Search of the Foundations of Theism," 127, below.
28 Quinn, "The Foundations of Theism Again," 146, below.
29 Adapted from Quinn, "In Search of the Foundations of Theism," 130, below.
30 Ibid. 131.

God speaking. Given this, Quinn concludes that with respect to (9) through
(11), "it is epistemically unimportant whether such propositions actually are
properly basic for that person at that time."[31]

Intellectually Sophisticated Theists. Perhaps the most important objection and the
deepest source of disagreement between Plantinga and Quinn concern the epistemic responsibilities of what Quinn calls 'intellectually sophisticated adult
theists'[32] who might form a properly basic belief in God but then are confronted with one or more putative defeaters for that belief, such as the problem of evil
or Freudian projection theories of religion. According to Quinn, the degree of
justification which the basic belief has is not high enough, at least in many cases,
to outweigh the justificatory status of a defeater like the problem of evil. What
the theist then needs to do is to appeal to some kind of non-basic justification for
theism to help supplement her original religious belief. This additional justification is likely to come in the form of evidential considerations offered by natural
theology for the truth of theism. With these evidential considerations in place,
however, the theist's belief will no longer continue to be a basic belief.

Religion and Political Liberalism

Towards the end of his life, Quinn participated in debates in political philosophy about the legitimacy of appeals to religious considerations in public political
discourse and decision making. His central contribution was his 1995 presidential address to the Central Division of the American Philosophical Association,
"Political Liberalisms and Their Exclusions of the Religious" (Chapter 8 in this
volume). Much of the paper is devoted to attacking views in political philosophy
that exclude certain kinds of religious appeals in the public square. In particular, Quinn first carefully summarizes and then criticizes Robert Audi's principles
of secular rationale and motivation, as well as John Rawls's claims about public
reason in *Political Liberalism*.

Also noteworthy are the final pages of the paper in which Quinn, following
Michael Perry, outlines his own positive proposal. Roughly, on Quinn's inclusivist theory citizens in a given society should be allowed to participate in political
discussions and decision making even if the only reasons they have for their
views stem from their own particular religious traditions. Quinn takes there to
be at least two considerations supporting this view. First, given his skepticism
about the likelihood of secular political arguments to reach an overlapping consensus, Quinn argues that allowing religious considerations into political debate
is unlikely to preclude possibilities for agreement that would have otherwise been
realized. And second, Quinn claims that being confronted with new and sometimes radically foreign modes of political discourse, in this case modes that stem

---

[31] Adapted from Quinn, "In Search of the Foundations of Theism," 132.   [32] Ibid. 135.

from divergent religious traditions, can sometimes enhance a person's thinking about his or her own position or even lead to its justified rejection. By way of conclusion, though, Quinn is quick to note that his inclusivist approach needs to put some limits on discourse, namely moral norms aimed at protecting free speech, equality, and mutual respect.

Six years later, in "Religious Citizens within the Limits of Public Reason" (Chapter 9 in this volume), Quinn reverses roles. After again carefully and systematically laying out the heart of Rawls's political philosophy as it pertains to the role of comprehensive religious and philosophical doctrines in questions of constitutional essentials and matters of basic justice, Quinn this time opts to defend Rawls from objections raised by Nicholas Wolterstorff. As Quinn presents them, Wolterstorff's criticisms revolve around three central themes:

(i) Rawls's ideal of public reason would require an implausibly high level of agreement in matters of political morality.
(ii) Rawlsian political liberalism would violate the free exercise of religion.
(iii) Rawlsian political liberalism, and indeed many other liberal positions as well, would violate the integrity of many religious persons and hence would be unfair if implemented.

Quinn is not very sympathetic to any of these lines of criticism, and mounts a sustained defense of Rawls against each of them.

This leaves the reader with a puzzle: Is Quinn merely defending a view against what he takes to be bad objections, even though he himself does not accept the view in question? Or has he had a change of heart since his presidential address and converted to something like Rawls's position? The final two paragraphs of "Religious Citizens within the Limits of Public Reason" provide an answer. Quinn is prepared to accept Rawls's ideal of public reason as just that, i.e. as an ideal that it would be good for us to strive to obtain given our actual political circumstances. However, merely as an ideal it does not impose moral obligations on us to act in the way that it outlines. Instead, in our present political environment, Quinn seems to think that there would be nothing either irrational or morally wrong with adopting the more inclusive model of political discourse and decision making outlined in his presidential address.

Topics in Christian Philosophy

Despite the resurgence of interest in philosophy of religion in the past thirty years, comparatively little attention has been paid by philosophers to claims which are specific to particular world religions. As a Christian, Quinn himself lamented the absence of work devoted to topics uniquely central to Christianity, and sought to address this absence in a number of papers. The papers reprinted in this section reflect his thinking on three topics of interest to Christians, namely original sin, atonement, and the church.[33]

Quinn's approach to these topics is not to consider them primarily in the context of purported biblical revelation, but rather to build on the work of previous thinkers such as Anselm, Kant, and Kierkegaard. In typical fashion, he first clearly and painstakingly reconstructs a given philosopher's view before submitting it to a penetrating critical discussion. Thus these papers here should also be of interest to historians of philosophy, including those who have no stake in the outcome of the particular debates. Because Quinn is so careful in his presentation of both the issues and the historical positions he discusses in these three papers, I will simply summarize briefly the central themes of each of them.

In " 'In Adam's Fall, We Sinned All' " (Chapter 10 in this volume), Quinn examines the writings of Anselm and Kant on the Christian doctrines of the fall and original sin. According to Quinn, anyone trying to make sense of original sin has to confront a basic puzzle. Original sin is supposed to be innate in all human beings. But if it is innate, it is plausible to think that original sin is not something human beings could have avoided. And on widely held views about moral responsibility, if something is unavoidable then it is not something for which we can be held accountable. Thus original sin is not something for which we would be punished or condemned by a just authority figure or judge, and so it is really no form of sin at all. Hence the doctrine of original sin, when conjoined with certain independently plausible assumptions, seems to lead to its own demise.[34]

According to Quinn, Anselm tries to salvage the doctrine by denying the connection between something's being unavoidable and its thereby being such that we cannot be held accountable for it. In response, Quinn does not address issues about moral responsibility directly, but instead argues by *reductio* that such a move on Anselm's part leads to a morally repugnant conclusion about the fate of unbaptized infants. Anselm believes that the proper condemnation for sin is eternal damnation in hell, and so it would thereby follow that all unbaptized infants would automatically be consigned to such a fate.

Kant, on the other hand, tries to avoid the above puzzle by denying the connection between something's being innate and its being unavoidable. On

---

[33] For additional papers by Quinn on these and related topics, see "Original Sin, Radical Evil and Moral Identity," *Faith and Philosophy*, 1 (1984), 188–202; "Does Anxiety Explain Original Sin?", *Noûs*, 24 (1990), 227–44; "Saving Faith from Kant's Remarkable Antinomy," *Faith and Philosophy*, 7 (1990), 418–33; "Aquinas on Atonement," in R. Feenstra and C. Plantinga (eds.), *Trinity, Incarnation, and Atonement* (Notre Dame: University of Notre Dame Press, 1990); "Abelard on Atonement: 'Nothing Unintelligible, Arbitrary, Illogical or Immoral about It'," in E. Stump (ed.), *Reasoned Faith* (Ithaca: Cornell University Press, 1993); "Swinburne on Guilt, Atonement and Christian Redemption," in A. Padgett (ed.), *Reason and the Christian Religion* (Oxford: Oxford University Press, 1994); and "Sin and Original Sin," in P. Quinn and C. Taliaferro (eds.), *A Companion to Philosophy of Religion* (Oxford: Blackwell, 1997), 541–8.

[34] For a formal statement by Quinn of this puzzle, see "Original Sin, Radical Evil and Moral Identity," 189–90.

Kant's view of radical evil, and simplifying greatly, all human beings as a matter of contingent fact have a propensity to evil. This is not a physical propensity, such as a disposition to eat ice cream, since all such propensities are for Kant subject to the laws of nature and so morally indifferent. Rather it is a moral propensity, and so in Kant's general framework it is one that must be the upshot of a rational agent's exercise of genuine libertarian free will. Thus the propensity to evil is something that human beings have freely bestowed upon themselves, and is not constitutive of human nature or causally determined by the laws of nature.

Kant's view can nicely avoid what Quinn takes to be the morally repugnant implication of Anselm's proposal. At the same time, if we are talking about original sin, the propensity to evil must be innate in human beings in some sense, and according to Quinn's reading of Kant, the sense is that in which "as the underlying ground of all morally evil actions in time, it is to be thought of as present in its possessors antecedent to all such actions."[35] In evaluating Kant's proposal, Quinn acknowledges the advantages of the view on ethical grounds, but notes that it suffers from a theological difficulty since it does not leave any role to be played by some historical catastrophe that Christians traditionally have believed led to the presence of evil in the world.[36]

Thus Quinn has helpfully illustrated two ends of a spectrum in thinking about original sin: one according to which original sin inheres in us at birth because of a causal chain of transmission from the first human beings, and the other according to which original sin is the product of our own exercises of free will. Quinn himself is clearly dissatisfied with both positions, but here does not offer a positive proposal of his own as a way of navigating between these two opposing approaches.[37]

A natural companion to this first paper is "Christian Atonement and Kantian Justification" (Chapter 11 in this volume), which was reprinted in *Philosopher's Annual* as one of the top ten papers of 1986. If sin is the problem, Christians claim that Christ's death and resurrection are supposed to be the solution. But how exactly should we make sense of atonement for sin from the Christian perspective? Again Quinn turns to Anselm and Kant for help, and again he finds their proposals wanting.

For Anselm, sinners are deeply in debt to God and must either fully satisfy their debt or be punished for their sins. Yet Anselm believes that left to their own devices, human beings cannot accumulate enough by way of positive merit or good works fully to pay back their debts to God. But all is not lost since, according to Anselm, God can satisfy the debts incurred through human sin, given that those debts are transferable and that God as Christ chose to atone vicariously for those

---

[35] "In Adam's Fall," 228, below.

[36] For additional critical discussion of Kant on original sin and radical evil, see Quinn's papers "Original Sin, Radical Evil and Moral Identity" and "Does Anxiety Explain Original Sin?"

[37] For some indication of where Quinn's own sympathies may lie, see "Does Anxiety Explain Original Sin?"

sins himself. To this proposal Quinn raises a number of objections, one of which is that unlike financial debts, moral debts are not transferable and so cannot be paid by anyone other than the original debtor himself.

Kant's view on atonement is complex, and the reader is urged to consult both Book Two of *Religion Within the Limits of Reason Alone* as well as Quinn's very helpful reconstruction of the relevant passages. Kant's two central claims seem to be the following. First, Kant believes that we must do what we can on our own to pay our debts for wrongdoing by exercising our freedom in order to carry out a moral revolution in our characters such that the propensity to evil is replaced by a propensity to goodness. But for Kant this isn't enough fully to satisfy the debt, and so secondly, the Christian hope is that through grace and mercy God will bestow a gift of righteousness on the individual who has undergone such a radical change of heart. These two actions, one human and one divine, are individually necessary and jointly sufficient for atonement according to Kant. To this proposal, Quinn again raises several objections, one of which is that God's bestowing righteousness on an individual as a gift would be a violation of the strictness of the moral law—unless someone is perfectly righteous, he or she must be condemned and punished at least to some extent.[38]

Thus Quinn has raised what he takes to be serious difficulties with two of the leading philosophical theories of Christian atonement. As he freely admits, he has not shown that no plausible theory can be devised. Yet here, too, he does not attempt to provide one of his own, but merely takes himself to have clearly outlined the parameters within which future investigation ought to proceed.

Finally, "Kantian Philosophical Ecclesiology" (Chapter 12 in this volume) is an attempt by Quinn to enrich Christian thinking about the role of the church in the Christian life. Here again the focus is on Kant, and specifically on his remarks about the church in the *Religion* and in *The Conflict of the Faculties*. According to Quinn's reading, the central image of Kant's ecclesiology is that of a pair of concentric circles. The inner circle is made up of the *a priori* principles of the pure religion of reason. The outer circle is made up of putative historical revelation, which is to be critically evaluated by reason and, if necessary, revised when conflicts arise. How do these claims pertain to the church? Kant's ideal is the establishment of an ethical commonwealth in which humans are guided by the commands of pure reason, commands that are self-legislated by reason and that at the same time are the true commands of God. Such an ethical commonwealth simply is the church in its perfected state, according to Kant. The true church, then, is "that which exhibits the (moral) kingdom of God on earth so far as it can be brought to pass by men."[39] Thus reason itself, insofar as it is not contaminated by any weakness, can bring about the perfected church

---

[38] For additional discussion of Kant on atonement, see Quinn's paper, "Saving Faith from Kant's Remarkable Antinomy."

[39] Quoted by Quinn, "Kantian Philosophical Ecclesiology," 258, below.

for Kant. But unfortunately, ordinary human beings struggle mightily with weakness, and so as a matter of empirical fact the church has been founded on revelation and historical contingency, and adorned with hierarchical structure, scripture, and tradition. Yet the order of priority remains the same—any and all empirical ecclesiastical practices should serve only to further the pure religion of reason.

Once again Quinn is not completely satisfied with this picture, and tries to convince us that we shouldn't be either, especially once we appreciate the fact that for Kant, the propositions within the inner circle are supposed to be such that we have very high epistemic confidence in them, whereas those in the outer circle have a much lower epistemic status. This difference in epistemic status between beliefs in the two sets of propositions is what for Kant grounds the priority claim between pure reason and historical revelation. But, Quinn argues, there are at least two problems here. First, in light of the reception that Kant's moral theory has received in subsequent decades, it is highly unlikely that it, or indeed any other moral theory, will acquire the epistemic status Kant claims for beliefs about moral propositions in the inner circle of pure reason. And second, Quinn argues that using the widely accepted methodology of reflective equilibrium, it is not at all clear that people will always resolve conflicts between their moral and theological beliefs in favor of the former. As a general matter, we should expect that resolutions will end up being made in a number of different ways, given widespread cultural and experiential diversity.

But all is not lost. According to Quinn, a 'chastened' Kantian ecclesiology should be accepted instead that "proceeds on a case by case basis to deploy moral beliefs of high epistemic status as levers, as it were, to move churches and their members in the direction of reforming ecclesiastical arrangements and reinterpreting scriptures."[40] Without elaborating on this alternative ecclesiology much beyond these brief remarks, Quinn concludes by evaluating the extent to which the Roman Catholic Church, and specifically the changes brought by Vatican II, have moved in the direction both of Kant's original view and of the 'chastened' Kantian alternative.

RELIGIOUS DIVERSITY

The final two papers in this collection center on another important topic in the philosophy of religion to which Philip Quinn turned his attention late in his professional career, namely the implications of widespread religious diversity. Quinn's central paper in this area is his "Toward Thinner Theologies: Hick and Alston on Religious Diversity," which is reprinted both here (Chapter 13) and in the excellent collection *The Philosophical Challenge of Religious Diversity*,

---

[40] Ibid. 271.

which Quinn edited with Kevin Meeker. As the title suggests, the paper is largely concerned with the work of John Hick and William Alston on religious diversity. However, Quinn also leaves several clues as to where his own sympathies lie, and so in what follows I briefly summarize his criticisms of Hick and Alston with the aim of trying to elucidate Quinn's positive view about the subject.

Alston argues that Christian doxastic practices of forming beliefs about God as a result of immediate religious experiences are not demonstrably unreliable and derive some support for themselves from the way in which they can lead to satisfying forms of spiritual development for some Christians. But Alston also acknowledges that the same is true of the religious experiences had by followers of many other major world religions, so that the beliefs formed as a result of such experiences all seem to be on equal epistemic footing. Perhaps independent evidence from natural theology, divine revelation, miracles, and the like could shift the balance in favor of Christianity, but Alston wants to consider what would happen to the degree of justification enjoyed by Christian beliefs in the worst case scenario in which there is no such supplemental evidence. Does epistemic parity render irrational the basic beliefs of any of the world's religious practitioners that are arrived at through religious experience?

Alston is prepared to admit that awareness of such religious diversity does lower the degree of justification that would otherwise be enjoyed by, say, Christian beliefs formed via religious experience. But using an analogy with sense perception, he argues that the degree of justification for such beliefs need not decrease to the level of irrationality. Alston asks us to imagine one society in which people form perceptual beliefs using a 'Cartesian' practice of understanding the objects of visual perception to be extended mediums with concentrations of points, whereas in a different society people have a 'Whiteheadian' practice in which the content of visual perception is understood to involve growing events. If I am a member of the first society, then according to Alston it is rationally permissible for me to retain my Cartesian framework even while being aware of the alternative Whiteheadian approach, provided I don't have any reason for thinking that the latter approach is more accurate. And the same is true of members of the second society vis-à-vis their Whiteheadian practice. So then by analogy it follows that Christians who formed their beliefs in God as a result of religious experiences can be rational in holding on to their beliefs in the face of religious diversity, provided there is no independent evidence for the veracity of any competing religious traditions.

Quinn agrees with Alston that this argument shows that it would be rationally permissible for the Christian (or Jew, Muslim, Buddhist, etc.) to retain his or her specific faith despite awareness of widespread religious diversity. However, he objects that Alston has not shown that this is the *only* rationally permissible thing to do. Returning to the example of sense perception, Quinn argues that it would also be rationally permissible to work from within, say, a Cartesian approach by gradually revising it in various ways and then attempting to establish this revised view in society. Similarly, then, by analogy it would also be rationally permissible for Christians to revise their view from within and work towards the revised view's widespread acceptance.

But how should this revision be undertaken? Here is where Quinn sees Hick as providing a promising starting point. According to Hick, behind the major world religions is an ultimate divine reality that has been interpreted in different ways by those religions. Using Kantian language, Hick's claim is that there is a noumenal Real that is manifested as different phenomena in the context of divergent religious traditions. Against this proposal, Quinn raises a number of objections, among them that Hick's view is ambiguous as to whether it is offering a construct model or a disguise model, that Hick does not provide any arguments for central negative assumptions of his view, and that Hick makes ontological claims about the noumenal Real to which he is not entitled by his own theory.

Interestingly, though, Quinn takes these problems to apply only to the details of Hick's own version of a pluralist approach to understanding religious diversity, and not to pluralism as such. Thus at the end of Section 1 of his paper, we find Quinn formulating a schematic version of religious pluralism that allegedly avoids the problems with Hick's view. Are, then, religious believers in the major world religions rationally required to work from within their own traditions towards such a pluralist view? Clearly not, according to Quinn, as such believers are rationally entitled to either revise their religious views or simply keep them as they are: "[e]each of these courses of action is rationally permissible in the light of religious diversity. Neither of them is irrational, but neither is rationally required."[41] Provided then that each option is merely permissible, is one of them nonetheless preferable by Quinn's own lights? Here the textual evidence is slim at best, but my own hunch is that Quinn would side with believers in the major religions making pluralistic revisions to their religious beliefs.

The final paper of this collection, "On Religious Diversity and Tolerance" (Chapter 14), was also the last paper Quinn completed before his death. It was published in *Daedalus*, the journal of the American Academy of Arts and Sciences, to which Quinn was elected a Fellow in 2003. This short paper is written for a general academic audience, and as the last paper of his philosophical career, it fittingly touches on a number of themes from Quinn's work. A central claim is one that Quinn borrows from Alston, namely that one's awareness of widespread religious diversity lowers the level of epistemic justification enjoyed by one's beliefs in the distinctive claims of one's own religion. Quinn suggests that this claim can be used to develop a new strategy for promoting tolerance among practitioners of different religions. More precisely, Quinn suggests that the Alstonian claim can be employed in an argument against the rationality of religious believers acting on the intolerant elements of their own particular religions, since

---

[41] "Toward Thinner Theologies," 298, below.

awareness of religious diversity may lower the epistemic status for such beliefs below the level of rational acceptability.[42]

FINAL REMARKS AND ACKNOWLEDGEMENTS

The papers in this collection attempt to represent what are, in my judgment, the central issues on which Philip Quinn concentrated in his published work in the philosophy of religion. However, I would be remiss if I did not mention that Quinn also had interesting and original things to say about a wide variety of other topics in the field ranging from Pascal's wager, to religious responses to torture, to Christianity and the meaning of life. A complete bibliography of his published work can be found at the end of this volume.

I am grateful to a number of people for their help in seeing this project through. A great deal of thanks is owed to Peter Momtchiloff at Oxford University Press for his initial interest in and invaluable assistance with the project. For her advice and willingness to write the foreword, I am also grateful to Eleonore Stump. For various forms of support, advice, and encouragement, I want to thank Joyous Miller, Jason Baldwin, LinDa Grams, Cheryl Reed, Mary Lou Solomon, and an anonymous referee for Oxford. Finally, my greatest debt is to Paul Weithman, the chair of the philosophy department at Notre Dame and the co-executor of Philip Quinn's estate. Paul was extremely helpful at every step of the way, and his advice was always clear, insightful, and wise. I very much doubt that this volume would have appeared without his patience and help.

I would like to end this introduction on a more personal note. I received my Ph.D. from Notre Dame in the summer of 2004, immediately before Phil was diagnosed with cancer. I was the last student at Notre Dame to finish a doctorate degree with Phil as a committee member, and I consider it an honor that he was willing to take the time to help me with my project. Not only was he a mentor, but by the end of my time at Notre Dame he was also one of my closest friends. We would routinely have lunch two to three times a week at a popular faculty cafe on campus, and those conversations make up some of my best memories of my time at Notre Dame. This volume is a symbol of my gratitude to a wonderful teacher, philosopher, and friend.[43]

---

[42] For related discussion of religious diversity, see two other papers by Quinn: "Religious Diversity and Religious Toleration," *International Journal for Philosophy of Religion*, 50 (2001), 57–80; and "Religious Diversity: Familiar Problems, Novel Opportunities," in William Wainwright (ed.), *The Oxford Handbook of Philosophy of Religion* (Oxford: Oxford University Press, 2005), 392–417.

[43] For comments on this introduction, I am very grateful to Joyous Miller and Jason Baldwin.

RELIGIOUS ETHICS

1

Religious Obedience and Moral Autonomy

It has become fashionable to try to prove the impossibility of there being a God. Findlay's celebrated ontological disproof has in the past quarter century given rise to vigorous controversy.[1] More recently James Rachels has offered a moral argument intended to show that there could not be a being worthy of worship.[2] In this paper I shall examine the position Rachels is arguing for in some detail. I shall endeavor to show that his argument is unsound and, more interestingly, that the genuine philosophical perplexity which motivates it can be dispelled without too much difficulty.

I

Rachels summarizes his position in the form of the following argument:[3]

(1) If any being is God, he must be a fitting object of worship.

(2) No being could possibly be a fitting object of worship, since worship requires the abandonment of one's role as an autonomous moral agent.

(3) Therefore, there cannot be any being who is God.

In order to test this argument for validity some uniform interpretation of its English modal auxiliaries in terms of a philosophically well understood set of modalities must be found. It seems clear that Rachels intends (1) to be read as a proposition of *de dicto* logical or conceptual necessity. He claims that "it is necessarily true that God (if he exists) is worthy of worship. Any being who is not worthy of worship cannot be God."[4] Hence, no violence is done to his intentions if we recast the argument in the following canonical form:

(4) Necessarily, if some being is God, then that being is worthy of worship.

It is a pleasure to thank my colleagues D. W. Brock and J. W. Lenz for helpful comments on an earlier version of this paper.

[1] J. N. Findlay, "Can God's Existence Be Disproved?", in A. Flew and A. MacIntyre (eds.), *New Essays in Philosophical Theology* (New York, 1964). See discussion in the replies to Findlay by G. E. Hughes and A. C. Rainer in *New Essays in Philosophical Theology* and in P. C. Appleby, "On Religious Attitudes," *Religious Studies*, 6 (1970), 359–68.

[2] J. Rachels, "God and Human Attitudes," *Religious Studies*, 7 (1971), 325–37.

[3] Ibid. 335. The argument (1)–(3) is expressed in Rachels's own words.   [4] Ibid. 325.

(5) It is not possible that some being is worthy of worship.

(6) It is not possible that some being is God.

In the restated argument all the modal operators are to be understood as express-ing *de dicto* logical necessity and possibility as explicated in one of the standard systems of alethic modal logic in order to avoid fallacies of equivocation. On this interpretation the argument is valid.[5] Furthermore, on Rachels's view that 'God' is not a proper name but a title,[6] there is no reason to object to (4). The sound-ness of the argument then hangs, as it should, on whether (5) is true.

Now (5) is certainly not an obvious modal truth, and so it is incumbent upon Rachels to argue for it. That he accepts this onus is evident from the since-clause in (2) which signals the argument that is the most interesting feature of Rachels's paper. Unfortunately, however, Rachels does not make this argument perfectly clear, and so it must be reconstructed for him. The following valid argument would suffice to establish (5) if it were sound:

(7) It is not possible that some being is worthy of worship and there are some moral agents.

(8) Necessarily, there are some moral agents.

(5) It is not possible that some being is worthy of worship.

To evaluate the soundness of this argument something more must be said about the concept of moral agency. Rachels's views on this matter place him squarely within what might be called, speaking loosely, the Kantian tradition. He asserts that "to be a moral agent is to be an autonomous or self-directed agent...The virtuous man is therefore identified with the man of integrity, i.e. the man who acts according to precepts which he can, on reflection, conscientiously approve in his own heart."[7] Let us suppose, for the sake of argument, that this view of moral agency is correct. Rachels admits that it is controversial and requires a detailed treatment which is beyond the scope of his paper. But he thinks it is sound, and since I agree with him on this point I shall grant him this conception without objection.

Unfortunately, on this view (8) seems to be false. Far from always being self-directed agents who act on principles they can conscientiously and reflectively approve, most people in fact often enough act in unprincipled and unreflective ways such that they cannot conscientiously approve all of their own conduct in their own hearts. And even if each of us is sometimes a moral agent in the requisite sense, this is a contingent truth and not a necessary one. It would be slightly unfair, however, to challenge what is intended as an *a priori* argument on empirical grounds, and so I propose to resort to the somewhat drastic expedient

    [5] My strategy is to reconstruct Rachels's arguments so that they turn out to be valid in order to focus my criticism on the truth value of their premisses. I have, therefore, checked to be sure that the reconstructed arguments are formally valid at least in the Feys system T and the Lewis systems S_4 and S_5.

    [6] Rachels, "God and Human Attitudes," 333.   [7] Ibid. 334.

of stipulating that (8) is a necessary truth about the possibility of moral agency. A more formal paraphrase of (8) can then be expressed as follows:

(9) Necessarily, it is possible that there are moral agents.

One must as a consequence of this stipulation accept the conclusion that most of us most of the time are not in fact full-fledged moral agents, but this is not, I think, an intolerable perversion of at least some of the evaluation uses of 'moral agent.' And we can now reformulate the argument in a more perspicuous way:

(10) It is not possible that some being is worthy of worship and that it is possible that there are moral agents.

(9) Necessarily, it is possible that there are moral agents.

(5) It is not possible that some being is worthy of worship.

This argument is also valid, and only the acceptability of (10) remains to be examined. Here we reach what is for Rachels's argument the heart of the matter; however, it also seems to be the heart of darkness.

Why should anyone be tempted to accept (10)? Rachels thinks he has found grounds for accepting it in certain features of the concept of worship. On his view, "That God is not to be judged, challenged, defied, or disobeyed, is at bottom a *truth of logic*; to do any of these things is incompatible with taking him as one to be worshipped."[8] He also says: "The point is not merely that it would be imprudent to defy God, since we certainly can't get away with it; rather, there is a stronger, *logical point* involved—namely, that if we recognise any being as God, then we are committed, in virtue of that recognition, to obeying him."[9] Hence, "in admitting that a being is worthy of worship we would be recognizing him as having an unqualified claim on our obedience."[10] We are then faced, according to Rachels, with "a conflict between the role of worshipper, which by its very nature commits one to total subservience to God, and the role of moral agent, which necessarily involves autonomous decision making."[11] In other words, there is, roughly speaking, supposed to be a conflict between regarding some being as worthy of worship and being a moral agent.

But, after all, role-conflict is not logical contradiction, and it is not clear just how the alleged conflict is supposed to enhance the plausibility of (10). For consider what someone who accepts Rachels's views on the logic of worship would be committed to. He would accept, I suppose, the following argument:

(11) Necessarily, God is worthy of worship.

(12) Necessarily, if God is worthy of worship, then for all persons p and all actions a if God commands a person p to do an action a, then p ought to do a.

(13) Necessarily, for all persons p and all actions a if God commands a person p to do an action a, then p ought to do a.

---

[8] Ibid. 333.   [9] Ibid. 332.   [10] Ibid. 334.   [11] Ibid.

This argument is valid with the modal operators taken, as before, to express *de dicto* logical necessity, '*a*' and '*p*' taken to be bound variables, and 'ought' in (12) and (13) taken to express a moral ought. Since 'God' is not taken to be a proper name, (11)–(13) should be understood as not implying the existence of God, parallel to our construal of (1) and (4). Hence, (13) does not imply by itself any existential claims about God, or for that matter about persons or actions, but merely expresses the logical connection between the concept of God and the concept of unqualified obedience. Let us also suppose, for the sake of argument, that (11)–(13) are true. The question which remains is how (13) is supposed to support (10). After all, since (13) is consistent with there being no divine commands, it hardly seems to conflict logically with the autonomy of any moral agent.

Rachels has anticipated an objection of this sort. His response is to claim that "even if God did not require obedience to detailed commands, the worshipper would still be committed to the abandonment of his role as a moral agent *if* God required it."[12] It is clear that, if God issues commands, then the worshipper is committed to obeying them; what is not so obvious is just how this is supposed to commit the worshipper to abandoning his role as a moral agent. In order to see whether this latter committment is involved in worship, let us suppose that God does issue a command:

(14) God commands P to do A

where 'P' and 'A' are constants substituted for the variables '*p*' and '*a*'. From (13) and (14) it follows:

(15) P ought to do A.

It should be noted that (14) is not a necessary truth but that it does imply the existence of God and at least one person. That (14) is not a necessary truth should be obvious from the fact that, even if God exists necessarily, it is not necessary that he ever issues any commands. Does the supposition expressed by (14) conflict with the autonomy of a moral agent?

Presumably a moral agent might, on reflection, conclude that (15) was unacceptable. He might assert:

(16) It is not the case that P ought to do A.

On the assumption that ought-statements can be incompatible, he would then be driven to denying (15) and, to preserve consistency, to denying either (13) or (14). Since (13) is a necessary truth, his only consistent option would be to deny (14). But denying (14) does not by itself compel him to deny the existence of God, for (14) is an internally complex proposition which can be partially analysed as follows:

(17) There is something which is God and which commands P to do A.

---

¹² Rachels, "God and Human Attitudes," 335.

The denial of (17) is equivalent to the following:

(18) Everything is such that either it is not God or it does not command P
to do A.

And a moral agent can assert (18) without denying the existence of God by asserting its second disjunct and claiming:

(19) God exists but God does not command P to do A.

In other words, an autonomous moral agent can admit the existence of God if
he is prepared to deny that any putative divine command which is inconsistent with his hard-core reflective moral judgments really is a divine command.
He can resolve the supposed role-conflict by acknowledging that genuine divine
commands ought to be obeyed unconditionally but maintaining that no directive
which he does not accept on moral grounds is a genuine divine command. For
the following three propositions are logically compatible:

(20) God exists.
(21) God sometimes commands agents to do certain things.
(22) God never commands anything an autonomous and well-informed
moral agent would, on reflection, disapprove.

Hence, since (13) does not entail or otherwise support (10) and because Rachels
has given no other reason for accepting (10), it is rational to reject (10). Indeed,
(10) seems to be demonstrably false. After all, Rachels would admit, as was noted
above, the following claim:

(23) It is possible that some being is worthy of worship and that this being
issues no commands and that it is possible that there are moral agents.

Furthermore, an obvious truth is the following:

(24) That some being is worthy of worship and that this being issues no
commands and that it is possible that there are moral agents entails
that some being is worthy of worship.

And, using the logical truth,

(25) (Possibly (p and q) and (p and q entail r)) entail possibly (p and r)

it can be validly inferred:

(26) It is possible that some being is worthy of worship and that it is possible that there are moral agents

which is the negation of (10). Therefore, the argument for (6) from (4), (5),
(9), and (10) is unsound. Rachels has failed to provide what he promised—a
valid and sound "*a priori* argument against the existence of God which is based
on the conception of God as a fitting object of worship."[13]

---

[13] Ibid. 325.

II

At this point the reader may suspect that, although Rachels' modal argument fails to show that there could not be anything worthy of worship, it does raise some philosophical issues which have not yet been dealt with adequately. This suspicion seems to me essentially correct, and so I shall press on in the attempt to get at the underlying perplexity which might have led Rachels to construct his argument.

One begins to appreciate what may be troubling Rachels when one asks whether someone who proposes to accept (18) is justified in all cases in asserting the second disjunct and denying the first. At first blush it would seem that the theist has a good reason for supposing that God would not, indeed could not, command anything which a well-informed autonomous moral agent should be unable to accept. After all, Rachels explicitly allows that "it has been admitted as a necessary truth that God is perfectly good; it follows as a corollary that He would never require us to do anything except what is right."[14] In other words, the theist is committed to the following claim:

(27) Necessarily, God is perfectly good

with (27) interpreted in the same way as (11). Hence, it seems open to him to argue that, because (27) is true, any command which is not acceptable to a well-informed and autonomous moral agent could not be a divine command. So the theist seems driven logically, for reasons which Rachels acknowledges, to accept the second disjunct of (18) and to deny that wicked commands could come from God.

It comes as a surprise, therefore, to find Rachels contending that this line of argument rests on a misunderstanding of (27). What he offers in support of this contention are the following remarks:

We cannot determine whether some being is God without first checking on whether he is perfectly good; and we cannot decide whether he is perfectly good without knowing (among other things) whether his commands to us are right. Thus our own judgment that some actions are right, and others wrong, is logically prior to our recognition of any being as God. The upshot of this is that we cannot justify the suspension of our own judgment on the grounds that we are deferring to God's commands (which, as a matter of logic, must be right); for if, by our own best judgment, the command is wrong, this gives us good reason to withhold the title 'God' from the commander.[15]

Now these remarks seem to be correct; one need only note that the situation being described involves epistemic rather than logical priority. What is puzzling is why Rachels thinks this description of the theistic moral agent's epistemic situation shows up a misunderstanding of (27). Surely the theist need only be

---

[14] Rachels, "God and Human Attitudes," 335.   [15] Ibid. 335–6.

committed to obeying God's commands because they are necessarily morally legitimate themselves; he need not be committed to obeying such commands simply because they are the decrees of a superior power.[16] What could be more natural, then, than using his reflective moral judgments as a touchstone for determining which claims to moral authority might plausibly be regarded as divine? Doubtless, many theists do in fact surrender their moral autonomy to human institutions and authorities, but then so do many nontheists. What seems clear is that the theist is not required by logic to suspend his moral judgment in the face of any human authority. Of course, the theist is committed to the view that if God commands then he should obey, but he may not be able to justify the belief that God has commanded a certain action without first having good moral reasons to think that he ought to do what has been commanded.

Why should Rachels be inclined to suppose that the theist should find this situation unsatisfactory? I suspect that it is because he imagines that a theist who uses his own moral judgments as a basis for deciding whether or not to obey commands cannot be yielding the appropriate sort of unqualified obedience which is owed to a being which is worthy of worship. To put the point crudely: if a moral agent sits in judgment on God's commands, accepting some and rejecting others, then he is not totally subservient to God.

If this is what Rachels supposes, then it is clear that he has misunderstood the position of the theist who is also an autonomous moral agent. This misunderstanding can be traced, I think, to a failure to make an important distinction between unqualified obedience to a command which is of divine origin and unqualified acceptance of the claim that a command is of divine origin. This distinction can be made clearer by examining the contrast between the following propositions:

(28) If God commands P to do A, then P ought to do A only if conditions C are satisfied.

(29) P ought to assent to the claim that God commands P to do A only if conditions C' are satisfied.

Presumably, since the theist accepts (13) and (27), he is committed to rejecting (28) for any nonvacuous specification of conditions C. This is what unqualified obedience amounts to. But the theist can accept (29) with rather strong nonvacuous specifications of the epistemic conditions C' which qualify his assent to the claim that a command is of divine origin. Since many theists believe that there are powerful evil spirits trying to deceive them, they ought to, and do, require that particularly stringent epistemic conditions be satisfied before they accept the claim that God has promulgated a certain decree. Frequently such conditions are formulated in terms of coherence with scripture and dogma, but there is no

---

[16] However, some theists, the so-called divine command theorists, among whom Descartes and perhaps Ockham are to be numbered, come perilously close to such a commitment.

logical reason why coherence with moral judgments about which the theist, on reflection, is very certain should not be included in such conditions. It is not as if the theist is sitting in judgment on commands which are known by him to be of divine origin and qualifying his obedience to God. Rather, he is endeavoring to determine whether certain commands are genuinely God's and, hence, ought to be obeyed and is qualifying his assent to claims of moral authority made on religious grounds. This he must do if he is not to become a fanatic or the victim of charismatic religious charlatans. Therefore, it is a mistake to suppose that the theist who is cautious about accepting putative divine commands as genuine is thereby qualifying his obedience to those commands which he does accept with justification as being divine.[17]

But, surely, it may be objected, in support of Rachels, God might command just anything; after all, he is necessarily omnipotent. In particular, it might seem that he could command a person to abandon his role as a moral agent, that is to say, to relinquish his moral autonomy. If so, then by instantiation of (13) it would follow:

(30) Necessarily, if God commands P to relinquish his moral autonomy, then P ought to relinquish his moral autonomy.

And if God did so command, it would be correct to assert:

(31) God commands P to relinquish his moral autonomy

and to infer by *modus ponens*:

(32) P ought to relinquish his moral autonomy.

Surely (32), though not a logical impossibility, seems to be troublesome at least to those theists who wish to subscribe to a Kantian view of moral agency. Except, of course, that such theists would be prepared to assert:

(33) It is not the case that P ought to relinquish his moral autonomy

and to infer by *modus tollens*:

(34) It is not the case that God commands P to relinquish his moral autonomy.

One person's *modus ponens* is another's *modus tollens*, and our Kantian theist is at no logical disadvantage in this argument. Indeed, since he accepts (27), he might assert the stronger proposition:

(35) It is not possible that God commands P to relinquish his moral autonomy

and justify this claim in terms of a theory of the divine attributes which has it that God's omnipotence is necessarily limited by his perfect goodness.

---

[17] A similar critical point has been elaborated in some detail in R. A. Oakes, "Reply to Professor Rachels," *Religious Studies*, 8, (1972), 165–7.

In any case, we have found no argument so far, *a priori* or empirical, which would pose a logical threat to the position of the theist who wishes to adopt a Kantian view of moral agency.

III

What does seem to threaten the position of the Kantian theist is not a matter of the logic of the concepts of moral agency or of worthiness of worship but rather of certain possible questions of fact and evidence. For it seems possible that a theist should have both good reasons for believing that God has commanded him to perform a certain action and good reasons for believing that it would be morally wrong for him to perform that action. Thus a theist can be confronted with moral dilemmas of a peculiar sort. The story of Abraham provides an illustration of the kind of moral problem which might arise. This story need not be interpreted in the idiosyncratic Kierkegaardian manner as involving a teleological suspension of the ethical in order for Abraham's dilemma to raise serious moral problems.[18]

We may imagine that Abraham accepts (13). He also has good reason to accept the following:

(36) God commands Abraham to kill Isaac.

After all, Abraham had reason to believe that God had made and kept some rather remarkable promises to him in the past, such as giving him a son when he was one hundred years old.[19] Thus Abraham, we may suppose, had what he took to be good inductive evidence to support his assent to (36). Hence, from (13) and (36) he could infer:

(37) Abraham ought to kill Isaac.

But now we may also imagine, anachronistically perhaps, that Abraham is a Kantian moral agent who is inclined to accept, on reflection, the following argument:

(38) One ought not to kill an innocent child.
(39) Isaac is an innocent child.
(40) Abraham ought not to kill Isaac.

Obviously, Abraham cannot consistently accept both (37) and (40). What is he to do? Well, supposing that he does not even consider doubting (39), he must reject either (36) or (38). But he has good reasons to accept both of these propositions. His reasons for accepting (36), being inductive, are admittedly less than logically conclusive. However, since even reflective moral judgments are

---

[18] For criticism of the Kierkegaardian interpretation see G. Outka, "Religious and Moral Duty: Notes on *Fear and Trembling*," in G. Outka and J. P. Reeder (eds.), *Religion and Morality* (Garden City, 1973).
[19] Genesis 21: 1–3.

fallible, his reasons for accepting (38) will also be logically inconclusive; perhaps his reflective moral judgments are slightly askew.

There is, of course, an easy way out of this dilemma. Kant was aware of it, and it is rather surprising that Rachels does not seem to be. In discussing the case of an inquisitor, Kant makes these remarks:

That it is wrong to deprive a man of his life because of his religious faith is certain, unless (to allow for the most remote possibility) a Divine Will, made known in extraordinary fashion, has ordered it otherwise. But that God has ever uttered this terrible injunction can be asserted only on the basis of historical documents and is never apodictically certain. After all, the revelation has reached the inquisitor only through men and has been intrerpreted by men, and even did it appear to have come to him from God Himself (like the command delivered to Abraham to slaughter his own son like a sheep) it is at least possible that in this instance a mistake has prevailed. But if this is so, the inquisitor would risk the danger of doing what would be wrong in the highest degree; and in this very act he is behaving unconscientiously. This is the case with respect to all historical and visionary faith; that is, the *possibility* ever remains that an error may be discovered in it. Hence it is unconscientious to follow such a faith with the possibility that perhaps what it commands or permits may be wrong, i.e., with the danger of disobedience to a human duty which is certain in and of itself.[20]

Kant's claim, which is bound to be attractive to many contemporary philosophers, is that Abraham is or can be certain of (38) but cannot have reasons good enough to warrant accepting (36). Needless to say, this is a very controversial thesis, and one which Abraham, and other theists, need not accept. For Abraham can reasonably judge that, in cases of conflict of duties, his actual duty is to obey God's commands because obedience to God's commands overrides his other prima facie duties in such cases. In so judging he would not abandon his role as an autonomous moral agent, for, as Rachels himself admits, "if we learn that God (i.e. some being that we take to be God) requires us to do a certain action, and we conclude on this account that the action is morally right, then we have *still* made at least one moral judgment of our own, namely that whatever this being requires is morally right."[21] Furthermore, Abraham might have very good reasons, at least, it seems, in terms of the evidential canons of his theistic conceptual framework, for believing that God has given him a command. Hence, he might be certain of (36) and dubious about (38).

Now it is fairly clear that this Abraham is no knight of faith; he is a moral rationalist who disagrees with Kant about the probative force of various sorts of evidence. His position is at least logically consistent. Is it utterly irrational?

[20] I. Kant, *Religion Within the Limits of Reason Alone*, tr. T. M. Greene and H. H. Hudson (New York, 1960), 175. Kant also says: 'That I ought not to kill my good son is certain beyond a shadow of a doubt; that you, as you appear to be, are God, I am not convinced and will never be even if your voice would resound from the (visible) heavens'. This remark from *Der Streit der Facultäten* is cited in G. Outka, 'Religious and Moral Duty,' 235.
[21] Rachels, "God and Human Attitudes," 336.

That depends, I suppose, on whether it is possible to have evidence which makes it certain that God has commanded a certain action. This question raises the hardest problems of religious epistemology, but, as far as I know, it is an open question. For I know of no argument which shows:

(41) It is not possible that there is evidence which makes it certain that God has commanded someone to kill an innocent child

with 'God' here taken to have existential import. Here we seem to reach an impasse at the epistemological chasm which separates theistic from nontheistic basic assumptions.

Of course, Abraham need not be certain of (36) in any very strong sense; Kant is surely correct in thinking that it is possible that Abraham is mistaken. But neither is the duty not to kill an innocent child "certain in and of itself" as Kant supposes, or at least there seems to be no good reason for the theist to subscribe to this variety of moral dogmatism. In the absence of logically conclusive evidence either way, Abraham can remain reasonable if for him (36) is epistemically preferable to (38). This may seem unlikely given Abraham's total evidence, or ours, but it is not impossible. It is not that Abraham need be thought of as acting unconscientiously; he is running grave risks of doing wrong no matter how he acts. If he kills Isaac and God has not commanded it, he acts wrongly, but equally if he does not kill Isaac and God has commanded it, he acts wrongly. His dilemma is an agonizing one, and ordinary theists should breathe a sigh of relief because it does not confront them. However, if a theist like Abraham confronts such a dilemma, then it does seem unfair to accuse him of being unconscientious simply because he must risk doing wrong and cannot be certain what would be wrong to do in his circumstances. Soldiers who had to decide whether to shoot a Vietnamese, not knowing whether he was a Viet Cong agent armed with grenades or an innocent peasant, also ran serious moral risks, but even if a soldier kills an innocent peasant he need not be regarded as having acted unconscientiously. Risky moral decisions made under uncertainty can have appalling consequences even if they are made in reasonable ways.

If our Abraham is neither conceptually confused nor provably irrational, is he wicked? It is not clear that this is the case. Abraham freely accepts the moral principle:

(42) If God commands someone to kill an innocent person, then he ought to kill that person.

Is this principle a manifestly repugnant one? The theist, arguing on his own ground, need not be driven to agree that it is. From a consequentialist point of view he can maintain that God, since he is omniscient, omnipotent, and perfectly good, can appropriately compensate both the killer and his victim in the relevant felicific or beatific respects either here or hereafter. Furthermore, on more formal grounds the theist can successfully apply the universalizability or reciprocity test to (42). He may acknowledge that if God commands someone to kill him then that person ought to kill him, for he may think that he would acquire special merit in the sight of God were he to be a willing sacrifice in such circumstances. He might, of course, consistent with this admission, also believe that no one who claims to have been commanded to sacrifice him has in fact been so commanded by God, and so resist vigorously all sorts of assassination attempts by religious fanatics. The most the theist can be forced to concede, provided he is moderately clever, is that (42) *sounds* harsh and inhumane. But then he will hasten to add that this is merely because we cannot understand why God does what he does, though we may trust that it is all for the best.

If correct, this establishes that our rationalistic Abraham has a way out of the moral dilemma posed by (37) and (40) which does not require him to abandon his role as an autonomous moral agent. Furthermore, this way out allows that he may consistently accept the command to sacrifice Isaac as specifying his actual moral duty and, within his own conceptual framework, correctly claim that he is neither irrational nor wicked. Of course, he may well be mistaken. And, naturally enough, the nontheist, who does not accept many of the assumptions of this framework, will be scandalized. He will, for instance, find the compensations and special merits alluded to above utterly fanciful and quite literally incredible. He may well claim that if the theist can swallow all this then he is a dangerous and undesirable sort of person to have around, and he may devoutly wish that there should be fewer theists so that the moral order should stand a chance of being stable and secure. What this shows is the depth of the differences which can separate some theists from some nontheists. Perhaps Kant's way out of the dilemma is the only exit the nontheist is prepared to tolerate on the part of the theist. This would show, if it were so, something about the limits of the nontheist's tolerance. It would not establish that the theist has confused or inconsistent beliefs. Nor would it prove, as Rachels may think, that theistic belief is bound to take the worshipper "beyond morality" or that theistic beliefs should, in this respect, be regarded as a source of "severe embarrassment."[22]

IV

Perhaps some embarrassment for the theist could be generated by means of a more careful scrutiny of some of the central concepts used in the argument so far. The terms 'obedience' and 'autonomy' have been used rather loosely, and artfully contrived definitions of these or related terms might produce a result that would bother the theist. In any case, this possibility seems interesting enough to warrant some further exploration.

Let us consider first the notion of obedience. When would it be appropriate to say that someone is actually obeying a command rather than merely doing what

<hr />

[22] Rachels, "God and Human Attitudes," 337.

has, in fact, been commanded? A suggestion as to how this question might be answered is found in the following remarks by Max Weber:

'Obedience' will be taken to mean that the action of the person obeying follows in essentials such a course that the content of the command may be taken to have become the basis of action for its own sake. Furthermore, the fact that it is so taken is referable only to the formal obligation, without regard to the actor's own attitude to the value or lack of value of the content of the command as such.[23]

As it stands, the suggestion is a bit nebulous; moreover, it seems stipulative rather than lexicographically descriptive. However, it does suffice to motivate the introduction of a technical notion of subservience, which may be formulated as follows:

(43) Agent p is subservient in doing action a if and only if p's only reason for doing a is p's belief that a has been commanded.

Now (43) does not quite capture the concept which is relevant to the problem at hand. After all, the theist need not be subservient to earthly commanders in anything he does; he may even consider himself obliged by conscience to engage in civil disobedience from time to time. What is wanted is a notion of religious subservience, which can be explicated as follows:

(44) Agent p is religiously subservient in doing action a if and only if p's only reason for doing a is p's belief that a has the property of being commanded by God.

'Religious subservience' is, of course, a term of art; however, it may express some of what Rachels has in mind when he speaks of the worshipper's 'total subservience to God'.[24] Even if it is not what Rachels intends, the concept of religious subservience has some interest in its own right.

It is a bit harder to see just how the notion of autonomy should be reshaped to suit present purposes. Since at this point no pretense to either lexicographical accuracy or historical fidelity is being made, misunderstanding will be avoided if technical locutions are introduced to pick out the concepts under discussion. A preliminary stab at what is wanted can be made using the following stipulation:

(45) Agent p is correct in doing action a if and only if p's only reason for doing a would, if true, suffice to show that a is what p ought to do.

The intuitive idea encapsulated in this stipulation is that an agent acts correctly provided that his reason for action provides epistemic warrant for the conclusion that he acts as he ought to do. The reason why (45) represents only a preliminary attempt to capture the concept being sought is that a particular agent can be both

---

[23] M. Weber, *The Theory of Social and Economic Organisation*, tr. A. M. Henderson and T. Parsons (New York, 1964), 327.
[24] Rachels, "God and Human Attitudes," 334.

religiously subservient and correct in doing a particular action. To show that this is the case the theist can deploy the following valid argument:

> (46) Necessarily, if God is perfectly good, then for all actions a and for all agents p, if a has the property of being commanded by God, then a is what p ought to do.
>
> (27) Necessarily, God is perfectly good.
>
> (47) Necessarily, for all actions a and for all agents p, if a has the property of being commanded by God, then a is what p ought to do.

Let us suppose, no reason to the contrary being obvious, that this argument is sound. Consider now a particular agent P and a particular action A. Assume that P is religiously subservient in doing A. This implies that P's only reason for doing A is his belief that A has the property of being commanded by God. If this belief were true, we could assert:

> (48) A has the property of being commanded by God.

But (47) and (48) together entail:

> (49) A is what P ought to do.

Hence, P's only reason for doing A would, if true, suffice to show, by a valid and sound deductive argument, that A is what P ought to do, and this implies that P is correct in doing A. Of course, this involves assuming that (47) is true, but that assumption seems unproblematic because (47) follows from (46), which is innocuous enough, and (27), which even Rachels will allow. Therefore, we must cast about for a concept rather different from correctness if we wish to make trouble for the religiously subservient theist.

The term 'moral correctness' will serve to pick out the required concept. It can be introduced using the following locution:

> (50) Agent p is morally correct in doing action a if and only if there is some property m such that (i) m makes a what p ought to do, and (ii) p's only reason for doing a is p's belief that a has m.

The idea behind this stipulation is that an agent acts morally correctly provided that his reason for action is the belief that the action in question has a certain property and that the very property he believes the action to have makes it the thing he ought to do. Of course, (50) and (44) are not inconsistent, for the property referred to in (50) might be identical with the property of being commanded by God. Thus, consider again a particular agent P and a particular action A. Suppose both that P's only reason for doing A is P's belief that A has the property of being commanded by God and that being commanded by God makes A what P ought to do. On these suppositions, P is morally correct in doing A, and P is religiously subservient in doing A. But notice that we have, in effect, imported a variant of the divine command theory into this argument in assuming that being commanded by God makes A what P ought to do. This assumption would be objectionable to many theists and to nontheistic moral theorists.

So let us rule out this possibility by means of the following stipulation:

(51) For all agents p, all actions a, and all properties m, it is not the case both that m makes a what p ought to do and that m is identical with the property of being commanded by God.

It is easy to see that (44), (50), and (51) are an inconsistent triad. Assuming (51), the proof goes as follows. Consider an arbitrary agent P and an arbitrary action A. Suppose, first, that P is morally correct in doing A. Then, according to (50), some M makes A what P ought to do and P's only reason for doing A is his belief that A has M. But then, by (51), M is not identical with the property of being commanded by God. Hence, it is not the case that P's only reason for doing A is his belief that A has the property of being commanded by God. Therefore, by (44), it is not the case that P is religiously subservient in doing A. Suppose, second, that P is religiously subservient in doing A. Then, according to (44), P's only reason for doing A is his belief that A has the property of being commanded by God. By (51), for arbitrary M, either M is not identical with the property of being commanded by God or M does not make A what P ought to do. If M makes A what P ought to do, then, since M is not identical with the property of being commanded by God, it is not the case that P's only reason for doing A is P's belief that A has M, in which case P is not morally correct in doing A by (50). On the other hand, if M is identical with the property of being commanded by God, M does not make A what P ought to do, in which case P is not morally correct in doing A by (50). In either case, P is not morally correct in doing A. Therefore, given (51), (44) and (50) are inconsistent.

What this shows, roughly speaking, is that, on the assumption that a certain version of the divine command theory is false, in doing an action A an agent P cannot be both religiously subservient and morally correct in the technical senses given to these notions. It is not surprising that, allowed enough latitude for stipulation, one can introduce incompatible terms into a philosophical vocabulary. The interesting question is whether the theist would, or should, be bothered by such contrivances. But it is easy to see that the theist need not be unduly perturbed by this particular set of maneuvers. After all, he may simply reject (51).[25] Moreover, even if he chooses not to reject (51), he can challenge (50) by pointing out that it places such stringent conditions on moral correctness that even secular moral theorists may find it embarrassing. Notice that (50) requires that an agent's only reason for doing an action be his belief that it has the very property which, as it happens, makes that action what he ought to do. But consider two agents P_1, a utilitarian, and P_2, a deontologist, and two actions A_1 and A_2 which are alike in all morally relevant respects. Suppose that P_1 does A_1 because he believes that A_1 has the property of maximizing expected utility and that P_2

---

[25] There are several variants of the divine command theory which might then be considered. For suggestive discussion see R. M. Adams, "A Modified Divine Command Theory of Ethical Wrongness," in Outka and Reeder (eds.), *Religion and Morality*.

does A_2 because he believes that A_2 has the property of being prescribed by a correct moral rule. On the assumption that both these properties would not make similar actions what one ought to do, at least one of these agents, and very possibly both, are not morally correct in doing what they do. But this would seem to be too harsh a judgment. Since most, perhaps all, agents frequently do what they ought to do for mixed reasons or the wrong reasons, when indeed they even manage to do what they ought to do, it would seem that (50) stipulates an unreasonably high standard for moral correctness in action. Perhaps it is a symptom of unhealthy scrupulosity when an agent is much concerned with moral correctness in the sense of (50); an agent might well do what he ought to do more often and with less strain, and lead a happier life to boot, if he aspired only to correctness in action in the sense of (45) and, in addition, took reasonable precautions to include many truths and few falsehoods among his reasons for action. If endorsing (50), or something like it, is the price that must be paid to bother the theist, then moral theorists may be unwilling to pay such a high price for such meagre benefits. And, even if some nontheists are willing to accept (50), there seems to be no compelling reason why a theist should accept it.

I shall conclude with a brief summary of my argument. In Section I I tried to show that Rachels's attempt to prove that no being could be a fitting object of worship rests on a false premiss and is, therefore, unsound. In Section II I contended that two other arguments, which can be constructed from premisses congenial to Rachels in order to embarrass the theist who would hold a Kantian view of moral agency, turn out on close inspection to be inconclusive or to rest on confusions. In Section III I attempted to elucidate how a theist might consistently deal with conflicts between divine commands and ordinary moral duties so as to make sense of the Abraham story without retreating to Kierkegaardian irrationalism. In Section IV I tried to show how with a bit of ingenuity one can construct contextually incompatible concepts of religious subservience and moral correctness, but I argued that there is no reason for the theist to be especially perturbed by such artifices. I have not undertaken to show that the views I attribute to the theist are plausible given the evidence base I share with Rachels; I suspect that I could not hope to succeed at that task. Instead, I have merely tried to defend the theist against some arguments which purport to demonstrate that his beliefs could not possibly be true.

2

Divine Command Ethics: A Causal Theory

What has God to do with human morality? According to divine command theories of ethics, his will determines, at least to some extent, its content. This general
conception of the source of morality has distinguished historical antecedents. In
the later middle ages both John Duns Scotus and William of Ockham endorsed
versions of the divine command conception. Lesser figures of the period who held
views of this sort include Gabriel Biel, Pierre d'Ailly, Jean Gerson, and Francisco Saurez. For the early modern period the list of divine command moralists
includes George Berkeley, René Descartes, John Gay, John Locke, and William
Paley. Among contemporary philosophers, divine command theories of one sort
or another have been defended by Robert M. Adams, Baruch A. Brody, Patterson
Brown, and Richard Swinburne. Recently I too have tried my hand at constructing and defending several divine command theories.[1]

Of course, this tradition in ethical theory has not lacked critics. Contemporary
philosophers often trace the line of critics all the way back to Plato's *Euthyphro*.
Early modern critics include Jeremy Bentham, Ralph Cudworth, Joseph Glan-
vill, Richard Price, and Shaftesbury. The contemporary critics are so numerous
that it would be pointless to try to list them all. Some of the more prominent among them are Keith Campbell, Eric D'Arcy, Graeme de Graaff, A. C.
Ewing, Anthony Flew, William K. Frankena, D. Goldstick, Kai Nielsen, and
P. H. Nowell-Smith.

The debate over the merits of divine command morality has been prolonged
and intense; the debaters have often been subtle and ingenious philosophers.
Nevertheless, I do not think anyone has conclusively settled the question of
whether there is a philosophically tenable divine command theory of ethics.
So in this paper I propose to set forth and defend as best I can yet another
divine command theory. My argument comes in three parts. First I shall discuss

In thinking about the topic of this paper two unpublished typescripts proved helpful to me:
Professor Edward Wierenga's "A Defensible Divine Command Theory," a paper read at the
American Philosophical Association's Eastern Division meetings in Dec. 1978; and Professor Janine
M. Idziak's "Divine Command Morality: A Guide to the Literature," a paper which is to serve as an
introduction to her anthology, *Divine Command Morality: Historical and Contemporary Readings*. I
read an earlier version of this paper at Dartmouth College; I am grateful to my audience there for
stimulating discussion.

[1] Philip L. Quinn, *Divine Commands and Moral Requirements* (Oxford: Clarendon Press, 1978).

and criticize metaethical divine command theories. Next I shall formulate a
normative divine command theory; it will be a causal theory of moral obligation.
Then I shall defend my theory against what seem to me to be four of the most
interesting of the many objections which might be directed against it.

I. METAETHICAL DIVINE COMMAND THEORIES

We may begin the discussion with a rough and ready distinction. There are ethical terms such as 'good', 'bad', 'right', 'wrong', and 'obligatory'; there are also
theological terms such as 'commanded by God', 'willed by God', 'decreed by
God', 'ordained by God', and 'approved by God'. A metaethical divine command theory is one which maintains that some or all ethical terms are definable in
terms of, or synonymous with, certain theological terms. I take Paley to be setting
forth part of a metaethical divine command theory in passages like the following:

Let it be remembered, that to be *obliged*, "is to be urged by a violent motive, resulting
from the command of another."
   And then let it be asked, Why am I obligated to keep my word? and the answer will
be, Because I am "urged to do so by a violent motive," (namely, the expectation of
being after this life rewarded if I do, or punished for it if I do not), "resulting from the
command of another" (namely, of God.)[2]

And Robert M. Adams is clearly enunciating part of a metaethical divine command theory in this passage:

I could say that by "X is ethically wrong" I mean "X is contrary to the commands of a
loving God" (i.e., "There is a *loving* God and X is contrary to His commands") and by
"X is ethically permitted" I mean "X is in accord with the commands of a *loving* God"
(i.e., "There is a *loving* God and X is not contrary to His commands").[3]

So when philosophers such as Graeme de Graaff and Kai Nielsen criticize
metaethical divine command theories, it is no straw man they are attacking.
   It would probably occur to most philosophers nurtured in the tradition of contemporary analytic philosophy that any attempt to define ethical terms by means
of theological terms is bound to commit the so-called 'naturalistic fallacy'. To
show that this is so, such philosophical critics might deploy a version of the celebrated 'open-question argument'. Suppose the divine command theorist asserts
things like this:

   (1) 'Lying is ethically wrong' means 'Lying is contrary to the commands of
       a loving God'.

[2] William Paley, *The Principles of Moral and Political Philosophy* (Boston: Richardson and Lord,
1825), 56.
[3] Robert M. Adams, "A Modified Divine Command Theory of Ethical Wrongness," in G.
Outka and J. P. Reeder (eds.), *Religion and Morality* (Garden City: Doubleday, 1973), 323.

The critic will note that the question:

> (2) Is lying, which is contrary to the commands of a loving God, ethically wrong?

is transformed by substitution of expressions alleged to be the same in meaning into the question:

> (3) Is lying, which is contrary to the commands of a loving God, contrary to the commands of a loving God?

And the critic will then urge that, whereas sentence (2) expresses an open question whose answer may not be obvious to someone who understands it, sentence (3) does not express an open question, since its answer must be trivially obvious to whoever understands it. From this, the critic will infer that (2) and (3) do not express the same question, and he will conclude that the transformation of (2) into (3) was not, after all, a case of substitution of expressions the same in meaning. On these grounds, he will take himself to be entitled to reject claims like that asserted by (1).

As it stands, this argumentative chain seems to me to have at least one weak link. It is the critic's assumption that whoever uses (2) must use it to express an open question. No doubt the critic himself uses that interrogative sentence to express an open question. But what reason do we have for assuming that the divine command theorist uses that sentence to express the same question his critic does? Perhaps for the divine command theorist the question expressed by (2) is not an open question at all. Indeed, he might be using (2) to express the same question he uses (3) to express, one to which the answer is trivially obvious. So I do not think the critic's objection is conclusive when presented in this form.

But the objection appears to contain a core of insight even if it is ineptly expressed. We might get at the crucial point more directly using this principle:

> (4) 'Lying is ethically wrong' means 'Lying is contrary to the commands of a loving God' only if the proposition expressed by 'Lying is ethically wrong' is identical with the proposition expressed by 'Lying is contrary to the commands of a loving God'.

Then we need to adopt this criterion of propositional identity:

> (5) The proposition that p is identical with the proposition that q only if, necessarily, for all S, S believes that p if and only if S believes that q.

And now the critic's point may be reformulated in a sharper way. It is evidently possible that some atheist believes that lying is ethically wrong and does not believe that lying is contrary to the commands of a loving God. Hence, by (5), the proposition that lying is ethically wrong is diverse from the proposition that lying is contrary to the commands of a loving God. But, in normal usage, the sentence, 'Lying is ethically wrong' expresses the proposition that lying is ethically wrong, and the sentence 'Lying is contrary to the commands of a loving

God' expresses the proposition that lying is contrary to the commands of a loving God. So, by (4), relative to normal usage, 'Lying is ethically wrong' does not mean 'Lying is contrary to the commands of a loving God'. To be sure, nothing forces the divine command theorist to stick to normal usage; he is free to use his sentences in a deviant fashion if he pleases. But, if (1) merely registers his decision to use 'Lying is ethically wrong' to express the proposition that lying is contrary to the commands of a loving God, then it is of little philosophical significance. Presumably (1) would be philosophically important only if it were offered as an analysis of standard meaning rather than a stipulative definition. What is of philosophical interest is the relation between the proposition normally expressed by 'Lying is ethically wrong' and the proposition normally expressed by 'Lying is contrary to the commands of a loving God'. Because the argument I have just laid out convinces me that this relation is not identity, I conclude that metaethical divine command theories are either incorrect or uninteresting specimens of trivial semantic conventionalism. For this reason, they merit being rejected, and I shall say nothing further about them in what follows.

II. A CAUSAL DIVINE COMMAND THEORY

The task before us, then, is to construct a normative divine command theory. An obvious first step is to assemble the terminological building blocks from which the theory is to be fabricated. We may begin to do this by distinguishing two families of moral predicates. The first might be thought of as the axiological family; it includes such predicates as 'is good', 'is bad', and 'is indifferent'. The predicates in this family express concepts of moral value. The second family might, by contrast, be regarded as deontological; it includes such predicates as 'is obligatory', 'is permitted', and 'is forbidden'. The predicates in this family express concepts connected with moral law and duty. Since traditional Judeo-Christian conceptions of God include the notion that he is a moral legislator, it would seem appropriate to make our theoretical connections, at least in the first instance, between divine commands and obligations, permissions and prohibitions. Indeed, some contemporary philosophers have argued that only in the context of divine command theories do the concepts related to moral obligation and duty really make any sense. G. E. M. Anscombe says:

To have a *law* conception of ethics is to hold that what is needed for conformity with the virtues failure in which is the mark of being bad *qua* man (and not merely, say, *qua* craftsman or logician)—that what is needed for *this*, is required by divine law. Naturally it is not possible to have such a conception unless you believe in God as a law-giver; like Jews, Stoics and Christians.[4]

---

[4] G. E. M. Anscombe, "Modern Moral Philosophy," in J. J. Thomson and G. Dworkin (eds.), *Ethics* (New York: Harper and Row, 1968), 192.

Because she thinks such beliefs no longer control philosophical thinking about morality, Anscombe recommends:

that the concepts of obligation and duty—moral obligation and *moral* duty, that is to say—and of what is *morally* right and wrong, and of the *moral* sense of "ought," ought to be jettisoned if this is psychologically possible; because they are survivals, or derivatives from survivals, from an earlier conception of ethics which no longer generally survives, and are only harmful without it.[5]

Although I am not convinced that there is no other way to theorize about the deontological family of concepts, I do believe that divine command theories provide natural and defensible accounts of obligations, permission, and prohibitions. Since I am not nearly so confident that I know how to account for moral value, I shall not here attempt to construct a theological theory of moral value. In particular, I will leave open the question of whether the terms in one of our two families are definable by means of, or in any other way reducible to, those in the other.

We will make use of three concepts from the deontological family in our theorizing. Let us begin with the primitive locution 'It is obligatory that *p*', where for the schematic letter '*p*' English declarative may be substituted. This primitive locution is intended to have the same meaning as the locution 'It is morally required that *p*'. Using it, we can define schematically two other deontological notions as follows:

(6) It is forbidden that *p* = def. It is obligatory that not-*p*

and

(7) It is permitted that *p* = def. It is not obligatory that not-*p*.

Only these three ethical locutions will enter into our divine command theory.

Next we should specify the theological vocabulary which will be employed in constructing the theory. Let us assume that the word 'God' functions non-rigidly as a title. More exactly, let us suppose that the word 'God' abbreviates the definite description 'the omniscient, omnipotent creator and sustainer of the universe'. We will need to make use of only a single theological locution, namely, 'God commands that *p*'. Alternative locutions which would serve our purposes equally well are 'God would have it that *p*', 'God wills that *p*', 'God decrees that *p*', and 'God wishes it to be the case that *p*'. A choice among these ways of speaking is, from our point of view, purely a matter of convenience.

Our theory must assert some general relationship to hold between things expressed in our ethical vocabulary and those expressed in our theological vocabulary. Different choices of the appropriate relationship will yield conceptually distinct divine command theories. Elsewhere I have investigated divine command theories based on logical relations such as strict equivalence. Here I propose to explore a somewhat different terrain. One intuitive picture that divine command theorists have found attractive presents God as an agent

---

[5] Ibid. 186.

bringing about moral obligations and prohibitions by means of his legislative activity. According to this picture, God imposes or creates moral obligations and prohibitions by his commands or acts of will. Moreover, moral obligations and prohibitions are depicted as being directly and solely dependent on acts of the divine will. This way of thinking about the connection between God's commands and moral obligations suggests a causal relation between divine commands and moral duty.

There are many difficult conceptual problems which arise when philosophers try to give an account or an analysis of causation. I shall ignore them in this paper. I shall merely introduce a vocabulary that I believe to be adequate to the task of formulating a causal divine command theory. I also believe this vocabulary does not beg any questions about the correct analysis of causation, though it clearly leaves some such questions unanswered. I begin by pointing out what is obvious, namely that there is a distinction between alethic and causal modalities. We will need to make use of one primitive alethic modal notion, expressed by the locution 'It is logically necessary that p'. In terms of that locution, we may define schematically two other familiar modal notions as follows:

(8) It is logically contingent that p = def. It is not logically necessary that not-p

and

(9) It is logically possible that p = def. It is not logically necessary that p, and it is logically possible that p.

I shall use these notions in an informal and intuitive fashion without a commitment to one among the formal systems of alethic modal logic which have been constructed to explicate them with greater precision. We will also need one primitive causal notion, expressed by the locution 'It is causally necessary that p'. I am inclined to doubt that an adequate theory of causation can do without some primitive notion of its own. But since I cannot argue for that claim here, I will simply leave open the question of whether this causal locution can be defined or further analyzed using some of our other primitive vocabulary (plus, perhaps, still other terms I have not mentioned). In terms of our primitive locution, we may schematically define two further causal notions which will enter into our theory in this way:

(10) A sufficient causal condition that q is that p = def. It is causally necessary but not logically necessary that if p then q

and

(11) A necessary causal condition that q is that p = def. It is causally necessary but not logically necessary that if q then p.[6]

---

[6] There are similar definitions in Roderick M. Chisholm, *Person and Object* (Lasalle: Open Court, 1976), 58, 68.

This technical vocabulary, consisting of four primitive locutions—one ethical, one theological, one alethic, and one causal—and six defined locutions, will suffice for the formulation of the causal divine command theory I wish to consider.

That theory consists of the following three principles:

(12) For every proposition which is such that it is logically possible that God commands that *p* and it is logically contingent that *p*, a sufficient causal condition that it is obligatory that *p* is that God commands that *p*, and a necessary causal condition that it is obligatory that *p* is that God commands that *p*.

(13) For every proposition which is such that it is logically possible that God commands that *p* and it is logically contingent that *p*, a sufficient causal condition that it is forbidden that *p* is that God commands that not-*p*, and a necessary causal condition that it is forbidden that *p* is that God commands that not-*p*

and

(14) For every proposition which is such that it is logically possible that God commands that *p* and it is logically contingent that *p*, a sufficient causal condition that it is permitted that *p* is that it is not the case that God commands that not-*p*, and a necessary causal condition that it is permitted that *p* is that it is not the case that God commands that not-*p*.

Is this theory philosophically tenable? What objections might its critics raise? What defensive moves might be made to meet such objections? In the remainder of this paper, I shall explore these questions.

III. OBJECTIONS AND REPLIES

Perhaps it will prove helpful to introduce this section of the paper with a few words about philosophical methodology. There are, I think, at least two strategies one might use to argue in support of a philosophical theory. One is to lay out positive considerations which would justify a reasonable person in accepting the theory. In the case of the divine command theory I have formulated, this would turn out to be an immense undertaking. As far as I can tell, it would involve justifying many of the central metaphysical beliefs of classical theism plus some highly controversial claims in religious ethics. And perhaps some of these beliefs, if they can be justified at all, cannot be justified by philosophically respectable techniques. The other strategy, which is defensive in character, aims more modestly at establishing that objections directed against the theory fail to refute it, that is, fail to prove its falsity. If successful, this strategy will only show that a reasonable person would, other things being equal, not be completely justified in regarding the theory under examination as false. It is in this fashion that I am prepared to defend divine command theories. I believe none of the objections usually urged against such theories suffice to refute them. Of course, objections must be handled one at a time and each considered on its own merits; I can think of no way to deal with all the possible objections to any theory in one fell swoop. So what I propose to do is to consider a series of objections which appear to have some initial plausibility and which raise issues of independent philosophical interest. If I can dispose of them, I will have shifted the burden of proof some distance toward the philosopher who wishes to reject divine command theories on rational grounds. It would then seem to be incumbent on such a philosopher to come up with better objections or, alternatively, to show that there are positive reasons to accept and no good reasons to reject some other theory incompatible with divine command theories.

III.1. Skeptical Problems

It is sometimes claimed that divine command theories inevitably generate insoluble problems in moral epistemology. Just what the problems are supposed to be is a matter about which the critics do not seem to be in complete agreement. I think we can discern at least three distinct complaints in the critical literature; I shall take up these three in what I think is the order of decreasing gravity.

The first is the claim that divine command ethics leads to moral skepticism. An argument in support of such a claim might run along these lines. According to divine command theory, we can come to know what is obligatory and forbidden only by first coming to know what God has commanded. But we cannot in this life ever come to know what God has commanded, for the divine will is inscrutable. Hence, we cannot ever come to know in this life what is obligatory and forbidden. A more modest version of this complaint would be that only those people who have religious knowledge can have moral knowledge. I take Eric D'Arcy to be expressing a worry of this sort when he says:

if immoral actions are immoral merely because God so wills it, merely because God legislates against them, it would be sheer coincidence if someone who knew nothing of God or his law happened to adopt the same views about particular actions as God did.[7]

But, of course, mere coincidence of views, even when it occurs, scarcely serves to justify moral beliefs.

One reply to this line of argument might be to claim that such things as scripture, tradition, personal revelation, and natural law itself are sources of knowledge concerning what God has willed. Although I do not wish to preclude this possibility, it is a controversial claim, and there is a much simpler way to defeat the present objection. Our theory asserts that divine commands are conditions

---

[7] Eric D'Arcy, " 'Worthy of Worship': A Catholic Contribution," in Outka and Reeder (eds.), *Religion and Morality*, 194.

causally necessary and sufficient for moral obligations and prohibitions to be in force. It makes no claims at all about how we might come to know just what God has commanded. For all the theory says, it might be that we can only come to know what God has commanded by first coming to know what is obligatory and forbidden. After all, it is a philosophical truism that the causal order and the order of learning need not be the same. Even if effects are sometimes known through their causes, causes are sometimes known from their effects. So it is consistent with our theory to maintain that we can come to know what is obligatory and forbidden without prior causal knowledge of why these things have the moral status they do.

The second complaint has it that divine command morality is useless as an ethical standard. This seems to be what Bentham is getting at in the following passage:

> We may be perfectly sure, indeed, that whatever is right is conformable to the will of God: but so far is that from answering the purpose of showing us what is right, that it is necessary to know first whether a thing is right, in order to know from thence whether it be conformable to the will of God.[8]

Now I do not wish to endorse the thesis that the only way to come to know God's will is by first coming to know what is obligatory and forbidden. That thesis is at best problematic and raises deep questions in religious epistemology. Instead, I should like to point out that our divine command theory makes no claim at all to provide a decision procedure for ethics. But ethical theories can perform other functions besides teaching us exactly where our duties lie. It would be theoretically interesting to find out that divine commands are necessary and sufficient causal conditions for moral obligations and prohibitions, regardless of the epistemic difficulties involved in scrutinizing the divine will. So even if Bentham's point is well taken, it constitutes no objection to our theory. Besides, it is worth noting, by way of an *ad hominem* against Bentham, that his own brand of utilitarianism seems to fare no better than our divine command theory in this respect. No one is in a position to calculate the exact hedonic values of all the consequences of all the alternative actions open to an agent in many circumstances where moral decisions must be made. Still, it would be of theoretical interest to find out that hedonistic act utilitarianism is correct, regardless of the practical difficulties involved in trying to use it as an instrument for decision-making.

The third complaint is that divine command theories will not help us to reach agreement on issues of ethical principle. William K. Frankena puts the point this way:

> However deep and sincere one's own religious beliefs may be, if one reviews the religious scene, contemporary and historical, one cannot help but wonder if there is any rational

---

[8] Jeremy Bentham, *An Introduction to the Principles of Morals and Legislation* (New York: Hafner, 1948), 22.

and objective method of establishing any religious belief against the proponents of other religions or of irreligion. But then one is impelled to wonder also if there is anything to be gained by insisting that all ethical principles are or must be logically grounded on religious beliefs. For to insist on this is to introduce into the foundations of any morality whatsoever all of the difficulties involved in the adjudication of religious controversies, and to do so is hardly to encourage hope that mankind can reach, by peaceful and rational means, some desirable kind of agreement on moral and political principles.[9]

Although Frankena is here discussing views according to which the relation between theology and morality is logical rather than causal, presumably he would have similar worries about theories like the one I have set forth. And, of course, it must be conceded to Frankena that religious controversies have in the past given rise to moral controversies and still do. However, at least in philosophical discussions of divine command theories there are theoretical issues of justification and correctness at stake, and if they introduce controversy into the foundations of morals, then philosophers ought to be prepared to deal with that situation by means of further analysis and argument, as they do in other areas of philosophy. Philosophically speaking, our goal should be agreement based on the best available reasons. Reasonable disagreement about theoretical questions at the foundations of morals might make consensus about the solutions to practical problems more difficult to achieve, at least for the time being. But the mere fact that a theory is controversial and provokes disagreement is by itself no reason for disbelieving that theory. Frankena, it ought to be noted in fairness, would probably agree with this conclusion; he acknowledges that if the view that morality is dependent on religion rests on good grounds, we must accept it.[10]

I conclude that this set of complaints against divine command theories generates no serious problems for the causal theory I have constructed. So I now turn to considerations of another kind.

III.2. The Nihilistic Problem

Suppose for the sake of argument that there is no God, that is, suppose the definite description 'the omniscient, omnipotent creator and sustainer of the universe' does not apply to exactly one thing. Or, alternatively, suppose that God exists but issues no commands. In either case, according to (12) and (13), every proposition which is logically contingent and such that it is logically possible that God commands it is also such that a necessary causal condition for it being either obligatory or forbidden is not satisfied. And, according to (14), every proposition which is logically contingent and such that it is logically possible that God commands it is also such that a sufficient causal condition for it being permitted is

---

    [9] William K. Frankena, "Is Morality Logically Dependent on Religion?" in Outka and Reeder (eds.), *Religion and Morality*, 313.
    [10] Ibid. 314.

satisfied. Hence, if there is no God or if God commands nothing, then, according to our theory, every such proposition falls into the category of the permitted.

I see no reason to doubt that each proposition which specifies a particular human action, that is, each proposition expressed by a sentence of the form '*x* does *A*', where '*x*' is an expression referring to a particular human agent and '*A*' is an expression which picks out a concrete action, is logically contingent and such that it is logically possible that God commands it. If this is the case, then if there are no divine commands, each such proposition is permitted. The point might be put vividly, although a bit crudely, by saying that one consequence of our theory is this:

(15) If there is no God, then everything is permitted.

Because it is customary to name theorems after those who first state them rather than those who finally prove them, I suggest we say that what sentence (15) expresses is "Karamazov's Theorem."

I tend to think that "Karamazov's Theorem" ought to be a consequence of any divine command theory worthy of the name. But its nihilistic flavor is almost certain to give offense to philosophers who believe that morality rests on non-religious foundations. Presumably such philosophers would hold that what (15) expresses is false. How should a defender of divine command theories react to this view?

Obviously, (15) expresses a falsehood just in case its antecedent expresses a truth and its consequent expresses a falsehood. I presume that the falsehood of what the consequent of (15) expresses is a relatively uncontroversial matter. Both religious and secular moralists are likely to reject nihilism and to insist that at least some things are forbidden. So let us grant for the sake of argument that the consequent of (15) expresses something false. The bone of contention will then be the truth-value of what the antecedent of (15) expresses.

To establish conclusively or to prove the truth of what the antecedent of (15) expresses would be to establish that there is no God, that is, no unique omniscient, omnipotent creator and sustainer of the universe. This would be tantamount to proving that classical theism is false or, equivalently, to constructing a successful argument in natural atheology. Moreover, such a proof could not be based on traditional versions of the problem of evil, because, as I am using the title 'God', a being to whom that title applies is not by definition perfectly good. Indeed, I deliberately refrained from including the predicate 'is perfectly good' in my definition of 'God'; had I included it I might have begged a question I said earlier I would leave open, namely, the question of whether moral value is dependent in some way on the divine will. But, apart from the problem of evil, there is no philosophical argument known to us which comes anywhere near to being a successful piece of natural atheology.[11] Hence, there is nothing in current

---

[11] For discussion, see Alvin Plantinga, *God and Other Minds* (Ithaca: Cornell University Press, 1967) and Richard Swinburne, *The Coherence of Theism* (Oxford: Clarendon Press, 1977).

philosophical lore which proves the truth of what the antecedent of (15) expresses and, thereby, refutes both (15) and a divine command theory, such as the one I have formulated, which has (15) among its consequences.

There may be, for all I have said, arguments available to us which establish agnosticism or which show that the proposition expressed by the antecedent of (15) is in some sense implausible or improbable. But if there are, they would not serve to refute (15). An argument which established agnosticism would presumably show that, relative to the available evidence, any rational epistemic subject ought to suspend judgment on the proposition expressed by the antecedent of (15) and, hence, on the proposition (15) expresses. And when withholding the proposition expressed by (15) is the best epistemic attitude toward it, then (15) has not been refuted. Similarly, an argument which renders the antecedent of (15) and (15) itself improbable falls short of a refutation of (15). However, all I am trying to do in defense of my theory is to show that alleged refutations of it fail, and arguments of the sort just described do not even purport to be refutations of (15) or of those theories which have (15) among their logical consequences.

Of course, the proposition expressed by (15) is controversial. Still, it is false only if its antecedent is true, and so it is refuted only if its antecedent is proved. So the battleground shifts. The critic must prove that there is no unique omniscient, omnipotent creator and sustainer of the universe and thereby establish the falsehood of classical theism. Otherwise his arguments fall short of refuting (15). However, no one has yet proved that there is no God, and so divine command theories have not so far been refuted by this line of argument.

III.3. Conflicts of Obligation

Notice that there seems to be no logical impossibility in the supposition that some propositions are such that God commands them and also commands their negations. Consider, by way of illustration, the strange case of Abraham and Isaac. We may imagine that the proper application of the command in the decalogue to this case is the following:

(16) God commands that Abraham does not kill Isaac.

But we also have scriptural authority for this claim:

(17) God commands that Abraham kills Isaac.

So let us imagine that both (16) and (17) express truths. From (10), (12), and (16) we may draw this conclusion:

(18) It is obligatory that Abraham does not kill Isaac.

But from (10), (12), and (17) we may also draw this conclusion:

(19) It is obligatory that Abraham kills Isaac.

So in the situation we are imagining Abraham is confronted with a conflict of obligations. Moreover, our theory offers Abraham no way out of this conflict, since it makes no provision for one obligation to override another. The point of the example is not to show that such conflicts do in fact occur; an omniscient God is undoubtedly smart enough never to command a proposition and also command its negation, if he so chooses. But nothing in our theory precludes such conflicts, and so for all our theory says they may arise.

And the mere possibility of such conflicts is the basis for another objection. Many philosophers have wished to include something like the following principle among the axioms of deontic logic:

(20) It is logically necessary that, for all propositions, if it is obligatory that *p*, then it is not the case that it is obligatory that not-*p*.

Or at least this principle expresses one plausible view of the intended interpretation of the formula '$Op \supset\sim O\sim p$'. Evidently (18), (19), and (20) are an inconsistent triad. If (20) expresses a truth, (18) and (19) do not express compossible propositions. But they were deduced from (10), (12), (16), and (17). Since (16) and (17) appear to express compossible propositions and (10) is a mere definition, it seems that the blame must fall on (12). Hence, if (20) expresses a truth, then it appears that (12), an essential part of our theory, must express a falsehood.

Now it may be that the propositions expressed by (16) and (17) merely appear to be compossible and are not really so. But no obvious considerations suffice to show that these propositions are not compossible. So a divine command theorist who merely stamps his foot and insists that they are not seems to be on weak ground. A ploy of this sort would appear to be counterintuitive and wildly ad hoc, even though logic alone does not rule it out. By contrast, a divine command theorist is, I think, on fairly strong ground if he rejects (20). Considerations of at least three kinds conspire to undermine rational confidence in the proposition expressed by (20). First, several respectable contemporary philosophers with no theological axes to grind do reject (20). For instance, Joel Feinberg makes this pertinent remark:

it is quite possible to be committed in two or more directions at the same time, so that, whatever you do, you will fail to discharge one of your duties. Clearly, in such a situation there is one best thing to do, one thing which you ought to do, even though there are several incompatible things you have an obligation to do.[12]

(Incidentally, if Feinberg is right about this, it is easy to locate what should perplex us about the case of Abraham and Isaac as I have described it. It is not that Abraham fails to do something he has an obligation to do; that must happen no matter what he does. Rather, it is that religious people venerate him just because he undertook to do what moral intuition tells most of us would not have

---

[12] Joel Feinberg, *Doing and Deserving* (Princeton: Princeton University Press, 1970), 8.

been the best thing to do, the thing he ought to have done.) Second, there are
perfectly respectable systems of deontic logic which do not include the formula
'$Op \supset \sim O \sim p$' or any other formal counterpart of (20) among their theorems.[13]
And, third, there are particular cases, other than that of Abraham and Isaac,
which seem to be counterexamples to (20). Antigone's conflict of obligations, as
Sophocles tells the story, is perhaps the clearest among them. Her moral dilemma
is that she has an obligation to bury a dead brother and an obligation not to bury
a dead brother, and there is no clear sense in which one of them overrides or
removes the other. Sartre's example of the young man who must choose between
joining the Resistance and caring for an aged relative is a similar case. For these
three reasons, then, I think a divine command theorist is entitled to regard (20)
as problematic at best. Thus, any objection to our theory which employs it as a
premiss is inconclusive and is not a refutation of the theory.

III.4. Cudworth's Objection

The most powerful objection to our causal divine command theory is one which
was anticipated by Ralph Cudworth. He advances the claim:

That it is not possible that any thing should Be without a Nature, and the Natures or
Essences of all things being Immutable, therefore upon Supposition that there is any
thing really Just or Unjust, Due or unlawful, there must of necessity be something so
both Naturally and Immutably, which no Law, Decree, Will nor Custom can alter.[14]

It is not too difficult to spell out the bearing of this doctrine on our theory.
Cudworth seems to have thought that, if there are any truths about obligation at
all, then there are some necessary truths about obligation. He might have supposed, for example, that this is obviously and incontrovertibly true:

(21) It is logically necessary that it is obligatory that everyone refrains from
gratuitous torture of innocents.

At least it is clear that many people today would be inclined to accept the proposition expressed by (21). And here is the rub: someone who accepts our causal
divine command theory as it stands must stoutly resist such inclinations.

It is certainly logically contingent that everyone refrains from gratuitous torture of innocents, and it is surely logically possible that God commands that
everyone refrains from gratuitous torture of innocents. So, according to (12), our
causal divine command theory commits us to this claim:

(22) A sufficient causal condition that it is obligatory that everyone refrains
from gratuitous torture of innocents is that God commands that everyone refrains from gratuitous torture of innocents.

---

[13] Some systems of this kind are discussed in Bas C. van Fraassen, "Values and the Heart's
Command," *Journal of Philosophy*, 70 (1973), 5–19.
[14] Ralph Cudworth, *Treatise Concerning Eternal and Immutable Morality*, Bk. II, ch. 1; repr. in
British Moralists, ed. L. A. Selby-Bigge (Indianapolis: Bobbs-Merrill, 1964), 258.

But from (10) and (22) we may draw this conclusion:

> (23) It is not logically necessary that, if God commands that everyone refrains from gratuitous torture of innocents, then it is obligatory that everyone refrains from gratuitous torture of innocents.

And (23), in turn, entails this:

> (24) It is logically possible that it is not obligatory that everyone refrains from gratuitous torture of innocents.

However, the definition expressed by (8), plus ordinary propositional logic, allows us to conclude that (24) is logically equivalent to the negation of (21).

So, at this point, anyone who wishes to defend a fully general causal divine command theory of the sort I have formulated must bite the bullet. Such a philosopher must resort to the desperate expedient of denying that there are any sentences analogous to (21) which express truths; he must affirm that there are no necessary truths about obligations and prohibitions. As a matter of historical interest, there may be a precedent for this move. Ockham apparently believed that the moral quality of an act can be detached from the act itself, so that acts cannot be taken to have moral characteristics necessarily or in themselves. He says:

God is able to cause all that pertains to X as such without anything else which is not identical with X per se. But the act of hating God, as far as the sheer being in it is concerned, is not the same thing as the wickedness and evilness of the act. Therefore, God can cause whatever pertains to the act per se of hating or rejecting God, without causing any wickedness or evilness in the act.[15]

Someone prepared to generalize this view of the separability of acts and their moral characteristics would be in a position to deny that there are any necessary truths expressed by sentences of the forms 'It is obligatory that p' and 'It is forbidden that p'. Only thus, it seems to me, can our causal theory escape entirely from Cudworth's Objection.

I must confess that I am not at all sure whether there are any necessary truths about obligations or prohibitions. So I am not persuaded that Cudworth's Objection is a refutation of my causal theory. I think it worth nothing, however, that even if one is convinced that there are, one need not abandon the whole framework of the causal conception of divine command ethics. One might, instead, opt for a middle way of the sort suggested by Richard Swinburne in this passage:

I have argued that, if God is the creator of man and of the inanimate world, his commands can impose obligations which did not exist before ... Some might urge that if God is our creator, he is so much more truly the author of our being and the owner of the

---

[15] William of Ockham, *On the Four Books of the Sentences*, Bk II, question 19. I am quoting a translation by Professor Janine M. Idziak.

land than are human parents and property-owners that there are no limits to the obligations which would be produced by his commands. But most would surely judge that even
God could not remove my obligation to keep a solemn promise when the keeping of it
would cause pain to no one, or my obligation not to torture the innocent.[16]

Modifying our theory in line with this suggestion would involve restricting the
class of propositions which are such that divine commands are both sufficient and
necessary causal conditions for their being obligatory or forbidden. I do not know
exactly how to formulate plausible restrictions of the appropriate kind. However,
I am convinced that this is the direction in which to move if one proposes both to
allow that Cudworth's Objection is decisive in some but not all cases and to assert
that a causal divine command theory like the one I have constructed accounts for
other cases of obligation and prohibition.

Imagine someone asking this question: Is promise-keeping obligatory because
God commands it, or does God command promise-keeping because it is obligatory? Someone who holds a causal divine command theory like the one I have
formulated will answer that promise-keeping is obligatory because God commands it. For all questions of this form about obligations and prohibitions, such
a person will, unlike Euthyphro, reject the answers Socrates was fishing for. If a
causal divine command theorist is prepared to pay the price of adopting the Ock-
hamistic tactic for dealing with Cudworth's Objection I sketched above, then I
can see no other grounds for accusing him of irrationality when he answers in
this way.

---

[16] Richard Swinburne, *The Coherence of Theism* (Oxford: Clarendon Press, 1977), 207–8.

3

The Primacy of God's Will in Christian Ethics

In this paper I argue that some form of theological voluntarism ought to be the ethical theory of choice for Christian moral philosophers. The audience I hope my argument will convince consists of Christians of a fairly traditional cast of mind, and so my assumptions are things I take to be widely shared in conservative Christian communities. They will not be shared by all communities of moral inquiry. Those who do not share them may be persuaded that they cohere well with theological voluntarism; they are not likely to be convinced of its truth by my argument. It should therefore be read as a contribution to a debate within a distinctively Christian tradition of moral reflection and as an attempt to promote progress internal to that tradition. It does not aim to convince the adherents of rival traditions that are not Christian.

The argument has two parts. The first part is an attempt to build a cumulative case for a divine command conception of Christian morality. The case has three elements. None of them by itself is decisive; together they have considerable force. The first element in the case appeals to a conception of the divine nature that is not restricted to Christian theism. I argue that a particularly strong form of the doctrine of divine sovereignty can be used to furnish theists of all sorts with a positive theoretical reason for divine command ethics. The second element in the case appeals to narratives from the Hebrew Bible that have some authority for Jews, Christians, and Muslims. I argue that the cases often described as the immoralities of the patriarchs have in Christian tradition been interpreted in a way that provides Christians with a positive historical reason for divine command ethics. And the third element in the case appeals to the Gospel accounts of the command to followers of Jesus to love their neighbors. I argue that these accounts should, for reasons that Kierkegaard made clear, be interpreted so as to provide a positive moral reason for divine command ethics. As I see it, then,

Much of what I say in the first two sections of this paper is a slightly revised version of material that was included in my "The Recent Revival of Divine Command Ethics," *Philosophy and Phenomenological Research*, 50 (1990). Some of the material in the final section, also revised, comes from my "A Response to Hauerwas: Is Athens Revived Jerusalem Denied?" *Asbury Theological Journal*, 45 (1990).

divine command ethics rests securely on a tripod whose legs come from philosophical theology, scriptural interpretation, and Gospel morality. But I make no
claim that mine is a complete cumulative case for a divine command conception of Christian morality. There are, no doubt, other considerations Christians
can mobilize that will also furnish positive reasons for divine command ethics.
The three elements of my case do, however, illustrate the range of factors that
converge in support of theological voluntarism.

Such considerations as these do, I think, suffice to show that a divine command conception of morality is a serious contender for the allegiance of Christian
moral philosophers. But there are rivals also in contention within the arena of
Christian ethical thought. So the second part of my argument is an effort to
show that theological voluntarism is superior to the rival contender that currently
enjoys the greatest popularity among Christian philosophers. It is a virtue theory
of Aristotelian provenance. Of course it would be silly to maintain that there is
no place in Christian ethics for virtues, but I shall argue that they should not have
pride of place in Christian moral philosophy. They should instead be confined
to a subordinate role. Making human virtue primary in ethics is an inversion of
the Christian order in which God's will is primary and the human response to it
is secondary. Seen from within a Christian perspective, virtue looks very different from what it appears to be when observed from the point of view of pagan
Aristotelianism. So incorporating parts of Aristotle's ethical legacy into Christian moral philosophy will inevitably involve radical transformation in order to
enforce the required theoretical subordination.

The first three sections of the paper will be devoted to the three elements of
my cumulative case for divine command ethics. The final section will concentrate on showing that the rivalry with virtue theory is best brought to an end by
assigning the virtues to a secondary and derivative place in the architecture of
Christian moral theory. One disclaimer is needed before the argument begins.
This paper does nothing by way of offering a defense of the divine command conception against various philosophical objections. It is not that I regard the task of
constructing such a defense as unimportant. On the contrary, I think it is sufficiently important that I have made it a central project in my previous work on
divine command morality.[1] And others who have made major contributions to
the recent revival of divine command ethics in the philosophical world have also
done much to show that it can be successfully defended against objections.[2] But I
think the time has come in the campaign to refurbish divine command morality

---

[1] Philip L. Quinn, *Divine Commands and Moral Requirements* (Oxford: Clarendon Press, 1978)
and "Divine Command Ethics: A Causal Theory," in Janine M. Idziak (ed.), *Divine Command
Morality: Historical and Contemporary Readings* (New York and Toronto: Edwin Mellen Press, 1979).
[2] See e.g. Robert M. Adams, "A Modified Divine Command Theory of Ethical Wrongness,"
repr. in his *The Virtue of Faith* (New York: Oxford University Press, 1987); Edward R. Wierenga,
The Nature of God (Ithaca and London: Cornell University Press, 1989), ch. 8; and Richard J.
Mouw, *The God Who Commands* (Notre Dame: University of Notre Dame Press, 1990), ch. 1.

when a purely defensive strategy no longer promises to yield the greatest benefits. It seems to me that the time is now ripe for supporters of the divine command conception to make the positive case on its behalf to the community of Christian philosophers. It is the chief aim of this paper to do part of what needs to be done on this score if the case is to succeed in persuading that community.

DIVINE SOVEREIGNTY

There are a number of reasons for including a strong doctrine of divine sovereignty in one's philosophical theology. Two of the most important among them pertain to creation and providence. Theists customarily wish to insist on a sharp distinction between God and the world, between the creator and the created realm. According to traditional accounts of creation and conservation, each contingent thing depends on God's power for its existence whenever it exists. God, by contrast, depends on nothing external to himself for his existence. So God has complete sovereignty over contingent existence. Theists usually also wish to maintain that we may trust God's eschatological promises without reservation. Even if God does not control the finest details of history because he has chosen to create a world in which there is microphysical chance or libertarian freedom, he has the power to insure that the cosmos will serve his purposes for it and its inhabitants in the long run. So God also has extensive sovereignty over contingent events. Considerations of theoretical unity of a familiar sort then make it attractive to extend the scope of divine sovereignty from the contingent to the necessary and from the realm of fact into the realm of value.

How far can such extensions be pushed? In recent philosophical theology, there have been speculative attempts to push them very far indeed. Thomas Morris has advanced the metaphysical thesis "that God is absolute creator of necessary as well as contingent reality, and thus that literally all things do depend on him."[3] As Morris sees it, in order to be absolute creator "God must be responsible for the necessary truth of all propositions with this modality as well as for their mere existence as abstract objects."[4] If this view is tenable, Morris notes, "moral truths can be objective, unalterable, and necessary, and yet still dependent on God."[5] Thus, for example, even if it is necessarily true that such things as murder, theft, and adultery are morally wrong, the absolute creationist holds that God is somehow responsible for the necessary truth of the proposition that murder, theft, and adultery are wrong. But is this view tenable? In order to answer this question, we need to look at the details of the accounts the friends of absolute creation propose of the relation of dependence that is supposed to hold between God and such propositions.

---

[3] Thomas V. Morris, *Anselmian Explorations* (Notre Dame: University of Notre Dame Press, 1987), 163.
[4] Ibid. 166.   [5] Ibid. 171.

As far as I can tell, it is Michael Loux who has provided the best worked out theory of how necessary truths might depend upon God. It is based on the idea that there is an asymmetrical relation of dependence between certain divine beliefs and facts being necessarily as they are. Taking notions of believing and entertaining as primitives, Loux defines a concept of strong belief as follows: a person S strongly believes that p if and only if S believes that p and does not entertain that not-p. Since God is omniscient, divine beliefs correlate perfectly with truth and divine strong beliefs correlate perfectly with necessary truth. But there is more than mere correlation here; there is also metaphysical dependency:

> God is not in the relevant strong belief states because the facts are necessarily as they are. On the contrary, the facts are necessarily as they are because God has the relevant strong beliefs. So it is the case that $2 + 2 = 4$ because God believes that $2 + 2 = 4$; and it is necessarily the case that $2 + 2 = 4$ because God strongly believes that $2 + 2 = 4$.[6]

And, of course, this idea can easily be extended to the moral realm. It is the case that murder, theft, and adultery are wrong, on this view, because God believes that murder, theft, and adultery are wrong; and if it is necessarily the case that murder, theft, and adultery are wrong, this is so because God strongly believes that murder, theft, and adultery are wrong.

Loux apparently means his account to be quite general, for he makes an explicit exception only for the case of free action. Thus he goes on to tell us that "if we turn to the realm of contingent facts (other than those consisting in rational agents freely performing actions), then, on the account I have given, it is most natural to suppose that the facts stand as they do because God has the beliefs God does."[7] It is an advantage of this way of thinking, he observes, that it furnishes a way to capture the dependence of the contingent on its divine creator and conserver. Similarly, it might be alleged by absolute creationists to be a merit of the claim that necessary facts are necessarily as they are because God has the relevant strong beliefs that it captures the dependence of the necessary on its divine absolute creator.

Unfortunately, however there are more exceptional cases than Loux acknowledges. Microphysical indeterminacy in the contingent realm is likely to be one sort of exception, but there are also theologically significant exceptions in the necessary realm. According to a leading theistic tradition, it is a necessary truth that God exists. Applied to this case, Loux's theory tells us that it is the case that

---

[6] Michael J. Loux, "Toward an Aristotelian Theory of Abstract Objects," *Midwest Studies in Philosophy*, 11, ed. P. A. French, T. E. Uehling, and H. K. Wettstein (Minneapolis: University of Minnesota Press, 1986), 510. It is important not to confuse Loux's notion of entertaining with other concepts of entertaining that are, perhaps, more familiar. He supposes that if S believes that p then S entertains that p. There seems to be a familiar sense of entertaining in which it is the case that if S entertains that p then S believes that it is possible that not-p. But if this principle were conjoined to Loux's suppositions, a consequence would be that God believes that it is possible that $2 + 2 \neq 4$, which is plainly false.

[7] Ibid.

God exists because God believes that God exists and that it is necessarily the case that God exists because God strongly believes that God exists. This is surely not correct and, indeed, seems to have the order of dependence backwards. God's beliefs neither produce nor explain his own existence. We cannot use Pirandello's slogan, 'Right you are if you think you are!', as a principle for bootstrapping God into existence from his own beliefs. Similarly, it is a necessary truth that God is omniscient. So, according to the theory, it is the case that God is omniscient because God believes that God is omniscient, and it is necessarily the case that God is omniscient because God strongly believes that God is omniscient. Again, the actual order of dependence appears to be just the reverse of what the theory claims. I take it that these and similar theological examples suffice to refute Loux's version of the absolute creationist claim that God is responsible for the necessary truth of all propositions with this modality. A little less absolutism is, I think, called for here.

I am not sure exactly how to restrict the scope of the absolute creationist thesis in order to lend it maximal plausibility, though I have set forth one suggestion elsewhere.[8] However, in the present context it is not necessary to solve this problem. We can, I believe, avoid it by narrowing our focus of attention from global questions about truth in general to local questions about moral truth, and we can then ask how the kinds of considerations that motivate Morris and Loux should be applied within the moral realm. At the very least, I suggest, they would lead one to hold that moral truth depends in some way on divine beliefs. A principle about wrongness proposed by Wierenga can be adapted to illustrate this idea.[9] The modified principle is this: For every agent x, state of affairs S, and time t, (i) it is wrong that x bring about S at t if and only if God believes that x ought not to bring about S at t, and (ii) if it is wrong that x bring about S at t, then by believing that x ought not to bring about S at t God brings it about that it is wrong that x bring about S at t. Less formally but more generally, the idea is that moral facts are as they are because God has the beliefs he does about what creaturely moral agents ought and ought not to do and necessary moral facts, if there are any, are necessarily as they are because God has the strong beliefs he does about what creaturely moral agents ought and ought not to do. This idea gets support from the doctrine of divine sovereignty because it extends God's sovereignty to cover the entire moral realm. I conclude from this that the doctrine of divine sovereignty provides a positive reason for a theoretical conception of this general kind.

So far I have been following the lead of Morris and Loux and discussing the dependence of morality on God in terms of divine doxastic states rather than

---

[8] Philip L. Quinn, "An Argument for Divine Command Ethics," in M. Beaty (ed.), *Christian Theism and the Problems of Philosophy* (Notre Dame: University of Notre Dame Press, 1990).

[9] Wierenga's original principle, which I quote a little later, is to be found on p. 217 of his *The Nature of God*.

divine volitional states. So it might be thought that the view I claim is supported by the doctrine of divine sovereignty is unconnected with theological voluntarism. My next task is therefore to elucidate the connections between them. There are several ways to do this; which of them is best will depend on other theological considerations.

If the doctrine of divine simplicity is true, intellect and will are not distinct in God, and so divine believings and divine willings are identical. If, for ease of exposition, we elide divine willings of a certain sort and divine commands, then to refer to a divine belief that an agent ought not to bring about a state of affairs at a time and to refer to a divine command that this agent not bring about that state of affairs at the time in question is to refer twice to just one thing. Divine strong beliefs will be identical with divine commands that are invariant across all possible worlds, which might be thought of as divine strong commands. Hence, to the extent that a strong doctrine of divine sovereignty is a positive reason for making moral truth dependent on divine beliefs across the board, it is also a positive reason for making such truth dependent on divine commands across the board. Wierenga's principle about wrongness, a modified version of which I set forth above, reads as follows: "For every agent x, state of affairs S, and time t (i) it is wrong that x bring about S at t if and only if God forbids that x bring about S at t, and (ii) if it is wrong that x bring about S at t, then by forbidding that x bring about S at t God brings it about that it is wrong that x bring about S at t." If the doctrine of divine simplicity is true, this principle and my modification of it are alternative formulations of what amounts to a single claim, and so whatever is a positive reason for one of them is also a positive reason for the other.[10]

If, as I tend to think, the doctrine of divine simplicity is not true, things are a bit more complicated. But intellect and will are nevertheless tightly integrated in God, and so divine normative believings and divine willings are perfectly correlated. Though I think it would smack of presumption to claim to know much about the internal mechanisms of the divine cognitive and conative apparatuses and their interactions, several simple models of the relations of divine beliefs and the divine commands I am assimilating to certain divine willings to moral truths can easily be constructed. One might suppose that moral truths are causally overdetermined and that perfectly correlated divine beliefs and divine commands operate independently to bring it about that moral propositions are true. Alternatively, one might assign causal priority either to the divine will or to the divine intellect. In the former case, divine volitions would bring about divine beliefs, which would, in turn, bring about the truth of moral propositions. By transitivity, divine volitions would bring about the truth of moral propositions, and

---

[10] For further discussion of the bearing of the doctrine of divine simplicity on the foundations of Christian ethics, see Norman Kretzmann, "Abraham, Isaac, and Euthyphro: God and the Basis of Morality," in D. V. Stump et al., *Hamartia: The Concept of Error in the Western Tradition* (New York and Toronto: Edwin Mellen Press, 1983).

so they would be remote causes of moral status. In the latter case, divine beliefs would bring about divine volitions and hence divine commands, which would in turn bring about the truth of moral propositions. Thus divine commands would be proximate causes of moral status. I favor the third of these ways of thinking in the present context because it seems to me to have a slight edge over the other two in terms of intuitive naturalness or plausibility. On this view, to the extent that a strong doctrine of divine sovereignty is a positive reason for making moral truth dependent on divine beliefs, which are remote causes of moral truth, it is also a positive reason for making moral truth dependent on divine commands, which are effects of divine beliefs and proximate causes of moral truth. Moral truth, one might say, is the product of commands in perfect conformity with divine normative beliefs; it is thus the product of a "supremely rational will."[11]

Quite recently William P. Alston has argued that the most plausible form of divine command ethics will be one in which moral obligation, but not moral goodness, is dependent on God's will.[12] If that is right, then considerations of theoretical unity will allow us to extend the scope of divine sovereignty into the moral realm but may not permit us to extend it so far that it covers the entire moral realm. Whether the latter extension can be made will depend on further considerations such as the plausibility of Alston's suggestion that God himself is the supreme criterion of moral goodness and whether, if this is true, God is sovereign over moral goodness in a sense analogous to that in which he is sovereign over moral obligation because it depends on his will. The upshot, I think, is that there is a positive reason to suppose that divine sovereignty has, at the very least, a large territory to rule in the realm of value. But its claim to rule the entire realm may have to be scaled back or qualified just as Loux's extravagant claims have to be cut back in the theological realm.

THE IMMORALITIES OF THE PATRIARCHS

Speculative theistic metaphysics is not the only source of support for the divine command conception to be found within Christian traditions. Another is scripture itself. When we turn our attention to its narratives of God's dealings with his human creatures, we discover a picture of a deity who commands extensively. And in a prominent medieval tradition of interpreting scriptural stories about divine commands we find independent positive reasons for favoring an account of morality in which the primacy of God's will is acknowledged.

[11] William E. Mann, "Modality, Morality, and God," *Noûs*, 23 (1989), 99. Mann's argument, like mine, starts from divine sovereignty, but the two arguments proceed along different paths to similar conclusions.

[12] William P. Alston, "Some Suggestions for Divine Command Theorists," included in his *Divine Nature and Human Language: Essays in Philosophical Theology* (Ithaca and London: Cornell University Press, 1989).

In medieval discussions it is sometimes disconcerting to see a philosophical question answered by appeal to the authority of scripture. For the most part, philosophers in our era would not make such appeals, but there is a good deal to be said for the practice, particularly in moral philosophy. The Hebrew Bible is authoritative for Judaism, Christianity, and Islam. I think this authority operates in two ways. First, scriptural narratives propose paradigms of moral good and evil. They thereby help train the theist's faculty of moral discrimination and even contribute to the constitution of theistic moral concepts. Second, within theistic traditions canonical scriptures are cognitive authorities because they are supposed to contain divine revelation. Of course interpreting scripture has always been a delicate task, and hermeneutical controversies are both abundant and persistent. But plausible interpretations must within these traditions be granted evidential force just because scripture is at least a source and, on some views, is the only independent and ultimate source of sound doctrine about God. There can be no serious doubt that the Hebrew Bible portrays God as a commander. He is to be obeyed.

The Pentateuch records divine commands laying down the law about all sorts of things, including but not restricted to matters such as homicide that are clearly moral. Both Exodus 20: 1–17 and Deuteronomy 5: 6–21, which recount the revelation of the Decalogue, picture God as instructing his people about what they are to do and not to do by commanding them. He reveals his will and does not merely transmit information. So it is natural enough to assume that the authority of the Decalogue depends upon the fact that it is an expression of the divine will. Even if one doubts some of the details of these narratives because one thinks, for example, that God would not bother to regulate diet or ritual to quite the extent they say he does, it can hardly be denied that the conception of God the stories embody is that of a lawgiver. This conception surely invites development along just the lines proposed by divine command theories of morality. But, though such a development coheres very well with the narratives, they do not force the conclusion that God is the source of moral obligation. They can be interpreted so as to portray God as merely promulgating to his people moral laws that hold independent of his will if there are good reasons to suppose that such laws exist. After all, if there were such laws, a perfectly good God would will that his people obey them. And divine commands governing such things as ritual could be thought of as imposing religious rather than moral obligations.

There are, however, scriptural stories that can serve as a basis for a direct argument to the conclusion that God is the source of moral obligation. These are the incidents sometimes described as the immoralities of the patriarchs. They are cases in which God commands something that appears to be immoral and, indeed, to violate a prohibition he himself lays down in the Decalogue. Three such cases come up again and again in traditional Christian discussions. The first is the divine command to Abraham, recorded in Genesis 22: 1–2, to sacrifice Isaac, his son. The second is the divine command reported in Exodus 11: 2, which was interpreted as a command that the Israelites plunder the Egyptians. And the third is the divine command to the prophet Hosea, stated first in Hosea 1: 2 and repeated in Hosea 3: 1, to have sexual relations with an adulteress. According to these stories, God has apparently commanded homicide, theft, and adultery (or at least fornication) in particular cases in a way that is contrary to the general prohibitions of the Decalogue. Such cases were bound to attract comments. How are we to interpret them?

The commentators I am going to discuss take scripture for literal truth; they assume that God actually did command as he is said to have done by the stories. They also suppose that these commands were binding on those to whom they were directed. In *The City of God*, Augustine uses the case of Abraham to make the point that the divine law prohibiting killing allows exceptions "when God authorizes killing by a general law or when He gives an explicit commission to an individual for a limited time." Abraham, he says, "was not only free from the guilt of criminal cruelty, but even commended for his piety, when he consented to sacrifice his son, not, indeed, with criminal intent but in obedience to God."[13] And in his *Questions on the Heptateuch*, Augustine disposes of the Exodus case with the remark that "the Israelites did not engage in theft, but, withG od commanding this, they performed an office."[14] It is clear that Augustine thinks Abraham did what he should do in consenting to kill Isaac and the Israelites did what they should do in plundering the Egyptians because these things had been commanded by God. He also thinks that these things, which would have been wrong in the absence of those commands, were not wrong given their presence. So Augustine holds that divine commands addressed to particular individuals or groups determine the moral status of actions they perform out of obedience.

This general line on the immoralities of the patriarchs crops up over and over again in the works of Augustine's medieval successors. In his *On Precept and Dispensation*, Bernard says this:

You shall not kill, You shall not commit adultery, You shall not steal, and the remaining precepts of that table, precepts which are such that, although they admit no human dispensation absolutely, and neither was it permitted nor will it be permitted to any human being to give release to something from those precepts in any way, yet God has given release from those which he wished, when he wished, whether when he ordered that the Egyptians be plundered by the Hebrews, or when he ordered the Prophet to have intercourse with a woman who was a fornicator. Certainly would nothing but a grievous act of theft be ascribed to the one, and nothing but the turpitude of a shameful act done in the heat of passion, to the other, if the authority of the commander should not have excused each act.[15]

---

[13] Augustine, *The City of God* I. 21.   [14] Augustine, *Questions on the Heptateuch* II. 39.
[15] Bernard, *On Precept and Dispensation* III. 6. I quote an unpublished translation by Janine M. Idziak.

So Bernard takes the Exodus case and the case of Hosea to show that God's
authority is such that by his commands, he and only he dispenses people from the
obligation to obey the precepts of the second table of the Decalogue. Plundering
the Egyptians and having intercourse with a woman who was a fornicator, which
would have been wrong in the absence of the divine commands to the Hebrews
and Hosea, respectively, because they violate the precepts of the Decalogue, were
in fact not wrong because God commanded them. Like Augustine, Bernard holds
that divine commands make all the difference in the moral status of these actions.

   The connection of these cases to a full-fledged divine command ethics is made
quite explicit in the work of Andreas de Novo Castro, a fourteenth century philosopher who is judged by Janine M. Idziak to have conducted "the lengthiest and
most sophisticated defense of the position."[16] He claims that there are actions
which, "known per se by the law of nature and by the dictate of natural reason,
are seen to be prohibited, as actions which are homicides, thefts, adulteries, etc.;
but, with respect to the absolute power of God, it is possible that actions of this
kind not be sins."[17] After citing the passage by Bernard I have quoted, which
he thinks makes this evident, de Novo Castro appeals to the case of Abraham
for additional confirmation. Abraham, he says, "wished to kill his son so that he
would be obedient to God commanding this, and he would not have sinned in
this if God should not have withdrawn the command."[18] For de Novo Castro,
God's absolute power is such that acts such as homicides, thefts, and adulteries,
which are seen to be prohibited and so sins when known per se by means of natural law and natural reason, would not be sins if they were commanded by God
as some in fact have been. He shares with Augustine and Bernard the view that
divine commands can and do determine the moral status of actions.

   What may be unexpected is that Aquinas too shares this view. He devotes an
article of the *Summa Theologiae* to the question of whether the precepts of the
Decalogue are dispensable, and in it he pronounces a verdict on our three cases.
Not surprisingly, Aquinas maintains that those precepts "admit of no dispensa-
tion whatever," and so he disagrees with Bernard on this point.[19] But when he
treats our three cases in the course of responding to an objection, he agrees with
Bernard in exonerating the patriarchs. How does he manage to pull off this trick?
The paragraph deserves to be quoted in full:

Consequently when the children of Israel, by God's command, took away the spoils
of the Egyptians, this was not theft; since it was due to them by the sentence of
God.—Likewise when Abraham consented to slay his son, he did not consent to murder,
because his son was due to be slain by the command of God, Who is Lord of life and

---

   [16] Janine M. Idziak, "In Search of 'Good Positive Reasons' for an Ethics of Divine Commands:
A Catalogue of Arguments," *Faith and Philosophy*, 6 (1989), 63.
   [17] Andreas de Novo Castro, *Primum Scriptum Sententiarum*, d. 48, q. 2, a. 2, concl. 2. I quote
from an unpublished edition and translation by Janine M. Idziak.
   [18] Ibid.   [19] Thomas Aquinas, *Summa Theologiae* I–II, q. 100, a. 8.

death: for He it is Who inflicts the punishment of death on all men, both godly and ungodly, on account of the sin of our first parent, and if a man be the executor of that sentence by Divine authority, he will be no murderer any more than God would be.—Again Osee, by taking unto himself a wife of fornications, or an adulterous woman, was not guilty either of adultery or of fornication: because he took unto himself one who was his by command of God, Who is the author of the institution of marriage.[20]

The main ideas in this passage are simple enough. Because God commanded the Israelites to plunder the Egyptians, what the Israelites took was due to them and not to the Egyptians. Since theft involves taking what is not one's due, the plunder of the Egyptians was no theft. Hence the Israelites needed no dispensation from the prohibition on theft because their action did not come within its scope. Similarly, because God, who is Lord of life and death, commanded Abraham to slay Isaac, Isaac was due to receive the punishment of death all humans deserve in consequence of original sin. Since murder involves slaying someone who is not due to be slain, the slaying of Isaac would have been no murder, and so Abraham did not consent to murder and needed no dispensation from the prohibition on murder. And because God, who is the Author of marriage, commanded Hosea to take the adulteress as his wife, she was his wife and so he was guilty of neither adultery nor fornication in having intercourse with her.

Aquinas and de Novo Castro differ in some respects about what the divine commands do in our three cases. De Novo Castro seems to think that God's command to Abraham brings it about that the slaying of Isaac would not be wrong while remaining a murder. By contrast, Aquinas clearly supposes that God's command to Abraham brings it about that the slaying of Isaac would be neither wrong nor a murder. But this disagreement should not blind us to the fact that they are of one mind in thinking that divine commands make a moral difference in all three cases. Both hold that the slaying of Isaac by Abraham, which would be wrong in the absence of the divine command to Abraham because of the Decalogue's prohibition, will not be wrong in the presence of that command if Abraham carries it out. And they think similar things about the plundering of the Egyptians by the Israelites and Hosea having intercourse with the adulteress. We might sum up the agreement by saying that what the divine commands do in all three cases is to make obligatory patriarchal actions that would have been wrong in their absence. And because divine commands make this kind of moral difference in virtue of something necessarily restricted to God alone such as absolute power or lordship over life and death, human commands could not make a moral difference of this sort.

It is worth noting that agreement with Augustine, Bernard, Aquinas, and de Novo Castro about these cases and others like them need not be restricted to those Christians who share their belief that there actually were such divine

---

[20] Ibid., ad 3. Aquinas also discusses these three cases, ibid., q. 94, a. 5; there the question is whether the natural law can be changed.

commands as the scriptural stories say there were. Some may choose to think of cases like these as merely possible but concur with the tradition of interpretation I have been describing in believing that divine commands would make a moral difference of the sort our medieval authorities thought they did in fact make. I think there would be enough agreement about some such cases among reflective Christians who considered them carefully to make it fair to claim that Christian moral intuitions about scriptural cases support the conclusion that God is a source of moral obligation. Moreover, it is only a contingent fact that there are at most a few such cases. The properties such as absolute power or lordship over life and death in virtue of which divine commands are authoritative would remain unchanged if such commands were more numerous or even universal. So it is hard to resist the conclusion that any act of homicide, plunder, or intercourse with a person other than one's spouse would be obligatory if it were divinely commanded. Most, if not all, such acts are not obligatory because God refrains from commanding anyone to perform them. Hence the moral intuitions that lie behind the tradition of scriptural interpretation I have been discussing also support the stronger conclusion that whether any action is obligatory or not depends on whether God commands it or refrains from doing so. Reflection on scripture and how it has been interpreted in an impressive tradition of Christian thought furnishes another positive reason for thinking that divine commands are both necessary and sufficient to impose moral obligations.

COMMANDED LOVE

It is a striking feature of the ethics of love set forth in the Gospels that love is the subject of a command. In Matthew's Gospel, Jesus states it in response to a question from a lawyer about which commandment of the law is the greatest. He says:

You shall love the Lord your God with your whole heart, with your whole soul, and with all your mind. This is the greatest and first commandment. The second is like it: You shall love your neighbor as yourself. On these two commandments the whole law is based, and the prophets as well.[21]

Mark 12: 29–31 tells of Jesus giving essentially the same answer to a question by a scribe, and Luke 10: 27–8 speaks of a lawyer giving this answer to a question from Jesus and being told by Jesus that he has answered correctly. And in his last discourse, recorded in John's Gospel, Jesus tells his followers that "the command I give you is this, that you love one another."[22] So the authors of those books concur in thinking that Jesus expressed, or approved others expressing, the ethical demand that we love one another in the form of a command.

It might be thought that this manner of expression is inessential to a Christian ethics of love of neighbor, arising merely from the fact that Jesus is portrayed as

---

[21] Matthew 22: 37–40.   [22] John 15: 17.

propounding the ethics of love in the course of discussion with lawyers or scribes who are concerned about his views on questions of law. Because the questions being discussed are legalistic in nature, it might be said, it is not surprising that Jesus uses or approves legalistic rhetoric involving talk of commands in the specific context of answering them. By itself, the fact that a Christian ethics of love can be put in terms of commands does not imply that it must be formulated or is best articulated in such terms. To be sure, Jesus commands love not only when addressing Pharisees who are hostile to him but also when addressing followers who are committed to him. But I suppose that even this consideration need not be regarded as decisive in the absence of a reason for thinking that the particular sort of love Jesus wants people to have must, at least in the first instance, be commanded. Is there such a reason?

I think there is. To a first approximation, it is that the love of neighbor of which Jesus speaks is unnatural for humans in their present condition. It does not spontaneously engage their affections, and so training, self-discipline, and, perhaps, even divine assistance are required to make its achievement a real possibility. For most of us most of the time, love of neighbor is not an attractive goal, and, if it were optional, we would not pursue it. It must therefore be an obligatory love with the feel of something that represents a curb or check on our natural desires and predilections. Because the divine command conception holds that all obligations depend on God's will, such an obligatory love is properly represented as subject to being commanded by a divine lawgiver. It is, then, no accident that the love of neighbor the Gospels propose to us is a commanded love.

In my opinion, no Christian thinker has seen with greater clarity than Kierkegaard just how radical the demands of love of neighbor are. In *Works of Love*, he addresses the reader in his own name, presenting, as the subtitle indicates, some Christian reflections in the form of discourses. The discourse on Matthew 22: 39, which was quoted above, draws a sharp contrast between erotic love and friendship, on the one hand, and Christian love of neighbor, on the other. Both erotic love and friendship play favorites; the practical love of neighbor Christians are commanded to display by performing works of love does not. Kierkegaard says:

The object of both erotic love and friendship has therefore also the favorite's name, *the beloved, the friend*, who is loved in distinction from the rest of the world. On the other hand, the Christian teaching is to love one's neighbor, to love all mankind, all men, even enemies, and not to make exceptions, neither in favoritism nor in aversion.[23]

One's neighbor is, in short, everyone. Since the command tells us that the neighbor is to be loved as we love ourselves, everyone without exception ought to be regarded as just as near to us as we are to ourselves according to Kierkegaard. In

---

[23] Soren Kierkegaard, *Works of Love*, tr. Howard and Edna Hong (New York: Harper Torchbooks, 1964), 36.

terms of this spatial metaphor, what is wrong with selfish self-love is that one is nearer to oneself than to anyone else. Erotic love and friendship represent only a partial break with selfish self-love because they are exclusive. The beloved or the friend is nearer to oneself than those who are not bonded to one by such relationships of partiality. Kierkegaard endeavors to drive the point home by putting it in terms that smack of paradox. His claim is this:

If there are only two people, the other person is the neighbor. If there are millions, everyone of these is one's neighbor, that is, again, one who is closer than *the friend* and *the beloved*, inasmuch as these, as objects of partiality, lie so close to one's self-love.[24]

The air of paradox is generated by the thought that the friend or the beloved is also one's neighbor, for this seems to have the consequence that one and the same person is nearer to us under one description than she or he is under another. But the point Kierkegaard is trying to make is not paradoxical at all, though it may seem shocking. I take it to be that the obligation to love imposed by the command places absolutely every human, including one's beloved, one's friend, and one's very self, at the same distance from one as one's worst enemy or millions of people with whom one has had no contact. And so it is an obligation that extends to all alike, excludes no one, and does not even permit distinctions among persons rooted in differential preferences. It is, perhaps, easy to imagine God loving all his human creatures in this undiscriminating way. It is much more difficult to see how it could be either desirable or feasible for humans to respond to one another in this fashion. But if Kierkegaard is right, this is exactly what the command to love the neighbor bids us to do.

The offense to common sense would be mitigated but not altogether removed if the scope of the obligation to love were narrowed. One might, for example, construe the command quoted above from the last discourse of Jesus as imposing an obligation to love that does not extend beyond those who are his followers. But even the first disciples of Jesus were a mixed bag; the members of the household of faith today are a very motley crew indeed. It would not square with the natural inclinations or predilections of the Christians of any era to love one another equally and without distinction. Not all Christians are alike in erotic attractiveness; nor are they all equal with respect to the charms of virtuous character. So a nondiscriminatory love of all alike is bound to go against the grain of our natural affections and their partialities.

Kierkegaard is acutely aware of this partiality. He insists that "in erotic love and friendship the two love one another in virtue of differences or in virtue of likenesses which are grounded in differences (as when two friends love one another on the basis of likeness in customs, character, occupation, education, *etc.*, consequently on the basis of the likeness by which they are different from other

---

[24] Soren Kierkegaard, *Works of Love*, 38.

men or in which they are like each other as different from other men)."[25] He is also sensitive to the fact that the dependence of erotic love and friendship on the characteristics of the beloved and the friend make them vulnerable to changes in their objects. If the beloved loses the traits in virtue of which she or he was erotically attractive, then erotic love dies. If the friend who was prized for having a virtuous character turns vicious, then the friendship is not likely to survive unless one is corrupted and turns vicious too. But love of neighbor is invulnerable to alterations in its object. Kierkegaard puts the point this way:

To be sure, you can also continue to love your beloved and your friend no matter how they treat you, but you cannot truthfully continue to call them beloved and friend when they, sorry to say, have really changed. No change, however, can take your neighbor from you, for it is not your neighbor who holds you fast—it is your love which holds your neighbor fast. If your love for your neighbor remains unchanged, then your neighbor also remains unchanged just by being.[26]

If there is to be such a love that alters not where it alteration finds, it cannot depend on mutable features of the neighbor or ways in which they engage our spontaneous and natural affections. According to Kierkegaard, it will have the requisite independence only if it is a duty, for only then can it be motivated by a sense of duty instead of by changeable affections or preferences. "In this way," he says, "the 'You shall' makes love free in blessed independence; such a love stands and does not fall with variations in the object of love; it stands and falls with eternity's law, but therefore it never falls."[27] Only if love of the neighbor is required of us will our response to that unvarying demand remain stable in the face of changes in the neighbor and our natural reactions to them.

There are, then, two reasons for supposing that Christian love of neighbor has to be a matter of duty or obligation. The first is that only a dutiful love can be sufficiently extensive in scope to embrace everyone without distinction. Erotic love and friendship are always discriminating and so exclusive. The second reason is that only a dutiful love can be invulnerable to alterations in its objects. Erotic love and friendship are apt to change when the valued features of their objects alter. "In love and friendship preference is the middle term," Kierkegaard says; "in love to one's neighbor God is the middle term."[28] In Christian love of neighbor God is the middle term in two ways. First, love of neighbor arises from loving God above all else and then loving his human creatures, including oneself, in the steadfast and nondiscriminating way in which he loves them. And, second, it is God's will, made known to us by Jesus, that we humans love one another in this manner. As Christians see it, Jesus is at least the Son of God who reveals the will of his Father by commanding love of the neighbor. Christians who also accept the astonishing claim that Jesus Christ is God Incarnate seem to be committed to

[25] Ibid. 69.   [26] Ibid. 76.   [27] Ibid. 53.   [28] Ibid. 70.

the view that the obligation to love the neighbor as oneself is a duty imposed by a direct divine command.

I think this commanded love is foundational for Christian ethics; it is what sets Christian ethics apart from all its rivals. There is nothing like it in the pagan ethics of antiquity or in the secular moralities of the modern era. The command is apt to give offense, and even Christians in their present condition find it difficult to acknowledge its full force. "Only acknowledge it," Kierkegaard exhorts his readers, "or if it is disturbing to you to have it put in this way, I will admit that many times it has thrust me back and that I am yet very far from the illusion that I fulfill this command, which to flesh and blood is offense, and to wisdom foolishness."[29] In our lucid moments all of us would have to agree with Kierkegaard on this point and admit that we as we love ourselves. But I concur with Kierkegaard in considering it important to highlight rather than downplay the stringency of the duty to love the neighbor even if in consequence some people are thrust back or offended. Loving everyone as we love ourselves is, I want to insist, obligatory in Christian ethics, and it has this status, as the Gospels show us, because God has commanded this all-inclusive love. So I find in what is most distinctive about the Christian ethics of the Gospels another reason for Christians to favor a divine command conception of moral obligation. It seems to me that Christians who take the Gospels seriously would be in no position to deny that they teach us that we have been commanded by God to love the neighbor and so are obliged to do our best to fulfill the command perfectly.

This completes my argument in three parts for the conclusion that a divine command conception of morality has in its own right a serious claim to be regarded as a good way to understand Christian ethics because it acknowledges the primacy of God's will in the moral realm. The strength of my case rests in part on the diversity of sources within Christian tradition to which it appeals. Considerations from speculative philosophical theology, Christian commentary on incidents portrayed in the Hebrew Bible, and the distinctively Christian ethical demands set forth by Jesus in the Gospels converge in supporting theological voluntarism. But it is a conception that has had rivals within the history of Christian moral thought, and so something must be said about how it stacks up against its competitors. I therefore conclude with a sketch of how the rivalry with currently fashionable virtue theories might be brought to an end by incorporating what is of lasting value from such theories into divine command morality.

DIVINE COMMANDS AND ARISTOTLE'S VIRTUES

Virtue ethics has undergone something of a renaissance in recent philosophical discussion. Virtue theorists agree in tracing their roots back to Aristotle, but he

---

[29] Soren Kierkegaard, *Works of Love*, tr. Howard and Edna Hong (New York: Harper Torchbooks, 1964), 71.

is a philosopher who can be used to serve many purposes. It is important to realize that not all philosophers who acknowledge having benefitted from studying him have learned the same lessons. On the contemporary scene, Aristotle is being appropriated by the adherents of at least two deeply divergent projects of moral inquiry.

One is wholly secular and is attracted by Aristotle's optimistic paganism. Martha Nussbaum represents this sort of interest in reviving Aristotle. She remarks that Aristotle "holds that human beings are naturally drawn toward virtue rather than vice, love more than repudiation—and that, given sufficient education, material support, and personal effort, most people will be able to make good and reasonable lives *for themselves*" (my emphasis).[30] On this view, the attractive prospect Aristotle's thought offers us is that, if fortune favors them, human beings can, operating on their own steam, so to speak, flourish and so be happy over the course of an earthly lifetime. And these achievements are independent of religion. Noting that Aristotle does not place piety on his list of virtues, Nussbaum conjectures that "this probably indicates his interest in separating practical reason from religious authority, and in keeping reason, rather than such authorities, in control of the most important matters."[31] Practical reason operating apart from religious influences offers humans their best shot at working out for themselves good lives.

All this is, needless to say, deeply alien to traditional Christian thought. It would insist that humans in their present condition are fallen and, if left to themselves, incapable of flourishing in this life. Such human flourishing as is possible must take place against a background of ceaseless struggle to overcome interior evil. It can never be a wholly human achievement, something people make for themselves if they are lucky. It must always be at least in part a divine gift. Nor is reason itself exempt from the infirmities of the present human condition; it too is fallen and enfeebled. A traditional Christian is therefore likely to regard as naive any confidence in the ability of unaided human practical reason to rule well in the most important matters in our lives.

Aristotle's perspective allows him to see nothing beyond completed earthly lives, and so he must judge human flourishing and happiness in secular terms. From this point of view, it is quite reasonable to emphasize the way in which good fortune is essential for human flourishing, for the activities that, according to Aristotle, constitute a happy life are not possible in the absence of such conditions as good health and a modicum of wealth. Christianity's larger eschatological vision opens up other possibilities. Misfortune, far from ruling out ultimate happiness, may prove a blessing in disguise by furnishing to the one who suffers it an opportunity to become more intimately related to the suffering Jesus on the

---

[30] Martha Nussbaum, "Recoiling from Reason," *New York Review of Books*, 36 (Dec. 7, 1989), 40.
[31] Ibid.

Cross. Providence may be giving to the wretched of the earth—those most sorely afflicted by disease and poverty—chances to imitate Christ that the comfortably situated ought to envy. Aristotle clearly would not have counted as blessed all the people Jesus did: the poor in spirit, the sorrowing, the lowly, those who hunger and thirst for holiness, the merciful, the simple-hearted, the peacemakers, and those who are persecuted for holiness's sake.[32] Not many such people would flourish in an ancient *polis* or, for that matter, in a modern secular polity. But Jesus promises them a great reward in heaven.

Moreover, Aristotelian friendships have just those characteristics in virtue of which a sharp contrast has to be drawn between even the best sort of friendship and genuine Christian love of the neighbor. Aristotle restricts the highest kind of friendship to good people who are equal in virtue and insists that we must rest content with only a few friends of this kind. "One cannot be a friend to many people in the sense of having friendship of the perfect type with them," Aristotle tells us, "just as one cannot be in love with many people at once (for love is a sort of excess of feeling, and it is the nature of such only to be felt towards one person); and it is not easy for many people at the same time to please the same person very greatly, or perhaps even to be good in his eyes."[33] But Christian love of neighbor, unlike both Aristotle's friendship of the perfect type and his love based on an excess of feeling, is something we are obliged to direct toward everyone. Aristotle also says this: "Now equality and likeness are friendship, and especially the likeness of those who are like in virtue; for being steadfast in themselves they hold fast to each other, and neither ask nor give base services, but (one may say) even prevent them; for it is characteristic of good men neither to go wrong themselves nor to let their friends do so."[34] But, again, Christian love of neighbor cannot be so exclusive; it must also be directed towards those who are not one's like in virtue. We are commanded to love not only our equals in virtue but also both those who are more virtuous and those who are less virtuous than we are. Aristotelian friendship between equals in virtue is, no doubt, an admirable thing, and secular moralists are right to praise it. It is, however, a far cry from Christian love of one's neighbor and the divine love for all humans that is its paradigm.

Another contemporary project of moral inquiry that treats Aristotle as a valuable resource is a tradition in Christian ethics whose distinguished ancestry can be traced back at least as far as Aquinas. Unlike the secular retrieval of Aristotle, this project must be very selective in appropriating Aristotelian materials, for Aristotle's optimistic paganism and the grim realities of the Christian drama of sin and salvation are worlds apart, as the contrasts I have mentioned above only begin to indicate. It can learn from Aristotle and other virtue theorists provided their insights are transformed by being situated in a theoretical context that focuses moral inquiry on discerning God's will.

---

[32] Matthew 5: 3–10.   [33] Aristotle, *Nicomachean Ethics*, 1158a10–14.
[34] Ibid. 1159b2–7.

Divine command moralists should, I think, be prepared to engage in such selective appropriation and transformation of Aristotelian conceptions of virtue. After all, divine command theorists will not wish to deny that there are such things as moral virtues; they will, however, want to dispute characteristic Aristotelian claims about their importance and centrality in moral thinking. For Aristotle, the virtues hold pride of place in ethical theory. They are not properly understood as dispositions to produce independently defined or recognizable good actions or states of affairs; rather good actions or states of affairs are defined as those a virtuous person would voluntarily produce in the appropriate circumstances. From the point of view of the divine command theorist, Aristotle has got things backwards. The will of God, the commands that express it, and the moral laws those commands establish are primary for ethics, and so obligations to obey God's moral legislation will be the fundamental facts of morality. The virtues will have a distinctly secondary role to play; they will be construed as habits of obedience to various standing divine commands or other expressions of God's will for humans. The virtue of obedience itself will be the master moral virtue and should occupy center stage in moral theory.

Aquinas recognizes the importance of obedience to God's will for Christian ethics. When engaged in moral thinking, he is a bit of a magpie, picking up bits and pieces of lore from a variety of sources. In portraying Aquinas as a moral *bricoleur*, Jeffrey Stout notes that "his real accomplishment was to bring together into a single whole a wide assortment of fragments—Platonic, Stoic, Pauline, Jewish, Islamic, Augustinian, and Aristotelian."[35] To be sure, he tries to assemble these fragments into a coherent pattern by subsuming them under a largely Aristotelian conceptual scheme. But scheme and content do not always fit well together, as the case of obedience shows. A single question is devoted to it slightly more than half way through the second part of the second part of the *Summa Theologiae*. It is classified as a part of a part of the virtue of justice. Yet Aquinas returns a positive answer to the question of whether obedience to God is the greatest of the moral virtues.

He argues that moral virtues are to be ranked in accord with the principle that the greater the thing a person contemns in order to adhere to God, the greater the virtue. Human goods that may be contemned for God's sake are, in order of increasing greatness, external goods, goods of the body, and goods of the soul. Among goods of the soul, the will is the highest because it is by the will that humans make use of all other goods. It follows that "properly speaking, the virtue of obedience, whereby we contemn our own will for God's sake, is more praiseworthy than the other moral virtues, which contemn other goods for the sake of God."[36] What is more, other acts of virtue have no merit in God's eyes

---

[35] Jeffrey Stout, *Ethics After Babel: The Languages of Morals and their Discontents* (Boston: Beacon Press, 1988), 76.

[36] *Summa Theologiae* II–II, q. 104, a. 3.

unless they are done out of obedience to God's will. "For were one to suffer even martyrdom, or to give all one's goods to the poor," Aquinas insists, "unless one directed these things to the fulfillment of the divine will, which pertains directly to obedience, they could not be meritorious."[37] Neither would such things be meritorious if they were done without charity, he continues, but that theological virtue "cannot exist apart from obedience."[38] So obedience to God's will is not only the most praiseworthy of the moral virtues but also a necessary condition of both merit before God and charity.

It is interesting to note that Aquinas returns to the immoralities of the patriarchs in the course of a discussion of the question of whether God is to be obeyed in all things. These cases now form the basis of an objection. No one, Aquinas assumes, is bound to do anything contrary to virtue. But it seems that the divine command to Abraham to slay his innocent son and the divine command to the Jews to plunder the Egyptians are contrary to justice and that the divine command to Hosea to take to himself a woman who was an adulteress is contrary to chastity. Hence it seems that God is not to be obeyed in all things. The reply to this objection puts the case for the primacy of God's will in Christian ethics in a striking and forceful way. "God can command nothing contrary to virtue," Aquinas assures us, "since virtue and rectitude of human will consist chiefly in conformity with God's will and obedience to His command, although it be contrary to the wonted mode of virtue."[39] And he proceeds to deal with the three cases in a manner that should by now seem quite familiar. God's command to Abraham to slay his innocent son is not contrary to justice because God is the author of life and death. God's command to the Jews to plunder the Egyptians is not contrary to justice because all things really belong to God and he gives them to whom he will. And God's command to Hosea to take unto himself an adulteress is not contrary to chastity because, God being the ordainer of human generation, the right manner of sexual intercourse is that which he appoints.

I am of the opinion that Christian moral philosophers ought to join Aquinas in holding that virtue consists chiefly in conformity with God's will and obedience to his commands. As I see it, this should be the ruling idea of any account of the virtues that claims it is part of a genuinely Christian ethics. Plausible claims about the virtues deriving from sources such as Aristotle should be incorporated into Christian ethics just to the extent that they can be made to cohere with and subordinated to this ruling idea. When this cannot be accomplished, Christian moral philosophers should reject such claims. So a Christian ethics of virtue would not be a rival of theological voluntarism but a proper part of a fully developed divine command morality. Such an account of the moral virtues may well, as the example of Aquinas suggests, overlap Aristotle's doctrine of the virtues at quite a few points. But those engaged in trying to construct such an account

---

[37] *Summa Theologiae* II–II, q. 104, a. 3.   [38] Ibid.   [39] Ibid., a. 4, ad 2.

ought to keep clearly in mind the thought that complete coincidence with Aristotle's ethics is out of the question. There are bound to be radical disagreements with Aristotle and with his contemporary secular heirs in any moral theory that insists, as I have argued Christian ethics should, on the primacy of God's will as a norm for human conduct and character.

RELIGION AND TRAGIC DILEMMAS

4

Moral Obligation, Religious Demand, and Practical Conflict

Almost all philosophers would concede that conflict among what are often described as prima facie moral obligations is possible and sometimes occurs. The question of whether there can be conflict among what are described, by contrast, as actual moral obligations is vexed. Some philosophers argue that such conflicts do occur, or at least are easily imaginable, and hence are possible.[1] Others argue that such conflicts cannot occur, or at least could not occur from the perspective of an ideally complete and adequate moral theory.[2] The arguments on both sides of the question are impressive. In my opinion, the philosophical contest so far has resulted in a standoff. Be that as it may, it is worth noting that, if such conflicts were to occur, they would be, as usually conceived, internal to the moral realm.

In this paper I discuss the possibility that there are conflicts between moral obligations and other practical requirements rooted outside the moral realm altogether. In particular, I intend to take seriously the possibility of conflict between actual moral obligations and the demands of religious living imposed by divine fiat. Many philosophers, myself included, have been tempted to assimilate all such religious demands to moral requirements and for that reason to suppose that a divine command theory might be needed to account for at least part of the moral realm.[3] But I now think that giving in to this temptation is likely to misrepresent, if not mask completely, an important philosophical issue by portraying all possible conflicts between moral obligations and religious demands as internal

Earlier versions of this paper were read at the University of Miami in Jan. 1984, in Lincoln, Nebraska, at the NEH Research Conference in the Philosophy of Religion in Apr. 1984, and at the University of Notre Dame in Nov. 1984. All three audiences engaged me in lively discussion, for which I am grateful. Keith Yandell's formal comments at the NEH conference were extensive and illuminating. I also received helpful criticism from Robert Audi, David Burrell, Clement Dore, C. Stephen Evans, William K. Frankena, Jorge Garcia, Ramon Lemos, Gary Rosenkrantz, Edward Wierenga, and others.

[1] On this side of the controversy, I find especially helpful Ruth Marcus, "Moral Dilemmas and Consistency," *Journal of Philosophy*, 77, (1980), 121–36, and Bas van Fraassen, "Values and the Heart's Command," *Journal of Philosophy*, 70 (1973), 5–19.

[2] On this side of the controversy, I find particularly illuminating Earl Conee, "Against Moral Dilemmas," *Philosophical Review*, 91 (1982), 87–97, and R. M. Hare, *Moral Thinking* (Oxford: Clarendon Press, 1981).

[3] Philip L. Quinn, *Divine Commands and Moral Requirements* (Oxford: Clarendon Press, 1978).

to the moral realm. And so I shall be exploring the possibility that some such conflicts are better depicted as pitting against one another claims stemming from the moral realm and claims whose source is external to the moral realm.

The paper has three parts. In the first section, I develop the technical apparatus I need to formulate several distinct theses about general conflicts of practical requirements. In the second section, I defend the claim that one of the stronger theses, when it is interpreted as a claim about possible conflicts of moral and religious requirements, is possibly true. And in the third section, I argue that, given a certain plausible epistemological view, one might be justified in believing that one was subject to such conflicting moral and religious demands. I confess at the outset to a painful awareness that the arguments of the second and third sections are far from conclusive. The best I can hope from them is that they will serve to render some claims—which otherwise would probably seem eccentric, if not obviously false—plausible enough to merit further consideration by those philosophers antecedently disposed to take religious demands seriously.

AN ANATOMY OF CONFLICTS OF REQUIREMENTS

I will employ the concept of requirement generically and somewhat technically to express the characteristic 'binding force' or 'compellingness' shared by moral obligations and religious demands. Since for me 'requirement' is a term of art, I do not claim my usage will correspond exactly with the use of the term 'obligation' in ordinary moral discourse. The letter p, primed when necessary, will serve as a variable ranging over states of affairs; the letter x, primed if necessary, will function as a variable ranging over individual human agents; and the letter a, primed when necessary, will play the role of a variable ranging over particular actions (which may or may not be performed). The symbol '+' will represent an operator that turns pairs of nouns or noun phrases into conjunctive nouns or noun phrases.

Following in most respects a procedure used previously by Roderick M. Chisholm, I take three schematic locutions as primitive and use them to formulate five schematic definitions.[4] The first primitive schema is $pRxa$; it may be read informally in English as 'p would require that x do a' or 'p, when it obtains, requires that x do a'. The second is Op; it may be read informally in English as 'p obtains'. And the third is MOp; it may be read informally in English as 'It is logically possible that p obtains'. The definition schemata are these:

(D$_1$) p requires that x do a = Df Op & $pRxa$.
(D$_2$) The requirement that x do a, which would be imposed by p, would be overriden by p' = Df $pRxa$ & $\sim (p + p'Rxa)$.
(D$_3$) The requirement that x do a, which is imposed by p, is overridden by p' = Df $pRxa$ & $\sim (p + p'\ Rxa)$ & $Op + p'$.

<hr>

[4] See Roderick Chisholm, "Practical Reason and the Logic of Requirement," in Stephan Körner (ed.), *Practical Reason* (Oxford: Basil Blackwell, 1974).

(D₄) p would indefeasibly require that x do a = Df $pRxa$ & $(\forall p')(MOp + p' \supset p + p'Rxa)$.

(D₅) p indefeasibly requires that x do a = Df $pRxa$ & $(\forall p')(MOp + p' \supset p + p'Rxa)$ & Op.

Although, as Chisholm has shown, other important practical concepts can be defined in terms of our three primitive locutions, I will need only those defined above to formulate the theses about conflicts of requirements I propose to discuss.

In order to formulate these theses, I need to add one primitive schematic locution to the stock I have adapted from Chisholm's discussion of requirement. It is *xIa*, and it may be read informally in English as '*x* and *a* are such that it is physically impossible that she or he does it'.[5]

The weakest thesis about conflicts of requirements I am going to consider may be formally stated as follows:

(T₁) $(\exists x)\ (\exists a)\ (\exists a')\ (\exists p)\ (\exists p')\ ((Op\ \&\ pRxa)\ \&\ (Op'\ \&\ p'Rxa')\ \&\ xIa + a')$.

Paraphrased into English, this thesis asserts that there are an agent, a pair of actions, and a pair of states of affairs which are such that (*a*) one of the states of affairs requires that the agent do one of the actions, (*b*) the other state of affairs requires that the agent do the other action, and (*c*) it is physically impossible for the agent to do both actions. So no matter what an agent of whom (T₁) is true does, there will be at least one thing the agent is required to do and does not do. Still, it should be noted that (T₁) only asserts the existence of conflict of requirements of a rather innocuous sort. It is consistent with (T₁) to claim that, in every case in which an agent is subject to two such conflicting requirements, at least one of the requirements imposed on the agent by a certain state of affairs is overridden by another state of affairs. If we were to define the notion of there being a prima facie requirement that an agent perform an action as there existing some state of affairs such that it requires that the agent perform the action, then we could say that (T₁) asserts no more than that there are cases of prima facie requirements that conflict in the sense that it is physically impossible for the agent on whom they are imposed to satisfy them both. Since most philosophers would allow that there are or can be conflicts of prima facie obligations internal to the moral realm, I take it that most philosophers would grant that something like (T₁) is true or, at least, possible within the moral realm.

A stronger and, therefore, more interesting and controversial thesis about conflicts of requirements may be stated formally in this way:

(T₂) $(\exists x)\ (\exists a)\ (\exists a')\ (\exists p)\ (\exists p')\ ((Op\ \&\ pRxa)\ \&\ (Op'\ \&\ p'Rxa')\ \&\ xIa + a'\ \&\ \sim (\exists p'')\ (Op''\ \&\ \sim (p'' + pRxa))\ \&\ \sim (\exists p''')\ (Op'''\ \&\ \sim (p''' + p'Rxa')))$.

---

[5] One could formulate stronger but parallel theses by using the notion of logical impossibility in place of the notion of physical impossibility.

Paraphrased into English, this thesis says that there are an agent, a pair of actions, and a pair of states of affairs which are such that (*a*) one of the states of affairs requires that the agent do one of the actions, (*b*) the other state of affairs requires that the agent do the other action, (*c*) it is physically impossible for the agent to do both actions, and (*d*) neither of the aforementioned requirements is overridden by any state of affairs. In other words, (T$_2$) asserts the existence of cases of conflicting prima facie requirements in which neither of the conflicting requirements is in fact overridden. If, by contrast to the notion of a prima facie requirement, we were to define the notion of there being an actual requirement that an agent perform an action as there being a prima facie requirement that the agent perform the action and there being no state of affairs that in fact overrides that prima facie requirement, then we could say that (T$_2$) asserts that there are cases of conflicting actual requirements. I take it that those philosophers who assert that there are or can be conflicts of actual moral obligations would grant that something like (T$_2$) is true or possible within the moral realm, and presumably philosophers who deny this would hold that, internal to the moral realm at least, nothing like (T$_2$) is true or possible. It is worth noting that (T$_2$) does not entail that there is no state of affairs such that, were it to obtain, one or the other of the conflicting actual requirements would be overridden; it entails only that no such state of affairs does obtain. Hence, it could be that (T$_2$) is true but only contingently so. If one thinks of conflicts of requirements of the sort whose existence is asserted by (T$_2$) as the stuff some tragedies are made of, the world could be only contingently endowed with such tragedies. Other possible worlds might be without conflicts of actual requirements of this sort and thus luckier than ours in virtue of being without tragedy of this kind.

As I see it, all the appearances that must be saved by an explanation of moral conflict can be saved, though perhaps in a somewhat Procrustean manner, by asserting that something like (T$_1$) is true within the moral realm and without postulating that something like (T$_2$) is true internal to the moral realm. After all, even if one of two conflicting prima facie moral requirements is overridden, it is not thereby rendered illusory or made to disappear. According to (D$_3$) and (D$_1$), if the requirement that an agent perform an action that is imposed by one state of affairs is overridden by another, it remains true that the former state of affairs does require that the agent perform the action. And so, for instance, if the agent fails to satisfy the overridden requirement, regret or even remorse may be an appropriate moral attitude or emotion.[6] But I also think there is real intuitive plausibility to the complaint, which would be made by those philosophers who hold that something like (T$_2$) is true internal to the moral realm, that such an

---

[6] In *Foundations of Ethics* (Oxford: Oxford University Press, 1939), 85, W. D. Ross says: "It remains hard fact that an act of promise-breaking is morally unsuitable, even when we decide that in spite of this, it is the act that we ought to do."

explanation, though it saves the appearances, is not the best explanation of the appearances, because to a certain extent it trivializes moral conflict by failing to face up to its tragic depths. However, since this paper is not about the possibility of conflict internal to the moral realm, I shall assume, for the sake of argument, that if we confine our attention to the moral realm, only conflicts of the sort whose existence is asserted by (T_1) and not those of the kind whose existence is asserted by (T_2) are to be discovered.

Many theists hold that divine commands impose requirements but not merely contingently. Requirements imposed by divine command are supposed to be indefeasible. And so, if I am to depict accurately the kind of conflict between religious requirements imposed by divine command and moral requirements I shall later on argue is possible, I believe I must first formulate some additional theses about conflict of indefeasibly imposed requirements with others.

The first of these theses may be formally stated in the following way:

$$(T_3) \ (\exists x) \ (\exists a) \ (\exists a') \ (\exists p) \ (\exists p') \ ((Op \ \& \ pRxa) \ \& \ (Op' \ \& \ p'Rxa' \\ \& \ (\forall p'')(MOp' + p'' \supset p' + p''Rxa')) \ \& \ xIa + a').$$

This thesis asserts that there are an agent, a pair of actions, and a pair of states of affairs which are such that (*a*) one of the states of affairs requires that the agent do one of the actions, (*b*) the other state of affairs indefeasibly requires that the agent do the other action, and (*c*) it is physically impossible for the agent to do both actions. Clearly (T_3), like (T_1), is fairly innocuous. Though the indefeasible requirement whose existence it asserts cannot be overridden, the requirement said to be in conflict with the indefeasible requirement is only asserted to be a prima facie requirement. (T_3) does not entail that the requirement which is not said to be indefeasible is in any case an actual requirement; for all (T_3) says, that requirement is overridden in every case where (T_3) holds.

There would be ineluctable conflict of the strongest sort if the following thesis were true:

$$(T_4) \ (\exists x) \ (\exists a) \ (\exists a') \ (\exists p) \ (\exists p') \ ((Op \ \& \ pRxa \\ \& \ (\forall p'') \ (MOp + p'' \supset p + p''Rxa)) \\ \& \ (Op' \ \& \ p'Rxa' \ \& \ (\forall p''') \ (MOp' + p''' \supset p' + p'''Rxa')) \ \& \ xIa \\ + a').$$

What this thesis says is that there are an agent, a pair of actions, and a pair of states of affairs which are such that (*a*) one of the states of affairs indefeasibly requires that the agent do one of the actions, (*b*) the other state of affairs indefeasibly requires that the agent do the other action, and (*c*) it is physically impossible for the agent to do both actions. Since both of the conflicting requirements said to exist by (T_4) are indefeasible, neither can be overridden, and so conflict of this sort can have no happy resolution.

I believe many of the classical discussions of alleged conflicts between moral and religious requirements can be consistently interpreted as involving the assertion of nothing stronger than (T_3). Thus, for example, when considering the persecution of heretics, Kant has this to say:

> That it is wrong to deprive a man of his life because of his religious faith is certain, unless (to allow for the most remote possibility) a Divine Will, made known in extraordinary fashion, has ordered it otherwise. But that God has ever uttered this terrible injunction can be asserted only on the basis of historical documents and is never apodictically certain. After all, the revelation has reached the inquisitor only through men and has been interpreted by men, and even did it appear to have come from God Himself (like the command delivered to Abraham to slaughter his own son like a sheep) it is at least possible that in this instance a mistake has prevailed.[7]

Ignoring for the time being the epistemological questions raised by this passage, we might read Kant as presupposing the following analysis of the situation. Some states of affairs morally require that the inquisitor refrain from each particular act of killing his victim. This is always at least a prima facie requirement, but one thing could override it. If God were to command the inquisitor to perform a particular act of killing his victim, such a divine command would indefeasibly require that the inquisitor perform that particular act of killing, but in that case the prima facie requirement to refrain from that act of killing would be overridden. Similarly, when Kierkegaard talks about the teleological suspension of the ethical in his discussion of the story of Abraham and Isaac, we might, by placing a lot of weight on the notion of suspension, interpret him as holding that God's command to Abraham imposes on Abraham an indefeasible requirement to perform a particular act of killing Isaac, that this requirement conflicts with the prima facie moral requirement that Abraham refrain from performing that action, and that the moral requirement in question is suspended in the technical sense of being overridden. So we could save the appearances, I think, without assenting to any thesis about conflicts of requirements stronger than (T_3).

But reflection on Kierkegaard's *Fear and Trembling* suggests to me an alternative that is both troublesome and philosophically interesting, namely, that what I shall call 'Kierkegaardian conflict' is possible.[8] Abstractly and formally stated, the thesis of Kierkegaardian conflict is this:

$$(T_5) \quad (\exists x)\,(\exists a)\,(\exists a')\,(\exists p)\,(\exists p')\,((Op \,\&\, pRxa$$
$$\&\, (\forall p'')\,(MOp + p'' \supset p + p''Rxa))$$
$$\&\, (Op' \,\&\, p'Rxa'$$
$$\&\, \sim (\exists p''')\,(Op''' \,\&\, \sim (p' + p'''Rxa')))\, \&\, xIa + a').$$

---

[7] Immanuel Kant, *Religion within the Limits of Reason Alone*, trans. T. M. Greene and H. H. Hudson (New York: Harper and Row, 1960), 175.

[8] Though I think Kierkegaard may be read as having some such possibility in mind, I adopt this epithet mainly for its suggestive value. I make no claim to have done the detailed exegetical work that would be needed to justify conclusively attributing (T_5) to Kierkegaard. It has been suggested to me that Kierkegaard does not claim that Kierkegaardian conflicts can or do occur but does hold that one can be prima facie justified in believing oneself to be in a situation of Kierkegaardian conflict. I argue in support of this claim about justification in the third section of this chapter.

What (T₅) asserts is that there are an agent, a pair of actions, and a pair of states of affairs which are such that (*a*) one of the states of affairs indefeasibly requires that the agent do one of the actions, (*b*) the other state of affairs requires that the agent do the other action, (*c*) this second requirement is in fact not overridden by any state of affairs and so is an actual requirement, and (*d*) it is physically impossible for the agent to do both actions. In the next section, I propose to offer a defense of the possibility of an instance of (T₅) in which the indefeasible requirement is a religious requirement imposed by divine command and the conflicting requirement that is not overridden is a moral requirement.

THE CASE FOR KIERKEGAARDIAN CONFLICT

In a Kierkegaardian spirit, the particular instance of (T₅) whose possibility I intend to defend is this:

(K) (i) God's commanding that Abraham perform a particular act of killing Isaac indefeasibly requires that Abraham perform that act of killing Isaac.

(ii) Isaac's being an innocent child requires that Abraham refrain from performing that act of killing Isaac.

(iii) The requirement that Abraham refrain from performing that act of killing Isaac, which is imposed by Isaac's being an innocent child, is overridden by no state of affairs.

(iv) Abraham and that act of killing Isaac are such that it is physically impossible that he both perform and refrain from performing it.

What is there to be said in support of the view that (K)(i)–(iv) are compossible? I shall endeavor to explain.[9]

One crucial assumption for my argument is that the moral realm is not the only source of ultimate values whose realization might be promoted by human actions. The tendency to moralize the whole of our lives is to be resisted. Of course, not all philosophers who accept this general way of looking at things would agree on how precisely the moral realm is to be circumscribed. Some would say it extends no farther than the regulation of interpersonal relations; others would push its limits to the welfare of all sentient beings. I will not here try to settle the question of how to fix the outer boundaries of the realm of moral value. I shall, however, make two plausible assumptions about the internal structure of the moral realm.

---

[9] Perhaps it is worth emphasizing at this point that I am arguing only for the possibility of Kierkegaardian conflict and that I use the case of Abraham and Isaac merely for illustrative purposes. I suppose most devout theists would hope, and perhaps even trust, that such a possibility, if it is a possibility, will never be actual. If such theists also believe that the story in Genesis 22 contains literal truth, they will need an interpretation of that story which reads it as something other than a case of Kierkegaardian conflict. But such interpretations abound, and some of them are independently plausible.

First, whenever an agent confronts a set of actions that are alternatives, there is at least one that is best from the point of view of promoting the values internal to the moral realm, even if a best action is only indifferent. I say that in each set of alternative actions there is *at least* one best because I wish to allow that in some such sets there are several tied for first place. The second assumption is that, in at least some cases where an agent confronts a set of alternative actions that contains a unique best from the point of view of promoting the values internal to the moral realm, the state of affairs in virtue of which that action is uniquely best imposes on the agent a moral requirement to do that action which is not overridden by any state of affairs. I do not say this is so for *all* such cases, in order to allow that the best may sometimes be supererogatory rather than required, because there are limits to what morality can demand by way of saintly or heroic behavior.[10]

Applying these assumptions to the case of Abraham and Isaac, I think we can see that (K)(ii)–(iv) are compossible. Of the two options available to Abraham, performing or refraining from performing a particular act of killing Isaac, refraining clearly can be morally better than killing. Refraining would not require any especially heroic or saintly behavior on Abraham's part. Isaac's being an innocent child is precisely the kind of consideration that is suitable for imposing moral requirements. And though there might be some states of affairs that would, if they obtained, override this requirement, it is surely possible that none of them do obtain and, hence, that the requirement is not overridden.

Since it is not an aim of this paper to argue for the coherence of theism, I shall take it for granted that (K)(i) is possible. What does need to be argued is that (K)(i), on the one hand, and (K)(ii)–(iv), on the other, are compossible. Even many theists will hold that the reason God's commanding Abraham to perform a particular act of killing Isaac indefeasibly requires that Abraham perform that act is that God is essentially perfectly good. They will then be tempted to suppose that God's commanding Abraham to perform that act of killing Isaac is a state of affairs that overrides the requirement imposed by Isaac's being an innocent child that Abraham refrain from performing the act. If this were correct, then (K)(i) and (K)(iii) would not be compossible.

I grant that God's being perfectly good explains why his commanding Abraham to perform a particular act of killing Isaac indefeasibly requires that Abraham perform that act. I deny, however, that God's goodness is exclusively moral goodness, and for that reason I deny that God's command that Abraham perform a particular act of killing Isaac overrides the moral requirement that Abraham refrain from performing that act. In short, because the requirements imposed by divine command spring from a realm of value not wholly coincident with the moral realm, they are not necessarily moral requirements at all. Hence, they are not

---

[10] A view supported in different ways by recent arguments in James S. Fishkin, *The Limits of Obligation* (New Haven: Yale University Press, 1982), and Samuel Scheffler, *The Rejection of Consequentialism* (Oxford: Clarendon Press, 1982).

necessarily moral requirements so stringent that they would override all other moral requirements, and so they do not necessarily override conflicting moral requirements.[11] Of course I do not claim that God is utterly careless of the welfare of his human creatures and altogether indifferent to the values of the moral realm. Sometimes divine commands do impose moral requirements indefeasibly, and sometimes moral requirements imposed by divine command do override other requirements, moral and nonmoral. But I think that this is not necessarily always the case, and so I hold that (K)(i) and (K)(iii) are compossible. Because the requirement indefeasibly imposed by God's command to Abraham is a religious requirement rooted outside the moral realm and not just a particularly stringent moral requirement, it does not override the supremely urgent moral requirement that Abraham refrain from killing Isaac imposed by the fact that Isaac is an innocent child. And so, I think, genuine Kierkegaardian conflict based on conflicting and incommensurable moral and religious values and requirements is possible.

Perhaps it will be allowed that my argument so far suffices to cast some doubt on the view that Kierkegaardian conflict is known to be impossible. But, it will be said, the defense of my view would be stronger if I could present a positive account of divine goodness that would serve as a basis for a positive insight into the possibility of requirements arising from divine commands coming into Kierkegaardian conflict with moral requirements. This I cannot do. Indeed, I think there are good religious reasons for believing that it is something no human is capable of doing. It would be presumptuous to suppose that any of us understands God well enough to give a complete account of his perfections; respectable traditions of religious thought hold that no human grasp of the divine nature can be adequate to exhaust any of its ingredient perfections. But I can do something less ambitious, namely, remind the reader that within orthodox theistic thought there are models of divine goodness that are supposed to enable us to get a partial insight into what divine goodness is but that do not identify divine goodness with moral goodness. One such model is the plenitude of being model. When God's perfections are summed up by saying that he is the *ens realissimum*, what is being asserted, I think, is at least this: God's goodness consists at least in part in his being metaphysically perfect in the sense of being metaphysically complete and self-sufficient and in his being the source of all existence and lesser metaphysical perfection in the creaturely domain.[12] Some such notion of metaphysical

[11] An interesting question is whether, apart from nonmoral requirements indefeasibly imposed by divine commands, moral requirements always override nonmoral requirements if there is conflict. In the absence of a detailed characterization of how the moral realm is to be circumscribed, it is clearly not possible to answer this question. But if one does not trivialize the question by defining moral requirements as those that would be overriding if there were conflict, then it seems to me that a negative answer is quite plausible. In support of such an answer, I would cite considerations of the kind presented by Bernard Williams, in "Ethical Consistency," collected in his *Problems of the Self* (Cambridge: Cambridge University Press, 1973).

[12] The plenitude of being model obviously also has implications for how the problem of evil can be treated, some of which are being worked out in unpublished research by Thomas V. Morris.

goodness seems to underlie the characteristic Leibnizian claim that, when God chooses to create the best of all possible worlds, it is the world that ranks highest on a scale combining considerations of simplicity of natural laws and variety of creaturely denizens. It is not at all obvious that a world that is best in this sense is also best in the sense of maximally realizing the values of the moral realm. For this reason it seems to me possible that some of the values God cares about having his human creatures pursue—enough that by command he imposes on them indefeasible requirements for certain actions—should be nonmoral values and that on this account those indefeasible requirements should possibly sometimes be in Kierkegaardian conflict with moral requirements.

Of course, the plenitude of being model is not the only alternative to thinking of divine goodness as exclusively moral goodness. Perhaps divine goodness has a dimension that is more akin to aesthetic goodness than to any other realm of goodness with which we humans are familiar. And maybe divine goodness has aspects that are and will always remain completely inscrutable to us. I do not intend to rule out such possibilities. Rather I wish to assert these two theses: (1) it is God's goodness that explains why his commands indefeasibly impose requirements, and (2) it is the fact that divine goodness has nonmoral components that explains why those indefeasibly imposed religious requirements can sometimes be in Kierkegaardian conflict with moral requirements.

The argument of this section will be complete when I have done what I can to fend off what I consider the most powerful objection to the defense I have been mounting of the possibility of Kierkegaardian conflict. Succinctly stated, the objection may be put this way. For the sake of argument, let it be granted that divine commands would indefeasibly impose requirements and that some of these requirements would be nonmoral, religious requirements. Let it also be granted that there are possible conflicts between such indefeasibly imposed religious requirements and moral requirements. It does not follow from these assumptions that any such cases are possible cases of Kierkegaardian conflict. It may yet be that in every such case the very state of affairs—namely, a certain divine command having been issued—which indefeasibly imposes a certain religious requirement also overrides any conflicting moral requirement. Hence, it may be conceded that there are distinctively religious values that impose nonmoral requirements indefeasibly and also denied that there are any cases, actual or possible, of Kierkegaardian conflict. Strictly speaking, all that must be granted if we accept the assumptions in question is that, in possible cases of conflict between indefeasible religious requirements and moral requirements, the religious requirements have priority and are the actual requirements to which one is subject. It need not also be granted that the conflicting moral requirements are not overridden.

Obviously, the objection has the logic of the situation right. The possibility of Kierkegaardian conflict does not follow from the assumptions so far made about diverse realms of value as sources for conflicting requirements. In effect, this is why I earlier acknowledged that one could save the appearances without asserting anything stronger than (T3). Moreover, the additional assumption that would be needed to complete a deductive argument for the possibility of Kierkegaardian conflicts, namely, that there are possible cases where indefeasible requirements rooted in the realm of religious values conflict with requirements that spring from the realm of moral values and yet are not overridden, seems to beg the question against the objector.

But, though I think the appearances can be saved without acknowledging the possibility of Kierkegaardian conflicts, I do not believe they are best saved in that fashion. As I see it, the best explanation of the appearances appeals to the possibility of Kierkegaardian conflict. In order to make a case for this claim, I can only ask the reader to reflect carefully on what the appearances are, as they manifest themselves in Kierkegaard's treatment of the story of Abraham and Isaac in *Fear and Trembling* or in similar vividly and imaginatively portrayed cases.[13] When I engage in such reflections, I am convinced that the moral requirement, imposed by Isaac's being an innocent child, that Abraham refrain from killing Isaac, is not overridden by God's command to Abraham, even though the command indefeasibly imposes a conflicting religious requirement. To suppose that the moral requirement is overridden in this case seems to me to involve a failure to acknowledge the ultimacy of certain moral values and our commitments to them. But to suppose that God's command to Abraham does not indefeasibly impose a religious requirement seems to me to involve a similar failure to acknowledge the ultimacy of certain religious values and our commitments to them. Either supposition strikes me as a response to the story that misses what is deepest and most poignant about it. And so I think the tables should be turned, so to speak, and the burden of proof placed squarely on the shoulders of the objector. Assuming that religious and moral values can conflict, what justifies the supposition that in each possible case of conflict of this sort pursuit of one of the two conflicting values must be better on some common scale of value than pursuit of the other? Why not allow that in certain possible cases of conflict the values of diverse realms are simply incommensurable? When requirements rooted in the realm of moral value and not overridden by anything internal to that realm conflict with requirements that spring from the realm of religious value and are not overridden by anything internal to that realm in certain possible cases, what justifies the assumption that there must be some more inclusive and more ultimate realm of value within which one or the other of the two conflicting requirements is overridden? My reflections on such questions convince me that there is no argument that would justify such assumptions without begging the question against the proponent of the thesis that Kierkegaardian conflicts are possible.

---

[13] But not everyone will agree with me about what the appearances are. A useful presentation of a contrasting view is G. Outka, "Religious and Moral Duty: Notes on *Fear and Trembling*," in G. Outka and J. P. Reeder (eds.), *Religion and Morality* (Garden City: Doubleday, 1973).

This concludes the case for Kierkegaardian conflict. It is, of course, not a proof that Kierkegaardian conflicts are possible. I think it likely that there is no proof of the claim that does not sooner or later beg the question against its opponents by appeal to some theoretical principle as open to doubt as the claim. But I consider it equally likely that there is no disproof of the claim that does not also beg the question against its proponents sooner or later by appeal to some theoretical assumption every bit as questionable as the negation of the claim is. As in the case of alleged conflicts of actual obligations within the moral realm, the direct philosophical arguments lead to a standoff, if I am right. However, the appearances of conflicts between moral and religious requirements, as I see them, are better explained on the hypothesis that Kierkegaardian conflicts are possible than on the hypothesis that they are not, and so I conclude that it is rational to believe that Kierkegaardian conflicts are possible. It is in this sense that I defend the claim that Kierkegaardian conflicts are possible. Because I have refrained from endorsing the parallel claim about the best explanation of the appearances of conflicts of obligations internal to the moral realm in this paper, I have not in this sense defended that possibility.

ON JUSTIFYING KIERKEGAARDIAN CLAIMS

In this section, I argue that it is possible in a certain sense to be justified in believing that one is in a situation of Kierkegaardian conflict. Though there are several ways to explain the concepts from normative epistemology I shall be using, the simplest procedure in the present context is to note their close analogy with the concepts involving requirement that I developed in the first section of this paper. One begins with the notion of a state of affairs being such that it would justify a belief for a person. A state of affairs justifies a belief for a person just in case it obtains and would justify that belief for that person. The justification of a belief for a person, which would be provided by one state of affairs, would be overridden by another just in case the first state of affairs but not the conjunctive state of affairs would justify the belief for the person. And the justification of a belief for a person, which is provided by one state of affairs, is overridden by another just in case (1) the first state of affairs would justify the belief for the person, (2) it is not the case that the conjunctive state of affairs would justify the belief for the person, and (3) the conjunctive state of affairs obtains. Since the formal definitions would exactly parallel those given in the first section, I do not bother to state them here. Because justification understood in this way may be overridden, it is a kind of prima facie justification. Though it may not in fact be overridden in a particular case, it is not indefeasible.

For the sake of vividness, I will conduct my argument for the possibility of being justified in believing one is in a situation of Kierkegaardian conflict in terms of the particular instance of (T_5) formulated as (K)(i)–(iv) in the preceding section. One is to suppose that the believer in question is Abraham or a counterpart of Abraham.

My first step is to argue that Abraham could be justified in believing (K)(iv). Abraham could grasp and accept the perfectly obvious truth that the particular act of killing Isaac referred to in (K)(iv) is such that it is physically impossible that he both perform and refrain from performing it. This for him would justify belief in (K)(iv). Hence, it is possible that Abraham is justified in believing (K)(iv).

My next step is to argue that Abraham could be justified in believing (K)(ii). Abraham could be justified in believing that Isaac is an innocent child, that killing Isaac would have a major negative impact on Isaac's welfare and, perhaps, the welfare of others as well, and that killing Isaac would have no positive impact on the welfare of sentient beings large enough to outweigh its negative impact on Isaac and others. Moreover, Abraham could be justified in believing that refraining from killing Isaac would involve no saintly or heroic behavior on his part. Taken together, these things would justify for Abraham belief in (K)(ii). Therefore, it is also possible that Abraham is justified in believing (K)(ii).

My third step is to argue that Abraham could be justified in believing (K)(i). Abraham could grasp and accept the conceptual truth that God, if he exists, is essentially perfectly good. This would justify for him the belief that God's commanding him to perform a particular act of killing Isaac would indefeasibly require that he perform that act. Moreover, Abraham could have an experience in optimal conditions that seemed to him to be an experience of God's commanding him to perform that particular act of killing Isaac. Appealing to recent arguments by Alston and Plantinga, whose general import is to show that sometimes beliefs about the contents made manifest in such experiences and based directly on such experiences are at least prima facie justified, I claim that the occurrence of such an experience in optimal conditions would justify for Abraham the belief that God commands him to perform that act of killing Isaac.[14] Taken together, these two beliefs, if justified, would in turn justify for Abraham belief in (K)(i). Hence, it is possible that Abraham is justified in believing (K)(i).

The next and, I suspect, most controversial step is to argue that Abraham could be justified in believing (K)(iii). Abraham could be justified in believing that no state of affairs bearing on the promotion of the values internal to the moral

[14] See William P. Alston, "Religious Experience and Religious Belief," *Noûs*, 16 (1982), 3–12, and Alvin Plantinga, "Is Belief in God Properly Basic?" *Noûs*, 15 (1981), 41–51. One might construe the Genesis story as saying that Abraham's epistemic blessings also included prima facie justified beliefs about the past history of his interactions with God that would serve as independent inductive backing for his belief that he had been divinely commanded. Thus, for example, Abraham had reason to believe that, when he was 99 years old, God had promised him a son (Genesis 17) and knew that, when he was 100 years old, he had astonishingly been given a son (Genesis 21). Such evidence would serve to strengthen the prima facie justification of his belief that he had been divinely commanded.

realm overrides the requirement that he refrain from performing the particular act of killing Isaac referred to in (K)(iii). Abraham could also, I claim, be justified (for instance, on the basis of considerations that went into the argument of the preceding section of this paper) in believing that no state of affairs pertinent to the promotion of the values internal to the religious realm, including the state of affairs of God's commanding that he perform that act of killing Isaac, overrides the moral requirement that he refrain from performing that act. And Abraham could be justified in believing that no state of affairs bearing on the promotion of values in any realm diverse from the moral and the religious, such as the aesthetic, overrides the requirement that he refrain from that particular act of killing Isaac. Taken together, these three beliefs, if justified, would further justify for Abraham belief in (K)(iii). Therefore, if my argument in the preceding section has enough force to provide prima facie justification for a belief by Abraham that God's command that he perform a particular act of killing Isaac would not override the moral requirement that he refrain from killing Isaac, as I think it does, it is also possible that Abraham is justified in believing (K)(iii).

The final step is to argue that Abraham could be justified in believing (K)(i)–(iv). By the arguments of the preceding four paragraphs, Abraham could be justified in believing each of (K)(i) through (K)(iv). By the argument of the preceding section, Abraham could be justified in believing that the hypothesis that (K)(i) through (K)(iv) are compossible is rational.[15] Taken together, these two beliefs, if justified, would in turn justify for Abraham belief in (K)(i)–(iv). Hence, it is possible that Abraham is justified in believing (K)(i)–(iv).

This concludes the argument for the claim that it is possible to be justified in believing one is in a situation of Kierkegaardian conflict. It is worth repeating that this is not a terribly strong claim, since the kind of justification in question is only prima facie justification. Though there are, I have argued, states of affairs that would justify for someone belief in (K)(i)–(iv), there are also states of affairs that would override such justification. For example, there are states of affairs that would for Abraham override the justification of the belief that God commands that he perform a particular act of killing Isaac provided by his religious experience. An interesting question is whether in every possible case in which Abraham is prima facie justified in believing (K)(i)–(iv) something does override his justification. Is it possible both that Abraham is prima facie justified in believing (K)(i)–(iv) and that Abraham's justification for believing (K)(i)–(iv) is not overridden? For all I know it is possible, since I can think of no argument that shows it to be impossible. So perhaps it is possible that Abraham has actual and not merely prima facie justification for believing (K)(i)–(iv). Hence, maybe it is even possible to have actual justification for believing oneself to be in a situation of

---

15 And, assuming the argument of the preceding section is sound, Abraham will have no grounds for supposing he will, and some grounds for supposing he will not, confront at this point in his reasoning an analogue of the lottery paradox, according to which the belief that no ticket in a large lottery will win is justified because each ticket probably will not win.

Kierkegaardian conflict. I shall conclude with the bold conjecture that this is indeed possible. And then I am prompted to ask: Is there an argument that shows that this conjecture is false?

EPILOGUE

One way in which philosophy can be edifying is to bring us to see new possibilities. When philosophy succeeds in performing this function, it teaches us that the world might be stranger by far than pedestrian common sense would allow. This paper has been an attempt to edify by broadening our horizon of possibilities.

In reading this paper to various groups, I have been struck by the fact that many in my audiences are preoccupied with actualities. They ask, But do situations of Kierkegaardian conflict actually occur? In response to this question, I have nothing helpful to say. Of course I hope they do not occur, but I cannot prove they do not. Or they ask, Do you think you will ever actually be justified in believing you are in a situation of Kierkegaardian conflict? Curiously enough, I do not think so.

When I try to imagine myself playing the role of Abraham, I cannot imagine I would ever regard myself as justified in believing that God had commanded me to kill Isaac. Were I to hear a voice issuing such an order, I am very sure I would conclude that the order was not a divine command. But when I ask myself why I would come to that conclusion, something interesting emerges. The conclusion would not rest on a confident belief that a perfectly good God could not issue such a command; it would be based on a deep skepticism about my ever being justified in believing that a divine command had been addressed directly to me.

Would the fact that such skepticism is bone-deep in me be of any special significance? Perhaps. Of course, maybe it would only betoken a properly humble appreciation of my own unworthiness to be the recipient of a direct divine command. But maybe it would show that, being situated as I am in a predominantly secular culture, I can conceive of certain possibilities for justified belief that I cannot quite imagine being actual for me. If it showed this, I would be under pressure to admit that my culture has the power to shut me off from understanding imaginatively and firsthand the kind of faith needed to play the role of Abraham. And I would be reluctant to concede so much influence in determining what I can imagine to the contingencies of my culture. Like many intellectuals, I am inclined to fancy I can transcend, if only in imagination, most of the limits of my culture. But perhaps the range of my imagination is severely constricted just because I am to a large extent the product of an incredulous culture. If so, then the fact that I can conceive possibilities I cannot quite imagine being actual for me may give me a hint about how grace might be needed to work certain kinds of religious transformations in my life.

5

Tragic Dilemmas, Suffering Love, and Christian Life

In weakness power reaches perfection.

2 Corinthians 12: 9

It has been one of the pretensions of philosophy, Bernard Williams[1] tells us, that it can answer the question of how one should live. Many philosophers have tried to answer the question by proposing ethical theories. Williams advocates an alternative procedure. As he sees it, the aim of ethical thought "is to help us to construct a world that will be our world; one in which we have a social, cultural, and personal life."[2] But we need plans for the construction, and they should be as detailed as we can make them. Drawing up such plans is bound to make heavy demands on our resources of understanding and imagination.

A life is a process with a narrative structure. The extent to which an ethical theory made in the image of the theories of science can generate a blueprint or model of a life is problematic. Theoretical descriptions of a life plan are usually very schematic and lacking in concrete detail; they seldom cast much light on what it would be like to lead a life as planned. Ethical theories are not narratives and do not seem apt to generate them. They seem at best to have a limited role in helping us to understand what it would be like to lead lives of various sorts. Nor does it seem likely that one will gain such understanding by bootstrapping up from an understanding of one's own life. As Kierkegaard reminds us, life must be lived forwards but can only be understood backwards. We are only in a position to understand our own lives when they draw to a close, and so this self-understanding inevitably comes too late to help us construct lives for ourselves prospectively. Fortunately there are other resources at our disposal. Among them

Earlier versions of this paper were presented at the University of Notre Dame and at the Midwest and Pacific Regional Meetings of the Society of Christian Philosophers. I thank my audiences on those occasions for lively and stimulating discussion. I am also grateful to David O'Connor and Alvin Plantinga for helpful oral comments and to Eleonore Stump and Linda Zagzebski for detailed written comments.

[1] Bernard Williams, *Ethics and the Limits of Philosophy* (Cambridge, Mass.: Harvard University Press, 1985).
[2] Ibid. 111.

are the lives narrated in history and literature. As models or analogies, they can contribute to our understanding of what it would be like to lead lives of various sorts and thereby help to guide us in constructing our own lives. Reflection on literature and history can in this way serve the ends of ethical thought.

Christian philosophers are advised[3] to set their own philosophical agenda. High on that agenda, I suggest, should be reflection on lives that hold promise of enriching Christian ethical thought. This paper is intended to be a contribution to that enterprise. In it, I narrate and then reflect upon the life of Sebastian Rodrigues, the main character in Shusaku Endo's striking novel, *Silence*.[4] Set in seventeenth-century Japan, *Silence* is the story of a Portuguese missionary priest captured by political authorities bent on eradicating Christianity from Japan. In order to force him to apostasy, they torture and kill Japanese Christians. Finally, to get them to stop this persecution of his flock, Rodrigues deliberately tramples upon an image of Christ. What is the significance of his apostasy for Christian ethical thought? Is it a matter of moral weakness, a failure of fidelity to religious vows binding no matter what the consequences? Or is it a matter of heroic self-sacrifice, a deep expression of Christian love of neighbor? Could it be both at once? These are among the questions the novel raises in a vivid way. I propose to use reflections on the details of Endo's narrative as a means of teasing out answers to them. In doing so, I hope to make a case for the claim that the philosophical study of literature has an important role to play in Christian ethical thought. In effect I shall be supporting with an argument by example a position others[5] have argued for on more theoretical grounds.

It is only to be expected that some philosophers will not find much ethical significance in the life of Sebastian Rodrigues. His values and commitments will strike some as absurd or ridiculous. No doubt there are secular ethical thinkers who would find it hard to work up much sympathy for the thought that his life has anything instructive to say about how we should construct our lives and the world in which we live them. Others will suppose that the solution to the problem he confronts is obvious to the point of triviality. But Christian philosophers may respect such reactions without sharing them. There are, it seems clear to me, lives that have significance for what is distinctive in Christian ethical thought and yet do not appear to have anything like the same significance when seen from other perspectives.

I now turn to the task of narrating the story of part of what I take to be one such life. It is a story that nicely illustrates Stanley Cavell's remark that "the moral

---

[3] Alvin Plantinga, "Advice to Christian Philosophers," *Faith and Philosophy*, 1 (July 1984), 253–71.

[4] Shusaku Endo, *Silence*, trans. William Johnston (New York: Taplinger Publishing Company, 1980).

[5] Stanley Hauerwas, *Character and the Christian Life* (San Antonio: Trinity University Press, 1975); see also Alasdair MacIntyre, *After Virtue: A Study in Moral Theory* (Notre Dame: University of Notre Dame Press, 1981).

of art, as of a life, is that you do not know in advance what may arise as a significant detail."[6]

THE ORDEAL OF SEBASTIAN RODRIGUES[7]

Word has filtered back to Europe that the Jesuit Christovao Ferreira, theologian and missionary to Japan, has apostatized after suffering the torture of the pit of Nagasaki. In Portugal, three of his former students at the monastery of Campolide lay plans to travel to Japan to investigate the matter. These priests, Francisco Garrpe, Juan de Santa Marta, and Sebastian Rodrigues, cannot believe that their teacher would grovel like a dog before the infidel. On March 25, 1638, they sail from Lisbon with the Indian fleet. After a stormy passage around the Cape of Good Hope, they reach Goa on October 9. There they learn that Japan has cut off trade with Portugal. They are also told that thirty-five thousand Japanese Christians, who had risen against the authorities, have been massacred at Shimabara. Undaunted, they proceed to Macao. There Valignano, Jesuit Provincial for Japan, informs them he has no intention of sending further missionaries to that dangerous land. The only report of Ferreira comes from Dutch sailors who left Nagasaki on the day that he was suspended in the pit. Beyond the fact that he was interrogated by the new magistrate Inoue, Lord of Chikugo, nothing definite is known of his fate.

Valignano consents to a secret mission to Japan. While waiting for a junk to be repaired, the three priests meet their first Japanese, Kichijiro, who agrees to accompany them on their mission. Kichijiro tells tales of Japanese Christians tortured by the water punishment, staked out at water's edge and battered by rising and falling tides, but he denies being a Christian himself. He also proves to be a drunkard and a coward. And then Santa Marta's health, undermined by the hardships of the voyage from Lisbon, breaks down completely. To go to Japan in his condition is unthinkable; he must remain in Macao for treatment, to his bitter disappointment. "The life of a priest can be sad," Rodrigues reflects. "There is no one more wretchedly alone than the priest who does not measure up to his task." The omens for the mission to Japan are not good, but Rodrigues remains firm in his commitment to it. As he meditates on the command to preach the gospel, the

---

6 Stanley Cavell, *The World Viewed*, enlarged edn. (Cambridge, Mass.: Harvard University Press, 1979), 145.

7 In his section of the paper, I tell an abbreviated version of the story of Shusaku Endo's *Silence*. Though I compress the narrative drastically and highlight salient ethical and religious features of the story, I stick as close to the language of the English translation as I can. If I were to indicate explicitly in the body of the text every use I have made of the language of the English translation, it would be hopelessly cluttered with quotation marks and page references. I have omitted such quotation marks and page references because I believe they would distract the reader. So let me here be quite clear about the debts I owe: the story is entirely Endo's, and much of the language in which it is expressed is that of Johnston, his translator. I am only retelling this story!

face of Christ rises up before his eyes. It is a face full of vigor and strength; he feels great love for that face. "I am always fascinated by the face of Christ," Rodrigues says, "just like a man fascinated by the face of his beloved."

Garrpe, Rodrigues, and Kichijiro set sail for Japan. A sudden night storm nearly sinks their junk. Kichijiro is so terrified he makes almost no attempt to help with the bailing. Wretchedly pale, lying in his own vomit, he is heard to mutter "Santa Maria." Could he be a Christian despite his denials? Garrpe and Rodrigues reject the thought. Their faith could not turn a man into such a coward. After nine days at sea, they reach the Japanese coast; at midnight they wade ashore. Kichijiro goes off to explore. Garrpe and Rodrigues fear that, like Judas, he has gone to betray them. But he soon returns with some Japanese Christians from Tomogi, a fishing village not too far from Nagasaki. These Japanese, who even speak a bit of Portuguese, make Garrpe and Rodrigues welcome and before dawn hide them in a charcoal hut in the hills behind their village. And so their mission to the Japanese begins. The people of Tomogi have been without a priest for six years but have managed to keep their faith alive. By day Garrpe and Rodrigues hide in their hut; at night they offer Mass, hear confessions, and give instruction. Things settle into a routine. Rodrigues thinks, "Never have I felt so deeply how meaningful is the life of a priest."

For a while the mission seems to be bearing good fruit. The conviction grows in Rodrigues that all is well and that God has extended his protection to it. He begins to understand the Japanese Christians. Persecuted by the authorities and treated like cattle by the bonzes, they live and die like beasts, in a cramped and desolate land. "Christianity has penetrated this land like water flowing into dry earth," he thinks, "because it has brought to its people a human warmth they never previously knew." As he performs his first baptism in Japan, he foresees for the child a miserable peasant existence face to face with the black sea. "Why," he asks, "has God given our Christians such burdens?" But Christ did not die for the good and beautiful alone. "It is easy enough to die for the good and beautiful," he tells himself. "The hard thing is to die for the miserable and corrupt." At the request of peasants from Fukazawa, Rodrigues travels to their village. From them he hears that Kichijiro is a Christian of their village who had once apostatized. Eight years before, he and his whole family had been betrayed to the authorities by an envious informer. Ordered to tread upon a picture of Christ, his brothers and sisters had firmly refused and had been burnt at the stake. Kichijiro, after a few threats from the authorities, had renounced his faith, watched his family being executed, and then disappeared from sight. Like an army marching through a parched desert to a oasis of water, the peasants of Fukazawa come to Rodrigues, thirsty and longing for spiritual refreshment. In a single day, he baptizes thirty adults and children and hears more than fifty confessions. As he leads the people in prayer, there often arises in his mind the face of Christ, and he imagines the people who sat or knelt fascinated by Christ's words. It is a beautiful face he imagines. From childhood, Rodrigues reveals, he has clasped that face to his breast just like the person who romantically idealizes the countenance of one he loves. As he sails back to Tomogi, he is filled with a sense of wellbeing. He feels that his life is of value and is accomplishing something. "I am," he thinks, "of some use to the people of this country at the ends of the earth."

And then disaster strikes. As Garrpe and Rodrigues watch from their hiding place in the hills, a samurai and his men take a hostage from the village. The white noonday sun beats mercilessly down on the village; an awful noonday silence envelops the whole place. Reeling and staggering, an old man, bound with ropes, is dragged off. An informer has told the authorities that there are secret Christians in Tomogi, and hostages are to be taken until the villagers betray them. Three days later a genial old samurai arrives in the village and demands that three more hostages be sent to Nagasaki. Ichizo and Mokichi, two of the leading Christians, volunteer. The villagers entreat Kichijiro, who is a stranger among them, to be the third man; they reason that the officials will not interrogate him so severely since he is not one of them. From sheer weakness Kichijiro gives in to the pressure of their pleas. Mokichi asks Rodrigues what they are to do if ordered to trample on the *fumie*, an image of Christ. Many Japanese Christians have gone to their death rather than do so. But is it possible to demand such sacrifices from these three unfortunate men? Overwhelmed by pity, Rodrigues shouts "Trample! Trample!" Immediately he realizes that those words should never have been on his lips. Kichijiro whines resentfully, "Why has Deus Sama given us this trial?" "We have done no wrong," he cries. Rodrigues is silent; he is pierced by those words. Gradually he comes to think they get at something sickening, the silence of God. After twenty years of persecution, the black soil of Japan is drenched with the red blood of martyrs; the walls of the churches have fallen down. "In the face of this terrible and merciless sacrifice offered up to Him," Rodrigues says, "God has remained silent."

Mokichi, Ichizo, and Kichijiro are brought before a magistrate and ordered to trample on the *fumie*. Following the advice given by Rodrigues, they do so, but their faces betray them. They are then ordered to spit on the *fumie* and to declare that the Blessed Virgin was a whore. This had been planned by Inoue, the man who interrogated Ferreira. Ichizo grasps the *fumie* with both hands but finds himself powerless to spit. He shakes his head as though caught in the throes of pain. A white tear of anguish rolls down Mokichi's cheek. Then both of them openly confess that they are Christians. Overcome by threats, Kichijiro gasps out the required blasphemy and spits on the *fumie;* he is set free and disappears from sight. Mokichi and Ichizo are returned to Tomogi to undergo the water punishment. As Rodriguez and Garrpe watch from the hut, they are staked out on the shore so that at high tide their bodies will be immersed to the chin in the sea. Their agony lasts for three days. As the afternoon tide comes in on the third day, the black, cold color of the sea deepens; the stakes seem to sink into the water. White foaming waves, swirling past the stakes, break on the sand; a white bird, skimming across the surface of the sea, flies away. With that it is over. The sea surges on in silence. Rodrigues finds he cannot bear the monotonous sound of the dark sea gnawing at the shore. "Behind the depressing silence of this sea," he thinks, "the silence of God . . . the feeling that while men raise their voices in anguish God remains with folded arms, silent."

Hearing that the hills are to be searched, Rodrigues and Garrpe decide to part and flee. Now Rodrigues is completely alone, filled with dread. The mouse-like face of Kichijiro, filled with terror, haunts his imagination. "Were I an ordinary Christian and not a priest," he asks himself, "would I have done what he did?" He returns to Fukazawa and finds it a scene of empty desolation. As he enters that village, he is struck by the stench of rotten fish and surrounded by a fearful, eerie silence. Wild cats stalk through the village, scavenging dry fish. Wandering deliriously through the empty landscape, he catches sight of his thin, hollow face, heavy with mud and with stubble, reflected in a pool of water. It is the face of a haunted man filled with uneasiness and exhaustion. At that moment he thinks of the face of Christ crucified, the most pure, the most beautiful that has claimed the prayers of man. It has corresponded with his own highest aspirations. Struck by the incongruity, he bursts into giddy laughter. In the woods a cicada is singing. Everywhere else there is silence. The sound of the roaring sea arises suddenly within his heart. This is the sea that washed over the dead bodies of Mokichi and Ichizo, the sea that swallowed them up, the sea that stretches out endlessly with unchanging aspect. And like the sea God is silent. His silence continues. "If God does not exist," Rodrigues asks himself, "how can man endure the monotony of the sea and its cruel lack of emotion?" How absurd it all becomes: the lives of Mokichi and Ichizo, the travails of the missionaries, his own wanderings. Suppressing these nauseating thoughts, he wanders on. He encounters Kichijiro, who follows him like a wild dog. From Kichijiro he learns that the magistrate will give a reward of three hundred pieces of silver for a priest. "Judas sold Our Lord for thirty pieces of silver," he reflects bitterly, "I am worth ten times as much." There spring up in his mind the terrible words Christ addressed to Judas: "What thou dost, do quickly." He has never fully understood those words. Walking wearily along beside Kichijiro, he keeps turning them over in his mind. What did Christ feel when he uttered them? Was it anger? Resentment? Or did they arise from his love? He cannot help suspecting that Judas was no more than the unfortunate puppet for the glory of the drama of Christ's death. He could not bring himself to say such words to Kichijiro. He wants to protect his own life, and he ardently hopes Kichijiro will not heap betrayal upon betrayal. Kichijiro complains that he, unlike Mokichi, is a weak shoot that will never grow. Moved by pity, Rodrigues offers him the opportunity to confess. As Kichijiro kneels, Rodrigues asks himself whether he would trample on the *fumie* if it were not for his priesthood and his pride. In the woods a cicada sings. Rodrigues hears then the sound of hastening footsteps. "Father, forgive me!" Kichijiro cries out in a voice choked with tears. "I am weak. I am not a strong person like Mokichi and Ichizo." Men seize Rodrigues and drag him to his feet. With a gesture of contempt, one of them flings in the face of the kneeling Kichijiro some tiny silver coins.

And now the ordeal of Sebastian Rodrigues begins in earnest. Inoue is bent on breaking him. First he is taken to a village where some Japanese Christians are being held. One of them, whose Christian name is Monica, gives him a small cucumber to eat. Her one-eyed companion is introduced to him as Juan. Monica, Juan, and the others put their manacled wrists on their knees and bow politely as a plump and elderly samurai approaches. It is the genial samurai who had delivered the ultimatum to Tomogi. "Peasants are fools," he says to Rodrigues. "It all depends on you whether they are to be set free." Rodrigues does not quite understand. "Apostatize! Apostatize!" the old man says, laughing and waving his fan. "Punish me alone," replies Rodrigues, shrugging his shoulders and laughing. This angers the old man. "It is because of you that they must suffer," he concludes.

Rodrigues is pushed into a small hut. A Portuguese-speaking interpreter is sent to him. Educated in a seminary, the interpreter thinks Christian doctrine should not be introduced into Japan. It is his opinion that foreign priests, filled with blind courage, only cause trouble for the Japanese, forcing on them things they do not really want. He tells Rodrigues that five peasants will be suspended upside down in the pit for several days unless Rodrigues apostatizes. He assures Rodrigues that he will eventually be interrogated by Inoue himself. Five priests, including Ferreira, have apostatized after Inoue's cross-examination. Rodrigues excitedly asks whether Ferreira is still alive. The interpreter informs him that Ferreira has taken a Japanese name and lives in a mansion in Nagasaki with a wife. Rodrigues is shocked. As the interpreter departs, he remarks casually to the guards that their prisoner is a selfish rascal who will end up by apostatizing anyhow. If even Ferreira has apostatized, Rodrigues asks himself, will he have the strength to endure the suffering now in store for him? A terrible anguish rises up within him. He tries to pray. But prayer cannot distract his attention from the agonizing question: "Lord, why are you silent? Why are you always silent . . .?"

Evening comes. Three guards take Rodrigues to a beach. While they are launching two small boats, he plays idly with some peach-colored shells he finds lying in the sand. Putting one to his ear, he hears a faint, muffled roar. Suddenly a dark shudder shakes him; he crushes the shell in his hand. As his boat pulls away from shore, he catches sight of Kichijiro, running wildly along the beach shouting in a loud voice. He finds in himself no inclination to hate Kichijiro. After all, he tells himself with resignation, sooner or later he was bound to be captured. As the boat moves on, Kichijiro's figure vanishes in the evening mist. Night falls. The boat passes Yokose-no-Ura, which had been a Portuguese port. It has been burnt to the ground, its inhabitants completely dispersed. "Why have you abandoned us so completely?" Rodrigues prays in a weak voice. "Have you just remained silent like the darkness that surrounds me? Why? At least tell me why." But the sea remains cold, and the darkness stays stubbornly silent. In the morning, they land at Omura. When Rodrigues is placed on horseback with his wrists tightly bound, a howl of derision arises from the spectators. Rodrigues and his guards start for Nagasaki. During a pause for the guards to eat, someone puts a few grains of rice in a broken dish in front of Rodrigues. He raises his eyes to the donor: it is Kichijiro. A black and cruel emotion sweeps over him. Seething with anger, he mutters in his heart: "What thou dost, do quickly!" The march to Nagasaki resumes, with Kichijiro trailing the procession.

For eight days Rodrigues is kept in isolation in a prison outside Nagasaki. At night, scenes from the life of Christ pass behind his closed eyelids. The face of Christ, which from childhood had embodied all his dreams and ideals, appears before him. When its soft, clear eyes are fixed on him, his fears vanish like tiny ripples of sea water sucked up by the sands of the shore. On the ninth day he is moved to another cell. Outside he hears other prisoners praying. As his lips move in unison with theirs, he thinks: "Yet you never break the silence. You should not be silent forever." His guards allow him to visit the other prisoners. He recognizes Monica and Juan among them. He assures them that the Lord will not be silent forever and hears their confessions. That evening he senses again the face of Christ looking intently at him. Its features are tranquil; the clear blue eyes are gentle with compassion. He seems to hear Christ saying: "I will not abandon you." He feels that for an instant his heart has been purified.

One day he is given new clothes, made of the material worn by Buddhist monks, and taken out into the prison courtyard to be interrogated. A cicada is singing. To encourage his fellow Christians, he enters into controversy with his interrogators. They argue that Christianity cannot flourish in Japanese soil. "If the leaves do not grow and the flowers do not blossom," he ripostes, "that is only when no fertilizer is applied." The cicada falls silent; the officials too are silent, as though at a loss for words. Carried away by emotion, he goads them. "No matter what I say I will be punished," he exclaims. "We will not punish the fathers without reason," replies one of the officials. This is an old man who has been following the argument in silence, smiling kindly and nodding as if in sympathy with Rodrigues. "If you were Inoue, you would punish me instantly," Rodrigues insists. The officials burst into laughter. One of them tells Rodrigues that the old man is Inoue, Governor of Chikugo. Inoue rises and departs, followed by the other officials. The cicada cries out. Feeling elated, Rodrigues tells himself that his conduct has not been base or cowardly. At least he has not confused the Japanese Christians; he has done nothing to disturb their faith.

Kichijiro appears outside the prison one afternoon. Telling the guards he is a Christian, he pleads to be put in prison. To Rodrigues, he screams, "One who has trod on the sacred image has his say too." Merely because he lives in a time of persecution, Kichijiro claims, he is despised as an apostate. Is it reasonable for God, who made him weak, to ask him to imitate the strong? "Do you think I trampled on it willingly?" he asks. "My feet ached with the pain." Rodrigues remains hard of heart. Closing his eyes, he begins to recite the *Credo*. Angry memories

of betrayal grip him; he feels a sense of joy in being able to abandon his betrayer. "Did Christ pray for Judas?" he wonders. He cannot bring himself to pray
for Kichijiro. But he has no right to refuse the sacrament of penance to anyone,
and so he agrees to hear Kichijiro's confession. As the stench of Kichijiro's filth
and sweat assails him, Rodrigues is struck by the thought that Christ loves and is
searching after this dirtiest of men. It is easy to love the beautiful and charming,
but true love also accepts humanity wasted like rags and tatters. Still he cannot
forgive Kichijiro, even though he has recited the words of absolution. Once again
the face of Christ appears to him. When the gentle eyes, wet with tears, look
straight into his, Rodrigues is filled with shame.

Now the Japanese Christians are asked to trample on the *fumie*. On this day,
too, a cicada sings. The officials keep insisting it is only a formality. "Just putting
your foot on the thing won't hurt your convictions," they say. But the Christians refuse. Juan, the one-eyed man, is executed. Trembling from head to foot,
Kichijiro is brought before the officials. He bows, places his thin, wasted foot
on the *fumie*, then runs away. The dazzling white rays of the sun beat down on
the still courtyard. The black blood of the executed man lies all around like the
sash of a garment. The cicada keeps up its song, dry and hoarse. Looking on
from his cell, Rodrigues clutches the bars and shivers. A fly buzzes around his
face. What he cannot understand is the stillness of the courtyard, the song of the
cicada, the buzzing of the fly. A man has died. Yet the world goes on as if nothing had happened. "Why are you silent?" he asks yet again. "Here this one-eyed
man has died—and for you. You ought to know. Why does this stillness continue? This noonday stillness. The sound of the flies—this crazy thing, this cruel
business. And you avert your face as though indifferent?" Rodrigues had always
thought of martyrdom as glorious. But the martyrdom enacted before him seems
as wretched as the rags the peasants wear, as miserable as the huts they live in.
"Am I looking for the true, hidden martyrdom," he wonders, "or just for a glorious death? On the day of my death, too, will the world go relentlessly on its way,
indifferent just as now?" The silence continues.

Five days later, in the evening, Rodrigues has his second meeting with Inoue.
Their conversation has a bantering tone. Inoue likens the missionary effort to the
persistent love of an ugly woman. In response, Rodrigues compares the persecution to tearing a husband away from his wife. Afterwards, Rodrigues compares
his appearance before Inoue to Christ's appearance before Pilate. Like Christ
betrayed by Judas, he has been sold by Kichijiro. At this thought, a tingling sen-
sation of joy wells up within him. Yet the thought that he has tasted none of the
physical suffering Christ had known makes him uneasy. Are his captors merely
using leniency to soften him up? He refuses extra food and straw mats to sleep on.
This provokes no response from Inoue.

Ten days after the meeting with Inoue, the remaining Japanese Christians
are chained together and taken away to do forced labor. They do not return
that evening. Next morning, before sunrise, Rodrigues is taken to a pine grove

overlooking an inlet from the sea. The sound of the waves reminds him of the deaths of Mokichi and Ichizo, and of the silence of the sea and God on that day. He recognizes the interpreter whom he had met on the day he was captured. The interpreter informs him that the Lord of Chikugo plans to have another Portuguese brought there to meet him. The name of Ferreira leaps to his mind. For a long time he has felt for Ferreira nothing but the pity a strong person feels for the wretched, but now he is agitated and his heart starts pounding. However, it is Garrpe who appears, following the Japanese Christians from the prison. Straw mats are rolled around the bodies of the Christians. Garrpe is told that they will be thrown into the water to drown if he does not apostatize. But if Garrpe gives in, thinks Rodrigues, it would mean the betrayal of his whole life. What is Garrpe to do? Two of the Christians, wrapped in straw, stumble forward as if to run away. A push from the officials sends them flying forward to fall prostrate in the sand. Monica, looking like a basket worm, stands staring dumbly at the sea. The taste of the cucumber she had once given him rises up in Rodrigues's heart. "Apostatize! Apostatize!" he silently cries to Garrpe. Turning away, he thinks: "You are silent. Even in this moment are you silent?" Prodded by the officials, the basket worms board a small boat. "I would apostatize. I would apostatize." The words rise up in Rodrigues's throat. Clenching his teeth, he bites them back. Two officials with lances, rolling their kimonos up to the waist, follow the prisoners into the boat. "There is still time!" thinks Rodrigues. "Do not impute all this to Garrpe and to me. This responsibility you yourself must bear." But now Garrpe rushes forward and plunges into the sea. Swimming toward the boat, he shouts, "Lord, hear our prayer. . . ." One by one, the Christians are pushed off the side of the boat with the tip of a lance. Finally waves from the boat cover Garrpe's head. Eyes filled with hatred, the interpreter says to Rodrigues: "Father, have you thought of the suffering you have inflicted on so many peasants just because of your dream, just because you want to impose your selfish dream upon Japan? Look! Blood is flowing again. The blood of those ignorant people is flowing again."

Back in his cell, Rodrigues stares at the wall and broods. He had come to this country to lay down his life for the Japanese, but instead they are laying down their lives for him, one by one. His pity for the dying Christians had been overwhelming, but long ago he had learned that pity, like passion, is only a kind of instinct. It is not action; it is not love. It occurs to him that the Christians had chosen to die for the sake of their faith, but this thought no longer has power to heal his wounds. Once more, at night, the face of Christ comes before his eyes. Now it is the sorrowful face of Gethsemane, a suffering, perspiring face with an emaciated expression. On that night had that man too felt the silence of God, Rodrigues wonders. Did he too shudder with terror at the silence? An image of the sad, rainy sea arises before him, and over this sea hangs an endless and unrelenting silence. Does God really exist? If not, how ludicrous is half his life spent traversing the limitless sea to plant the seed of faith on this barren island! How ludicrous the deaths of Garrpe and the Japanese Christians! And yet, when the morning sun comes, his spirits revive and the night's loneliness departs. He whispers in a sorrowful voice: "My heart is steadfast, O God, my heart is steadfast!"

At last the time of his confrontation with Ferreira arrives. With the interpreter, Rodrigues travels to a small Buddhist temple. On the heels of an old monk, Ferreira, in a black kimono, enters, his eyes cast down. His first upward glance reveals a servile smile of shame, which is quickly replaced by a deliberately challenging look. Rodrigues tries to force a smile to his lips. Nostalgia, anger, sadness, and hatred mix within his heart. A white tear drops from his eye and rolls slowly down his cheek. Asked how he occupies himself, Ferreira replies that he is translating a book of astronomy into Japanese. It is something he can do, he says, to be of use to the Japanese. To help others, thinks Rodrigues, this is the one wish and the only dream of one who has dedicated himself to the priesthood. "Are you happy?" he murmurs. A flash of pain crosses Ferreira's face. The interpreter remarks that Ferreira is also writing a book to show the errors of Christianity. "Cruel!" exclaims Rodrigues. As Ferreira tries to turn his face away, a white tear glistens in his eye. Rodrigues thinks: "And yet this man is still alive! Lord, you are still silent. You still maintain your deep silence in a life like this!" The interpreter snaps at Ferreira to get on with his job. "I've been told to get you to apostatize," says Ferreira. He describes the pit. You are bound hand and foot and hung upside down in a pit. Small cuts are made behind the ears to delay loss of consciousness; the blood trickles out drop by drop. It is a torture invented by Inoue. As he listens, Rodrigues feels only pity for Ferreira; he can summon up no contempt.

But then Ferreira launches his serious attack. He confesses that twenty years of missionary work have defeated him. The one thing he knows is that Christianity does not take root in Japan. The country is a swamp. Whenever you plant a sapling in it, the roots begin to rot; the leaves grow yellow and wither. Clenching his fists in anger, Rodrigues tells himself desperately not to be deceived by this sophistry. A defeated man, he thinks, will use any self-deception he can to defend himself. Ferreira presses relentlessly on. The Japanese have never accepted the God of Christianity, he insists. It was always their own gods they worshipped. "But I have seen martyrs," Rodrigues thinks. "With my own eyes I have seen them die, burning with faith," he says. Memories crowd in upon him: the rain-drenched sea with two stakes at its edge, black blood on the prison courtyard floor, the woman who had given him a cucumber trussed into a basket. "They did not believe in the Christian God," Ferreira says now, speaking clearly and with self-confidence, emphasizing every word. "The Japanese till this day have never had the concept of God; and they never will." And in these words Rodrigues senses a sincerity unlike the self-deception of a defeated man. But later he is able to tell himself that Ferreira was merely trying to increase the number of weaklings like himself, to share with others his cowardice and loneliness. So he prays: "Lord, will you not save him? Turning to Judas you said, 'What thou dost, do quickly.' Will you number this man, too, among the abandoned?" Comparing his own loneliness and sadness with Ferreira's, Rodrigues feels self-respect and even a certain satisfaction, and is able to sleep.

Two days later he is taken from his cell for the last time. "At last the time has come," he tells himself. As his hands are being bound behind him, he feels a sense of elation he has never before experienced. A smile of triumph passes over his face. "No matter what the circumstances, no man can completely escape from vanity," he reflects. But, as they ride together through the streets of Nagasaki, the interpreter tells him: "Tonight, you will apostatize." Inoue has predicted it, and Inoue has never been wrong. Rodrigues drives these words from his mind. He finds joy in the thought that he will soon be united with the Japanese martyrs, with Garrpe, and with Christ crucified. The patient, suffering face of Christ pursues him, and he prays that his face may draw near to that face. The interpreter pleads with him to go through the formality of apostatizing. Biting his lip, Rodrigues sits silently on his horse; blood flows down his chin. And so they proceed onward to the office of the magistrate Inoue.

Rodrigues is placed in a dark cell. As he finds his way around it by touch, his fingers discover the words LAUDETE EUM carved into the wall. In the darkness, the face of Christ, filled with sorrow, appears to be close beside him. It seems to say to him: "When you suffer, I suffer with you. To the end I am close to you." The sound of a snoring guard distracts him. It strikes him as ludicrous that he should be facing death while another man snores in this carefree way. He laughs. Waves of terror wash over him. He tries to pray. Seeing the emaciated face of Christ, covered with sweat like drops of blood, brings no consolation. He paces the cell to distract himself. In the distance, he hears a voice. It is Kichijiro shouting: "Let me meet the father! Let me meet the father!" Again Kichijiro begs for absolution. As Rodrigues silently utters the words of absolution, a bitter taste fills his mouth. Kichijiro laments: "I was born weak. One who is weak at heart cannot die a martyr. What am I do? Ah, why was I born into the world at all?" Then his voice trails off. Again Rodrigues thinks of the words of command Christ had addressed to Judas. If Christ was love itself, why had he driven Judas from him in this fashion? Had Judas been cast aside to sink down into eternal darkness? These doubts seem like dirty bubbles rising from the waters of a swamp. Again the sound of snoring drives him to laughter. He pictures the cruel face of the snoring guard, bloated and heavy with sake. He is filled with sudden rage that such a vile noise should disturb the most important night of his life. He feels he is being trifled with and begins to beat wildly on the wall. "Father, what is wrong?" asks the interpreter in the voice of a cat toying with its prey. "Isn't it better for you not to be so stubborn? If you simply say, 'I apostatize,' all will be well." Rodrigues replies, "It's only that snoring." From the darkness, in a low and pitiful voice, it is Ferreira who enlightens him: "That's not snoring. That is the moaning of Christians hanging in the pit."

"I was here just like you," Ferreira says. "I, too, heard those voices." As Ferreira speaks, the voices like snoring, the gasping and groaning of suffering men, beat upon their ears. Rodrigues is bewildered. While they had been in agony, he had uttered no prayers; he had laughed. In his pride, he had believed he alone in this night was sharing that man's suffering, but just beside him others were sharing in that suffering much more than he. "And you," he thinks, "call yourself a priest who takes upon himself the sufferings of others!" "Lord, until this moment have you been mocking me?" he cries aloud. " 'Laudete Eum!' I engraved those letters on the wall," Ferreira tells him. "I was put in here and heard the voices of those people for whom God did nothing. God did not do a single thing. I prayed with all my strength; but God did nothing." Shaking his head wildly, Rodrigues stops up his ears with his fingers. But the groaning of the Christians breaks in upon his prayer. "Stop! Stop! Lord, it is now that you should break the silence. You must not remain silent. Prove that you are justice, that you are goodness, that you are love." Ferreira tells Rodrigues that the five people who had been suspended in the pit when he was brought there had already apostatized many times. The groaning goes on. "In return for these earthly sufferings, those people will receive a reward of eternal joy," Rodrigues says to Ferreira. "Don't deceive yourself!" Ferreira insists. "Don't disguise your own weakness with those beautiful words." Angrily Ferreira continues: "You make yourself more important than them. You are preoccupied with your own salvation. If you say that you will apostatize, those people will be taken out of the pit. They will be saved from suffering. And you refuse to do so. It's because you dread to betray the church. You dread to be the dregs of the church, like me." For a moment Ferreira is silent. Then he says in a strong voice: "Certainly Christ would have apostatized for them." Gradually the first light of day begins to filter into the cell. "Christ would certainly have apostatized to help men," he says confidently. "No, no!" says Rodrigues, covering his face with his hands. "For love Christ would have apostatized. Even if it meant giving up everything he had," Ferreira insists. "Go away, away!" shouts Rodrigues wildly. Now the door of the cell swings open and the white light of morning floods in. Taking Rodrigues gently by the shoulder, Ferreira says: "You are now going to perform the most painful act of love that has ever been performed." Dragging his feet as if his legs were bound with leaden chains, Rodrigues allows Ferreira to guide him down the corridor. At the end stand the interpreter and two guards, looking like black dolls. The interpreter places a large wooden plaque on the ground. "Now you are going to perform the most painful act of love that has ever been performed," Ferreira repeats gently. Rodrigues now sees the *fumie* at his feet. A simple copper medal is attached to a grey plaque of dirty wood. On it is the ugly face of Christ, crowned with thorns, thin arms outstretched. It is the first time Rodrigues has seen a physical image of Christ since coming to Japan. "Whenever I prayed, your face appeared before me," he thinks. "When I was alone I thought of your face imparting a blessing; when I was captured your face as it appeared when you carried your cross gave me life. This face is deeply ingrained in my soul—the most beautiful, the most precious thing in the world has been living in my heart." The first rays of morning sun appear. Rodrigues grasps the *fumie* and brings it close to his eyes. Sadly he stares at the man in its center, worn down and hollow from constant trampling. "It's only a formality," the interpreter urges excitedly. "Only go through with the exterior form of trampling."

Rodrigues lifts his foot. In it he feels a dull, heavy pain. This is no mere formality. He is about to trample on the most beautiful thing in his life, the focus of his ideals and dreams. The pain in his foot is agonizing. And then the Christ in bronze speaks to him: "Trample! Trample! I more than anyone know of the pain in your foot. Trample! It was to be trampled on by men that I was born into this world. It was to share men's pain that I carried my cross!" Rodrigues places his foot on the *fumie*. Dawn breaks. In the distance a cock crows.

So ends the ordeal of Sebastian Rodrigues. A few things remain to be said about its effects on him.

Rodrigues is kept for a while in a small house in Nagasaki. Children stare at him as he gazes out a window. "Apostate Paul! Apostate Paul!" they shout. He wonders if word of his apostasy has reached the missionaries at Macao and Goa. Do they regard him as a renegade? But it is not they, he thinks, who judge his heart. He imagines the Inquisition pursuing him. How can they, who live in tranquil security in Europe, judge him? Generals should not reproach the privates who are taken prisoner. Is this thought self-deceit? "Why even now am I attempting this ugly self-defense?" he asks himself. "I fell," he admits. "But, Lord, you alone know that I did not renounce my faith!" He had been driven beyond endurance by the moaning of the prisoners in the pit. As Ferreira spoke, he had thought they would be saved if he apostatized. But is all this talk of love, after all, just an excuse to justify his own weakness? He wonders whether there is any real difference between him and Kichijiro. "I know," he tells himself, "that my Lord is different from the God that is preached in the churches." And once more the face of Christ rises up behind his eyelids. It is not a face filled with majesty and glory; neither is it a face made beautiful by enduring pain; nor is it a face filled with the strength that conquers temptation. It is the face of the *fumie*, sunken and exhausted. Looking up at him in sorrow, those eyes had said: "Trample! Trample! It is to be trampled on by you that I am here."

From time to time he encounters Ferreira at the magistrate's office. He feels hatred for Ferreira, but it is self-hatred. In Ferreira, he finds his own deep wound, a reflection of his fall. There is Ferreira in front of him, clad in the same Japanese clothes, using the same Japanese language, and like himself expelled from the church. He feels pity too, but it is self-pity. They are like two ugly twins, he thinks. They hate one another's ugliness; they despise one another; but they are inseparable. It is unbearable to him to see his own ugly face in the mirror of Ferreira. They do not speak to one another. Neither can plumb the depths of the other's solitude. As they depart, each glances furtively back at the other.

He has a final meeting with Inoue. Oddly, he feels no sense of disgrace in Inoue's presence. He has realized that it was against his own faith and not against the Lord of Chikugo that he had fought. Inoue informs him that he is to live permanently in Edo and to take the Japanese name Okada San'emon. "Father, you were not defeated by me," Inoue says. "You were defeated by this swamp of Japan." He replies that his struggle was with Christianity in his own heart. With a cynical smile, Inoue expresses disbelief that the Christ of the *fumie* had told the priest to trample. "Isn't this just your self-deception? Just a cloak of your weakness?" Inoue insists. Other priests have told him that the difference between the mercy of the Christian God and that of the Buddha is that the Christian believer must retain with all his might a strength of heart in order to deserve salvation. The priest wants to reply that Christianity is not what Inoue takes it to be. But the words stick in his throat. It occurs to him that no matter what he says no one could understand his present feelings. So, eyes blinking, he sits before the magistrate listening to his words in silence. Inoue announces that he has no desire to apprehend the remaining Japanese Christians. In the swamp of Japan, the sapling will wither and the leaves die once the roots have been cut. "The Christianity you brought to Japan has changed its form and has become a strange thing," sighs Inoue with resignation. The priest recalls that Ferreira had said the same thing. With a gesture of farewell, Inoue departs.

That evening the priest encounters Kichijiro again. Kichijiro shows up at his house, pleading once more for absolution. He voices the familiar complaint: "The strong never yield to torture, and they go to Paradise; but what about those, like myself, who are born weak, those who, when tortured and ordered to trample on the sacred image. . . . " The priest, too, had stood on the sacred image, on the face of the one he had always longed to love. "Trample! Trample!" those eyes of pity had said. "Your foot suffers in pain; it must suffer like all the feet that have stepped on this plaque. But that pain alone is enough." The priest had said, "Lord, I resented your silence." "I was not silent; I suffered beside you," had been the answer. "But you told Judas to go away: What thou dost, do quickly. What happened to Judas?" "Just as I told you to step on the plaque, so I told Judas to do what he was going to do. For Judas was in anguish as you are now." The priest had felt a tremendous onrush of joy as he lowered his foot onto the sacred image. Now he thinks, "There are neither the strong nor the weak. Can anyone say that the weak do not suffer more than the strong?" He hears Kichijiro's confession. "Go in peace," he says. Weeping softly, Kichijiro leaves the house. The priest tells himself he did not betray his Lord in administering the sacrament. He loves Christ now in a different way from before, and everything that has taken place until now has been necessary to bring him to this love. "Even now I am the last priest in this land," he affirms. "But Our Lord was not silent. Even if he had been silent, my life until this day would have spoken of him."

The records of the Christian residence at Edo show that Okada San'emon lived there quietly under guard for thirty years. Kichijiro was among his attendants. He died of illness at the age of 64. His corpse was cremated.

ETHICAL CONFLICT AND SUFFERING LOVE

Literature abounds with narratives of conflict among ideals and obligations. Some spring from a tragic vision. Agamemnon is torn between military necessity and parental love, and Antigone is forced to choose between the claims of familial piety and those of civic duty. Some reflect the dark side of bourgeois domesticity. Nora must decide between the security of home and the risks of freedom. And some serve to illustrate philosophical theses. Sartre's young man has to create himself in making the choice between the bonds of kinship and the demands of resistance. The story of Sebastian Rodrigues shows that the ideals and obligations involved in following Christ can give rise to such conflicts. He is torn between the demand for loyalty to his priestly vows and to his church and the claim the suffering of the Japanese Christians makes on his capacity for love of neighbor. At first glance, the result of the conflict appears to be tragic. Driven by dire necessity, Rodrigues fights a battle with Christianity in his own heart, and it appears that Christianity emerges from this struggle defeated. The terror Rodrigues feels at the silence of God makes him vulnerable to doubts that sap the strength of his faith, and he apostatizes. But Rodrigues seems to be a loser, too, for it appears that Inoue has been able to break him. His life seems to come to an abrupt end when he tramples on the face of Christ, though the life of Okada San'emon drags on in seclusion for another thirty years. As Inoue has insisted, the consolation he takes in the thought that the Christ of the *fumie* has spoken to him and through his life may seem to be no more than a pitifully thin cloak of self-deception.

One might respond to the story by judging it to be an unnecessary tragedy. Trampling on an image of Christ, Rodrigues is assured over and over again by his interpreter, is only a formality. If he wishes, he can go through the motions with a mental reservation, but his tormenters will be satisfied. They make it appear that they do not care whether he steps on the *fumie* with the intention of renouncing or dishonoring Christ, so long as he presses his foot on the image of Christ's face. So it looks as if he has a chance to save the Japanese Christians from being tortured on his account while remaining faithful to the spirit of his vows. Is it not terribly quixotic, at best, for him not to take advantage of this opportunity to avoid betraying Christ in his heart?

Perhaps there are Christians who could trample on an image of Christ without meaning thereby to apostatize. But Sebastian Rodrigues is not among them; for him, pressing a foot on the *fumie* must signify betrayal. The image of Christ's face is the focus of all his deepest ideals and aspirations, dreams and desires. From childhood, he had treasured that face as the romantic lover adores the face of his beloved. It appears to him over and over again, sometimes strong and beautiful, sometimes suffering and sorrowful. In it he has invested the commitments that bestow meaning on his life. He could not detach this significance from that image by a single act of will, even if he wished to do so. His whole life has made it a stubbornly sacred symbol for him, and in the crunch its power will not be denied. Ferreira is aware of this when he tells Rodrigues that trampling on the image of Christ's face will be the most painful act of love that has ever been performed. It becomes irrevocably clear to Rodrigues when he raises his foot to trample and feels agonizing pain in it. For him, just going through the motions is not an option; the accumulated weight of the loyalties of a lifetime has ruled out that possibility. The causistry of mental reservations is bound to be powerless against such a weight. His life has made Rodrigues a man who cannot step on the *fumie* and not have what he is doing be an act of betrayal.

And, of course, this betrayal involves self-betrayal. Rodrigues had thought himself strong and fantasized for himself a glorious martyr's death. He had been willing to advise Japanese Christians to trample on the *fumie* because he pitied their misery, but he then had no thought of following his own advice. He had silently cried out to Garrpe to apostatize to save the basket worms from drowning, but he had made no move to deny his own faith for their sake. He had pitied Ferreira for his weakness; his attitude toward Kichijiro had been a mixture of pity, disgust, and anger. Rodrigues had considered himself stronger than all these people. He had taken pride in not doing anything base or cowardly that would shake the faith of Japanese Christians. He had hoped and prayed to be strong enough to succeed where Ferreira had failed, to resist apostasy even under physical torture in the pit. But instead he came to tread upon an image of Christ without even having been subjected to the explicit threat of physical torture. In so doing, he betrayed something deep in himself, his sense of himself as a man with the vocation to lead a life of exemplary Christian courage. It was this picture of what his life was all about that had sustained him through the earlier parts of his ordeal. After apostatizing, he is no longer in a position to think that he is even stronger than Kichijiro. He has broken off the thread that had given his life up to now continuity.

But there is a strain in Christian ethics that leads to the conclusion that this sacrifice of his own ideals is required of him. It is suggested by this brief comment James F. Gustafson makes about the situation in which Rodrigues finds himself:

A rigoristic response might be that his vows were unconditional, and should provide the reasons as well as the strength of will to maintain fidelity to them regardless of the consequences to others. That would seem to me, however, to be a curious way of loving one's neighbor, and particularly those who are of the household of faith. It does not follow from this case, however, that vows, contracts, promises, and other time-binding commitments are without motivating force, or that they always can be ignored because they can in this extreme case.[8]

---

[8] James F. Gustafson, *Ethics from a Theocentric Perspective*, ii. *Ethics and Theology* (Chicago: University of Chicago Press, 1984), 312. Though I have discovered that some devout Christians are horrified by this thought, one might concede to Gustafson that apostatizing to spare the Japanese

Christians are enjoined to love of neighbor. Rodrigues has come to Japan to serve the Christians there and to suffer for them, if necessary. Instead they suffer because he will not trample on the *fumie*. Is his refusal a matter of stubborn pride? On the night before his apostasy, when he recognizes the sound that has disturbed him as the groaning of Japanese Christians in the pit, he realizes that he has been so preoccupied with his own terrors that he has not even prayed for them. This recognition is the significant detail that he had not foreseen. It had not even occurred to him that others might be suffering more than he that night. Ferreira angrily insists that Rodrigues is motivated by fear of looking bad in the eyes of the Church and claims that Christ himself would have apostatized for love of the suffering Japanese Christians. If Rodrigues had found it in himself to reject Ferreira's argument, would that bespeak a kind of self-absorption inconsistent with the full measure of love a Christian should have for his fellow men and women in their hour of agony? As the groaning from the pit continues, the demand that Rodrigues express love for the Christians suffering there by acting to bring their anguish to an end grows more urgent. Beyond a certain point, further resistance to that demand would seem to reflect callous indifference in the face of suffering. Maybe finding within oneself the strength of will to resist such a demand for love would only be possible if one could destroy in oneself capacities for sympathetic response essential for human love of neighbor to take root and flourish. If so, then the outcome of Rodrigues's struggle would have been terrible even if he had resisted apostasy to the bitter end, for he would have killed in himself the capacity to cultivate the love of neighbor required by his own Christian commitments. Indeed, we can see that capacity atrophy in the course of his struggle as his heart hardens toward Kichijiro. So perhaps Christian love of neighbor requires Rodrigues to act as he does to stop the torture of the Japanese Christians. And maybe he begins to realize this when he sees that there has been a barrier to love in his inordinate preoccupation with his own strength of will and the issue of how it will fare when put to the test.

But we should not be too quick to endorse Gustafson's suggestion that Rodrigues may ignore his vows on account of the extremity of his situation. Christian ethical thought also has a strand that supports the claim that he has an absolute duty to hold out against apostasy. It is not he, after all, but Inoue who is responsible for the suffering of the Japanese Christians, and he need not take upon himself the responsibility for relieving it. His faith allows him to leave to God the responsibility for the ultimate care of them. Indeed, he would display lack of trust in God's providence if he were not convinced that God was going to reward them fully if they remained steadfast under torture. Then, too, his apostasy will have dreadful consequences. It will cause scandal throughout the

Christians suffering is the better course for Rodrigues. Even so, it does not follow that his obligation not to apostatize is overridden or nullified, and so it does not follow that he does not confront a dilemma.

Christian world. It will also be fatal for the beleaguered community of Japanese Christians. Inoue is so confident Christianity will wither in the swamp of Japan after its roots are cut that he sees no need to apprehend the remaining Japanese Christians once the last foreign priest apostatizes. More important, Rodrigues has dedicated himself to living the life of a religious hero for whom apostasy is unthinkable. If he can be brought to think that his vows do not bind him provided the stakes are high enough, he has already failed by his own standards. If the groaning of a few Japanese in the pit is not sufficient to break him, Inoue has only to raise the stakes. Once Rodrigues makes himself susceptible to moral blackmail by the wicked of this world, he is no longer fit for the heroic part demanded by missionary activity in a time and place of persecution. He has no choice but to regard his apostasy as a fall, and he rightly does so. The thought of pleading duress to the Inquisition strikes him as an ugly form of self-defense. What he sees after the fall in the mirror of Ferreira is his own ugly flaw. What he feels toward Ferreira is a pity that is also self-pity for being a weakling and a hatred that is also self-hatred on account of his own shameful weakness.

When Rodrigues tramples on the *fumie* what he does, I think, is both to violate a demand of his religious vocation binding on him no matter what the consequences and to satisfy an equally pressing demand for an expression of love of neighbor. The case resists subsumption under one but not the other of these descriptions. Both demands are characteristic of a distinctively Christian ethic. They spring from a single source: the commandment that we both love God with total devotion and love our neighbors as ourselves.[9] The misfortune is that Rodrigues cannot, given that he is the kind of person his life has made him, satisfy one of these demands without violating the other. He is, I suggest, trapped in an ethical dilemma. There is an ethical dilemma when a person is subject to two ethical demands such that he cannot satisfy both and neither demand is overridden or nullified. The ethical demand that I play tennis with you on Friday imposed by my having promised to do so would be overridden by the more stringent demand that I stay home to comfort my mother if she were dying on Friday. The ethical demand that I play tennis with you on Friday imposed by my having promised to do so would be nullified if you were to break a leg on Thursday. Demands that are neither overridden nor nullified are in force. When one confronts two conflicting ethical demands both of which are in force, one is caught in an ethical dilemma. It seems to me that this is the situation of Sebastian Rodrigues.

Elsewhere[10] I have argued abstractly that there can be dilemmas in which religious demands created by divine fiat conflict with the demands of ordinary

---

[9] A related problem to which the Great Commandment gives rise is sensitively treated in Robert M. Adams, "The Problem of Total Devotion," in Robert Audi and William J. Wainright (eds.), *Rationality, Religious Belief, and Moral Commitment* (Ithaca and London: Cornell University Press, 1986), 169–94.

[10] Philip L. Quinn, "Moral Obligation, Religious Demand, and Practical Conflict," in Audi and Wainwright (eds.), *Rationality*, 195–212.

morality. Here the suggestion is rather different and, perhaps, more radical. It is that the possibility of a dilemma arising is built into Christian ethics at its foundations. A Christian ethics of love is presumably based on the command both to love God with total devotion and to love the neighbor as oneself. The two parts of the command are conjoined. Neither is said to override the other.[11] But it seems clear that it is possible for a situation to arise in which the two parts of the Great Commandment are in conflict.

Much of the interest Endo's *Silence* has for Christian ethical thought derives from the fact that it presents what looks like such a situation in rich and realistic detail. Love of neighbor demands that Rodrigues trample on the *fumie* in order to get Inoue to call a halt to the torture of the miserable Japanese Christians. Given the role the image of Christ's face has played in his spiritual life, it is not open to him to treat stepping on a copper image of that face as a mere formality. For him, trampling on the *fumie* cannot be anything other than apostasy. But he has constructed his whole life around his priestly vocation and committed himself to remaining true to his vows come what may. Given also what fidelity to his vows signifies in his life as an expression of his devotion to Christ, it is not an option for him to think of himself as released from those vows by the gravity of his situation. For him, apostasy just is betraying something constitutive of his character and essential to the way in which total devotion to God has come to express itself in his life. So the response he makes to the demand of love of neighbor must, given what his life has been, be a fall away from total devotion to God. It is bound to be both a painful act of love and a shameful act of disloyalty. He is choosing between love of neighbor and total devotion to God in circumstances in which he cannot satisfy the demands both make on him. And, because he confronts a hard, forced choice of this sort, things would not have been any better if he had chosen the other way. Total devotion to God demands that he refrain from trampling on the *fumie* in order to prove the strength of his faith and the depths of his loyalty to his chosen way of serving God. Given the sensitivity he has developed to the sufferings of the Japanese Christians and the claim the groans of those in agony next to him in the pit makes on his instinctive sympathies, it is not open to him just to remain oblivious to their suffering. For him, to refrain from trampling on the *fumie* could not be anything other than to turn his back on their cry of anguish. But his life has also been constructed on an ideal of serving others and suffering even unto death for their sake, if necessary. Given also what living up to

---

[11] When a lawyer asks him which is the greatest commandment of the law, Jesus replies: "'You shall love the Lord your God with your whole heart, with your whole soul, and with all your mind.' This is the greatest and first commandment. The second is like it: 'You shall love your neighbor as yourself.' On these two commandments the whole law is based, and the prophets as well" (Matthew 22: 37–40). Though the two commandments are ordered, it does not seem to me that Jesus says or implies that the second is to be subordinated to the first or that the first would override the second in case of conflict. See also Mark 12: 29–33, in which Jesus first orders and then conjoins the two parts of the Great Commandment.

that ideal has come to mean to him in the arduous course of his mission to the persecuted Japanese Christians, it is not an option for him to think of himself as released from that commitment to serve by the extremity of his plight. For him, to turn his back on their cry of anguish would be to betray another ingrained part of his character, one which has come to determine the way in which love of neighbor can find expression in his life. So the response he would make to the demand of total devotion to God would have to be, given the course his life had taken, an unloving rejection of claims of the neighbor upon him. It would be both a painful expression of loyalty and a shameful act of denial.

Indeed, there are indications that it might come to something a good deal worse than that. As Rodrigues draws nearer to having to face the torture of the pit in his own flesh, he becomes more and more wrapped up in his own fears and less and less apt to attend and respond to the claims others have on him. Immediately after his capture he has no hatred for Kichijiro; he is resigned to thinking he was bound to be captured sooner or later anyway. But gradually his heart hardens. When Kichijiro visits him in prison to beg forgiveness for the betrayal, he cannot even bring himself to pray for Kichijiro. Though he recites the words of absolution he is unable to forgive Kichijiro, and this makes him feel shame. In the night prior to his apostasy, he is so preoccupied with the torments he is enduring that, until he recognizes the groaning from the pit, it does not even occur to him that the Japanese Christians might be suffering worse than he is, and he neglects to pray for them. Steeling himself to hold out under torture comes to absorb all his strength; his struggle to refrain from doing anything base or cowardly consumes all his energy. The danger is that he will no longer have anything to give to others. If we imagine his ordeal indefinitely protracted, we fear that he may lose the resources and then the ability to love his neighbors. And, in the limit, the ultimate threat is that he may lose his love for Christ as well. If that were to happen, resisting apostasy at all costs would prove to be a hollow victory for him.

Resistance to reading the plight of Rodrigues as an ethical dilemma might be expected to take many forms. One that deserves a certain amount of attention is this. It may be thought that neighbor love does not demand that Rodrigues act to relieve the suffering of the Japanese Christians being tortured in the pit; rather it requires him to do what is best for them. If the Japanese Christians die in their torments, they die for their faith, and so they die as martyrs. A martyr's death is something many early Christians considered the greatest of earthly goods. Glory awaits martyrs after death. Because it is best for the Japanese Christians in the pit that they die as martyrs, neighbor love demands that Rodrigues refrain from intervening to spare them. But, though this response must be respected, it should also, in my opinion, be resisted. The Japanese Christians in the pit are merely pawns in Inoue's game. They do not seek or wish for martyrdom. Ferreira had been explicitly told that the five Japanese Christians in the pit at the time of his final ordeal were being tortured despite the fact that they had already apostatized many times. Doubtless Inoue's fiendish cleverness extends to making similar arrangements to turn the screws on Rodrigues. If such people die under torture, they will not be dying for the Christian faith. They are not the stuff glorious martyrs are made of. So it is not best for them that their torture in the pit be prolonged, and Rodrigues does not go contrary to what is best for them when he acts to relieve their suffering. To be sure, he falls, but in falling he expresses and preserves his capacity for love.

Another reason for resistance is this. Christianity enjoins the imitation of Christ. But if Christ had been in the place of Rodrigues, there is exactly one thing he would have done. Perhaps, as Ferreira insinuates, he would have apostatized. Whatever he would have done, Rodrigues ought to do that thing, and it is not the case that he ought to do anything else. So, the objection concludes, there could be no genuine dilemma for Rodrigues. This objection seems to me to over-simplify considerably the relation of imitation that is supposed to hold between our lives and Christ's. No one imagines that we are obliged to imitate the life of Christ in all its concrete details. What we are called to imitate is something more abstract, a pattern deriving from the life of Christ, and this pattern represents the life of Christ as it has been refracted through scriptural traditions and our culture's interpretations of those traditions. In short, it is a cultural construction. And such cultural constructions can give rise to dilemmas when one tries to apply them in circumstances very different from those they were constructed to fit. An illustration of this point is the following, somewhat contrived example. Imagine a society in which the pattern for men to imitate is the life of the heroic warri-or who is hard toward all enemies and tender toward all women. How will this pattern apply to the case of these men encountering for the first time women sol-diers in the armies opposed to them? They will confront a dilemma, because the pattern of the heroic warrior directs them to be both hard and tender toward the women soldiers in the enemy armies. Of course, this society may eventually get rid of its dilemma by revising the pattern to make the heroic warrior one who is hard toward all enemies and tender toward women except when they are enemy soldiers. But I can see no parallel to such a revision in the case of Rodrigues. I think there is no revision in the pattern of the life of Christ that would both remove his dilemma and remain faithful to our cultural traditions or his.

A third kind of response would be to concede that Rodrigues faces a dilemma but argue that this is his own fault. According to Alan Donagan,[12] Aquinas was of the opinion that moral dilemmas can arise only when, as a result of violating one or more moral demands, a person would find that there is a moral demand he or she can obey only if he or she violates another. The trouble with this response is that it seems not to be true to the story of Rodrigues. To be sure, he is portrayed as being a bit too proud of his own strength and a bit too paternalistic toward the Japanese for contemporary tastes. But it is not suggested that these flaws are in

---

[12] Alan Donagan, "Consistency in Rationalist Moral Systems," *Journal of Philosophy*, 81 (1984), 291–309.

any way his fault. Indeed, it is clear that it is Inoue's fault, and not his, that he confronts a dilemma. It might, of course, be held that the pride and paternalism Rodrigues exhibits are consequences of original sin rather than results of his personal sins. Departing from Aquinas, one might then go on to claim that moral dilemmas can also arise when, as a result of flaws due to original sin, a person would find there is a moral demand he or she can obey only if he or she violates another. However, this appeal to fallen human nature implies that even the best of us are, through no personal fault of our own, liable to being confronted with moral dilemmas.

Doubtless there are other ways of resisting my claim that Rodrigues confronts a moral dilemma. Instead of discussing more of them, however, I shall return now to exploring the consequences of reading the narrative as the representation of a dilemma.

So perhaps there is something providential in this fall. Though it is so painful to him that Rodrigues seems thereafter a broken man, he might have lost everything he valued and been utterly destroyed if he had managed somehow to hold out against apostatizing to the bitter end. But if something providential is shepherding Rodrigues toward the choice he makes, it works in the most appallingly risky ways. It operates on Rodrigues, paradoxically enough, through the medium of the silence of God, which might drive him to despair or flush him into open rebellion. The whole affair must be managed like the most delicately calibrated balancing act.

Inoue, Ferreira, and the interpreter try to crack Rodrigues's self-confidence with argument. The interpreter insinuates that Rodrigues is only making trouble for the Japanese by bringing them as a gift they do not want. Ferreira insists that Christianity has mutated and become something alien in Japan. Inoue proclaims that Christianity will wither in the Japanese swamp if its foreign roots are cut off. Rodrigues is not shaken by any of these attacks on the sense of his mission. He ignores the interpreter, banters with Inoue, and writes off Ferreira's argument as the sophistical self-defense of a proven weakling. But the silence of God pierces him. It sickens him that God has remained silent through twenty years of persecution. When Mokichi and Ichizo die staked out in the sea, the silence of the sea reminds him of the silence of God. He is nauseated by the thought that the cruel indifference of the sea would be unbearable if God did not exist. When he wonders whether he will have the strength to withstand tortures that broke Ferreira, he asks God why he is always silent. As he passes the ruins of Yokose-no-Ura, he prays to God to tell him why he remains silent like the surrounding darkness. When he hears Japanese Christians praying outside his prison cell, he tells God that he should not be silent forever. The execution of one-eyed Juan provokes him to ask again why God is silent, averting his face as though indifferent. When the basket worms are about to be killed, he insists that God must not remain silent and leave everything up to him and Garrpe, and shortly thereafter he even wonders whether God exists. If not, he thinks, his life is absurd and the deaths of the Japanese martyrs are ludicrous. The cruelty of making Ferreira write a book about the errors of Christianity leads him to exclaim to himself about God's continuing silence. And, finally, as he listens to the groaning from the pit, he demands that God break his silence and prove that he is just, good, and loving.

Only the face of Christ seems to have the power to give him temporary relief from the oppressive burden of God's silence. At one point he even wonders whether Christ too had shuddered at the terror of that silence on the night of his agony in Gethsemane. This silence is a horrifying mystery. Thousands of Christians have suffered and died for their faith. Men have been pushed to the limits of their endurance and beyond. Yet God has not spoken out to comfort them or to rebuke their persecutors. It is as though God is indifferent to the tribulations of his servants. He does not even speak to vindicate himself. The cumulative effect of the suffering he has witnessed is to make this situation intolerable to Rodrigues. He can no longer stand it. It is not that he thinks that the suffering he has witnessed is logically incompatible with the existence of God; nor does he suppose that suffering provides conclusive evidence against the existence of God. Denying the existence of God is not to be his way out of a situation he can no longer endure. Like Job, he quarrels with God. He insists that God break his silence to vindicate himself and demands that God prove that he is just, good, and loving. But no voice answers him out of a whirlwind. So he pushes the quarrel one step further. If God will do nothing to end the suffering of those groaning Christians in the pit, he will do what has to be done. Like Ferreira before him, he seems stuck with that painful responsibility in virtue of the continuing silence of God. He is prepared to sacrifice himself, if necessary, in rebellion against his vows and against the grain of some of the strongest loyalties of his life. Only some dire necessity, something whose terrors haunt him as persistently as the silence of God does, could have driven him to this point. And so he falls, and his fall seems to break him. True, he seems to hear the Christ of the *fumie* speaking to him, urging him to trample as he had urged others. But that could be an illusion, perfectly understandable in someone in his over-wrought state. And, in any case, it appears to come too late to do him any good. What a cruel irony it seems for God to break the long silence only after Rodrigues has raised his foot to trample! His fate appears to be sealed once he lifts his foot and feels the agonizing pain in it.

But it is not. If the story of Sebastian Rodrigues had ended when he pressed his foot on the face of Christ, it would have been a complete tragedy. The narrative would have been the story of a man whose Christian life ended in catastrophe, and nothing more. Pulled by love for suffering humanity and goaded by the silence of God, Rodrigues betrays what he loves best and seems to be broken in the process. Yet, though he is sorely wounded by his fall, it does not destroy him utterly. He does not emerge from his trial fixed, like Satan, in enmity against God, and so it is possible for him to go on loving God. Something of the deepest ideal of his life can be salvaged from the shipwreck. This, I think, gives us a clue to a distinctively Christian hope for goods to be found even in otherwise tragic circumstances.

Reflecting on his fall, Rodrigues is able to affirm that he did not renounce his faith, though God alone knows it. But he also arrives at an even more remarkable conclusion. He has come to love Christ in a new way. And, more important, everything he had been through had been necessary to bring him to this new love. Moreover, it seems that he is not self-deceived on this point, for his new love bears good fruit. He is able to love his neighbor in a new way too. Before the fall, he had been proud of his own strength and looked down with contempt on Kichijiro's weakness; after the fall, his strength and Kichijiro's weakness no longer impose a barrier between them. Both of them have trampled on the *fumie*, and both felt that terrible pain in their feet when doing so. He is now weak and wounded like Kichijiro, and so he can now forgive Kichijiro for betraying him. He tells Kichijiro to go in peace. The distinction between strength and weakness has lost its salience for him; his love can now extend beyond the beautiful to humanity wasted in rags and tatters. So, in one respect, he can find consolation in the upshot of his fall. He has been empowered to love his neighbors in a way that better imitates the way in which Christ loves them.

It will be clear to Christians that Rodrigues can forgive Kichijiro because Christ has first forgiven him. What needs emphasis is that it is a remarkable achievement for Rodrigues to accept this forgiveness and to continue loving the one who offered it to him. All of us find it hard to acknowledge the need for forgiveness. We would prefer to have our faults and weaknesses treated with indulgence. But those whose strength and luck allow them to lead upright lives in favorable circumstances have a special problem. When they come to grief, they are apt to see their lapses as particularly shameful betrayals of all that has given their lives meaning and value. Resenting keenly the weakness in themselves, they are also apt to think of themselves as unforgivable. It can be too much to bear to have another appreciate the grievousness of an offense and yet to offer the gift of forgiveness, if one is unable to forgive oneself. There is an inclination to reject the gift and then to turn away from the giver in rage. We may imagine such tendencies in a man like Rodrigues. Product of a militant church and a confidently colonizing culture, his whole life prepared him for missionary triumph or martyrdom. He felt only anger and hatred mixed with sadness and pity toward the weakness he found in the defeated Ferreira. Confronting the same weakness in himself, he could easily have seen himself as unforgivable, been overwhelmed with self-loathing, and trampled on the *fumie* with anger and hatred in his heart. When the Christ of the *fumie* urged him to trample, he might have taken that to be a mocking invitation to damn himself, of a piece with the previous silence of God, and trampled in defiance or from spite. But these things, either of which would have been perfectly understandable, did not happen. He recalls having felt a tremendous onrush of joy as he lowered his foot to the *fumie*. Why?

What exactly did happen remains rather obscure. During his last encounter with Inoue, Rodrigues finds himself unable to explain it and is reduced to silence. Somehow Rodrigues was able to see in the words of the Christ of the *fumie* an end to the terrible silence of God, even though those words did nothing to justify or explain the suffering of the Japanese Christians. When Christ said to him that it was to share men's pain that he carried his cross, perhaps this convinced Rodrigues that his pain was understood. As Rodrigues later remembers it, Christ also said that the pain he suffered in trampling was enough. So maybe Rodrigues was also persuaded that the very painfulness to him of his apostasy went some way toward atoning for it. Thus it could be that Rodrigues, even as he apostatized, felt assured of an offer of forgiveness for his apostasy.

But what prompts him to accept the offer? Earlier he had demanded that God prove himself to be just, good, and loving. His estrangement from God had been spurred by God's silence in the face of that demand. Now it seems that, even though his demand has not been met, Rodrigues can be reconciled with God. What brings about this change in him? I think the answer must have to do with roles love and suffering combined play in both Christ's life and his. As I see it, there is at the very center of the life of Sebastian Rodrigues a mystery concerning the operations and powers of suffering love. It is, I think, no accident that the one from whom Rodrigues can accept forgiveness is the weak, exhausted, suffering Christ of the *fumie*. A tangled knot of love and suffering ties the two of them together. Christ, wounded by the apostasy of Rodrigues, steadfastly offers love in return. For Rodrigues too love has led to suffering. Suffering himself as a result of having tried to love in imitation of Christ, Rodrigues can accept forgiving love from the Christ who suffers for love of him, and perhaps he could accept it from no one else. Suffering together, they are held together by bonds of reciprocal love. It is as though shared suffering is strong enough to overcome almost any obstacle to accepting forgiving love that may be lodged in Rodrigues's heart. Because the gift comes from one who suffers for love to another who suffers for love, Rodrigues can accept it, and it may be that he could not otherwise have brought himself to do so. Once accepted, the gift of love can then be returned and extended to others. But how suffering love, which appears in the lives of both Christ and Rodrigues at the times when they seem to be at their weakest, can forge such a powerful bond is far from being obvious.

In a sense, then, it turns out, surprisingly, that Rodrigues gets what he most wanted in life. He had wanted his life to express Christian love. But Christian love is paradigmatically Christ's love, and it works through suffering and apparent defeat. Though he emerges from his ordeal a wounded and broken man, Rodrigues arrives at a love for Christ that, like Christ's love for him, has been tested in the fires of calamity and survived. He comes to think that the ordeal was necessary to bring him to this new kind of love, and he may be right about this. Perhaps nothing short of being caught in his dilemma could have taught him suffering love. So maybe it is providential rather than wholly tragic that there can be ethical dilemmas in the sort of Christian life Rodrigues chose for himself. Before he disappears into the Christian residence at Edo, Rodrigues affirms that God has spoken through his life, and he may be right about this too. Indeed, perhaps there is, underneath his apparent weakness, a new and hidden source of strength, and maybe this provides a thread of continuity beyond what otherwise looks for all the world just like a terminal catastrophe for his life. It is, of course, quite fitting that he should live out the last thirty years of his life in seclusion and silence in the Christian residence at Edo. The story of his life makes dramatic sense only if his life ends in defeat in the eyes of the world and even in the eyes of his own church. Endo tactfully tells us nothing about what goes on in his mind during those long years, and so we must speculate. But perhaps Rodrigues finds an odd sort of contentment at last. I like to imagine that he comes to understand and to be able to apply to his own life something paradoxical St. Paul says of himself. "Therefore," Paul (2 Corinthians 12: 10) says, "I am content with weakness, with mistreatment, with distress, with persecutions and difficulties for the sake of Christ; for when I am powerless, it is then that I am strong." And perhaps, like Kichijiro, who remains his companion, he falls over and over again. On two occasions his guards in Edo inform their masters that he has begun composing a denunciation of Christianity.

CONCLUSIONS

Tragic ethical conflict speaks of the fragility of goodness.[13] Unless goodness consists of the kind of stoic apathy that can render one invulnerable to the slings and arrows of fortune, the good person is at the mercy of things he or she cannot wholly control. In a tragic ethical dilemma, a person is forced to act contrary to an ethical demand of such high priority that the consequences will be calamitous no matter how the person chooses. They may include the destruction or corruption of the good person's character and thereby involve shattering the fragile goodness painfully acquired over the course of a lifetime. And if goodness shattered is goodness beyond repair or replacement, then a tragic ethical dilemma is bound to be an ethical tragedy for the life of one caught in it.

Endo's *Silence* shows us how a tragic dilemma can arise internal to a distinctively Christian form of ethical life. Sebastian Rodrigues is forced to choose between betraying his assiduously cultivated aspiration toward total devotion to God and betraying his equally firm and longstanding commitment to loving and serving his neighbor. Catastrophic consequences for his character threaten no matter which way he goes. He may lose the capacity for loving if he turns away from the suffering Japanese Christians to keep his attention fixed on God alone, but he may wind up fixed in enmity toward God if he tramples on an image of

[13] Expressions of this thought in Greek drama and philosophy are eloquently discussed in Martha C. Nussbaum, *The Fragility of Goodness* (Cambridge: Cambridge University Press, 1986).

Christ's face in hatred, anger, defiance, or spite. The choice shatters something strong and admirable in him. He emerges from the dilemma wounded and weak, full of ugly self-hatred and self-pity; never again will he be self-confident and proud, burning with missionary zeal. He has insulted the most beautiful thing in his life, Christ, the focus of his noblest dreams and desires, and as a result the life he has constructed for himself lies in ruins around him. And so it may appear that his life has been destroyed by tragedy.

It is, I think, a typically audacious Christian hope that even a tragic ethical dilemma need not spell tragedy for the whole of one's ethical life. Providence may provide a replacement for shattered goodness. *Silence* illustrates this possibility in a striking way. Although the consequences of his choice are bad enough for Rodrigues, they are not the worst things that could have befallen him. He has not renounced his faith, and he has discovered a new kind of love for Christ. Because his new love is a suffering love just as Christ's love for him is a suffering love, he is in some ways closer to Christ than he has ever been before. He is able to offer forgiveness to Kichijiro, who betrayed him in agony, just as he supposes Christ offered forgiveness even to Judas, another anguished betrayer. Astonishingly, Rodrigues is even able to affirm that his whole life, including his dilemma and its tragic consequences, was necessary to bring him to this new love. And since his deepest desire had always been to draw close to Christ in love, his life's most important thread of continuity is not cut off at the point of his tragic dilemma, though it may seem to the rest of the world to end there. His life's project continues beyond that point, transformed in ways he could not have anticipated, and the whole of his ethical life need not be seen as a tragedy after all. For him, there remains the possibility of constructing the remainder of his life as a narrative of continued striving for goals he had always sought. The fact that the defeat of his apostasy is not final for him makes the audacious Christian hope concrete in a way that can give it some purchase on one's imagination.

But, of course, Endo's *Silence* is only a story, set long ago and far away. It may not be clear how it is supposed to bear on the lives today's Christians are called to construct and on Christian ethical thought about those lives. There are three ways in which my own thought has been enriched by reflecting upon Endo's novel. First, my awareness of how the silence of God threatens faith has been heightened. There are, to be sure, other examples that might serve this purpose; the survivors of the Holocaust, for instance, testify eloquently about the silence of God.[14] Nevertheless, I find Endo's novel particularly helpful as an aid to imagining vividly how the silence of God may come to try the religious loyalties of a Christian. Second, my appreciation of the possibilities for tragic conflict within Christian ethics and of what such conflict may do to transform the life of a

---

[14] Interesting philosophical reflections on this testimony are to be found in John K. Roth, "The Silence of God," *Faith and Philosophy*, 1 (1984), 407–20. It is worth remarking, however, that, even in the midst of the Holocaust, there continues to be testimony to God's speech.

Christian has been reinforced and deepened. The accumulation of concrete detail a narrative provides helps one to get a better imaginative grip on what it would be like to be caught up in such a conflict than the rather schematic presentations of dilemmas found in most philosophical writing. Such imaginative exercises remind us how frightful tragic dilemmas really are and recommend caution about rushing in, like fools, to situations in which they are likely to arise. And, third, my sense that Christianity must, even in the face of the worst tragedies, remain optimistic about the prospects for life in accord with its commands and ideals has been sharpened and strengthened. Embodied in Endo's novel is an expression of the hope that no tragic dilemma is so destructive that God cannot use it providentially to offer a benefit that advances the sufferer along the path toward identification with Christ in love.[15] Such hope seems to me to be what most decisively marks off Christianity from pessimistic views according to which tragedy must sometimes have the last word in human life.

Ideas like these do not appear likely to contribute directly to the edifice of Christian ethical theory. But, by providing thick, rich, and realistic descriptions of some of the possibilities for Christian life, they add to our resources for constructing in the imagination models of what it can be like to lead a Christian life. And such models may, in turn, help to guide us through the perplexities we encounter in trying to make of our own lives Christian stories. The life of Sebastian Rodrigues both shows something close to the worst that can happen to a Christian in this life and hints at the saving power of Christian love in the midst of such a life. And so, perhaps, it can help support the hope poignantly expressed in the mystical exclamation that "all will be well, and all will be well, and every kind of thing will be well."[16]

In our time this is a fragile hope. Many think it foolish, and some profess to find it unintelligible. It is hard to imagine it taking root and flourishing in the slaughterhouse of the twentieth century. But books like *Silence* testify to its stubborn power to survive.

---

[15] Eleonore Stump has recently suggested that "Christian doctrine is committed to the claim that a child's suffering is outweighed by the good for the child which can result from that suffering" ("The Problem of Evil," *Faith and Philosophy*, 2 (Oct. 1985), 410). Though I am inclined to doubt that Christian doctrine is committed to so strong a claim about the suffering of children, it would appear that such a claim could be supported only if the afterlife were brought into the picture. A nice feature of the case of Sebastian Rodrigues is that we can see in it, in spite of the fact that his defeat at first appears total, a good for him in this life that results from his suffering.

[16] Julian of Norwich, *Showings* (New York: Paulist Press, 1978), 225.

RELIGIOUS EPISTEMOLOGY

6

In Search of the Foundations of Theism

Foundationalism comes in two varieties. Descriptive foundationalism is a thesis about the structure of a body of beliefs, and normative foundationalism is a thesis about the structure of epistemic justification for a body of beliefs. Both varieties partition a body of beliefs into two subclasses, a foundational class and a founded class. For descriptive foundationalism, the foundational class is the class of basic beliefs. A belief is basic for a person at a time provided it is accepted by that person at that time but is not accepted by that person at that time on the basis of any of his or her other beliefs at that time. For normative foundationalism, the foundational class is the class of properly basic beliefs. A belief is properly basic for a person at a time just in case it is basic for the person at the time and its being basic for the person at the time is contrary to no correct canon of epistemic propriety and results from no epistemic deficiency on his or her part at that time. For descriptive foundationalism, the founded class is the class of beliefs based on basic beliefs, and, for normative foundationalism, the founded class is the class of beliefs properly based on properly basic beliefs.

It surely is possible that, for some human persons at some times, certain propositions which self-evidently entail that God exists are basic. But is it also possible that, for some human persons at some times, certain propositions which self-evidently entail that God exists are *properly* basic? In other words, could such propositions *be*, or at least *be among*, the normative foundations of theism, at least for some people at some times? The answers to these question depend, of course, on what the correct criteria for proper basicality turn out to be.

Recently Alvin Plantinga has been arguing that it is in order for a religious epistemologist to return affirmative answers to these questions.[1] There are two

Some of the material in this paper was included in comments on Plantinga's "Is Belief in God Properly Basic?" I read at the 1981 meeting of the Western Division of the American Philosophical Association. Robert Audi was the other commentator on Plantinga's paper. Earlier versions of the present paper were read in 1984 at the Greensboro Symposium on the Logic of Religious Concepts, where Jonathan Malino was my commentator, and at the University of Notre Dame, where Alvin Plantinga was my commentator. In making various revisions, I have profited by the comments of Audi, Malino, and Plantinga and also by written criticism from William P. Alston, Roderick M. Chisholm, George I. Mavrodes, and Ernest Sosa.

[1] Alvin Plantinga, "Is Belief in God Properly Basic?" *Noûs*, 15 (1981). Additional discussion related to the charge that modern foundationalism is self-referentially incoherent may be found

prongs to Plantinga's argument. The first is destructive: it is an attempt to show that certain criteria for proper basicality, according to which propositions which self-evidently entail the existence of God could not be properly basic, are seriously defective and must be rejected. The second is constructive: it is an attempt to elaborate a procedure for justifying criteria for proper basicality which will allow that some propositions self-evidently entailing that God exists could turn out to be properly basic.

This paper has two aims. The first is to criticize Plantinga's argument. In the first section of the paper, I argue for two claims: (1) that Plantinga has failed to show that the criteria for proper basicality he proposes to reject are in any way defective; and (2) that Plantinga's procedure for justifying criteria for proper basicality provides no better reason for adopting criteria according to which some propositions which self-evidently entail the existence of God can be properly basic than for adopting a criterion according to which no such propositions can be properly basic. The paper's second aim is exploratory. Although Plantinga's argument is unsuccessful, it may nevertheless be true that some propositions which self-evidently entail that God exists could be properly basic. And so, in the second section of the paper, I go on to argue, on the hypothesis that this is true, for two additional claims: (1) that actually being properly basic would be a relatively unimportant feature of such propositions because they would be at least as well justified if properly based on other properly basic propositions and could always be so based; and (2) that such propositions would seldom, if ever, be properly basic for intellectually sophisticated adult theists in our culture.

CRITIQUE OF PLANTINGA

The criteria for proper basicality Plantinga proposes to reject are those of classical foundationalism. Classical foundationalism is the disjunction of ancient or medieval foundationalism and modern foundationalism. The criterion for proper basicality of ancient or medieval foundationalism is the triply universal claim:

> (1) For any proposition p, person S, and time t, p is properly basic for S at t if and only if p is self-evident to S at t or is evident to the senses of S at t.

And the criterion for proper basicality of modern foundationalism is this triply universal claim:

in Alvin Plantinga, "Is Belief in God Rational?" in C. F. Delaney (ed.), *Rationality and Religious Belief* (Notre Dame: University of Notre Dame Press, 1979). Material from both these papers has subsequently been incorporated into Alvin Plantinga, "Rationality and Religious Belief," in Steven M. Cahn and David Shatz (eds.), *Contemporary Philosophy of Religion* (New York: Oxford University Press, 1982). And some of the same themes are further amplified in Alvin Plantinga, "Reason and Belief in God," in Alvin Plantinga and Nicholas Wolterstorff (eds.), *Faith and Rationality* (Notre Dame: University of Notre Dame Press, 1983).

(2) For any proposition p, person S, and time t, p is properly basic for S at t if and only if p is incorrigible for S at t or is self-evident to S at t.

Although Plantinga thinks the propositions expressed by both (1) and (2) should be rejected on grounds of self-referential incoherence, he actually discusses only the latter proposition at any length. However, it is clear that if his argument for self-referential incoherence succeeds against the proposition expressed by (2), a similar argument will, *mutatis mutandis*, work equally well against the proposition expressed by (1). But what exactly is the argument? And how much does it really prove?

Consider the proposition expressed by (2). What place does it have in the modern foundationalist's own structure of epistemic justification? Is it in the foundational class? Does the modern foundationalist suppose that it is ever properly basic for anyone? If he or she does, then he or she must hold that for someone at some time it is either incorrigible or self-evident. Plantinga believes it to be "neither self-evident nor incorrigible."[2] I agree. I think the proposition expressed by (2) is never incorrigible for or self-evident to me. Are Plantinga and I idiosyncratic in this respect? Could the modern foundationalist claim with any plausibility that we are just plain mistaken on this point? I think the answer to these questions has to be negative. It seems to me perfectly clear that the proposition expressed by (2) is never incorrigible for or self-evident to anyone. Hence, no one, not even a modern foundationalist, is entitled to suppose that the proposition expressed by (2) is ever properly basic for anyone.

Does this suffice to show that modern foundationalism is self-referentially incoherent? Obviously it does not. What would be self-referentially incoherent would be to affirm the proposition expressed by (2), to assert that it is itself never incorrigible for or self-evident to anyone, and also to claim that it is itself properly basic for someone at some time. But this leaves the modern foundationalist with the option of continuing to affirm the proposition expressed by (2) while conceding that it is itself never properly basic for anyone. For all that has been said so far, the proposition expressed by (2), though never properly basic for anyone, is for some people at some times properly based on propositions which, by its own lights, are properly basic for those people at those times. In discussion, Plantinga has claimed that no modern foundationalist has ever given a good argument for the view that the proposition expressed by (2) is, for some people at some times, properly based on propositions which, by its own lights, are properly basic for them then. Maybe this is so. But, even if it is, this does not show that modern foundationalism is self-referentially incoherent. All it shows is that the modern foundationalist has so far not completed the task of justifying the proposition expressed by (2) in the only way that remains open to him or her, namely, by showing how it can, for some people at some times, be properly based

---

[2] Plantinga, "Is Belief in God Properly Basic?" 49.

on propositions which are, by its own lights, properly basic for them at those times. Can this be done, and, if so, how? More generally, how could any criterion for proper basicality be justified?

Plantinga offers us an explicit answer to the more general question. He says:

the proper way to arrive at such a criterion is, broadly speaking, *inductive*. We must assemble examples of beliefs and conditions such that the former are obviously properly basic in the latter, and examples of beliefs and conditions such that the former are obviously *not* properly basic in the latter. We must them frame hypotheses as to the necessary and sufficient conditions of proper basicality and test these hypotheses by reference to those examples.[3]

As I understand the proposed procedure, it requires that we do two things. First, we are to assemble the data upon which the induction will be based. A datum may be represented as an ordered pair whose first member is a belief and whose second member is a condition. Positive data are data such that the beliefs that are their first members are obviously properly basic in the conditions that are their second members; negative data are data such that the beliefs that are their first members are obviously not properly basic in the conditions that are their second members. Call the set of data, presumably finite, so assembled 'the initial set.' Second, we are to frame hypotheses stating necessary and sufficient conditions for proper basicality and test them against the data in the initial set. An hypothesis will pass the test posed by the data in the initial set if and only if all of the positive data in the initial set and none of the negative data in that set satisfy its necessary and sufficient conditions for proper basicality. So far, so good.

However, two questions about this procedure quickly arise. First, how do we know that there will be *any* hypothesis at all stating non-trivial necessary and sufficient conditions for proper basicality which will pass the test posed by the data in the initial set? Maybe the initial set will itself be inconsistent or in some other way subtly incoherent. So perhaps we should be allowed to throw data out of the initial set should we discover that it is in some fashion incoherent. But, second, how do we know that there will be *only one* hypothesis stating non-trivial necessary and sufficient conditions for proper basicality which will pass the test posed by the data in the initial set? If the initial set is finite and our hypotheses are universally quantified, as the classical foundationalist's criteria are, then the data in the initial set will underdetermine the truth of hypotheses. In that case, there may very well be several interesting hypotheses which all pass the test posed by the data in the initial set and yet disagree radically about the proper basicality of examples outside the initial set. So perhaps we should also be allowed to add data to the initial set if this will help us to eliminate at least some of those hypotheses that have passed the test posed by the data in the initial set. These considerations make one thing very clear. Plantinga has so far given us only the

---

[3] Plantinga, "Is Belief in God Properly Basic?" 50.

rough outlines of the first stage of a broadly inductive procedure for arriving at a uniquely justified criterion of proper basicality. Many more details would need to be filled in before we could have any rational assurance that correct application of the procedure would yield exactly one hypothesis about conditions necessary and sufficient for proper basicality that are inductively best supported by, or most firmly based upon, the data in the initial set or in some suitable revision of the initial set.

But, rough though it be, Plantinga's sketch of the first stage of a procedure for justifying criteria of proper basicality is nonetheless well enough developed to permit us to see that it confronts at the outset at least one important difficulty. This is because, as Plantinga himself acknowledges, there is no reason to assume in advance that everyone will agree on what is to go into the initial set. Plantinga says:

> The Christian will of course suppose that belief in God is entirely proper and rational; if he doesn't accept this belief on the basis of other propositions, he will conclude that it is basic for him and quite properly so. Followers of Bertrand Russell and Madelyn Murray O'Hare (*sic!*) may disagree, but how is that relevant? Must my criteria, or those of the Christian community, conform to their examples? Surely not. The Christian community is responsible to *its* set of examples, not to theirs.[4]

The difficulty is, of course, that this is a game any number can play. Followers of Muhammad, followers of Buddha, and even followers of the Reverend Moon can join in the fun. Even the modern foundationalist can play. When a modern foundationalist, under optimal conditions for visual perception, seems to see a green beachball in front of her, she can claim that one thing which is obviously properly basic for her then is this:

> (3) I am being appeared to greenly.

And one thing which is obviously not properly basic for her then, she can say, is this:

> (4) I am seeing a green beachball.

After all, as she sees it, the proposition expressed by the latter sentence is for her then properly based, at least in part, on the proposition expressed by the former. And she can then mimic Plantinga's own argument in this fashion: "Followers of G. E. Moore and Alvin Plantinga may disagree, but how is that relevant? Must my criteria, or those of the community of modern foundationalists, conform to their examples? Surely not. The community of modern foundationalists is responsible to *its* set of examples, not to theirs." It would seem that what is sauce for Russell's goose should also be sauce for Plantinga's gander. Turn about *is*, in this case, fair play.

Ad hominem arguments to one side, the problem is that fidelity to the data in an initial set constructed from intuitions about what is obvious is a very weak

---

[4] Ibid.

constraint on the justification of a criterion for proper basicality. The modern foundationalist can easily choose the data in his or her initial set so that his or her criterion for proper basicality passes the test they pose by making sure (1) that only beliefs that nearly everyone would admit are, in the associated conditions, incorrigible or self-evident are the first members of positive data, and (2) that all beliefs that nearly everyone would, in the associated conditions, not consider incorrigible or self-evident are either the first members of negative data or outside the initial set altogether. How is this to be accomplished?

Suppose a modern foundationalist is contemplating believing that she is being appeared to redly in conditions optimal for visual experience in which she is being appeared to redly. Surely she can plausibly say that it is self-evident to her that that belief would be properly basic for her in those conditions, and clearly she can also reasonably claim that it is self-evident to her that that belief would be self-evident to her in those conditions. Now suppose the same modern foundationalist is contemplating believing that Jove is expressing disapproval in conditions optimal for auditory experience in which she is being appeared to thunderously. Surely she can plausibly say that it is self-evident to her that that belief would not be properly basic for her in those conditions, and clearly she can also reasonably claim that it is self-evident to her that that belief would be neither incorrigible for nor self-evident to her in those conditions. After having assembled a rich initial set of positive and negative data by ringing the changes on these two thought experiments, the modern foundationalist is then in a position to claim, and properly so, that his or her criterion, though not itself properly basic, is properly based, in accord with what Plantinga has told us about proper procedures for justifying criteria for proper basicality, on beliefs that are properly basic by its own lights.

It is important to understand that the data I am supposing the modern foundationalist might use to justify his or her criterion of proper basicality derive from thought experiments about hypothetical situations. My claim is not that when, for instance, a person in fact believes that Jove is expressing disapproval in conditions optimal for auditory experience in which she is being appeared to thunderously, it will then in fact be self-evident to her that that belief is not properly basic for her in those conditions. After all, she may not even wonder whether that belief is properly basic for her in those conditions when she happens to have the belief in the conditions. Rather my claim is that when a modern foundationalist contemplates the hypothetical situation of believing that Jove is expressing disapproval in conditions optimal for auditory experience in which she is being appeared to thunderously, then she can with plausibility maintain that it is self-evident to her that that belief would not in those conditions be properly basic for her. Because I hold that our intuitions about such hypothetical situations often provide the ultimate and decisive test of philosophical generalizations, I think the role of such beliefs about hypothetical situations in confirming or disconfirming philosophical generalizations is best explained on the supposition that they can be, in the right circumstances, self-evident.

In discussion, Plantinga has objected to this line of argument. If I understand his objection, it goes as follows. To say that a belief is properly basic in a set of circumstances is to say, among other things, that in those circumstances a person could accept the belief without displaying some kind of noetic defect. But what constitutes a noetic defect depends upon what constitutes the proper working of one's noetic equipment. So a proposition to the effect that a certain person on a certain occasion is displaying no such defect cannot possibly be self-evident because it cannot be self-evident to one that all one's noetic equipment is in proper working order. Hence, a proposition to the effect that a certain belief is properly basic on a certain occasion cannot possibly be self-evident either.

I concede, of course, that it is not usually self-evident to one that all one's noetic equipment is in proper working order. But if Plantinga's objection is to have any force against my argument, it must apply to the particular hypothetical case I have described above. I believe it does not. Our modern foundationalist is supposed to be contemplating believing that she is being appeared to redly in conditions optimal for visual experience in which she is being appeared to redly. It seems quite clear to me that it could be self-evident to her that she would display no noetic defect in accepting that belief in those conditions. To be sure, her noetic equipment might then have some defects of which she was unaware. She might then, for example, not be able to recognize the taste of ordinary table salt. But that is irrelevant provided she would display none of these defects in accepting the belief that she is being appeared to redly in the specified circumstances. For all that is required is that it could be self-evident to her that she would display no such defect in accepting that belief in those circumstances. Because I believe this requirement can be met, I conclude that Plantinga's objection fails. In short, it can be self-evident to one that one is displaying no noetic defect in accepting a certain belief on a certain occasion without it also being self-evident to one then that all one's noetic equipment is in proper working order.

I do not expect that this reply will bring Plantinga's objections to an end. I suspect Plantinga will continue to think the modern foundationalist has made some mistake if he or she proceeds in this fashion to justify his or her criterion for proper basicality. But it is not obvious that this is so; nor is it obvious what precisely the mistake might be. After all, one of the rules of the game specifies that the community of modern foundationalists is permitted to be responsible to *its* set of examples. Hence, absent a good argument by Plantinga which establishes that a mistake must occur in such a procedure, I think we are entitled to hold that Plantinga's own procedure for justifying criteria for proper basicality provides no better reason for adopting criteria according to which some propositions which self-evidently entail the existence of God can be properly basic than for adopting a criterion, namely, the one proposed by the modern foundationalist, according to which no such propositions can properly basic.

Of course, nothing I have said rules out the possibility that Plantinga could use the inductive procedure he advocates to justify a criterion of proper basicality according to which some propositions which self-evidently entail that God exists can be properly basic. Indeed, if, as his talk about being responsible to the examples of the Christian community suggests, he would take some such propositions to be the first members of positive data in his initial set and thereafter not delete all such positive data in revising his initial set, it is pretty obvious that Plantinga can succeed in this task, though success at so cheap a price may be thought by some to come uncomfortably close to question-begging. But if Plantinga does succeed in performing this exercise, then I think the conclusion we should draw is that his fight with classical foundationalism has resulted in a stand-off.

WHAT IF BELIEF IN GOD COULD BE PROPERLY BASIC?

If my critique of Plantinga has been successful, I have shown that he fails to prove that belief in propositions which self-evidently entail God's existence could ever be properly basic for anyone. But it might be true that belief in such propositions could be properly basic, even if Plantinga has not proved it. And if it were, what would be the consequences for religious epistemology? I now turn to an exploration of this issue.

Plantinga's examples of beliefs which could be properly basic in the right conditions include the following items:

(5) God is speaking to me.
(6) God disapproves of what I have done.

And:

(7) God forgives me for what I have done.

And according to Plantinga, the right conditions include a component which is, broadly speaking, experiential. He says:

Upon reading the Bible, one may be impressed with a deep sense that God is speaking to him. Upon having done what I know is cheap, or wrong, or wicked I may feel guilty in God's sight and form the belief *God disapproves of what I've done*. Upon confession and repentance, I may feel forgiven, forming the belief *God forgives me for what I've done*.[5]

It strikes me that part of what makes the suggestion that beliefs like those expressed by (5)–(7) could be properly basic in conditions like those partially described in the quoted passage seem attractive is an analogy with an extremely plausible view about how certain Moorean commonsense beliefs are often justified. When I have the experience of seeming to see a hand in front of me in the right conditions, I may be justified in believing:

(8) I see a hand in front of me.

---

[5] Plantinga, "Is Belief in God Properly Basic?" 46

This justification may be direct in the sense of being grounded directly in the experience itself without passing through the intermediary of a belief about the way I am being appeared to such as:

(9) It seems to me that I see a hand in front of me.

For I may not in the circumstances have entertained, much less accepted, the proposition expressed by (9), but, on the view under consideration, my justification for believing the proposition expressed by (8) is in no way defective on that account. Hence, the proposition expressed by (8) may be basic, and quite properly so, in the right conditions. And if this is, as I believe it to be, an attractive view about how believing the proposition expressed by (8) can be, and sometimes is, justified, then there is an argument from analogy for supposing that propositions like those expressed by (5)–(7) may also be properly basic in conditions which include an experiential component of the right sort for grounding such beliefs. To be sure, there are significant disanalogies. The direct justification of the belief expressed by (8) is grounded in a mode of sensory experience which is now generally believed by non-skeptical epistemologists to be reliable in the right conditions. By contrast, the direct justification of the beliefs expressed by (5)–(7) is grounded in a mode of experience which, though it may be reliable in the right conditions, is not now generally believed by non-skeptical epistemologists to be so. But, although such considerations might be taken to show that the analogical argument is not very strong, it does not deprive the positive analogy of heuristic and explanatory capabilities. I am going to make use of these capabilities in the remainder of the discussion.

When I have the experience of seeming to see a hand in front of me in the right conditions, though the proposition expressed by (8) could then be properly basic for me, it could instead be the case that the proposition expressed by (9) is then properly basic for me and the proposition expressed by (8) is then properly based, at least in part, on the proposition expressed by (9). For when I have that experience in those conditions, I might well be attending mainly to the qualitative aspects of my visual experience with the result that the proposition expressed by (9) is then basic for me. If this happens, the proposition expressed by (9) would clearly be properly basic for me. I might well also then base the proposition expressed by (8) in part on the proposition expressed by (9). And, if this too happens, then the proposition expressed by (8) would be properly based, in part, on the proposition expressed by (9) because the latter proposition does nothing more than serve to articulate that part of the content of my visual experience which is relevant to justifying the former. If the proposition expressed by (8) were indirectly justified by being properly based on the proposition expressed by (9), it would be no less well justified than if it were directly justified by being directly grounded in visual experience. Since, by hypothesis, my visual experience in those conditions suffices to confer a certain degree of justification on the proposition expressed by (8), the amount of justification that reaches the proposition expressed by (8) from that experience will not be less in those conditions if it passes by way of the proposition expressed by (9) than if it is transmitted directly without intermediary. But neither would its justification be any better if indirect in this way. Moreover, it could happen that at a certain time the proposition expressed by (8) is properly basic for me and at a later time it is no longer properly basic, though still justified, for me because in the interval it has come to be properly based on the proposition expressed by (9). For in the interval I might, for example, have come to wonder whether I was justified in believing the proposition expressed by (8) and as a result come to believe the proposition expressed by (9) and to base properly on this belief my belief in the proposition expressed by (8). And if such a process did occur, I think the degree to which the proposition expressed by (8) was justified for me would, other things remaining unaltered, stay constant through it.

By analogy, similar things seem true of the examples that are Plantinga's prime candidates for religious beliefs which could be properly basic. When I am impressed with a deep sense that God is speaking to me, if the proposition expressed by (5) could then be properly basic for me, then it could instead be the case that some other proposition is among those then properly basic for me and the proposition expressed by (5) is then properly based in part on it. Such a proposition is:

(10) It seems to me that God is speaking to me.

If the proposition expressed by (5) were indirectly justified for me by being properly based on the proposition expressed by (10), its justification would be no better, and no worse, than if it were properly basic and directly justified for me by being directly grounded in my experiential sense that God is speaking to me, other things remaining the same. And it could happen that in the course of time the proposition expressed by (5) changes from being properly basic for me to being properly based in part for me on the proposition expressed by (10) without gain or loss of degree of justification.

So, oddly enough, if certain propositions which self-evidently entail the existence of God can be properly basic for a person at a time, it is epistemically unimportant whether such propositions actually are properly basic for that person at that time. Without loss of degree of justification, such theistic propositions can just as well be properly based, at least in part, on others which are descriptive of the person's experience at the time and are then properly basic for the person. Although such theistic propositions would not need to be based on the evidence of other propositions, they always could be so based. So the cautious philosopher who did so base them would be every bit as justified in believing in the existence of God as the reckless mystic who did not.

There is another salient feature of directly justified Moorean beliefs like the one expressed by (8) which would have an analogue in the case of religious beliefs like those expressed by (5)–(7) if they could be properly basic in the right conditions. This is that the kind of justification conferred on such Moorean beliefs by direct grounding in experience of the right sort is defeasible. So, for example, a potential defeater for the proposition expressed by (8) is this:

(11) I am now hallucinating a hand.

If propositions such as (8) are taken to be properly basic in the right conditions, then a full specification of those conditions must include reference to the status of potential defeaters such as (11). What would it be reasonable to say about potential defeaters when specifying in fuller detail the right conditions for proper basicality of the proposition expressed by (8)? Several possibilities come to mind.

It might be suggested that conditions are right for the proposition expressed by (8) to be properly basic for me only if none of its potential defeaters is true. This suggestion clearly misses the mark. When I have the experience of seeming to see a hand in front of me, it may be that the proposition expressed by (8) is true and the proposition expressed by (11) is false, and yet I am justified in rejecting the former and accepting the latter because, for instance, I remember taking a large dose of some hallucinogen only an hour ago and hallucinating wildly in the interval. Merely to insist that potential defeaters be false in order for conditions to be right for proper basicality is to require much too little.

Alternatively, it might be suggested that conditions are right for the proposition expressed by (8) to be properly basic for me only if each of its potential defeaters is such that I have some reason to think it is false. Clearly this suggestion errs in the direction of demanding too much. I have never exhaustively enumerated the potential defeaters of the proposition expressed by (8), and I am inclined to doubt that I would ever complete such a task if I began it. I have certainly never mobilized or acquired a reason against each of them. No one I know has ever tried to do such a thing in defense of all of his or her Moorean commonsense beliefs. So if such beliefs frequently are properly basic in virtue of being directly grounded in sensory experience, as I think they are, conditions are often right for proper basicality without such an elaborate structure of reasons for the falsity of potential defeaters having been mobilized.

It does, however, seem initially plausible to suppose that conditions are right for the proposition expressed by (8) to be properly basic for me only if I have no sufficiently substantial reasons to think that any of its potential defeaters is true and this is not due to epistemic negligence on my part. Two features of this claim require a bit of explanation. First, if the only reason I have to think that some potential defeater of the proposition expressed by (8) is true is, for instance, that I remember once, long ago, having mistaken a tree's branches for a hand, then that will not usually suffice to undermine the prima facie justification the proposition expressed by (8) has in the right experiential conditions to such an extent that that proposition is not properly basic. More generally, since prima facie justification comes in degrees, although any good reason one has for thinking one of a proposition's potential defeaters is true will undermine that proposition's prima facie justification to some degree, slight reasons will usually not singly undermine it to the extent that it is no longer prima facie justified. Instead, it will usually remain prima facie justified in the presence of one or a few such reasons but to a lesser degree than it would be in their absence. It takes a sufficiently substantial reason for thinking one of its potential defeaters is true to rob a proposition of proper basicality in conditions in which it would otherwise be properly basic.[6] Second, if I happen to lack sufficiently substantial reasons to think that any potential defeater of the proposition expressed by (8) is true merely because, for example, I have negligently failed to recall that I ingested some hallucinogenic substance only an hour ago and have been hallucinating wildly in the interval, then clearly conditions are not right for the proposition expressed by (8) to be properly basic for me, even though it may in fact be basic for me. More generally, a proposition is not prima facie justified if one negligently ignores good reasons for thinking one of its potential defeaters is true which would be sufficiently substantial to undermine the proposition's prima facie justification to such an extent that it would not be prima facie justified. Such epistemic negligence would constitute an epistemic deficiency.

By analogy, it also seems initially plausible to say that conditions are right for the propositions expressed by (5)–(7) to be properly basic for me only if I have no sufficiently substantial reasons to think that any of their potential defeaters is true and this is not due to epistemic negligence on my part. But there is the rub. A potential defeater of the propositions expressed by (5)–(7) is this:

    (12) God does not exist.

And, unfortunately, I do have very substantial reasons for thinking that the proposition expressed by (12) is true. My reasons derive mainly from one of the traditional problems of evil. What I know, partly from experience and partly from testimony, about the amount and variety of non-moral evil in the universe confirms highly for me the proposition expressed by (12). Of course, this is not indefeasible confirmation of the proposition expressed by (12). It could be defeated by other things I do not know. Perhaps it is not even undefeated confirmation. Maybe it even is defeated by other things I do know. Nevertheless, it does furnish me with a very substantial reason for thinking that the proposition expressed by (12) is true. Moreover, I dare say that many, perhaps most, intellectually sophisticated adults in our culture are in an epistemic predicament similar to mine. As I see it, an intellectually sophisticated adult in our culture would have to be epistemically negligent not to have very substantial reasons for thinking that what (12) expresses is true. After all, non-trivial atheological reasons, ranging from various problems of evil to naturalistic theories according to which theistic belief is illusory or merely projective, are a pervasive, if not obtrusive, component of the rational portion of our cultural heritage.

---

[6] I came to appreciate this point as a result of reflecting on comments by Jonathan Malino and William P. Alston.

But, even if such reasons are very substantial, are they sufficiently substantial to make it the case that the propositions expressed by (5)–(7) would no longer be properly basic in conditions of the sort described by Plantinga in which, we are supposing, they could have been properly basic but for the presence of such substantial reasons? On reflection, I am convinced that such reasons are, taken collectively, sufficiently substantial, though I confess with regret that I cannot at present back up my intuitive conviction with solid arguments. But I conjecture that many, perhaps most, intellectually sophisticated adults in our culture will share my intuitive conviction on this point. And so I conclude that many, perhaps most, intellectually sophisticated adult theists in our culture are seldom, if ever, in conditions which are right for propositions like those expressed by (5)–(7) to be properly basic for them.

It does not follow from this conclusion that intellectually sophisticated adult theists in our culture cannot be justified in believing propositions like those expressed by (5)–(7). For all that I have said, some such propositions are such that, for every single one of their potential defeaters which is such that there is some very substantial reason to think it is true, there is an even better reason to think it is false. And so, for all I know, some intellectually sophisticated adult theists in our culture could be, or perhaps even are, in the fortunate position, with respect to some such propositions and their potential defeaters, of having, for each potential defeater which some epistemically non-negligent, intellectually sophisticated adult in our culture has a very substantial reason to think is true, an even better reason to think it is false. But if there are such fortunate theists in our culture, they are people who have already accomplished at least one of the main tasks traditionally assigned to natural theology. Although they may know of no proof of the existence of God, they possess reasons good enough to defend some proposition which self-evidently entails the existence of God against all of its potential defeaters which epistemically non-negligent, intellectually sophisticated adults in our culture have very substantial reasons to believe. I tend to doubt that many intellectually sophisticated adult theists in our culture are in this fortunate position for any appreciable portion of their lives.

But suppose someone were in this fortunate position. Such a person would have reasons good enough to defend theistic belief against all of its potential defeaters which epistemically non-negligent, intellectually sophisticated adults in our culture have very substantial reasons to believe, and such reasons would be parts of such a person's total case for the rationality of theistic belief. But would such a person's theistic belief have to be based on such reasons? That depends, of course, on exactly what is involved in basing one belief on others. Plantinga is prudently reticent about describing the basing relation; he says only that, "although this relation isn't easy to characterize in a revealing and non-trivial fashion, it is nonetheless familiar."[7] On the basis of the examples Plantinga gives,

---

[7] Plantinga, "Is Belief in God Properly Basic?" 41.

I once conjectured in discussion that he thinks the relation is characterized by something like the following principle:

> (13) For any person S and distinct propositions p and q, S believes q on the basis of p only if S entertains p, S accepts p, S infers q from p, and S accepts q.[8]

If Plantinga does have in mind some such narrow conception of the basing relation, then our hypothetical fortunate person's theistic belief clearly need not be based on all the reasons, including defenses against potential defeaters which have very substantial support, in the person's total case for the rationality of theistic belief. After all, some such defenses may consist only of considerations which show that certain atheological arguments are unsound or otherwise defective, and our fortunate person's belief need not be based, in this narrow sense, on such considerations. Indeed, for all I know, it is possible that all our fortunate person's successful defenses against potential defeaters which have substantial support are of this sort. Hence, for all I know, our fortunate person could have a successful total case for the rationality of theistic belief made up entirely of reasons such that belief in some proposition which self-evidently entails the existence of God needs none of them for a basis. Thus, for all I know, on this narrow conception of the basing relation, our fortunate person's theistic belief might be properly basic in the right conditions.

If I were to endorse some such narrow conception of the basing relation, I would have to revise my earlier proposal about when it is plausible to suppose conditions are right for propositions to be properly basic for me. I am inclined to believe that the appropriate thing to say, in light of the line of reasoning developed in the previous paragraph, is that it seems plausible to suppose that conditions are right for propositions like those expressed by (5)–(7) to be, in the narrow sense, properly basic for me only if (i) either I have no sufficiently substantial reason to think that any of their potential defeaters is true, or I do have some such reasons but, for each such reason I have, I have an even better reason for thinking the potential defeater in question is false, and (ii), in either case, my situation involves no epistemic negligence on my part. I could then put the point I am intent on pressing by saying that, depending on which of the two disjuncts in the first clause of this principle one imagines me satisfying, I would have to be non-negligently either rather naive and innocent or quite fortunate and sophisticated in order for conditions to be right for propositions like those expressed by

---

[8] In a more thorough treatment, it would be important to worry about the temporal references in this principle. If I have just looked up the spelling of 'umbrageous' in my dictionary, then my belief about how that word is spelled may now be based on my belief about what *my* dictionary says. But if I last looked up its spelling many months ago, then my belief about how 'umbrageous' is spelled may now only be based on my belief that I seem to remember seeing it spelled that way in *some dictionary or other*. Presumably bases of the sort specified by this principle can and sometimes do shift with time.

(5)–(7) to be, in the narrow sense, properly basic for me. When I examine my epistemic predicament, I find myself forced to conclude that I am in neither of those extreme situations. Since I have very substantial reasons for thinking the proposition expressed by (12) is true, innocence has been lost. But, because I have not yet done enough to defend theistic belief against potential defeaters which have substantial support, I have not reached the position of our hypothetical fortunate person. Innocence has not, so to speak, been regained. Hence, conditions are not now right for propositions like those expressed by (5)–(7) to be, in the narrow sense, properly basic for me. My conjecture is that many, perhaps most, intellectually sophisticated persons in our culture are in an epistemic predicament similar to mine in this respect for most of their adult lives.

There is, of course, nothing wrong with construing the basing relation in some such narrow fashion provided one is tolerably clear about what one is doing. Surely there is such a relation, and Plantinga is free to use it in his theories if he wishes. But I think it may be more perspicuous, or at least equally illuminating, to look at matters in a slightly different way. Consider again our hypothetical fortunate person who has reasons good enough to defend theistic belief against all of its potential defeaters which epistemically non-negligent, intellectually sophisticated adults in our culture have very substantial reasons to believe. I would say that, for such a person, theistic belief would be based, in a broad sense, on all the reasons which are parts of the person's total case for the rationality of theistic belief. In employing this broad conception of the basing relation, I am aiming to draw attention to the fact that, if the person did not have all those reasons and were like many, perhaps most, intellectually sophisticated adults in our culture, theistic belief would not be rational for the person, or at least its rationality would be diminished to an appreciable extent if some of those reasons were absent. On this broad conception of the basing relation, I would not need to revise the principle concerning the right conditions for certain propositions to be, in the broad sense, properly basic for me, to which I had ascribed initial plausibility, in order to accommodate the hypothetical fortunate person, for the fortunate person's theistic belief would be, in the broad sense, properly based on all the reasons which comprise his or her total case for the rationality of theistic belief. Reasons which are, in the broad sense, part of a basis for theistic belief need not be related to a proposition which self-evidently entails the existence of God in the same way that the premisses of an inference are related to its conclusion. They may instead provide part of a basis for theistic belief roughly in the same way a physicist's demonstration that the so-called "clock paradox" does not reveal an inconsistency in Special Relativity provides part of a basis for Special Relativity. Or, to cite what may be a more helpful analogy in the present context, they may provide part of a basis for theistic belief in much the same way Richard Swinburne's argument in *The Coherence of Theism* that the claim that God exists is not demonstrably incoherent provides part of the basis for Swinburne's claim in *The Existence of God* that God's existence is more probable than not.[9] And if I am right about the epistemic predicament of many, perhaps most, intellectually sophisticated adult theists in our culture, for them theistic belief stands in need of at least some basis of this kind if it is to be rational. This may, in the end, be a point on which Plantinga and I have a disagreement which is not merely verbal. I would insist, and Plantinga, for all I know, might not, that many, perhaps most, intellectually sophisticated adult theists in our culture must, if their belief in God is to be rational, have a total case for the rationality of theistic belief which includes defenses against defeaters which have very substantial support.

CONCLUSION

If theistic belief can be prima facie justified by experience at all, then there may be less difference between Plantinga and his opponents than one might at first have thought.[10] Plantinga locates a proper doxastic foundation for theistic belief at the level of propositions like that expressed by (5); a modern foundationalist would wish to claim that there is a subbasement in the truly proper doxastic structure at the level of propositions like that expressed by (10).

Plantinga's view has the advantage of psychological realism. I doubt that most theists generate their doxastic structures by first entertaining and accepting propositions like that expressed by (10) and then inferring from them, together perhaps with some epistemic principles, propositions like that expressed by (5). Nonetheless, I think there is something to be said on behalf of what I take to be an important insight captured by the modern foundationalist's position, though perhaps not perfectly articulated there. Although it may be a mistake to suppose that a phenomenological belief like the one expressed by (10) must always mediate between experience and a belief like the one expressed by (5) in a properly constructed structure of *prima facie* justification for a belief like the one expressed by (5), experience of the sort that could serve to ground a belief like the one expressed by (5) is itself so thoroughly shaped and penetrated by conceptual elements that, if it grounds a belief like the one expressed by (5) directly, then that belief is based on a cognitive state of the believer, even if that state is not an explicit belief with a phenomenological proposition for its object. Perhaps it is at the level of such cognitive states that we may hope to discover the real evidential foundations in experience for theistic belief.

[9] See Richard Swinburne, *The Coherence of Theism* (Oxford: Clarendon Press, 1977) and Richard Swinburne, *The Existence of God* (Oxford: Clarendon Press, 1979).

[10] A recent defense of the view that theistic belief can be prima facie justified by experience of certain kinds may be found in William P. Alston, "Religious Experience and Religious Belief," *Noûs*, 16 (1982).

7

The Foundations of Theism Again: A Rejoinder to Plantinga

During the past dozen years Alvin Plantinga has published an impressive series of papers in which he advocates a point of view on questions of religious epistemology that has, on account of its Calvinian inspiration, come to be called "Reformed Epistemology."[1] A few years ago I tried my hand at criticizing some of the characteristic claims and arguments of Reformed Epistemology and succeeded in provoking a forceful reply by Plantinga.[2] I have recently been persuaded that some philosophical progress might be made if my discussion with Plantinga were continued. So I have returned to the issues raised by Plantinga's reply and have thought my way through them again. This rejoinder is a product of that effort.

Before I turn to those issues, let me note two limits on what I hope to achieve in this paper. First, in order to keep the paper within reasonable bounds of length, I restrict my attention to just the four sets of problems that Plantinga raised in his reply to my earlier paper. Much ink has already been spilled over Reformed Epistemology, and doubtless more is to come. But I make no attempt here to treat other philosophers whose work, published and unpublished, has stimulated my thinking on this topic.[3] Second, I make no attempt to bring the discussion

I am grateful to Alvin Plantinga for spending most of an afternoon discussing a draft of this paper with me. It takes a rare kind of generosity to help one's critics improve their arguments.

[1] Alvin Plantinga, "Is Belief in God Rational?" in C. F. Delaney (ed.), *Rationality and Religious Belief* (Notre Dame: University of Notre Dame Press, 1979); Alvin Plantinga, "Is Belief in God Properly Basic?" *Noûs*, 15 (1981); Alvin Plantinga, "Rationality and Religious Belief," in Steven M. Cahn and David Shatz (eds.), *Contemporary Philosophy of Religion* (New York: Oxford University Press, 1982); Alvin Plantinga, "Reason and Belief in God" (hereafter RBG), in Alvin Plantinga and Nicholas Wolterstorff (eds.), *Faith and Rationality* (Notre Dame: University of Notre Dame Press, 1983); Alvin Plantinga, "Coherentism and the Evidentialist Objection to Belief in God," in Robert Audi and William J. Wainwright (eds.), *Rationality, Religious Belief, and Moral Commitment* (Ithaca: Cornell University Press, 1986); and Alvin Plantinga, "Justification and Theism," *Faith and Philosophy*, 4 (1987). I include page references to RBG parenthetically in the body of my text.

[2] Philip L. Quinn, "In Search of the Foundations of Theism," *Faith and Philosophy*, 2 (1985); Alvin Plantinga, "The Foundations of Theism: A Reply" (hereafter FT), *Faith and Philosophy*, 3 (1986). I include page references to this paper of mine and to FT parenthetically in the text.

[3] I do however need to acknowledge the work I have found especially helpful, including the following published papers: William P. Alston, "Plantinga's Epistemology of Religious Belief," in

Religious Epistemology

to closure, but only to advance it a step or two. I have no doubt that there will remain plenty more for Plantinga to say if he, in turn, decides there would be some profit in carrying the discussion beyond where I leave off at the end of this paper. But I do hope to narrow the gap between us by indicating points on which I think we are already close to agreement and by acknowledging points on which he has persuaded me to change my mind. And I also aim to sharpen the focus on the remaining disagreements by explaining why I find some of his arguments unpersuasive and by presenting objections to some of the things he says in his reply.

The paper is divided into four parts. In the first, I discuss the particularistic, quasi-inductive method of justifying epistemic criteria that Plantinga recommends. In the second, I consider the question of whether the criterion for proper basicality proposed by the Classical Foundationalist could be justified by means of this method. These sections of the paper cover terrain on which lie substantial disagreements between us, but I think there are opportunities for progress toward resolving them. In the third part, I explore the issue of whether properly basic beliefs can also, without loss of justification, be properly based on other beliefs. And, finally, I return in the last part to the vexed question of whether belief in God, or theistic beliefs that self-evidently entail the existence of God, can be or are properly basic for intellectually sophisticated adult theists in our culture. In these last two sections of the paper I treat issues on which, as I see it, such deep disagreements are to be found between us that we have almost no hope of achieving a mutually satisfactory resolution. But even on these topics there is room, I think, to make some progress in the direction of achieving greater clarity about the issues.

1. JUSTIFYING EPISTEMIC CRITERIA

Following Chisholm, Plantinga endorses a particularistic and broadly inductive method of arguing for epistemic criteria. Applied to the case of criteria for proper basicality, the claim is this:

> We must assemble examples of beliefs and conditions such that the former are obviously properly basic in the latter, and examples of beliefs and conditions such that the former are obviously not properly basic in the latter. We must then frame hypotheses as to the necessary and sufficient conditions of proper basicality and test these hypotheses by reference to those examples. (RBG, p. 76)

James Tomberlin and Peter van Inwagen (eds.), *Alvin Plantinga* (Dordrecht: D. Reidel, 1985); Robert Audi, "Direct Justification, Evidential Dependence, and Theistic Belief," in Audi and Wainwright (eds.), *Rationality, Religious Belief, and Moral Commitment*; and Stephen J. Wykstra, "Toward a Sensible Evidentialism: On the Notion of 'Needing Evidence'," in William L. Rowe and William J. Wainwright (eds.), *Philosophy of Religion: Selected Readings*, 2nd edn. (New York: Harcourt Brace Jovanovitch, 1989). I have also found helpful unpublished work by Anthony Kenny, Norman Kretzmann, James F. Sennet, Stephen J. Wykstra, and Linda Zagzebski.

So we are to begin with examples that serve as data for the induction. They can be expressed as instances of the following two schemata:

(1) The belief that *p* is properly basic in conditions *C*.

And:

(2) The belief that *p'* is not properly basic in conditions *C'*.

Let the set of examples thus assembled be the initial set. The next step is to frame hypotheses that specify necessary, sufficient, or necessary and sufficient conditions for proper basicality. They can be expressed as instances of the following three schemata:

(3) A belief is properly basic only if it is *P*.
(4) A belief is properly basic if it is *Q*.

And:

(5) A belief is properly basic if and only if it is *R*.

And then, according to Plantinga, we are to test these hypotheses against those examples.

There is, of course, no guarantee that there will be a perfect fit between the first hypotheses we frame and the data in the initial set. Neither our first hypotheses nor the examples in the initial set of data are immune from revision. It might, as I pointed out, turn out that the initial set itself is inconsistent or otherwise incoherent, in which case "perhaps we should be allowed to throw data out of the initial set should we discover that it is in some fashion incoherent" (p. 472). More generally, as Plantinga observes, the initial set "should be revisable in the light of theory and under the pressure of argument" (RBG, p. 76). In short, the initial set of examples is not an Archimedean fixed point that has to remain unchanged throughout the process of making revisions.

Plantinga also notes that applications of this method are constrained in other ways. Thus, "various constraints on such criteria may indeed be self-evident; more important, there are theoretical constraints arising from one's general philosophical views as to what sorts of beings human beings are" (FT, p. 313). One theoretical constraint needs to be made explicit because it will be important in the subsequent discussion. The constraint is required to insure the coherence of our final hypotheses with the examples in our final set of data. If the instances of (1) and (2) that wind up in the final set of data are basic beliefs, they must at least satisfy any necessary conditions for proper basicality specified by instances of (3) and (5) among the final hypotheses. And if such instances of (1) and (2) are not basic beliefs, then there must be a path from them in the inquirer's noetic structure to other beliefs that are basic and at least satisfy any such necessary conditions for proper basicality.

There is a lot more that could be said about this method. One might, for example, discuss the similarities it bears to the procedure for getting to narrow reflective equilibrium that has been debated in recent moral epistemology.[4] But I do not have the space to say such things here. So let me just acknowledge that, as thus far characterized, it is a perfectly legitimate method of arriving at, and justifying, epistemic criteria.

In fact, I even think the method could be employed in constructing a rationally persuasive argument for the conclusion that theistic beliefs which self-evidently entail the existence of God can be properly basic. Imagine someone who starts out by being genuinely puzzled and uncertain about whether such theistic beliefs can be properly basic. Not being firmly convinced they cannot be, she is willing to let further inquiry settle the matter for her. Since it is not obvious to her that there are any conditions in which such theistic beliefs are properly basic, she includes no instance of (1) involving such a theistic belief among the examples in her initial set of data. Assume that these two things do not change in the course of the inquiry and that it terminates successfully with a final set of data that includes no instance of (1) involving a theistic belief and final hypotheses that have among them an instance of (4), all appropriate constraints on the process having been satisfied. Now our inquirer notices that there are circumstances in which a theistic belief satisfies the sufficient condition for proper basicality specified by the instance of (4) among her final hypotheses and concludes that this theistic belief is in those circumstances properly basic. She is in a position at this point to argue inductively from the examples in her final set of data to a criterion for proper basicality and from that criterion to the conclusion that some theistic beliefs are, and hence can be, properly basic. Because there are no theistic beliefs in her final set of data, this argument is not circular and does not beg the question. I can see no reason for thinking that such an argument would not be rationally persuasive for our inquirer. She had been disposed to let the outcome of her inquiry settle the matter, and it has done so.

No argument of this sort appears in Plantinga's papers. He does not actually try to justify any criteria for proper basicality by putting the quasi-inductive method to work; indeed, he does not even frame any hypotheses about the necessary and sufficient conditions of proper basicality. Instead, he assumes that the Reformed Epistemologist will include instances of (1) involving theistic beliefs in his initial set of data. Why not? After all, Plantinga insists:

there is no reason to assume, in advance, that everyone will agree on the examples. The Christian will of course suppose that belief in God is entirely proper and rational; if he does not accept this belief on the basis of other propositions, he will conclude that it is basic for him and quite properly so. Followers of Bertrand Russell and Madelyn Murray O'Hare [*sic*] may disagree; but how is that relevant? Must my criteria, or those of the

---

[4] See e.g. John Rawls, *A Theory of Justice* (Cambridge, Mass.: Harvard University Press, 1971), 19–21, 48–51; and Norman Daniels, "Wide Reflective Equilibrium and Theory Acceptance in Ethics," *Journal of Philosophy*, 76 (1979).

Christian community, conform to their examples? Surely not. The Christian community is responsible to *its* set of examples, not to theirs. (RBG, p. 77)

In response to these claims, I had said: "The difficulty is, of course, that this is a game any number can play. Followers of Muhammad, followers of Buddha, and even followers of the Reverend Moon can join in the fun" (p. 473). In his reply, Plantinga interpreted these remarks as an allegation that the method is defective. This interpretation is not utterly unreasonable because I had said that "Plantinga's sketch of the first stage of a procedure for justifying criteria of proper basicality is nonetheless well enough developed to permit us to see that it confronts at the outset at least one important difficulty" (p. 473).

Plantinga's response to the allegation that the method is defective is right on target:

It is indeed true that if people start with different beliefs as to which propositions are properly basic in various circumstances, then following the method I sketched, they may well come to different conclusions. But why think this is a defect in the proposed method? If it is, it is a defect this method shares with such paragons of propriety as deductive reasoning. (FT, p. 303)

I agree that a flawless method can yield different outputs for different inputs. That was not the aspect of Plantinga's procedure which bothered me. He himself comes very close to expressing my concern in the following passage:

And hence criteria for proper basicality arrived at in this particularistic way may not be polemically useful. If you and I start from different examples—if my set of examples includes a pair < B, C > (where B is, say, belief in God and C is some condition) and your set of examples does not include < B, C >—then we may very well arrive at different criteria for proper basicality. Furthermore I cannot sensibly use my criterion to try to convince you that B is in fact properly basic in C, for you will point out, quite properly, that my criterion is based upon a set of examples that, as you see it, *erroneously* includes < B, C > as an example of a belief and condition such that the former is properly basic in the latter. You will thus be quite within your rights in claiming that my criterion is mistaken, although of course you may concede that, given my set of examples, I followed correct procedure in arriving at it. (RBG, pp. 77–8)

There are, however, two rather different reasons why I might have decided to exclude the pair < B, C > from my initial set of examples. I might be antecedently convinced that it is an example of a belief and condition such that the former is *not* properly basic in the latter. If that were the case, I would indeed conclude that the Reformed Epistemologist's criterion is mistaken, and quite properly so. It would therefore be polemically useless in a dispute with me. But, like the puzzled and uncertain inquirer previously described, I might begin by being unconvinced that it is an example of a belief and condition such that the former is properly basic in the latter but be open to being persuaded that it is. If that were the case, I would not necessarily conclude that the Reformed Epistemologist's criterion is mistaken, for I might well consider it an open question whether it could be properly based on other examples. So I would object to how the Reformed Epistemologist applies the particularistic method because I find his procedure philosophically unhelpful in the extreme. Here I am, like the inquirer of my example, open to being persuaded that B is properly basic in C if the particularistic method is applied in a way that generates a good argument for this conclusion, and the Reformed Epistemologist tells me that the way he applies the method involves assuming at the outset the very thing I need an argument for. Hence all I can expect from his application of the method is an argument that begs the question by my lights.

Plantinga urges the Christian community to be responsible to its set of examples. The trouble is that not all Christians who have considered the matter agree with the Reformed Epistemologist's claim that pairs like $< B, C >$ belong in that set. It does not follow that such Christians are not open to being persuaded that belief in God is properly basic. Some, like the inquirer of my example, might welcome an argument to that effect and even be willing to apply the particularistic method in way that could give rise to one. But the Reformed Epistemologist's use of the particularistic method is not likely to be helpful to such people, for it appears to be committed to assuming without argument that belief in God is properly basic.

Moreover, even if it is granted that the Reformed Epistemologist is within his epistemic rights in including instances of (1) involving theistic beliefs which self-evidently entail the existence of God in his initial set of data, this is not enough to guarantee that application of the quasi-inductive method will ultimately vindicate the claim that those theistic beliefs are properly basic in the conditions specified. Suppose the Reformed Epistemologist stumbles across an hypothesis that is an instance of (3) which satisfies the following condition: (i) all the nontheistic beliefs in the initial examples that are said to be properly basic possess the feature the hypothesis claims is a necessary condition for proper basicality; (ii) all the nontheistic beliefs in the initial examples that are said not to be properly basic lack the feature the hypothesis claims is a necessary condition for proper basicality; and (iii) all the theistic beliefs in the initial examples, both those that are said to be properly basic and those that are said not to be properly basic, lack the feature the hypothesis claims is a necessary condition for proper basicality. I do not see how this possibility could be ruled out in advance. Indeed, being properly basic and nontheistic is trivially a feature of the required kind. But even if we make the supposition interesting by resolving not to appeal to such trivial features, I still do not see how to rule out the possibility in question. Nor do I see how to rule out in advance the possibility that the simplest thing to do in such circumstances would be to revise the initial set of data by deleting from it the instances of (1) involving theistic beliefs. And, of course, if this were done, subsequent inquiry might terminate with criteria for proper basicality according to which no theistic beliefs are properly basic. To be sure, the Reformed Epistemologist has another option open to him at this point; to reject the hypothesis in question and continue the search for criteria of proper basicality. But, in that case, I do not see how to rule out in advance the possibility that the search goes on interminably without coming up with anything as good as the rejected hypothesis. Nor do I see how to rule out in advance the possibility that the instances of (1) involving theistic beliefs that were at the outset among the Reformed Epistemologist's basic beliefs and go into his initial set on that account will themselves fail to satisfy the necessary conditions for proper basicality specified by all the otherwise plausible instances of (3) and (5) he manages to generate in the course of his search for hypotheses.

So it should not be taken for granted that once the Reformed Epistemologist gets down to business and puts the particularistic method to work, he is bound to succeed in justifying criteria for proper basicality according to which theistic beliefs are properly basic. We should pass judgment on the success of this enterprise only after it has been completed.

2. CLASSICAL FOUNDATIONALISM REVISITED

Plantinga's energies have not been devoted to this enterprise in his papers on Reformed Epistemology. Instead he has concentrated them on attacking the criterion for proper basicality of Classical Foundationalism. It may be put as follows:

> (6) A proposition *p* is properly basic for a person *S* if and only if *p* is either self-evident to *S* or incorrigible for *S* or evident to the senses for *S*. (RBG, p. 59)

Since theistic beliefs that self-evidently entail the existence of God are neither self-evident, nor incorrigible, nor evident to the senses, such beliefs will not be properly basic if this criterion is correct. So it must be discredited in order to clear the ground for Reformed Epistemology.

The main thrust of Plantinga's attack on Classical Foundationalism is an attempt to show that it is, or at least is likely to be, self-referentially incoherent. What does the charge of self-reverential incoherence amount to in this case? Consider, by way of contrast, the following proposal for a criterion of truth:

> (7) An English sentence is true if and only if it contains fewer than ten English words.

Now (7) itself is an English sentence that contains more than ten English words. So if we assume that it is true, it follows that it is not true. In short, (7) is self-refuting. But (6) is not like (7) in this respect. Plantinga and I agree that it is neither self-evident, nor incorrigible, nor evident to the senses for the Classical Foundationalist. So if we assume that (6) is true, what follows is that it is not properly basic for her. But this does not suffice to refute (6) or even to show that the Classical Foundationalist is irrational in accepting it. For all that has been said so far, it could be that (6) is both true and rationally acceptable for her because it is properly based on beliefs that are for her self-evident, incorrigible, or evident to the senses.

After acknowledging that it could be the case that (6) is properly based on beliefs that are for the Classical Foundationalist self-evident, incorrigible, or evident to the senses, Plantinga goes on to contend that this seems unlikely (RBG, p. 62). Maybe so. But even if we suppose that (6) is initially not thus properly based for the Classical Foundationalist, fairness demands that we give her a chance to conduct an inquiry designed to find out whether her noetic structure can be transformed in such a way that by inquiry's end (6) has come to be properly based on beliefs that satisfy the conditions for proper basicality it itself lays down. And, of course, she is entitled to make use of the particularistic method described above, though it cannot be guaranteed in advance that the method will yield an inductive justification of (6) if it is correctly applied. As for the Reformed Epistemologist, so too for the Classical Foundationalist: we should await the results and only then evaluate the success of the enterprise.

Trying to lend a hand to the Classical Foundationalist in getting this project started, I had suggested a couple of examples she might want to put in her initial set of data.[5] Thus, I imagined her contemplating believing that she is being appeared to redly in conditions optimal for visual experience in which she is being appeared to redly. My claim was this: "Surely she can plausibly say that it is self-evident to her that the belief would be properly basic for her in those conditions" (p. 474). So my suggestion was that the following instance of (1) could go into her initial set of data:

> (8) The belief that I am being appeared to redly is properly basic in conditions optimal for visual experience in which I am being appeared to redly.

Similarly, I had imagined her contemplating believing that Jove is expressing disapproval in conditions optimal for auditory experience in which she is being appeared to thunderously. And so I had suggested that the following instance of (2) could also be put in her initial set:

> (9) The belief that Jove is expressing disapproval is not properly basic in conditions optimal for auditory experience in which I am being appeared to thunderously.

My proposal was that the Classical Foundationalist proceed to build up a large and rich set of data by ringing the changes on thought experiments such as these.

In his reply, Plantinga argues that this proposal does not have much real promise. If such things as (8) and (9) are basic beliefs for the Classical Foundationalist, they must satisfy her criterion for proper basicality in order to be rationally acceptable. Clearly neither of them is incorrigible or evident to the senses for

---

[5] It is important to bear in mind that I took these examples to involve thought experiments about hypothetical situations.

anyone. Could they be self-evident? Plantinga is prepared to grant, if only for the sake of argument, that (8) can be self-evident, but he insists that (9) is not. The argument goes as follows:

> But if it is self-evident that this belief is not properly basic in those circumstances, then it must be self-evident that a person who accepted it in those circumstances would either be going contrary to an epistemic duty or be displaying a cognitive defect or malfunction in accepting it in those circumstances. It seems to me entirely clear that neither of these nor their disjunction could be self-evident to a human being. Obviously a person need not be going contrary to his epistemic duties in accepting the relevant proposition. Indeed, it may be *impossible* for him not to accept the proposition on an occasion when he does accept it; our beliefs are not for the most part within our direct control. And how could it be just *self-evident* that in accepting such a proposition one would be displaying some cognitive malfunction? It is not self-evidently false that there is such a person as Jove; and not self-evidently false that he has created us in just such a way as to be aware of his disapproval upon being appeared to thunderously. (FT, pp. 301–2)

I am persuaded by this argument that (9) is not self-evident.

But I do not think this suffices to show that my proposal lacks promise. By Plantinga's own admission, the initial set of data can be revised under the pressure of argument. So the next move for the Classical Foundationalist is to revise (9) in such a way that Plantinga's objection to its being self-evident is no longer telling. One such revision yields the following result:

> (10) The belief that Jove is expressing disapproval is not properly basic in conditions optimal for auditory experience in which I am being appeared to thunderously and I can refrain from believing that Jove is expressing disapproval.

Plantinga's stated reason for considering it obvious that one need not be going contrary to epistemic duty in accepting the proposition in question is that it may be impossible for one not to accept it. By the ought–implies–can principle, if this is impossible, one does nothing contrary to duty in accepting it. But since it is not impossible in the conditions specified in (10), Plantinga has given us no reason to think that one need not be going contrary to epistemic duty in accepting that proposition in those conditions. Hence Plantinga's argument does not put intolerable pressure on the claim that (10) is self-evident. Of course he might be able to come up with another argument that does put such pressure on that claim. If he did, the Classical Foundationalist could try to revise (10) in such a way as to relieve that pressure, and I see no way to guarantee in advance that she could not succeed.

Thus, for example, suppose I could have been born and raised in ancient Rome where worship of Jove was common. On this supposition, belief that Jove is expressing disapproval could have been properly basic for me in the conditions specified in (10); if I had been a Roman youth, my situation would have been much like that of the Christian youth in one of Plantinga's examples for whom belief in God is properly basic. Of course, the Classical Foundationalist might want to reject the supposition on the Kripkean grounds that our biological origins are essential to us. But she might also respond with a successor to (10) that adds further conditions to those explicitly stated in it. Perhaps such conditions would include my living in a society in which Jove is not worshiped and children are taught in grade school courses that cover mythology that the deities of the Roman pantheon do not exist. The Classical Foundationalist is, after all, entitled to respond to challenges to her examples as they come up, one by one, either by attacking some assumption of the challenge or by making additional revisions in the example.

So I believe it remains open to the Classical Foundationalist to claim that (10) or some successor to it is self-evident.[6] Suppose she does. Speaking for myself, I think (10) is not self-evident, and I doubt that I will be persuaded that any of its successors is self-evident; on this point I am in agreement with Plantinga's position. If we are right on this score, she is mistaken. But I have no proof that we are right. And if she is right, it is we who are mistaken. This is just another instance of disagreement about the examples, which does not differ in kind from the disagreement between the Reformed Epistemologist and someone who is firmly convinced that theistic beliefs that self-evidently entail the existence of God cannot be properly basic. In both disputes one party is mistaken, but in neither dispute is it obvious which party that is.

Plantinga challenges another instance of (1) that he supposes the Classical Foundationalist may wish to include in her initial set of data. He puts it this way:

(11) The belief that $2 + 1 = 3$ is properly basic in circumstances C. (FT, p. 301)

According to Plantinga, if she assumes that (11) is self-evident:

she must accordingly suppose that it is self-evident that in those circumstances her intellectual and cognitive equipment is functioning properly in producing such beliefs in her. It would therefore have to be self-evident to her that, for example, her accepting those beliefs is not due to the malevolent activity of a Cartesian evil demon. (FT, p. 301)

Clearly it is not self-evident to the Classical Foundationalist that she is not being deceived by a Cartesian demon. But whether or not this would have to be self-evident to her in order for (11) to be self-evident to her cannot be determined in

---

[6] When I say that this option remains open to her, I do not mean to deny that she may have to bite the bullet in exercising it. The situation here seems to be on a par with an example that Plantinga discusses. Though my memorial belief that I had lunch this noon is neither self-evident nor evident to the senses nor incorrigible for me, it is basic for me. Will this putative counterexample convince the Classical Foundationalist to abandon (6)? According to Plantinga, perhaps she "will bite the bullet and maintain that if I really *do* take it as basic, then the fact is I *am*, so far forth, irrational" (RBG, p. 60).

the absence of a specification of the circumstances referred to in (11). Suppose they are spelled out in the following way:

(12) The belief that $2 + 1 = 3$ is properly basic in conditions optimal for grasping mathematical truths in which that proposition is clearly and distinctly conceived.

If one is being deceived by a Cartesian demon, one is not in conditions optimal for grasping mathematical truths. But even though it is not self-evident to the Classical Foundationalist that she is, in fact, in such conditions, it could, I think, be self-evident to her that the belief that $2 + 1 = 3$ would be properly basic if she were in such conditions and conceived that proposition clearly and distinctly. And I also think it could be self-evident to her that her intellectual and cognitive equipment would be functioning properly in producing this belief in her if she were in the circumstances specified in (12). In other words, if (12) is construed hypothetically, as I think it may be, then Plantinga's argument does not prove that it could not be self-evident to the Classical Foundationalist.

I conclude that the arguments of Plantinga's reply do not demonstrate that the Classical Foundationalist is bound to fail in justifying her criterion for proper basicality if she makes use of the particularistic method. Responses to the objections he brings to bear on the examples are available to her. Of course it does not follow that she is bound to succeed in this enterprise. So I must confess I was excessively optimistic when I wrote that, after assembling an initial set of examples, the Classical Foundationalist "is then in a position to claim, and properly so, that his or her criterion, though not itself properly basic, is properly based, in accord with what Plantinga has told us about proper procedures for justifying criteria for proper basicality, on beliefs that are properly basic by its own lights" (p. 474). As I now see, the Classical Foundationalist has a lot more work to do before she will be in a position to make any such claim with propriety. She must defend her examples against objections of the sort Plantinga has set forth or revise them under the pressure of such arguments. And I see no way to guarantee in advance that she will ultimately be able to assemble and defend a sufficiently large and varied stock of examples to justify her criterion inductively, for it could turn out that the examples in her final set are so few that the weak inductive support they give to her criterion is insufficient to provide a proper basis for it. But the Reformed Epistemologist is in the same boat. He, too, has a lot more work to do before he can properly make such a claim; after all, he has not yet framed any hypotheses about the necessary and sufficient conditions for proper basicality. Nor can it be guaranteed in advance that he will succeed in justifying his criterion inductively once he tells us what it is. If we judge by what has been done so far by the contending parties in this dispute to apply the particularistic method, I think we should conclude that neither party has yet done enough to give us a good reason to adopt its criterion for proper basicality. Hence I am of the opinion that we thus far have no better reason for adopting criteria according to which some beliefs that self-evidently entail the existence of God can be properly basic than for adopting criteria according to which no such beliefs can be properly basic.

3. JUSTIFYING THEISTIC BELIEFS

For Plantinga properly basic beliefs are not groundless. Upon having an experience of a certain sort, I form the belief:

(13) I see a tree before me.

My having the experience of being appeared to treely plays a crucial role in justifying that belief. According to Plantinga, "my being appeared to in this characteristic way (together with other circumstances) is what confers on me the right to hold the belief in question; this is what justifies me in accepting it" (RBG, p. 79).[7] We may say that this experience is the ground of my justification and, by extension, the ground of the belief itself. There is, then, one sense in which properly basic beliefs are not supported by evidence. Since they are basic, they are not based on other beliefs and so are not supported by doxastic or propositional evidence. But there is another sense in which properly basic beliefs are supported by evidence. Because they are grounded in experience, they are supported by nonpropositional experiential evidence. In the case of perceptual beliefs such as (13), the experiential evidence in question is often spoken of as the evidence of one's senses. And, on Plantinga's view, properly basic memorial beliefs and beliefs ascribing mental states to other persons are similarly grounded in experience and hence supported by experiential evidence.

Something analogous appears to be at work in the case of theistic beliefs that self-evidently entail the existence of God. Plantinga supposes there are conditions in which such beliefs as the following are properly basic:

(14) God is speaking to me.
(15) God disapproves of what I have done.

And:

(16) God forgives me for what I have done.

He offers a partial description of such conditions in the following passage:

Upon reading the Bible, one may be impressed with a deep sense that God is speaking to him. Upon having done what I know is cheap, or wrong, or wicked, I may feel guilty in God's sight and form the belief *God disapproves of what I have done*. Upon confession and repentance I may feel forgiven, forming the belief *God forgives me for what I have done*. (RBG, p. 80)

---

[7] According to Plantinga, a belief is justified for a person at a time "if (a) he is violating no epistemic duties and is within his epistemic rights in accepting it then and (b) his noetic structure is not defective by virtue of his then accepting it" (RBG, p. 79).

These conditions all include an experiential component, and, indeed, Plantinga speaks of exploring their phenomenology. So it seems fair to attribute to him the assumption that such beliefs as (14)–(16) are, when properly basic, grounded in such experiences, which, together with other circumstances, justify one in accepting them. And, if this is correct, the experiences in which such theistic beliefs are grounded are nonpropositional evidential support for them.

According to the argument of the previous sections of this paper, Plantinga's supposition that such theistic beliefs are properly basic in such conditions has not yet been established by means of the particularistic method. But it seems to me to be prima facie plausible in its own right. So I am prepared to grant it for the sake of argument and to explore the consequences of adopting it.

Plantinga and I disagree rather sharply about what the consequences are. Suppose the belief in (13) is properly basic for me in conditions that include my being appeared to treely. On that assumption, my experience of being appeared to treely grounds the belief and is nonpropositional evidence for it, and the belief is justified for me in those conditions. Assume next that, after reflecting upon my experience, I form this belief, which I had not previously had:

(17) I am being appeared to treely.

Suppose further that I then proceed to change my noetic structure in such a way that (13) comes to be based on (17). And assume, finally, that there are no other changes in the conditions in which (13) was properly basic for me. Now (17) is properly basic for me. My experience of being appeared to treely grounds it and is nonpropositional evidence for it, and it is justified for me in these circumstances. But what of (13)? Though it is no longer basic for me, my claim is that it is now properly based on (17) and is now no less justified for me than it was when it was properly basic for me. The reason I gave for this claim in my earlier paper goes as follows:

Since, by hypothesis, my visual experience in those conditions suffices to confer a certain degree of justification on the proposition expressed by (13), the amount of justification that reaches the proposition expressed by (13) from that experience will not be less in those conditions if it passes by way of the proposition expressed by (17) than if it is transmitted directly without intermediary. (p. 478)[8]

After quoting a passage that includes this sentence, Plantinga charges that I am mistaken here.

What, he asks, is the reason for the "Since" in the quoted sentence? This query suggests that Plantinga means to challenge the claim that visual experience is

---

[8] I change numerals within this and some subsequent quotations in order to produce conformity with the numbering system of the present paper. Also, I used a different example in my earlier paper. In order to allude to G. E. Moore I there spoke of seeing a hand and seeming to see a hand.

strong evidence or, perhaps, is evidence at all for (13). Such a challenge is implicit in what he says next:

Thus what justified me in believing the corresponding conditional of *Modus Ponens*, say, is my having a certain sort of experience; and no doubt *Modus Ponens* has a great deal of warrant for me. It does not follow, however, that my having that sort of experience is much by way of *evidence* for *Modus Ponens;* that I am appeared to in a certain way is weak evidence indeed, if it is evidence at all, for the truth of *Modus Ponens*. (FT, p. 306)

I think it is Plantinga who is mistaken here.

Perhaps he is right in saying that experience does not provide much by way of evidence for simple logical truths. So maybe my being appeared to in a certain way is weak evidence, if evidence at all, for the corresponding conditional of *Modus Ponens*. It does not follow that visual experience does not provide much by way of evidence for certain perceptual truths. In other words, it does not follow that my being appeared to treely in certain circumstances is, in those circumstances, weak evidence, if evidence at all, for (13). Moreover, if Plantinga is right in saying that my having a certain sort of experience is weak evidence, if evidence at all, for the conditional corresponding to *Modus Ponens*, then he is wrong in saying that what justifies me in believing that conditional is my having that sort of experience. If I nonetheless do come to be justified in believing that conditional in circumstances in which I have that sort of experience, what does the justifying is not the experience in question but something else about those circumstances. And if what justifies me in believing that conditional is my having a certain sort of experience, my having that sort of experience is evidence strong enough to justify me in believing it rather than weak evidence, if evidence at all. Or, at any rate, so it seems me.

Plantinga's reply suggests another line of argument that might succeed without leading to a denial of the truism that sensory experience is good evidence for perceptual beliefs. It aims to show that such beliefs as (17) are not good evidence for such beliefs as (13), not that such experiences as my being appeared to treely are not good evidence for such beliefs as (13). According to Plantinga, the whole development of modern philosophy from Descartes to Hume and Reid shows that Reid was correct "in agreeing with Hume (as he understood him) that such beliefs as (17) do not in fact constitute much by way of (non-circular) *evidence* for such propositions as (13)" (FT, p. 305). But why does he think Reid was right about this? The only remark he makes that even hints at an answer is this: "It is exceedingly hard to see how to construct a cogent argument—deductive, inductive, abductive or whatever—from experiential beliefs (beliefs like (17)) to propositions which, like (13), entail the existence of such material objects as tables, houses, and horses" (FT, p. 305).[9] I agree with this remark. But how

---

[9] Even if (17) is good evidence for (13), an argument for (13) whose only premiss is (17) will not effectively refute a kind of Humean skepticism about the external world and so will lack the sort of cogency I assume Plantinga has in mind.

is this difficulty relevant to the issue of whether (17) is good evidence for (13)? Plantinga does not say.

So at this point I can only conjecture about how he might flesh out the argument. Perhaps he would say something like this:

> (18) (17) is good evidence for (13) only if someone has constructed a cogent argument from (17) to (13).

I am prepared to admit that no one has constructed such an argument. Hence if I were to accept (18), I would have to conclude that (17) is not good evidence for (13). But what reason is there for me to accept (18)? It is not obviously true. The only such reason I can think of is that (18) is a deductive consequence of some general principle that is itself inductively supported by other examples. One principle worth looking at in this connection is the following:

> (19) For all p and q, p is good evidence for q only if someone has constructed a cogent argument from p to q.

Is (19) an acceptable principle?

I think not. It seems to me there are counterexamples to (19). Suppose that, as I look out over my class, I observe a fidgety student. Upon noticing this, I form the following belief:

> (20) That student is moving restlessly about.

I also form this belief:

> (21) That student feels uncomfortable.

Now it is exceedingly hard to see how to construct a cogent argument from (20) to (21), as anyone who has studied Plantinga's *God and Other Minds* must admit.[10] If the problem of other minds is as yet unsolved, as I think it is, no one has constructed such an argument. But (20) is good evidence for (21), and so (19) is false. It follows that the valid deductive argument from (19) to (18) is unsound. Hence it does not give me any reason to accept (18). Since I can think of no other reason for me to accept (18), I conclude that I am within my epistemic rights in not accepting it. And because I can think of no better way to flesh out Plantinga's argument for the conclusion that (17) is not good evidence for (13), I also conclude that I am within my epistemic rights in affirming that (17) is good evidence for (13).

Where does this leave us? My claim is that if (13) is properly basic for me in conditions in which I am being appeared to treely, then it can in those conditions also be properly based on (17) without loss of justification. I am in agreement with Plantinga that my claim is true only if (17) is good evidence for (13), and I

---

[10] Alvin Plantinga, *God and Other Minds: A Study of the Rational Justification of Belief in God* (Ithaca: Cornell University Press, 1967). Even if (20) is good evidence for (21), an argument for (21) whose only premise is (20) will not effectively refute skepticism about other minds and so will not solve the philosopher's problem of other minds.

have argued that I am within my epistemic rights in affirming this consequence of my claim. Plantinga, of course, may be within his epistemic rights in denying what I affirm even if he has as yet offered no argument that should convince me to change my mind. I am prepared to grant that he is, and so I do not think either of us fails in doing his epistemic duty when we differ about what are, after all, difficult and contested philosophical issues. And clearly one of us is mistaken. He thinks it is I, but I continue to think it is he.

The disagreement carries over from perceptual beliefs grounded in sensory experience to experientially grounded theistic beliefs. Suppose I base the belief in (14) on the following belief:

(22) It seems to me that God is speaking to me.

The claim I made about this case goes as follows: "If the proposition expressed by (14) were indirectly justified for me by being properly based on the proposition expressed by (22), its justification would be no better, and no worse, than if it were properly basic and directly justified for me by being directly grounded in my experiential sense that God is speaking to me, other things remaining the same" (pp. 478–9). I do not think that anything Plantinga has said in his reply shows that this claim is indefensible. No doubt in this case Plantinga and I will disagree about whether (22) is good evidence for (14). As in the previous case, though one of us is mistaken, neither of us need be undutiful or irrational from an epistemic point of view when we thus differ. And at present I do not see how to resolve such disagreements or even how to advance the discussion of them.

Fortunately, I do not need to resolve our disagreements about examples of this kind in order to make the point with which I am going to conclude this section of the paper. Following Plantinga, let us call the property such that enough of it turns true belief into knowledge "warrant." Warrant comes in degrees. When a belief is properly basic, it has a certain amount of warrant at minimum, but it need not then have the highest degree it is capable of acquiring or enough to make it knowledge. So there will be cases in which beliefs have more warrant when they are properly based on other beliefs than when they are properly basic. Here, I think, is one such case. When I was a senior in high school an older friend, who was then a college sophomore, told me that there are infinite sets larger than the set of all natural numbers but teasingly refused to show me a proof. I took his word for it and formed the belief that there are such sets. It was then among my basic beliefs. I did not reason to it as follows: "Tony tells me that there are infinite sets larger than the set of all natural numbers, and most of what he tells me is true; so probably there are indeed such sets." Suppose that it then was, as I tend to think, properly basic but not knowledge. Later on, when I was a college sophomore, I was exposed to Cantor's Diagonal Argument, studied it, and came to understand it. I thereby came to base my belief that there are infinite sets larger than the set of all natural numbers on the premises of that argument. As a result my belief that there are such sets acquired additional warrant, enough of it, I would say, to make it knowledge.

There are conditions, let us suppose, in which theistic beliefs that self-evidently entail the existence of God have, when properly basic, enough warrant to make them knowledge. But there are also conditions in which such beliefs, when properly basic, do not have enough warrant to make them knowledge. If I were initially in conditions of the second sort and discovered a deductive argument for the existence of God whose premises were known to me and whose validity was self-evident to me, I could improve the epistemic status of my belief in God by basing it on the premises of that argument. If I did so base it, it would become knowledge, which it had not previously been, and would have more warrant than it had when it was properly basic. So there is a way in which a successful piece of natural theology could improve the epistemic status of belief in God even for some theists who do not, if Plantinga is right, need it in order to be within their epistemic rights in believing in God. And, of course, as Plantinga notes, "natural theology could be useful in helping someone move from unbelief to belief" (RBG, p. 73).

4. DEFEATING THEISTIC BELIEFS

The intellectually sophisticated adult theist in our culture is an ideal type I constructed in my earlier paper for the purpose of making vivid certain questions about the defeasibility of theistic beliefs such as (14)–(16). Such a person is supposed to know a good deal about standard objections to belief in God. These objections include various versions of the problem of evil as well as the tradition of explaining theistic belief projectively that stems from Feuerbach and comes down to us through Freud and Durkheim. Can such theistic beliefs as (14)–(16) be properly basic for the intellectually sophisticated adult theist in our culture? If so, under what conditions?

The answer I proposed to the latter question was framed in terms of the following principle:

(23) Conditions are right for propositions like (14)–(16) to be properly basic for me "only if (i) either I have no sufficiently substantial reason to think that any of their potential defeaters is true, or I do have some such reason, but for each such reason I have, I have an even better reason for thinking the potential defeater in question is false, and (ii) in either case any situation involves no epistemic negligence on my part." (p. 483)

Plantinga's reply contains an attack on this principle; he thinks it is pretty clearly false and can be shown to be so. Suppose, he says, an atheologian gives me an initially convincing argument for thinking that:

(24) God exists and is omniscient, omnipotent, and wholly good

is extremely improbable on:

(25) There are 10^{13} turps of evil.[11]

Plantinga's analysis of the situation proceeds as follows:

Upon grasping this argument, perhaps I have a substantial reason for accepting a defeater of theistic belief, namely that (24) is extremely improbable on (25). But in order to defeat this potential defeater, I need not know or have very good reason to think that it is *false* that (24) is improbable on (25); it would suffice to show that the atheologian's argument (for the claim that (24) is improbable on (25)) is unsuccessful. To defeat this potential defeater, all I need to do is refute this argument; I am not obliged to go further and produce an argument for the denial of its conclusion. (FT, p. 309)

There are, he reminds us in terminology borrowed from John Pollock, undercutting defeater-defeaters as well as rebutting defeater-defeaters.

But does this show that (23) is false? I think not. Suppose that the only potential defeater of theistic belief I need to worry about is

(26) (24) is extremely improbable on (25),

and assume also that the only reason I have for accepting (26) is the argument the atheologian gives me. On these assumptions, if I do show that the atheologian's argument is unsuccessful by refuting it, then I have no sufficiently substantial reason to think that any potential defeater of theistic belief is true, for surely an argument I know to be unsuccessful because I myself have refuted it gives me no reason to accept its conclusion. So it is not a consequence of (23) that, once I encounter the atheologian's argument, theistic belief ceases to be properly basic for me unless I have a good reason for thinking that (26) is false. Even if I have no argument for the denial of (26), I can satisfy both (ii) and the first disjunct of (i) in the consequent of (23) by showing that the atheologian's argument fails. Hence even if I lack a good reason for the falsity of (26), (23) does not preclude theistic belief from being properly basic for me both before I am given the atheologian's argument and after I have refuted it. It seems to me that Plantinga has failed to notice the fact that, although the atheologian's argument is a substantial reason for accepting a defeater or theistic belief if it is undefeated, it is not a substantial reason for accepting such a defeater if it has been undercut by a successful refutation. Therefore I am not persuaded that he has shown (23) to be false by means of this line of argument.

Nor am I persuaded by the possibility of there being intrinsic defeater-defeaters, though I must admit that this possibility had not occurred to me before Plantinga pointed it out. An intrinsic defeater-defeater is a basic belief that has more by way of warrant than some of its potential defeaters. Suppose that one of my basic theistic beliefs has so much warrant that it remains properly basic for me even after I have acquired a substantial reason for thinking one of its potential defeaters is true because that reason, though substantial, confers less

---

[11] A turp is $1/10^{13}$ times all the evil there is in the actual world.

warrant on the defeater in question than my basic theistic belief has in its own right. On this assumption, the antecedent of (23) is satisfied. But if I am not epistemically negligent, the consequent of (23) holds as well because the second disjunct of condition (i) is satisfied. Though I do have a substantial reason for thinking that a potential defeater of my basic theistic belief is true, for the only such reason I have, I have an even better reason, namely, my basic theistic belief itself, for thinking the potential defeater in question is false. The existence of intrinsic defeater-defeaters would falsify (23) if it were read in such a way that my reason for thinking the defeater in question is false has to be an extrinsic defeater-defeater. But since, as I have acknowledged, I did not have the distinction between extrinsic and intrinsic defeater-defeaters in mind when I formulated (23), it was certainly not my intention that it be so understood. Nor need it be read in that way.

But are there such things as intrinsic defeater-defeaters? The example Plantinga gives convinces me that there are. A letter that could embarrass me disappears from my department chair's office under mysterious circumstances. I had motive, means, and opportunity to steal it, and a reliable member of the department testifies to having seen me furtively entering the office around the time the letter must have disappeared. I have been known to steal things in the past. This circumstantial evidence persuades my colleagues, who are fair-minded people, that I am guilty, and I have all the evidence they do. Yet the fact of the matter is that I spent the whole afternoon in question on a solitary walk in the woods, and I clearly remember having done so. It is one of my basic beliefs that:

> (27) I was alone in the woods all that afternoon, and I did not steal the letter.

The evidence I share with my colleagues gives me a substantial reason to believe a defeater of (27), but the warrant (27) has for me in virtue of my memory is greater than that conferred on this defeater by that evidence. Hence (27) is an intrinsic defeater-defeater.

It is worth noting that the power of this example to persuade depends critically on what we may assume about the case. One such assumption is quite explicit; it is said that my memory of the walk in the woods is clear. If it were not clear, the warrant (27) has for me in virtue of my memory might well be less than that conferred on its defeater by the circumstantial evidence I share with my colleagues. But there are also some tacit assumptions. Thus, for example, I suppose (27) would not have much, if any, warrant for me if I suffered from certain sorts of memory disorder or even had a sufficiently substantial reason to consider myself thus afflicted and no reason to think otherwise.

And, of course, from the fact that some basic memorial beliefs are intrinsic defeater-defeaters, it does not follow without further ado that basic theistic beliefs are ever intrinsic defeater-defeaters. Nonetheless I am willing to grant that some basic theistic beliefs are or, at least, could be intrinsic defeater-defeaters. Another example Plantinga gives illustrates the point. He remarks, with what I take to be some asperity: "When God spoke to Moses out of the burning bush, the belief that God was speaking to him, I daresay, had more by way of warrant for him than would have been provided for its denial by an early Freudian who strolled by and proposed the thesis that belief in God is merely a matter of neurotic wish fulfillment" (FT, p. 312). But having the experience of being spoken to out of a burning bush is one thing; having a deep sense that God is speaking to one upon reading the Bible is quite another. Even if the former experience is part of a condition in which (14) has more warrant for Moses than would have been provided for its denial by the casual proposal of an early Freudian, it does not follow that the latter experience is part of a condition in which (14) has more warrant for a contemporary theist than is provided for its denial by the results of current psychoanalytic inquiry. So from the assumption that (14) is an intrinsic defeater-defeater for Moses it does not follow that it is also an intrinsic defeater-defeater for the intellectually sophisticated adult theist in our culture. It may be; but, then again, it may not. For all that has been said so far, when contemporary theists form the belief that God is speaking to them upon reading the Bible, that basic theistic belief has less warrant for them than at least some of its potential defeaters and so is not a defeater of all its defeaters. And perhaps basic theistic beliefs such as (14)–(16) do not have enough warrant in the circumstances described by Plantinga, in which the believer reads the Bible, feels guilty or feels forgiven, to defeat any potential defeaters of theism but those the believer has only relatively insubstantial reasons to think true.

If basic theistic beliefs such as (14)–(16) do not in such circumstances have enough warrant to serve as intrinsic defeater-defeaters of all the potential defeaters of theism, natural theology might come to the theist's rescue. Suppose there is a sound deductive argument for the existence of God. If the theist comes to see that it is valid and to know its premises and bases belief in God on those premises, belief in God will come to have a great deal of warrant for the theist. The increment in warrant might well be sufficiently large that belief in God comes to have more warrant for the theist than all its potential defeaters. So this is another way in which natural theology might improve the theist's epistemic situation. Its fate, then, may turn out to be no small matter even if it is conceded to the Reformed Epistemologist that belief in God can be properly basic in certain special conditions.

Whether or not basic theistic beliefs such as (14)–(16) are intrinsic defeater-defeaters depends both on how much warrant they have and on how much warrant potential defeaters of theistic belief have. How much warrant do basic theistic beliefs have? It is not easy to say. For what it is worth, my view is that they do not have a great deal of warrant except in extraordinary conditions such as those we may imagine to be present in Plantinga's Moses example. As I see it, such basic theistic beliefs as (14)–(16) have only modest amounts of warrant in conditions in which the theist reads the Bible, feels guilt, or feels forgiven. Plantinga says: "It could be that your belief, even though accepted as basic, has more warrant than the proposed defeater and thus constitutes an intrinsic defeater-defeater" (FT, p. 312). It could indeed; this might even be the case for all proposed defeaters, not just for one. I accept this weak modal claim because I think the Moses example establishes it. But I have never been spoken to out of a burning bush. Nor, I daresay, have many other contemporary theists been thus addressed. Of course, even if I am right in thinking that basic theistic beliefs such as (14)–(16) have only modest amounts of warrant in ordinary conditions, they would still be intrinsic defeater-defeaters if the potential defeaters of theistic belief had even less warrant.

How much warrant do potential defeaters of theistic belief have? Much needs to be said on this topic, and I have space here to say only a little bit of it. I think both the evidential problem of evil and projective explanations of theistic belief provide substantial reasons for thinking the following defeater of theistic belief is true:

(28) God does not exist.

In his reply Plantinga argues that these reasons for rejecting theism warrant a good deal of skepticism. I do not find his arguments convincing for reasons I shall briefly explain.

My claim about evil is this: "What I know, partly from experience and partly from testimony, about the amount and variety of non-moral evil in the universe confirms highly for me the proposition expressed by (28)" (p. 481). It is worth bearing in mind that this claim is consistent with (28) being highly disconfirmed by my total evidence. Plantinga's counterclaim is this: "So far as I can see, no atheologian has given a successful or cogent way of working out or developing a probabilistic atheological argument from evil; and I believe there are good reasons for thinking that it can't be done" (FT, p. 309).[12] But even if it is the case that it cannot be shown that (28) is highly probable given the amount and variety of non-moral evil in the universe, it does not follow that it cannot be shown that (28) is highly confirmed by that evil unless it is also assumed that confirmation is to be understood probabilistically. I do not accept this additional assumption. It seems to me that the failure of philosophers of science in the Carnapian tradition to work out a satisfactory probabilistic confirmation theory gives me reason enough not to accept it. I do not for a minute doubt that in science, observation statements sometimes confirm theoretical hypotheses. I take intuitively clear cases of scientific confirmation and disconfirmation as data against which philosophical accounts of confirmation are to be tested. Such data have an epistemic presumption in their favor, as I see it, and so should be rejected only for good reasons. And I am inclined to think that the claim that (28) is highly confirmed by the non-moral evil in the universe is another such datum for confirmation theory.

---

[12] In a footnote Plantinga refers the reader who is interested in finding out what those reasons are to Alvin Plantinga, "The Probabilistic Argument from Evil," *Philosophical Studies*, 35 (1979).

The treatment of projection theories in Plantinga's reply is very harsh. He dismisses them with this remark: "Freud's jejune speculations as to the psychological origin of religion and Marx's careless claims about its social role can't sensibly be taken as providing argument or reason for (28), i.e., for the nonexistence of God; so taken they present textbook cases (which in fact are pretty rare) of the genetic fallacy" (FT, p. 308). There are, I admit, some textbook cases of the genetic fallacy in Freud's writings; I enjoy seeing students discover this in class discussions of *The Future of an Illusion*. But to construe Freud's contribution to our understanding of religion as nothing but jejune speculation and bad argument strikes me as uncharitable in the extreme. There is, I suggest, a great deal more to his legacy than that, and things get even more complicated when we take into account sociological projection theories such as Durkheim's.

I believe it is useful to think of projection theories of religious belief as constituting a research program in the human sciences.[13] This research program has not and is not likely to come up with a theory having the explanatory power of Newtonian mechanics, but that is probably too much to hope for in any research in the human sciences. The unifying idea of the research program is that there is in us a mechanism of belief formation and maintenance that involves projecting attributes of individual humans or their societies outwards and postulating entities in which the projected attributes are instantiated. The existence of the postulated entities is supposed to play no role in explaining the formation or persistence of belief in the postulates. The various theories that make up this research program attempt to specify in some detail the workings of the projection mechanism; typically they consist of hypotheses about its inputs and outputs. If such hypotheses can explain religious beliefs in a wide variety of circumstances, leaving unexplained no more anomalies than other good theories, then appeal to some principle of economy such as Ockham's razor can be made to justify the conclusion that the entities whose existence is postulated as a result of the operation of the projection mechanism do not exist because they are explanatorily idle. To the extent that such hypotheses have explained religious beliefs, that conclusion has warrant. I believe that projection hypotheses have so far achieved a real, but limited, success in explaining religious beliefs of some sorts, and I think this success does give the intellectually sophisticated adult theist in our culture a substantial reason for thinking that (28) is true.

This is another point at which natural theology might perform useful services. Suppose the natural theologian presented us with an abductive argument for the

---

[13] In this paragraph and the next I make use of ideas derived from Imre Lakatos, "Falsification and the Methodology of Scientific Research Programmes," in Imre Lakatos and Alan Musgrave (eds.), *Criticism and the Growth of Knowledge* (Cambridge: Cambridge University Press, 1970). Those who doubt that there are such things as human *sciences* could, I believe, translate my talk about research programs into talk about traditions of inquiry of the sort contained in Alasdair MacIntyre's recent writings. See Alasdair MacIntyre, *Whose Justice? Which Rationality?* (Notre Dame: University of Notre Dame Press, 1988); and Alasdair MacIntyre, *Three Rival Versions of Moral Enquiry* (Notre Dame: University of Notre Dame Press, 1990).

existence of God according to which divine activity is the best explanation of a wide variety of phenomena, including, but not restricted to, theistic beliefs. The successes of the projection theorist's research program would undercut this argument to some extent, but they would leave untouched the claim that divine activity is the best explanation of phenomena other than theistic beliefs. Though the strength of the abductive argument would be diminished, it might retain enough force to confer a good deal of warrant on belief in the existence of God. If that were so, theists could accept the successes of projection theories with equanimity, for they could view the projection mechanisms discovered by the human sciences as secondary causes divinely ordained to serve as generators of theistic belief.

Of course the research program of the projection theorists is open to being criticized in the same ways that other scientific research programs are criticized by scientists and philosophers of science. Thus, for example, it might be argued that although the program was progressive back around the beginning of the century, when Freud and Durkheim were making contributions to it, it has more recently been degenerating and ought now to be abandoned. Or it might be argued that projection hypotheses explain only religious beliefs that are "primitive" or "pathological" and that the best explanation of the religious beliefs of mature theists involves the truth of theism and the existence of God. I myself am inclined to believe that an argument for the conclusion that the truth of theism is part of the best explanation of theistic belief might well be, when all is said and done, the best way for theists to reply to projection theorists. But I think it is a mistake to ignore the explanatory successes of projection theories and the warrant they confer on a potential defeater of theistic belief such as (28). Dismissing the work of projection theorists as a combination of jejune speculation and bad argument would not do justice to their real accomplishments.

So I am convinced that defeaters of theistic belief have a good deal of warrant. It seems to me they have enough to insure that, for the intellectually sophisticated adult theist in our culture, basic theistic beliefs such as (14)–(16) are not intrinsic defeater-defeaters unless such a theist is in extraordinary circumstances of the sort that are assumed in Plantinga's Moses example. If such a theist is not thus circumstanced, then theistic beliefs such as (14)–(16) will be properly basic only if the theist has extrinsic defeater-defeaters for defeaters of theism like (28).

For simplicity's sake, I have up to this point been conducting the discussion in terms of the idealized figure of the intellectually sophisticated adult theist in our culture. How should my conclusions be applied to actual adult theists? In considering this question I wish to proceed more cautiously than I did in my previous paper. An answer to this question is bound to be speculative unless it is based on empirical knowledge of the doxastic situations of adult theists.

Imagine a large research project whose first phase aims at finding out how many adult theists there are in the United States who both have propositions such as those expressed by (14)–(16) among their basic beliefs and know a good deal about non-moral evil and projective theories of religious belief. A follow-up phase of the project is designed to learn more about such people in order to subdivide them into three groups. In the first group will be people in conditions in which their basic theistic beliefs are intrinsic defeater-defeaters of the defeaters of theism that derive warrant from what they know of non-moral evil and projective theories. In the second group will be people who have extrinsic defeater-defeaters of such defeaters of theism. Anyone who satisfies both these conditions will be arbitrarily placed in the first group. Those who satisfy neither conditions will be placed in the third group; they are people whose basic theistic beliefs are not properly basic and who are to some extent irrational. In determining the membership of the second group, a generous communitarian account of what it is to have the requisite defeater-defeaters is to be adopted. That one know exactly how to solve the evidential problem of evil or to respond on behalf of theism to projection theorists is not necessary. It would suffice to have it on the authority of a reliable informant that the experts had reached consensus on these matters, the trouble of course being that, as things actually stand at present, it is well known that there is no such expert consensus and so testimony to that effect could hardly come from a reliable informant.

Now it strikes me as rather silly to try to predict, in advance of doing the imagined research, the actual numbers of people who would wind up in each of the three groups. But, given his views, I would expect Plantinga to predict that a very large percentage of the total will be in the first or second groups, leaving the third group sparsely populated. So it is understandable that he should think little of importance hangs on the fate of natural theology, since few people need it in order to escape from irrationality in theistic belief. Given my views, however, I am willing to predict that a large percentage of the total will be in the third group, rendering it thickly populated. Therefore I believe a great deal hangs on the fate of natural theology, for it seems to me that many people need it, or, at least, need assurances that the experts of the relevant community have it, if their theistic beliefs are to avoid irrationality. My hunch is that this is the issue on which Plantinga and I disagree most deeply, and the prospects of progress toward agreement do not seem to me good.

But I wish to conclude by paying tribute to Plantinga's achievement. I think he has succeeded in identifying a view of theistic belief that, though it may be inchoately present in the Calvinian theological tradition, has never before been seriously discussed by analytic philosophers of religion. And I think he has by this time said enough about the view to show that it has real promise of developing coherently into a religious epistemology worthy of respect. What he has not shown, in my opinion, is that it is superior to alternatives that display similar promise of coherent development.

RELIGION AND POLITICAL
LIBERALISM

8

Political Liberalisms and Their Exclusions of the Religious[1]

Writing a Presidential Address provides a fine opportunity to set aside for a while the small puzzles that tend to preoccupy us in our increasingly specialized discipline and to spend time on larger issues of general interest. I have taken full advantage of my opportunity. I shall be speaking about the role of religion in the politics of a pluralistic democracy. A growing literature in political philosophy addresses this issue, but it is also much discussed in other academic disciplines, particularly law, political science, religious studies, and theology. And, of course, educated citizens of a pluralistic democracy such as ours have a stake in and should, though they often do not, take an interest in the course of academic discussions of this issue. So I do not worry about there being considerable interest in my topic, both within and beyond philosophy.

I do however worry about the prospects for making a contribution that has any real chance of advancing the discussion. Politics and religion are a dangerous mixture; combining them, even in academic discussion, risks generating more heat than light. Any substantive view on the proper role of religion in democratic politics will, in present circumstances, be highly controversial. My position will, I am sure, be no exception to this general rule. I shall be dissenting from the views of a great many philosophers, including those of three past divisional

I owe thanks to many people for help at various stages in the preparation of this Address. For suggesting or giving to me things to read, I am grateful to Michael Byron, Thomas D'Andrea, Jean Hampton, Alasdair MacIntyre, Suzanne Marilley, Michael Perry, John Robinson, and Paul Weithman. For comments on a draft, I am indebted to Robert Audi, C. F. Delaney, Martin Golding, Jeff Jordan, J. B. Kennedy, Janet Kourany, Richard Kraut, Stephanie Lewis, Alasdair MacIntyre, Suzanne Marilley, Kevin Meeker, Mary Mothersill, Martha Nussbaum, David O'Connor, John Rawls, Hans Reinders, Robert Rodes, Jr., Richard Rorty, Nevan Sesardic, Eleonore Stump, Paul Weithman, and several members of an audience at Notre Dame. Responding adequately to all the points raised by the people who gave me comments would involve expanding the address to such an extent that the Editor of the APA *Proceedings* might well balk at publishing it. So I have set aside for use on other occasions the comments that suggest, quite correctly, that much more needs to be said on certain topics I treat briefly in the Address.

[1] *Editor's note*: Philip Quinn's paper was his Presidential Address to the American Philosophical Association's Central Division, delivered April 28, 1995.

presidents of this association. I cannot hope to advance the discussion if doing so requires coming up with arguments that are apt to produce consensus on my views. But perhaps discussion of controversial issues can be advanced without producing much progress toward agreement. Hence maybe I can hope to advance the discussion if no more is required of me than to enrich a lively conversation by adding a distinctive and reasonable voice to it. What I aim to accomplish is at least to satisfy this modest requirement.

Several prominent philosophers who support one version of political liberalism or another have recently proposed excluding religion from our political life in various ways. Richard Rorty is an example. In a recent discussion of Stephen Carter's book, *The Culture of Disbelief*, Rorty advocates what he describes as the happy, Jeffersonian compromise that the Enlightenment reached with the religious, which "consists in privatizing religion—keeping it out of what Carter calls 'the public square,' making it seem bad taste to bring religion into discussions of public policy."[2] And he attributes to contemporary liberal philosophers the view that "we shall not be able to keep a democratic political community going unless the religious believers remain willing to trade privatization for a guarantee of religious liberty."[3] But of course many religious believers do not regard the proposed exclusion of religion from the public square as an acceptable compromise or a source of happiness. It strikes them as unreasonable and unfair. Thus a question political liberals need to answer is this: Can any exclusion of religion from the public square be defended by showing that it is neither unreasonable nor unfair? I am going to take a few steps toward an answer to this general question by examining critically three fairly specific proposals by contemporary liberals for excluding religion from politics.

In order to provide a unifying thread to my discussion, I shall focus on proposals involving claims that there are moral duties to refrain from appealing to religious reasons in certain political contexts. I shall concentrate on the question of whether ordinary citizens of pluralistic democracies have such duties, leaving aside the question of whether public officials such as legislators or judges have role-specific, special duties of this sort and the question of whether ecclesiastical officials such as bishops have related special duties. I shall also restrict my attention to discussion of these topics by philosophers and legal theorists, passing over in silence a large and interesting literature in religious ethics and moral theology because of limitations of time and space.

The first proposal I wish to consider comes from Robert Audi. In recent publications, he has formulated and defended two principles of individual conduct that would, if scrupulously followed by all citizens of a democratic society, have the effect of excluding some religious believers from full participation in political debate and action on some important issues. In order to understand these

---

[2] Richard Rorty, "Religion as Conversation-Stopper," *Common Knowledge*, 3/1 (1994), 2.
[3] Ibid. 3.

principles, one needs first to grasp Audi's idea of what is involved in having an adequate secular reason to advocate or support a law or public policy. He tells us that "a secular reason is, roughly, one whose normative force, that is, its status as a prima facie justificatory element, does not (evidentially) depend on the existence of God (for example, through appeals to divine command) or on theological considerations (such as interpretations of a sacred text), or on the pronouncements of a person or institution qua religious authority."[4] I shall refer to reasons that are not secular in this sense as religious reasons. Audi goes on to say that "an adequate reason for a law or policy is a proposition whose truth is sufficient to justify it."[5] Combining the notions of secularity and adequacy yields the result that an adequate secular reason to advocate or support a law or public policy is a proposition such that (i) it is evidentially independent of religious reasons and (ii) its truth confers justification on the law or public policy.

Audi employs the idea of adequate secular reason in formulating his two principles. The weaker is the principle of secular rationale. It says that "one should not advocate or support any law or public policy that restricts human conduct unless one has, and is willing to offer, adequate secular reason for this advocacy or support."[6] A slightly different formulation says that "one has a prima facie obligation not to advocate or support any law or public policy that restricts human conduct unless one has, and is willing to offer, adequate secular reason for this advocacy or support."[7] The stronger is the principle of secular motivation. It says that "one should not advocate or promote any legal or public policy restrictions on human conduct unless one not only has and is willing to offer, but is also *motivated by*, adequate secular reason, where this reason (or set of reasons) is motivationally sufficient for the conduct in question."[8] An alternative formulation says that "one also has a prima facie obligation to abstain from such advocacy or support unless one is sufficiently *motivated* by adequate secular reason."[9] According to Audi, these principles are not merely counsels of prudence; they are not merely specifications of what it would be best for religious believers to do if they hope to persuade or form alliances with their nonreligious fellow citizens. They are, he says, "principles of conscience,"[10] and are intended to express "constraints on conscience."[11] And he concludes that "a conscientious citizen strongly committed to preserving religious and other liberties should probably strive to follow the stronger principle, which requires that one do one's best to have sufficient secular motivation, particularly for actions in support of laws or policies that would restrict human conduct."[12] Of course many conscientious citizens devoted to

[4] Robert Audi, "The Separation of Church and State and the Obligations of Citizenship," *Philosophy and Public Affairs*, 18 (1989), 278.

[5] Ibid.   [6] Ibid. 279.

[7] Robert Audi, "The Place of Religious Argument in a Free and Democratic Society," *San Diego Law Review*, 30 (1993), 691–2.

[8] Audi, "Separation," 284.   [9] Audi, "Place," 692.   [10] Audi, "Separation," 278.

[11] Audi, "Place," 691.   [12] Audi, "Separation," 286.

preserving religious and other liberties would not always succeed in complying with Audi's stronger principle even if they always tried to follow it. Ordinary citizens cannot be expected to be perfect judges of the adequacy of secular reasons or flawless in understanding and managing their own motivations.

An interpretive issue must be resolved before Audi's principles can be evaluated. At one point he remarks that he has "not meant to suggest that, for example, there is no *right* to base one's vote on a religious ground. But surely we can do better than guide our civic conduct merely within the constraints imposed by our rights."[13] This remark suggests that the prima facie obligations specified by the two principles may never be actual obligations because they are always overridden by a right not to comply with the principles. Since Audi describes his views on individual conduct as laying out "what we ought to do in something like an ideal case,"[14] we might do well to understand his two principles not as principles of obligation but as principles fleshing out a supererogatory ideal of good citizenship. If they are construed as counsels of perfection, compliance with them would always be better than failure to comply but would never be obligatory. However, thus construed, they would lack constraining power. What is more, this interpretation does not fit well with other things Audi says. After all, he formulates the two principles as specifications of prima facie obligation and describes them as principles governing "duties as citizens."[15] And, in discussing the principle of secular motivation, he says that "I leave open whether, as I am inclined to grant, there is a moral *right* to act otherwise; but I assume that rights do not exhaust oughts—that there are things one ought not to do even if one has a right to do them."[16] It seems to me that Audi is best understood as claiming that the secular motivation principle is a principle of obligation specifying what one ought to do, all things considered, in at least some cases and hence determining one's actual obligations in those cases. In short, I think Audi intends his principles to have considerable constraining power—real teeth, so to speak—and I shall proceed on that assumption.

If Audi's intentions are understood in the way I have proposed, I do not find it plausible to suppose that every conscientious citizen strongly committed to preserving religious and other liberties should probably strive to follow the secular motivation principle in all cases. Reflection on an example will help to explain my view. Imagine a person sufficiently motivated to take part in peacefully advocating more restrictive abortion laws solely by the belief that God has made it known through the teaching authority of the Roman Catholic Church that almost all abortions are wrong. Because this person is not motivated by any secular reason, she is a fortiori not motivated by adequate secular reason, and so she violates the principle of secular motivation. But I think it a mistake to suppose that she fails on this account to be a conscientious citizen, particularly if we further specify

---

[13] Audi, "Place," 700.   [14] Ibid.
[15] Audi, "Separation," 278.   [16] Ibid. 284.

the case by adding that she firmly opposes illegal violence of the sort involved in bombing abortion clinics or killing physicians who perform abortions. Furthermore, if she is to come into compliance with this principle, she must either cease her advocacy or acquire a sufficient secular motivation for it. As Audi emphasizes, the intent of the principle "is to require that one either not perform the relevant acts or see to it that one's secular, for instance purely moral, motivation is strong enough so that (other things being equal) one would do the thing in question even if one had no further motive."[17] But our advocate of restrictive abortion laws might also believe that, apart from religious reasons, there simply are no true propositions that confer justification on more restrictive abortion laws or their advocacy and so consider it unconscientious to try to comply with the principle by acquiring secular motives, which by her lights either would fail to confer justification or would be false beliefs. She might therefore be able to comply with the principle in good conscience only by ceasing to engage in her advocacy of restrictive abortion laws, and I do not think it reasonable to suppose that she is under an obligation to refrain from advocacy in her circumstances. More generally, I doubt that good citizens must in all or even most cases abide by self-denying ordinances according to which being motivated by beliefs of certain sorts is a precondition of political speech in support of restrictive laws or policies.

There is, of course, room in Audi's position for him to agree with my view of this and similar cases. He could acknowledge that in such cases one ought, all things considered, to exercise one's moral right to act otherwise than as the principle of secular motivation directs. In other words, he could say that the principle specifies in such cases only a prima facie obligation but not one's actual obligation. So perhaps the principle of secular motivation will exclude fewer people from political participation than one might have initially supposed. However, if it is to have any teeth at all, it will have to exclude some people who are not sufficiently motivated by adequate secular reasons. I regard the principle as dubious for this reason alone.

Audi's weaker principle of secular rationale also appears to be problematic. One difficulty is technical. Consider two secular moralists who offer contrary nonreligious reasons in support of the policy on abortion enunciated in *Roe v. Wade*. One argues that, though it does not protect a woman's right to make early abortion decisions free from state interference, there being no such right, it does maximize utility. The other argues the opposite, contending that the policy does not maximize utility but does adequately protect the right in question. Since both these claims cannot be true, both cannot be adequate reasons if we follow Audi in holding that an adequate reason is a proposition whose truth is sufficient to justify a law or policy. So at least one of our secular moralists must not have and be offering an adequate secular reason to support the policy being discussed. And because even this fairly liberal policy is restrictive in comparison to some alternatives, at least

---

[17] Ibid.

one of them must therefore be failing to comply with the principle of secular rationale. But it seems excessively harsh to suppose that either fails to comply with a principle of conscience binding on good citizens. After all, each may be perfectly reasonable, even if both cannot be correct, in accepting the propositions she offers in support of the policy under consideration. Such disagreement about reasons is commonplace in moral argument between reasonable people.

No doubt this technical problem in Audi's account can be solved. One might, for example, weaken his condition for adequacy by stipulating that reasons are adequate for purposes of advocacy or support of restrictive laws or policies if they are reasonably held and would justify the law or policy in question if they were true. But then we must ask why citizens who have religious but not secular reasons that satisfy a condition of this sort should ever consider themselves by conscience bound not to advocate or support laws or policies their reasonably held beliefs would, if true, serve to justify. Such self-denial on the part of religious believers would be an extraordinary thing to demand. What could justify such a demand for self-denial?

Some people fear that religious argument is apt to be dangerously divisive. This fear seems to be behind Audi's remark that "conflicting secular ideas, even when firmly held, can often be blended and harmonized in the crucible of free discussion: but a clash of gods is like a meeting of an irresistible force with an immovable object."[18] No doubt religious conflict has in the past been dangerous and continues to be so in some parts of the world. However it does not seem that religious disagreement in a democracy must be dangerous or that it is a danger in all democratic societies. Students in Holland told Kent Greenawalt in 1991 that "very few people took religion seriously any longer, that tolerance was high and religious tension was virtually nonexistent, that religious arguments for political positions would be wholly ineffective."[19] If these students are correct, there is no need in Holland at present for exclusionary principles of constraint of the sort proposed by Audi. And, following Greenawalt, I think we should acknowledge that what principles of constraint on the use of religious reasons in political argument, if any, are needed to prevent dangerous conflict will "depend on time and place, on a sense of present realities within a society, its history and its likely evolution."[20] If that is the case, an argument that Audi's principles are needed for this purpose in the United States at the present time should rest on appeals to empirical realities and possibilities here and now instead of appealing to an abstract ideal of good

[18] Audi, "Separation," 296. It also seems to animate Jeffrey Stout's argument that we should probably not try to revive the theological presuppositions of the traditional moral conscience. Stout asserts that "the risks of reviving religious conflict like that of early modern Europe are too great," and supports his assertion by pointing to contemporary evidence "from Belfast to Beirut, from Teheran to Lynchburg, Virginia." See Jeffrey Stout, *Ethics after Babel: The Languages of Morals and Their Discontents* (Boston: Beacon Press, 1988), 223.

[19] Kent Greenawalt, "Grounds for Political Judgment: The Status of Personal Experience and the Autonomy and Generality of Principles of Restraint," *San Diego Law Review*, 30 (1993), 674.

[20] Ibid.

citizenship and its duties. I doubt that a good argument in such empirical terms will be forthcoming because current political debate in the United States exhibits failure to comply with Audi's principles on a massive scale and yet shows no tendency to reignite the Wars of Religion of the early modern era. Of course, current political debate in the United States contains more verbal conflict than it would if Audi's principles were agreed to by all parties. But constrained verbal conflict is probably healthy in a deeply pluralistic democratic society provided it rarely spills over into violence and does not seriously threaten the stability of fundamental constitutional arrangements.

But perhaps the self-denial required of the religious by the principle of secular rationale could be argued for on the grounds that in a religiously pluralistic society religious reasons cannot justify laws or policies that restrict conduct in terms of considerations all citizens can share or cannot reasonably reject. Such an argument is suggested by Audi's remark that "adherence to the principle of secular rationale helps to ensure that, in determining the scope of freedom in a society, the decisive principles and considerations can be shared by people of differing religious views, or even no religious convictions at all."[21] However, if the fact that religious reasons cannot be shared by all in a religiously pluralistic society suffices to warrant any exclusion of religious reasons for advocating or supporting restrictive laws or policies, then much else ought in fairness also to be excluded on the same grounds. For example, justification of a restrictive law or policy by an appeal to its maximization of utility should be excluded because many citizens reasonably reject utilitarianism. Indeed, it would seem that the appeal to any comprehensive ethical theory, including all known secular ethical theories, should be disallowed on the grounds that every such theory can be reasonably rejected by some citizens of a pluralistic democracy. And if justification of restrictive laws or policies can be conducted only in terms of moral considerations no citizen of a pluralistic democracy can reasonably reject, then in a pluralistic democracy such as ours very few restrictive laws or policies can be morally justified, a conclusion that would, I suspect, be welcomed only by anarchists.

At one point Audi raises the possibility of going beyond the principle of secular rationale to something stronger. He says that "if there is secular reason which is esoteric in a sense implying that a normal rational person lacks access to it, then a stronger requirement is needed; one might thus speak of public reason, as Rawls and others do."[22] But he has made it clear that in saying this he "was taking account of the possibility that the secular may be esoteric, and not asserting that secular beliefs sometimes are."[23] He has not acknowledged that many secular beliefs are on a par with religious beliefs in not being shared by all citizens or in

---

[21] Audi, "Separation," 290.   [22] Audi, "Place," 690.

[23] This remark, contained in a letter to Michael Perry, is quoted in Michael J. Perry, "Religious Morality and Political Choice: Further Thoughts—and Second Thoughts—on *Love and Power*," *San Diego Law Review*, 30 (1993), 716.

being reasonably rejected by some citizens. If such features of religious beliefs are grounds for demanding that citizens who have religious but not secular reasons for restrictive laws or policies refrain from advocating or supporting such laws or policies, they are equally grounds for demanding that citizens whose secular reasons for such laws or policies also possess these features refrain from advocating or supporting such laws or policies. In other words, religious believers will rightly regard Audi's principle of secular rationale as making an unfair demand on them unless it is coupled with corresponding principles that make similar demands on people whose secular reasons are no better off than their religious reasons in terms of being shared or not being reasonably rejected. If the exclusion of the religious in Audi's variety of liberalism is to be fair, it must be accompanied by other exclusions.

As Audi's allusion to him indicates, John Rawls stresses the distinction between public and nonpublic reasons, rather than the contrast between secular and religious reasons, in formulating his idea of public reason. An advantage of this way of proceeding is that it allows Rawls both to include religious beliefs within public reason in some circumstances and to exclude many secular beliefs from public reason. Thus, although public reason does impose limits on the kinds of considerations to which it is legitimate to appeal in certain political contexts, it need not be systematically unfair in its exclusion of the religious. Rawls aims at an account of public reason in which all reasonable comprehensive doctrines, whether they be religious or not, are treated in the same way.

For Rawls, public reason is connected with an ideal conception of citizenship for a constitutional democratic regime. As such, "it presents how things might be, taking people as a just and well-ordered society would encourage them to be."[24] Yet it is not an ideal for the whole of life of a democratic citizen; it is only meant to regulate a citizen's participation in political affairs. And even within the political sphere "the limits imposed by public reason do not apply to all political questions but only to those involving what we may call 'constitutional essentials' and questions of basic justice."[25] Constitutional essentials consist of "fundamental principles that specify the general structure of government and the political process: the powers of the legislature, executive and the judiciary; the scope of majority rule; and equal basic rights and liberties of citizenship that legislative majorities are to respect: such as the right to vote and to participate in politics, liberty of conscience, freedom of thought and of association, as well as the protections of the rule of law."[26] When what is at stake in politics is these things or questions of basic justice, "the ideal of public reason does hold for citizens when they engage in political advocacy in the public forum, and thus for

---

[24] John Rawls, *Political Liberalism* (New York: Columbia University Press, 1993), 213. Nonpublic reasons are said to "comprise the many reasons of civil society and belong to what I have called the 'background culture,' in contrast with the public political culture" (p. 220).
[25] Ibid. 214.   [26] Ibid. 227.

members of political parties and for candidates in their campaigns and for other groups who support them. It holds equally for how citizens are to vote in elections when constitutional essentials and matters of basic justice are at stake."[27] Yet it is not a supererogatory ideal, asking for conduct above and beyond the call of duty. The ideal of citizenship with which it is connected "imposes a moral, not a legal, duty—the duty of civility—to be able to explain to one another on those fundamental questions how the principles and policies they advocate and vote for can be supported by the political values of public reason."[28] And such explanations are to be given "in terms each could reasonably expect that others might endorse as consistent with their freedom and equality."[29] The content of public reason will therefore have to be restricted under conditions of pluralism if mutuality of endorsement is to be hoped for or achieved.

The restrictions Rawls proposes become clear when he specifies the content of public reason. It has three components, all of which are tied to distinctly liberal political conceptions of justice. A liberal conception of justice does three things: "first, it specifies certain basic rights, liberties, and opportunities (of the kind familiar from constitutional democratic regimes); second, it assigns a special priority to these rights, liberties, and opportunities, especially with respect to claims of the general good and of perfectionist values; and third, it affirms measures assuring all citizens adequate all-purpose means to make effective use of their basic liberties and opportunities."[30] To say that a conception of justice is political is to say three things: "that it is framed to apply solely to the basic structure of society, its main political, social and economic institutions as a unified scheme of social cooperation; that it is presented independently of any wider comprehensive religious or philosophical doctrine; and that it is elaborated in terms of fundamental political ideas viewed as implicit in the public political culture of a democratic society."[31] The three components of public reason are the substantive principles of justice of a liberal political conception, the guidelines of inquiry of a liberal political conception, which specify "principles of reasoning and rules of evidence in the light of which citizens are to decide whether substantive principles properly apply and to identify laws and policies that best satisfy them,"[32] and rules determining the kinds of considerations to which it is legitimate to appeal in advocacy and voting on matters of constitutional essentials and basic justice. Since the purpose of public reason is to justify laws and policies regarding such matters to all citizens of a pluralistic democratic society, the rules will have to exclude considerations about which there is reasonable disagreement in such a society. As Rawls states them, "we are to appeal only to presently accepted general beliefs and forms of reasoning found in common sense, and the methods and conclusions of science when these are not controversial"[33] and "we are not to appeal to comprehensive religious and philosophical doctrines—to what we as

---

27 Ibid. 215.   28 Ibid. 217.   29 Ibid. 218.   30 Ibid. 223.
31 Ibid.   32 Ibid. 224.   33 Ibid.

individuals or members of associations see as the whole truth—nor to elaborate economic theories of general equilibrium, say, if these are in dispute."[34] Within the bounds of public reason, then, we may appeal to the substantive principles and guidelines of inquiry of a liberal political conception of justice, and to political values associated with it, as well as to shared common sense and undisputed science, but we may not appeal to comprehensive doctrines, religious or secular, or to disputed science. And the duty of civility requires us to stay within the bounds of public reason when we are trying to justify laws and policies bearing on constitutional essentials and questions of basic justice unless we are in special circumstances Rawls later discusses or others like them.

Rawls considers it desirable that the substantive principles and guidelines of inquiry of a liberal political conception of justice should be complete in the sense that its values, when suitably combined or balanced, will "alone give a reasonable public answer to all, or to nearly all, questions involving the constitutional essentials and basic questions of justice."[35] If this is to occur, the resources of public reason must be rich enough to justify answers to all, or nearly all, such questions. But since public reason denies itself the resources of all comprehensive doctrines, including comprehensive liberal doctrines, it is not obvious that it has enough content to yield such answers in almost all cases. It must be applied to hard cases to determine whether it yields reasonable public answers.

Rawlsian political liberalism thus excludes the religious by drawing the boundaries of public reason so that comprehensive religious doctrines fall outside them for the most part. But it also excludes comprehensive secular doctrines in the same way and so cannot be accused of unfairly privileging the secular over the religious. Instead it privileges liberal conceptions of justice over their rivals by including the substantive principles, guidelines of inquiry, and political values of a liberal conception of justice, or a family of such conceptions, but not those of competing, nonliberal conceptions, within the bounds of public reason. Those whose comprehensive doctrines endorse such nonliberal conceptions of justice can be expected to object that their views are being unfairly excluded from the domain of public reason. Of course, if there were an overlapping consensus of all the reasonable comprehensive doctrines present in a pluralistic and democratic society on a liberal conception of justice, or on a family of them, there would be no unfairness in such an exclusion. But even if one agrees with Rawls that the *hope* for such an overlapping consensus on a liberal conception is not utopian,[36]

---

[34] John Rawls, *Political Liberalism*, 224–5. Because Rawls excludes secular comprehensive doctrines from public reason while Audi does not insist upon a parallel exclusion of secular reasons, there is one way in which Audi's view is more permissive than that of Rawls. But since they do not benefit from this permissiveness, religious believers are apt to see it as an instance of secularist bias.

[35] Ibid. 225.

[36] Ibid. 158–68, presents a reply by Rawls to the objection that the hope for an overlapping consensus is utopian. His argument proceeds in two stages. The first shows how liberal arrangements that are merely an acceptable modus vivendi at first might come to enjoy the status of being the

one should be willing to acknowledge that no such consensus exists in our society here and now. Hence those whose reasonable comprehensive doctrines do not at present support any liberal conception of justice will find it natural to object that they have no sufficient reason to honor the limits of public reason or to affirm the duty of civility, as these things are specified by Rawlsian political liberalism. Though I have considerable sympathy with this objection, I am not going to press it on this occasion. My interest is in political liberalism's exclusion of the religious and not in whether its other exclusions may be unfair.

I am, however, going to press an objection based on the way in which Rawls uses public reason to discuss a hard case. In a footnote that has already attracted some attention and is bound to attract more, Rawls considers the question of abortion. It is worth quoting at length:

Suppose first that the society in question is well-ordered and that we are dealing with the normal case of mature adult women. It is best to be clear about this idealized case first; for once we are clear about it, we have a guide that helps us to think about other cases, which force us to consider exceptional circumstances. Suppose further that we consider the question in terms of these three important political values: the due respect for human life, the ordered reproduction of political society over time, including the family in some form, and finally the equality of women as equal citizens. (There are, of course, other important political values besides these.) Now I believe any reasonable balance of these three values will give a woman a duly qualified right to decide whether or not to end her pregnancy during the first trimester. The reason for this is that at this early stage of pregnancy the political value of the equality of women is overriding, and this right is required to give it substance and force. Other political values, if tallied in, would not, I think, affect this conclusion. A reasonable balance may allow her such a right beyond this, at least in certain circumstances. However, I do not discuss the question in general here, as I simply want to illustrate the point of the text by saying that any comprehensive doctrine that leads to a balance of political values excluding that duly qualified right in the first trimester is to that extent unreasonable; and depending on details of its formulation, it may also be cruel and oppressive; for example, if it denied the right altogether except in the case of rape and incest. Thus, assuming that this question is either a constitutional essential or a matter of basic justice, we would go against the ideal of public reason if we voted from a comprehensive doctrine that denied this right. However, a comprehensive doctrine is not as such unreasonable because it leads to an unreasonable conclusion in one or even in several cases. It may still be reasonable most of the time.[37]

As it happens, I agree with the conclusion Rawls arrives at by means of this reasoning concerning the qualified right to decide whether or not to abort during

---

object of a constitutional consensus. The second shows how a constitutional consensus might evolve into an overlapping consensus. The argument, if successful, shows that evolution to an overlapping consensus on a liberal conception of justice, or a family of them, is, in some sense, possible. As far as I can tell, it does not show that evolution to an overlapping consensus is likely, will occur, or is inevitable.

[37] John Rawls, *Political Liberalism*, 243–4.

the first trimester of pregnancy. But the question I want to ask is whether public reason alone dictates the conclusion he and I share. I do not think so.

Let us assume that the question of abortion is a matter of constitutional essentials or basic justice. On that assumption, the duty of civility requires us to respect the limits of public reason in answering it. The conception of justice that well-orders our society provides the political values we are to balance in coming to an answer. Let us further suppose, to simplify the discussion, that two of the values Rawls mentions, due respect for human life and equality of women as citizens, are so great that the balance between them is enough to determine our conclusion, leaving it unaffected when all other political values are taken into account. How are these two values to be balanced for the first trimester of pregnancy? Let us suppose that one of the two values is overriding and the other overridden: Either the value of equality of women is overriding and the value of respect for human life is overridden or vice versa. Rawls claims that the value of equality of women is overriding, arguing that the right to abortion is needed to give that value substance and force. Some who agree with Rawls about the values at stake will claim that the value of respect for human life is overriding and argue that a fetal right to life is required to give substance and force to that value. There is a conflict of intuitions about how two great values are to be balanced in a hard case. Does public reason have the resources to resolve it?

I think it does not. Comprehensive doctrines lie outside the limits of public reason. So those who oppose Rawls cannot appeal to comprehensive religious or metaphysical doctrines according to which the fetus is during early pregnancy a full-fledged person to support their intuition that the value of respect for human life is overriding. But, by the same token, those who side with Rawls cannot appeal to comprehensive doctrines according to which the early fetus is not a full-fledged person to support their intuition that the value of respect for human life is overridden. If they are to honor the limits of public reason, both sides must accept the discipline of restricting their appeals to generally accepted common sense beliefs and uncontroversial science. However, common sense is divided on or simply perplexed by the question of abortion and probably will remain so, and uncontroversial science is and is likely always to be silent on the question of whether the early fetus is a person and so should be protected by a strong right to life. Hence it seems that resources of public reason cannot get us beyond a standoff between the two sides in this debate, a standoff that is likely to persist.

If this is correct, there appear to be two ways of describing the situation. One could say that public reason in this case yields no reasonable balance of the values of respect for human life and equality of women because its resources are too weak to determine any reasonable balance. Or one could say that public reason permits two reasonable balances of those values because its resources are too weak to single out just one reasonable balance. In either case, public reason does not determine a unique reasonable balance of the values in question and so is incomplete to that extent. And that being the case, one may not infer, as Rawls does, that any comprehensive doctrine whose balance of those values excludes the duly qualified right to abortion in question is to that extent unreasonable. But neither may one infer that any comprehensive doctrine whose balance supports such a right is to that extent unreasonable. My suspicion is that public reason will fairly often fail to determine a balance of liberal political values that can be seen to be reasonable by all citizens of a democracy as deeply pluralistic as ours is. I have little confidence in its resolving power, its ability to provide "guidance where guidance is needed."[38]

Of course Rawls uses the example in the footnote to illustrate how political values may be balanced within public reason, not as a full argument about abortion and certainly not as a decisive argument. Indeed, as he has subsequently made clear, such a balancing of values yields only a *pro tanto* political justification that "may be overridden by citizens' comprehensive doctrines once all values are tallied up."[39] This is because "it is left to each citizen, individually or in association with others, to say how the claims of political justice are to be ordered, or weighed, against nonpolitical values" and "the political conception gives no guidance in such questions, since it does not say how nonpolitical values are to be counted."[40] Thus Rawls acknowledges that public reason cannot determine, by itself, a unique reasonable balance of political and nonpolitical values. What is more, as I see it, it does not even in hard cases determine a unique reasonable balance of political values.

Rawls himself acknowledges that public reason may sometimes fall short of providing uniquely reasonable answers to troubled questions. The ideal asks us to try for a balance of values we think can be seen to be reasonable by fellow citizens:

Or failing this, we think the balance can be seen as at least not unreasonable in this sense: that those who oppose it can nevertheless understand how reasonable persons can affirm it. This preserves the ties of civic friendship and is consistent with the duty of civility. On some questions this may be the best we can do.[41]

If we are to test the proposition that our opponents can understand how reasonable persons can affirm the balance we favor, however, we may have to introduce

---

[38] John Rawls, *A Theory of Justice* (Cambridge, Mass.: Harvard University Press, 1971), 20. Jean Hampton and Peter de Marneffe have recently arrived by independent arguments at similar critical conclusions about the way Rawls treats the abortion issue. According to Hampton, "the abortion issue would seem to be a paradigm case of an issue on which reasonable people can reach different conclusions, by virtue of the fact that they weight the relevant considerations differently" (Jean Hampton, "The Common Faith of Liberalism," *Pacific Philosophical Quarterly*, 75 (1994), 209). And according to de Marneffe, "The issue of abortion suggests, then, that there are important liberal positions on the scope of basic liberty that cannot be adequately defended in terms of liberal political values alone" (Peter de Marneffe, "Rawls' Idea of Public Reason," *Pacific Philosophical Quarterly*, 75 (1994), 235).

[39] John Rawls, "Reply to Habermas," *Journal of Philosophy*, 92 (1995), 143.   [40] Ibid.

[41] Rawls, *Liberalism*, 253. In a footnote, Rawls expresses indebtedness to Robert M. Adams for instructive discussion of this point.

into the discussion enough of our comprehensive doctrine to enable them to see that the part of it on which we rely in arriving at the balance we favor is itself not unreasonable and does support that balance. Thus there are circumstances in which the appeal to comprehensive doctrines, including religious doctrines, may be consistent with the duty of civility and the ideal of public reason and, what is more, may even serve to support the ideal.

Rawls agrees that there are such circumstances, which is why he endorses an inclusive view of the limits of public reason "allowing citizens, in certain situations, to present what they regard as the basis of political values rooted in their comprehensive doctrine, provided they do this in ways that strengthen the ideal of public reason itself."[42] He gives two examples. The first is a case of a serious dispute in a nearly well-ordered society. Suppose the dispute concerns the constitutionality of state aid to church schools. In the course of such a dispute, citizens on different sides of the issue might come to doubt the sincerity of one another's allegiance to fundamental political values, such as separation of church and state that order the society. According to Rawls, "one way this doubt might be put to rest is for leaders of the opposing groups to present in the public forum how their comprehensive doctrines do indeed affirm those values."[43] The second example is a case of a society that is not well ordered and in which there is profound disagreement about constitutional essentials. Rawls mentions in discussing this case the abolitionists of the nineteenth century and civil rights leaders, such as Martin Luther King, Jr., who appealed to comprehensive religious doctrines in the public forum. As Rawls sees it, "the abolitionists and leaders of the civil rights movement did not go against the ideal of public reason; or rather, they did not provided they thought, or on reflection would have thought (as they certainly could have thought), that the comprehensive reasons they appealed to were required to give sufficient strength to the political conception to be subsequently realized."[44] And once we have grasped the principle underlying these examples, we can construct others, even if they are only hypothetical, that satisfy the proviso that an appeal to comprehensive doctrine must strengthen, or least must not go against, the ideal of public reason. It would not be contrary to the spirit of the Rawlsian enterprise to be open to altering the proviso.

Indeed, Rawls has altered it in a forthcoming paper in which he moves from the inclusive view of public reason to what he calls "the wide view of public political discourse." Its principle is that "in public political discourse citizens (though not judges and other government officials) may freely introduce their reasonable comprehensive doctrines, with one crucial proviso: namely, that in due course they support the political measures they propose in terms of the principles and values of a public political conception of justice." The new proviso separates the wide view from what Rawls calls "the open view," according to which anything goes in public political discourse. He explicitly rejects the open view, saying

---

[42] Rawls, *Liberalism*, 247.   [43] Ibid. 249.   [44] Ibid. 251.

that "political liberalism cannot, then, accept the open view, for this abandons the ideal of public reason: namely, that citizens in a democratic regime owe one another a public and mutually acceptable justification for their political actions on fundamental questions."[45] I suppose the new proviso is not vacuous because there are, for example, comprehensive religious doctrines whose adherents can support some political measures they propose only by appeal to principles or values, for instance, an interpretation of scriptural texts that is authoritative only for a particular religious denomination, that are not included within any public political conception of justice. Since adherents of such comprehensive doctrines cannot justify some of their political actions in terms acceptable to their fellow citizens who do not regard such scriptural texts, thus interpreted, as authoritative, the wide view precludes them from introducing their comprehensive doctrines into public political discourse about measures or actions of this sort. If this supposition is correct, then, even on the wide view, the ideal of public reason will rule out some appeals to comprehensive religious doctrines, and so Rawlsian liberalism will remain committed to excluding the religious from the public forum to some extent. Religious pacifists whose opposition to war is justified only by nonpublic reasons drawn from their comprehensive doctrines would seem to be precluded by the wide view's proviso from appealing to those reasons to support a constitutional amendment they might propose to prohibit the United States from waging any wars.

As I have tried to show, the political liberalisms of philosophers such as Audi and Rawls involve exclusions of the religious from political activity under certain conditions. For Audi, what is involved is exclusion from advocacy or support of restrictive laws or policies if one has only religious motives or reasons for such advocacy or support. For Rawls, what is involved is exclusion of religious comprehensive doctrines from the things to which it is legitimate to appeal in ultimately justifying answers to questions about constitutional essentials and matters of basic justice. To be sure, both philosophers soften the exclusions, so to speak, by allowing for or explicitly making exceptions. But one cannot help wondering whether the strategy of exclusions tempered by exceptions is one liberals must adopt or the best one for them to adopt. A growing literature suggests an alternative. Since much of it is in books by legal theorists or in law reviews, I expect that it will not be familiar to most philosophers. For this reason, I shall not try to present or discuss its details. I shall instead report briefly on the direction in which it seems to me moving—a direction I find attractive—with the hope that some of you will be drawn to look at it for yourselves.

One important contribution to this literature is Kent Greenawalt's book, *Religious Convictions and Political Choice*. Greenawalt argues that "when people

[45] John Rawls, "Public Reason Revisited," *University of Chicago Law Review* (forthcoming). My quotes are from pp. 12 and 16 of the copy of the manuscript in my possession. I am grateful to Rawls for permission to attribute the wide view to him in advance of the publication of this paper.

reasonably think that shared premises of justice and criteria for determining truth cannot resolve critical questions of fact, fundamental questions of value, or the weighing of competing benefits and harms, they do appropriately rely on religious convictions that help them answer these questions."[46] In a footnote, however, Rawls maintains that his ideal of public reason is consistent with Greenawalt's views, though Greenawalt thinks otherwise. Rawls may be right because, as he says, the requirements of public reason "are limited to our conduct in the public political forum and how we are to vote on constitutional essentials and questions of basic justice."[47] Some of Greenawalt's most convincing examples of cases in which reliance on religious convictions is appropriate do not concern constitutional essentials or matters of basic justice; these include issues concerning our treatment of nonhuman animals and problems in environmental ethics. To be sure, Greenawalt considers abortion to be a case in which reliance on religious convictions is appropriate, and Rawls is willing to assume that the question of abortion is either a constitutional essential or a matter of basic justice. But even if reliance on religious convictions is appropriate in answering for oneself the question of abortion, it does not follow immediately that reliance on such convictions is appropriate in determining one's conduct in the public political forum when the question of abortion is at issue or how one is to vote on that question. Besides, Greenawalt has recently told us that factors he discerns on the contemporary American religious and political scene "counsel some restraint about casting public political issues in terms of competing religious grounds."[48] Even if this is only a counsel of prudence and has nothing to do with moral duty or obligation, it leaves Greenawalt on the side of those who think it good that there should be some exclusion of the religious from our political life.

For my purposes, the most interesting contribution to this literature is the work of Michael J. Perry, and responses to it, starting with his book, *Love and Power*. In that book Perry proposed a model of ecumenical political dialogue that was meant to be inclusive of the religious. He describes it as "an ideal of religious (and nonreligious) participation in political dialogue—specifically, in the political dialogue of a religiously and morally pluralistic society."[49] Ecumenical political dialogue has existential prerequisites because, according to Perry, "a certain constellation of attitudes and virtues or habits of character is prerequisite to fruitful participation in the practice of ecumenical political dialogue."[50] Two of them are fallibilism and pluralism. To be a fallibilist "is essentially to embrace the ideal of self-critical rationality."[51] In other words, fallibilists treat their own beliefs as questionable and revisable in the light of reason. To be a pluralist "is to

---

[46] Kent Greenawalt, *Religious Convictions and Political Choice* (Oxford and New York: Oxford University Press, 1988), 12.

[47] Rawls, *Liberalism*, 244.   [48] Greenawalt, "Grounds," 675.

[49] Michael J. Perry, *Love and Power: The Role of Religion and Morality in American Politics* (Oxford and New York: Oxford University Press, 1991), 141.

[50] Ibid. 99.   [51] Ibid. 100.   [52] Ibid.

understand that a morally pluralistic context, with its attendant variety of ways of life, can often be a more fertile source of deepening moral insight—in particular, a more fertile soil for dialogue leading to deepening moral insight—than can a monistic context."[52] In other words, pluralists attribute positive value to moral diversity because they consider it instructive. Many religious believers today are fallibilists and pluralists and so can participate fruitfully in ecumenical political dialogue.

But some religious believers even today regard fallibilism and pluralism as vices rather than virtues when they are extended to moral and religious matters. Even before Perry's book had been published, David M. Smolin, a law professor who identifies himself as an evangelical Christian, complained about the religious exclusiveness of the ideal of ecumenical political dialogue in correspondence with Perry. According to Smolin, Perry's prerequisites of fallibilism and pluralism have the effect of "excluding from dialogue a number of culturally significant religious communities in America, including various Christian groups (evangelicals, fundamentalists, pentecostals, traditionalist Roman Catholics) and theologically conservative representatives of other monotheist[ic] religions (Orthodox Jews, and certain Muslims)."[53] In the conclusion of the book, which contains a brief response to Smolin, Perry backed off a bit, suggesting that "perhaps fallibilism and pluralism are better understood, not as prerequisites *to* ecumenical political dialogue, but as attitudes or positions for which it is sometimes fitting to contend, depending on the particular question at issue, *in* ecumenical political dialogue."[54] This retreat indicates, I think, that Perry had grown uncomfortable with an ideal of the middle ground according to which some religious believers can participate happily in ecumenical political dialogue but others are or feel themselves to be excluded from participation.

There is, however, another chapter in the story of the development of Perry's views on this topic. Pressing his case in print, Smolin wrote that "Perry has used his own vision of good religion as the standard for admission to political and legal debate."[55] After expressing agreement with Smolin on several points, Sanford Levinson, who is not an evangelical Christian, set forth his own criticism of the limited tolerance of Perry's ecumenical politics, arguing that "Perry seems to impose his own version of 'epistemic abstinence' on those religions that are less modernist (and politically liberal) than his own."[56] Levinson went on to ask whether the search for criteria that would exclude certain types of discourse from the public square is misguided. His question is this: "Why doesn't liberal democracy give everyone an equal right, without engaging in any version of epistemic abstinence, to make his or her arguments, subject, obviously, to the prerogative of

---

[53] Ibid. 139, quoting a letter from David M. Smolin to Michael J. Perry.   [54] Ibid. 140.

[55] David M. Smolin, "Regulating Religious and Cultural Conflict in Postmodern America: A Response to Professor Perry," *Iowa Law Review*, 76 (1992), 1076–7.

[56] Sanford Levinson, "Religious Language and the Public Square," *Harvard Law Review*, 105 (1992), 2075.

listeners to reject the arguments should they be unpersuasive (which will be the case, almost by definition, with arguments that are not widely accessible or are otherwise marginal)?"[57] Second thoughts have prompted Perry to give an answer to this question that is worth quoting in detail:

I now see that we Americans should not accept any exclusivist ideal, either of public political argument or of political choice—not even any "middle ground" ideal. Instead we should accept the inclusivist ideal, according to which neither any controversial moral belief nor supporting belief—including (and this is what I want to emphasize here) any supporting religious belief—is excluded. This includes any supporting religious belief. There is no good reason to accept any middle ground exclusivist ideal. In particular, there is no good reason to exclude religious beliefs—religious beliefs that, in the view of those who embrace them, support controversial moral beliefs—as a basis for political choice *even when no other basis is available.*[58]

And, to lay my own cards on the table, I think Perry, who is a liberal Roman Catholic, has here come close to the position it would be best for all contemporary American liberals to endorse.

Two sets of considerations make Perry's inclusivist ideal more attractive to me, all things considered, than the ideal of public reason proposed by Rawls or its close kin.[59] One I share with Robert M. Adams; the other I share with Jeremy Waldron. I shall sketch both briefly.

Adams points out that "nothing in the history of modern secular ethical theory gives reason to expect that general agreement on a single comprehensive ethical theory will ever be achieved—or that, if achieved, it would long endure in a climate of free inquiry."[60] Though the substantive principles of justice of liberal political conceptions are not comprehensive, they are, when stated with precision, theoretical. For example, they go well beyond what might be regarded as the shared common sense of Americans to make distinctively liberal claims about justice that not all reasonable American citizens share or are likely to come to

---

[57] Sanford Levinson, "Religious Language and the Public Square," *Harvard Law Review*, 2077.

[58] Perry, "Religious Morality," 713. The restriction to "we Americans" is important. There would clearly be at least prudential or strategic reasons for some exclusions if the introduction of religious beliefs into public political argument without limits were to produce or exacerbate destructive social conflict on a large scale. But I judge that such conflict is unlikely here and now.

[59] For example, the one proposed by Lawrence B. Solum, "Constructing an Ideal of Public Reason," *San Diego Law Review*, 30 (1993), 729–62. As I understand it, the ideal Solum endorses does not completely exclude nonpublic reasons. But it "implies that nonpublic reasons could only be given in two circumstances: (1) if the nonpublic reason were the foundation for a public reason, and (2) if the nonpublic reason were an additional sufficient justification for a policy that would be given an independent and sufficient justification by a public reason" (p. 748). These conditions restrict the use of religious reasons in much the same way that Audi's principle of secular rationale does, though they also restrict the use of nonpublic secular reasons in a way that Audi's principle does not. They also insure that Solum's ideal is less inclusive than Perry's ideal. Solum also argues for these restrictive conditions in "Inclusive Public Reason," *Pacific Philosophical Quarterly*, 75 (1994), 217–31.

[60] Robert M. Adams, "Religious Ethics in a Pluralistic Society," in Gene Outka and John P. Reeder, Jr. (eds.), *Prospects for a Common Morality* (Princeton: Princeton University Press, 1993), 97.

share. By parity of reasoning, then, nothing in the history of modern secular political theory should lead us to expect that an overlapping consensus on a single liberal political conception of justice, or a small family of such conceptions, will ever be achieved or would long endure in a pluralistic democracy if achieved. Because the chances of agreement in ethical theory are so slim, Adams concludes that "the development and advocacy of a religious ethical theory, therefore, does not destroy a realistic possibility of agreement that would otherwise exist."[61] Similarly, on my view, allowing nonpublic reasons, whether religious or secular, into political debate about restrictive laws or policies or about matters of constitutional essentials or basic justice is unlikely, here and now, to destroy a realistic possibility of agreement that would otherwise exist. So I am skeptical about there being any assured real (as opposed to merely possible) costs associated with being guided by Perry's inclusivist ideal rather than the Rawlsian ideal of public reason. And if there are none, the inclusivist ideal is more attractive than its rival because, being less restrictive, it allows all citizens to express themselves and their deepest values more fully in the political sphere and is apt to mitigate the problem of alienation from the political. Adams suggests that "Rawls underemphasizes the combative aspects of a democratic polity and tends to overestimate the level of theoretical agreement in political ethics needed for an attainably just society."[62] I concur. Of course we let ourselves in for something more like debate than like dialogue on many issues if we adopt the inclusivist ideal, but I consider that no bad thing when there is disagreement in a pluralistic democracy.

There are benefits to be gained from adopting an inclusivist ideal of public political discourse that permits more than argument from shared premises by shared modes of reasoning. For one thing, it is open to the possibility that agreement may emerge from political discourse that does not presuppose it. As Jeremy Waldron points out, "moves may be made in political argument that bear no relation to existing conventions or commonly held opinions, but which nevertheless gain a foothold as soon as they are considered and discussed by persons with open minds."[63] Even if this does not occur, there is the possibility that one's own view may be improved in its subtlety and depth by contact and confrontation with an alien religion or metaphysics that one is initially inclined to reject. In this connection, Waldron says:

I mean to draw attention to an experience we all have had at one time or another, of having argued with someone whose world view was quite at odds with our own, and of having come away thinking, "I'm sure he's wrong, and I can't follow much of it, but, still, it makes you think..." The prospect of losing that sort of effect in public discourse is, frankly, frightening—terrifying, even, if we are to imagine it being replaced

---

[61] Ibid. 91.   [62] Ibid. 112.
[63] Jeremy Waldron, "Religious Contributions in Public Deliberation," *San Diego Law Review*, 30 (1993), 838.

by a form of "deliberation" that, in the name of "fairness" or "reasonableness" (or worse still, "balance") consists of bland appeals to harmless nostrums that are accepted without question on all sides. That is to imagine open-ended public debate reduced to the formal trivia of American television networks.[64]

Even if one considers Waldron's portrait of the imagined replacement tinged with rhetorical excess or finds it merely depressing, rather than terrifying, one can appreciate the loss of value to which he is pointing.

Commitment to Perry's inclusivist ideal, as stated above, probably needs to be qualified in one way. Liberals typically subscribe to norms of respect for fellow citizens as free and equal persons. So a narrowly drawn moral but not legal restriction on contributions to public political discourse that express disrespect, such as certain forms of hate speech, or that assert or imply a lack of equality of groups of citizens, such as racist and anti-Semitic speech, is certainly in the spirit of liberalism and may be required to capture its limits of moral toleration.[65] History teaches that religion has not, to put it mildly, been altogether free of lack of respect for others as free and equal persons.[66] So in the end liberalism will probably have to practice a minimal exclusion of the religious. If it does so, then in the interests of fairness the many secular doctrines that are committed to such lack of respect will also have to be excluded. Spelling out the details of such a restriction in such a way that it could survive testing against examples would, of course, be a large task. And the claim that the restriction should be moral but not legal would have to be defended against the arguments of those nonliberals who are prepared to support legal prohibitions of such forms of speech. I do not on this occasion have time or space even to begin these projects of explication and defense.

There are, then, political liberalisms that advocate extensive exclusions of the religious from the public forum, but there are also political liberalisms that put forward a more inclusive ideal. Being both a liberal and a religious believer myself, I naturally favor liberalisms of the latter sort. I think religious believers who are now American citizens should not acknowledge prima facie obligations to be sufficiently motivated by or even to have and be willing to offer adequate secular reasons for advocating or supporting restrictive laws or policies. Nor should they affirm a duty of civility according to which they may not appeal to their comprehensive religious doctrines to justify answers to questions about constitutional

---

[64] Jeremy Waldron, "Religious Contributions in Public Deliberation," *San Diego Law Review*, 842.

[65] Perry, of course, knows that giving reasons of certain sorts is a failure to show equal respect. On p. 711 of "Religious Morality" he cites the example of a Nazi offering a Jew as a reason for acting as the Nazi does his sincere belief that the Jew has an inferior nature and credits Charles Larmore with having brought the point to his attention. But this knowledge did not prompt him to qualify the statement of the inclusivist ideal I have quoted.

[66] Closest to home, in my own case, are the many shameful episodes in the history of Christianity in which Christians have failed to show respect, most notably to Jews. It is no consolation that secular ideologues such as the Nazis have done worse.

essentials or basic justice unless they satisfy some restrictive proviso. And they should not think that political liberalism is the exclusive possession of secular forces opposed to religion, even if they cannot help being aware that plenty of liberals are in fact hostile to religion.

As I see it, among religious people only liberals will even be tempted to acknowledge such obligations or to affirm such a duty of civility. Religious conservatives, particularly those who belong to the so-called Religious Right in the United States, will predictably decline to acknowledge or affirm such things. If religious liberals were to give in to the temptation, political debate in the public square in the United States would continue to be polarized between secular liberals and religious conservatives. Secular liberals would have an excuse for thinking in terms of the stereotype according to which all religious people are illiberal, and religious conservatives would have an excuse for thinking in terms of the stereotype according to which all liberals are secularists. But if religious liberals were to resist the temptation, they would have a way to challenge this polarization. They would be in a position to argue for liberal laws and policies from religious premises and thereby show secular liberals that some religious people are their allies, and they would also be in a position to dispute the political agenda of the Religious Right on religious grounds. I am convinced that such a challenge would be good for the health of the American body politic.

According to an attractive ideal of good citizenship, being a good citizen of a political community involves having some allegiance to the values that are most deeply embedded in it. I, for instance, think the Establishment Clause of the First Amendment to the Constitution of the United States expresses one of the deepest values of the political community to which we belong, and so I am prepared to acknowledge that peacefully advocating repeal of the Establishment Clause in order to clear the way for making Christianity the official religion of the United States would represent a failure to live up to that ideal. But I do not think American citizens have a prima facie moral obligation to refrain from peacefully advocating the repeal of the Establishment Clause. Hence I do not concede that American citizens have a prima facie moral duty to live up to the ideal in question. Though I endorse this ideal, I also believe that living up to it is supererogatory. The ideal imposes no moral requirements on American citizens, and one is not a bad citizen if one fails to live up to it. However one is a better citizen if one lives up to it than if one does not, and so I would want to encourage religious citizens to refrain from advocating repeal of the Establishment Clause or trying to make the United States into a "Christian nation," whatever that might mean. And I would make similar claims about other, less dramatic cases in which it is morally permissible but less than ideal for citizens to introduce their religious concerns into politics.

If we look away from the debates about liberal theory in the academy, we will notice that, in the rough and tumble of American politics, liberalism has recently suffered serious reverses. If they are to overcome these setbacks, liberals need new allies. They might find some in America's religious communities if their ideals were more inclusive. Thus it may be important for the future of American liberalism that something like the inclusivist ideal should prevail in the practice, even if it remains disputed in the theory, of liberalism for our time and place. I hope it will prevail.

9

Religious Citizens within the Limits
of Public Reason

It was a surprising discovery of modern liberal politics. As John Rawls puts it, "the success of liberal constitutionalism came as a discovery of new social possibility: the possibility of a reasonably harmonious and stable pluralist society."[1] There was, he thinks, no way of knowing in advance of that possibility. Moreover, this pluralism is itself reasonable. Modern democratic societies are characterized, according to Rawls, "not simply by a pluralism of comprehensive religious, philosophical and moral doctrines but by a pluralism of incompatible yet reasonable comprehensive doctrines."[2] So liberals should now start from the assumption that such pluralism is the normal result of the exercise of human reason within the context of the free institutions of a democratic society. The assumption is supported by the modern history of secular philosophical ethics. As Robert M. Adams notes, "nothing in the history of modern secular ethical theory gives reason to expect that general agreement on a single comprehensive ethical theory will ever be achieved—or that, if achieved, it would long endure in a climate of free inquiry."[3] And, needless to say, the prospects for agreement on a single comprehensive religious doctrine are, at best, equally dim.

I share with Adams the view that the discovery of this new social possibility was "an important moral discovery," though, as he notes, Rawls is "more explicit about discovery of possibility than about discovery of value."[4] In particular, it seems to me that liberal societies in which there is a pluralism of reasonable comprehensive religious doctrines realize some very significant values. Among them is the availability to those who live within such societies of a variety of sources of insight into human spirituality and a transcendent dimension of reality as well

I am grateful to Jeffrie G. Murphy, who was my commentator at the fourth Henle Conference, and to members of the conference's audience for stimulating discussion.

1 John Rawls, *Political Liberalism* (New York: Columbia University Press, 1993), p. xxv. (Hereafter cited as *PL*.)

2 *PL*, xvi.

3 Robert M. Adams, "Religious Ethics in a Pluralistic Society," in Gene Outka and John P. Reeder, Jr. (eds.), *Prospects for a Common Morality* (Princeton: Princeton University Press, 1993), 97. (Hereafter cited as REPS.)

4 Robert M. Adams, *Finite and Infinite Goods: A Framework for Ethics* (New York and Oxford: Oxford University Press, 1999), 368. (Hereafter cited as *FIG*.)

as ample social space for criticism and reform of religious traditions. Of course, like Rawls, who attributes this thought to Isaiah Berlin, I believe "there is no social world without loss."[5] And, like Adams, I think that "some social arrangements seem to have few advantages, but all have disadvantages."[6] I can appreciate the values, especially those connected with social and cultural integration, that can be realized in a religiously homogeneous society but are bound to be lost, at least to some extent, in a religiously pluralistic society such as ours. But if I had a choice about which sort of society I would inhabit, I would opt for a religiously pluralistic society. So I am a supporter of the religious arrangements commonly found under modern liberal constitutional regimes. Believing what I do about loss, however, I consider it incumbent on me to be attentive to the costs such regimes impose on religion and their religious citizens. A big question for me therefore is how to arrange such costs so that they are not an excessive burden on religious citizens.

In my opinion, the version of political liberalism developed in the past two decades by Rawls is the best attempt so far to work out in detail a liberal political theory according to which the costs liberal regimes should impose on religious citizens are, though real, close to minimal. An important innovation in that theory is its distinctive idea of public reason, which is explained in Lecture VI of the book *Political Liberalism* and then refined in the article "The Idea of Public Reason Revisited." Can religious citizens live comfortably within the limits of public reason and should they be willing to do so? Some philosophers favor negative answers to these questions. In a pair of powerfully argued book chapters, "Why We Should Reject What Liberalism Tells Us" and "The Role of Religion in Decision and Discussion of Political Issues," Nicholas Wolterstorff has directed critical fire against Rawls's version of the liberal position. I think much of this critical fire misses the mark, and I argue for that conclusion in this paper. Its first part is devoted to explaining the Rawlsian idea of public reason; its second part defends that idea against some of Wolterstorff's critical assaults.

I. THE RAWLSIAN IDEA OF PUBLIC REASON EXPLAINED

For Rawls, public reason is the reason of democratic citizens, who share the status of equal citizenship, on the subject of the good of the public. It is to be contrasted with the reasons of rulers in aristocratic and autocratic regimes and with the nonpublic reasons, within a democratic society, of churches, universities, and many other associations within civil society. Two structural features Rawls attributes to it deserve to be emphasized. The first is the fundamental political questions to which it applies; they are questions of constitutional essentials and matters of basic justice. Constitutional essentials concern the general structure of government and political processes as well as the equal basic political rights and

---

[5] *PL*, 197.   [6] *FIG*, 334.

liberties of citizens. Matters of basic justice have to do with the basic structure of society and, in particular, how it ought to respond to social and economic inequalities. The second feature is the persons to whom the idea of public reason applies; they are persons who conduct discussions of the fundamental political questions in the public political forum. Rawls specifies this forum quite narrowly. He says it "may be divided into three parts: the discourse of judges in their decisions, and especially of the judges of a supreme court; the discourse of government officials, especially chief executives and legislators; and finally, the discourse of candidates for public office and their campaign managers, especially in their public oratory, party platforms, and political statements."[7] To get around the problem of drawing a line separating candidates and those who run their campaigns from other politically engaged citizens, Rawls by stipulation makes candidates and those who run their campaigns responsible for what others say or do on behalf of candidates. It is thus important to be clear at the outset that the idea of public reason is meant to apply *only* to questions of constitutional essentials and matters of basic justice and *only* to discussions of them in the public political forum, narrowly circumscribed.

Public reason helps to specify an ideal conception of citizenship for a constitutional democratic regime. Rawls thinks it is a normative ideal. Thus it imposes on citizens "a moral, not a legal duty—the duty of civility—to be able to explain to one another on those fundamental questions how the principles and policies they advocate and vote for can be supported by the political values of public reason."[8] How do citizens live up to the ideal and fulfill the duty? Judges, chief executives, legislators, and candidates for public office do so when they "act from and follow the idea of public reason and explain to other citizens their reasons for supporting fundamental political positions in terms of the political conception of justice they regard as the most reasonable."[9] And how do citizens who are not government officials comply with the duty of civility? Recently Rawls has said that they "fulfill their duty of civility and support the idea of public reason by doing what they can to hold government officials to it."[10] But earlier he had presented his ideal of democratic politics as asking more than that. One of the tasks of all democratic citizens is that they should at least try to "be ready to explain the basis of their actions to one another in terms each could reasonably expect that others might endorse as consistent with their freedom and equality."[11] It is not clear, at least to me, whether he then thought that performing this task is required by the duty of civility and, if he did, whether he has since backed off from that view. What does seem clear is that the duty of civility requires government officials and political candidates to use the political conception of justice they find most reasonable to explain to their fellow citizens why they support the

---

[7] John Rawls, "The Idea of Public Reason Revisited," *University of Chicago Law Review*, 64 (1997), 767. (Hereafter cited as IPRR.)

[8] *PL*, 217.   [9] IPRR, 769.   [10] Ibid. 769.   [11] *PL*, 218.

positions they do on constitutional essentials and matters of basic justice, and requires other citizens to try to hold government officials and political candidates to conducting themselves in this manner. And it also seems clear that Rawls once thought that citizens who are not government officials or political candidates should, in order to realize fully the ideal of public reason, do what they can to make themselves ready to explain to one another their positions and actions regarding constitutional essentials and matters of basic justice in terms each could reasonably expect that the others might endorse as consistent with their freedom and equality. What kinds of normative constraints do the ideal of public reason and the duty of civility it imposes actually involve? In order to address this question, it is important to understand Rawls's idea of a political conception of justice and how he specifies the reasonable.

Let us begin with the idea of a political conception of justice. While a political conception is a moral conception, it is restricted in some significant ways. According to Rawls, political conceptions have the following three features: "First, their principles apply to basic political and social institutions (the basic structure of society); second, they can be presented independently from comprehensive doctrines of any kind (although they may, of course, be supported by a reasonable overlapping consensus of such doctrines); and finally, they can be worked out from fundamental ideas seen as implicit in the public political culture of a constitutional regime, such as the conceptions of citizens as free and equal persons, and of society as a fair system of cooperation."[12] The first feature insures that political conceptions are limited in scope; they do not apply to every issue where justice is at stake. The second guarantees that they are freestanding relative to comprehensive philosophical and religious doctrines in the sense that presentations of them need not appeal to such comprehensive doctrines. And the third specifies a source for political conceptions that is generally accessible to and widely shared by citizens of a constitutional democracy. Rawlsian political liberalism is, of course, particularly concerned with liberal political conceptions of justice. Liberal political conceptions are political conceptions with the following additional features: "First, a list of certain basic rights, liberties, and opportunities (such as those familiar from constitutional regimes); Second, an assignment of special priority to those rights, liberties, and opportunities, especially with respect to the claims of the general good and perfectionist values; and Third, measures ensuring for all citizens adequate all-purpose means to make effective use of their freedoms."[13] These features help to configure distinctively liberal substantive principles of justice for political conceptions. In addition to their substantive principles of justice, liberal political conceptions also contain guidelines for inquiry that "specify ways of reasoning and criteria for the kinds of information relevant for political questions."[14] The substantive principles of justice and the guidelines for inquiry in turn specify political values of two sorts. The substantive principles give rise to values of political

12 IPRR, 776.   13 Ibid. 774.   14 *PL*, 223.

justice; they include equal political and civil liberty and equality of opportunity. The guidelines generate values of public reason, which include political virtues such as reasonableness and a readiness to honor the duty of civility. Rawls also insists that liberal political conceptions should be complete. For him, this means that "each conception should express principles, standards, and ideals, along with guidelines of inquiry, such that the values specified by it can be suitably ordered or otherwise united so that those values alone give a reasonable answer to all, or to nearly all, questions involving constitutional essentials and matters of basic justice."[15]

It is worth calling attention at this point to the fact that Rawls has deliberately characterized liberal political conceptions of justice rather abstractly. It follows directly that "the content of public reason is given by a family of political conceptions of justice, and not by a single one."[16] Even the liberal political conception Rawls himself prefers, justice as fairness, which makes use of the representational device of the original position in specifying its substantive principles of justice, is only one liberal political conception among many. To be sure, such conceptions are united in their endorsement of the general ideas of citizens as free and equal persons and of society as a fair system of cooperation over time. However, as Rawls hastens to add, "since these ideas can be interpreted in various ways, we get different formulations of the principles of justice and different contents of public reason."[17] Rawlsian political liberalism does not aspire to fix public reason in the form of just one liberal political conception. Even if one or a few conceptions were, in the course of a society's historical development, to become dominant, "the forms of permissible public reason are always several."[18] In short, public reason does not demand of citizens of a constitutional democracy, even at the level of principle, unanimity on political questions, even when constitutional essentials or matters of basic justice are at stake.

As we have seen, the idea of the reasonable enters into Rawls's characterization of the duty of civility as it applies to government officials and political candidates, into his description of a task he once thought the ideal of public reason sets for democratic citizens who are not government officials or political candidates, into his specification of the political values of public reason, and into his definition of completeness for liberal political conceptions of justice. So let us now turn to what he has to say about this idea. Rawls contrasts the reasonable with the rational, and he does not try to define the reasonable directly. Instead, he specifies two of its aspects as virtues of persons. The first is this: "Persons are reasonable in one basic aspect when, among equals say, they are ready to propose principles and standards as fair terms of cooperation and to abide by them willingly, given the assurance that others will likewise do so."[19] Proposing principles and standards as fair terms of cooperation involves taking them to be reasonable

---

[15] IPRR, 777.   [16] Ibid. 773.   [17] Ibid. 774.
[18] Ibid. 49.   [19] *PL*, 775.

for everyone to accept. The second aspect is "the willingness to recognize the burdens of judgment and to accept their consequences for the use of public reason in directing the legitimate exercise of political power in a constitutional regime."[20] The burdens of judgment are factors that contribute to explaining reasonable disagreement under conditions of free inquiry. According to Rawls, they include conflicting and complex evidence, disagreement about the weights to assign to various considerations, conceptual vagueness or indeterminacy, the influence of differing total life-experiences on how we balance values, difficulties in coming up with an overall assessment of competing normative considerations, and being forced to select among values that compete for room in a social space that cannot fully realize them all. Accepting the consequences of these burdens, and others like them, involves acknowledging that reasonable people can disagree about how to order or balance political values when they are applied to cases even if they agree about which political values are applicable. As Rawls observes, liberal political conceptions differ not only about substantive principles but also "in how they order, or balance, political principles and values even when they specify the same ones."[21] What is more, even within a single liberal political conception, there can be reasonable disagreement about how to order or balance its political values in particular cases. Thus it is only to be expected that "reasonable political conceptions of justice do not always lead to the same conclusion; nor do citizens holding the same conception always agree on particular issues."[22] In other words, public reason itself often allows more than one reasonable answer to a particular question. What are we to do in such situations?

Rawls is aware that some will be tempted to say that, since public reason has failed to resolve the question, "citizens may legitimately invoke principles appealing to nonpolitical values to resolve it in a way they find satisfactory."[23] But he thinks the ideal of public reason urges us not to proceed in this way on questions of constitutional essentials and basic justice. We should instead stick to considering the question exclusively in terms of what we regard as our political conception. In other words, "we should sincerely think that our view of the matter is based on political values everyone can reasonably be expected to endorse."[24] The question can then be resolved by a vote. When we vote, however, the ideal of public reason is sustained if the question has been debated by appeal to political values and citizens vote on the basis of political values they sincerely believe everyone might reasonably endorse. In such cases, "what public reason asks is that citizens be able to explain their vote to one another in terms of a reasonable balance of public political values, it being understood by everyone that of course the plurality of reasonable comprehensive doctrines held by citizens is thought by them to provide further and often transcendent backing for those values."[25] So even in situations of reasonable disagreement in which questions are to be settled

---

[20] *PL*, 54.	[21] IPRR, 774.	[22] Ibid. 798.
[23] *PL*, 240.	[24] Ibid. 241.	[25] Ibid. 243.

by a vote the ideal of public reason has some bite. It proposes to democratic citizens a task of abstinence; they should abstain from going outside the realm of political values in search of a basis for discussion and voting. It also proposes to them a task of articulateness; they should be prepared to explain their votes to each other in terms of a reasonable balance of political values.

Perhaps an example will serve to make it clear that the task of abstinence is not trivial. Consider the issue of capital punishment. It is obviously a matter of basic justice, and so the ideal of public reason urges us to consider it exclusively within our political conceptions. Suppose the main political values that bear on the issue are respect for human life, public safety, and compensation for victims of serious crimes or their relatives. I myself think that the most reasonable balance of these values, one that gives very great weight to respect for human life, supports opposition to capital punishment. In his comments on this paper at the fourth Henle Conference, Jeffrie G. Murphy constructed an argument for opposing America's harsh system of criminal punishment, particularly the death penalty, that appeals to comprehensive Christian doctrine. No doubt some Christians will believe that Murphy's argument, or something like it, articulates their deepest reasons for opposing capital punishment. Even if they agree with my judgment about the most reasonable balance of political values, it may seem to them to provide only relatively shallow reasons for opposition to capital punishment. I sympathize with this point of view. So I am prepared to grant that performing the task of abstinence will in some cases involve appealing only to shallow reasons even though one has deeper reasons for one's position. For Rawls, of course, this is simply a price that must be paid if, given the fact of reasonable pluralism, we are to realize the ideal of living politically with one another in the light of reasons all might reasonably be expected to endorse. Yet it is a real price, and it may not always be a small one.

I think the deepest consideration Rawls mobilizes in support of this way of responding to reasonable disagreement about questions of constitutional essentials and matters of basic justice is an appeal to a criterion of reciprocity. When citizens propose fair terms of cooperation to one another according to what they regard as the most reasonable political conception, he tells us, the criterion of reciprocity requires that they "must also think it at least reasonable for others to accept them, as free and equal citizens, and not as dominated or manipulated, or under the pressure of an inferior political or social position."[26] To be sure, citizens will disagree about which political conception is the most reasonable, and so public reason can lead to a stand-off on particular issues. Yet Rawls hopes that citizens will agree that several political conceptions are reasonable, even if some of them are barely so. When citizens appeal to the political conceptions they regard as most reasonable and a stand-off results, they can think it reasonable that others, who disagree with them about what is most reasonable, can

[26] IPRR, 770.

at least agree that their proposals are reasonable. If citizens appeal beyond such political conceptions to other parts of their comprehensive doctrines as a basis for their proposals, they will not, according to Rawls, reasonably think others could reasonably accept those proposals. Hence when stand-offs occur and are to be resolved by vote, "citizens must vote for the ordering of political values they sincerely think the most reasonable. Otherwise they fail to exercise political power in ways that satisfy the criterion of reciprocity."[27] And to violate reciprocity is to flout the ideal of public reason.

Or at least this is so under what we might think of as the best-case scenario. In *Political Liberalism*, Rawls distinguishes between the exclusive view and the inclusive view of public reason. According to the exclusive view, "reasons given explicitly in terms of comprehensive doctrines are never to be introduced into public reason."[28] Rawls suggests that the exclusive view would be appropriate for the highly idealized case of a more or less well-ordered society untroubled by deep disputes. To claim that a society is well ordered is to say three things: first, it is a society in which everyone accepts, and knows that everyone else accepts, the same principles of justice; second, its basic structure is publicly known, or with good reason believed, to satisfy these principles; and third, "its citizens have a normally effective sense of justice and so they generally comply with society's basic institutions, which they regard as just."[29] Hence in a more or less well-ordered society there is just one political conception. Rawls supposes that "in this case the values of the political conception are familiar and citizens honor the ideal of public reason most clearly by appealing to those values."[30] Even in a more or less well-ordered society there is, of course, room for reasonable disagreement, as a consequence of the burdens of judgment, about how to apply the shared principles and balance the values of the political conception in particular cases. But, absent deep disputes, there is no need for citizens to go outside the political conception they share to locate a balance of values they consider most reasonable and also sincerely regard as reasonable for their fellow citizens to accept. So the exclusive view, which in effect has been the focus of my discussion thus far, seems well suited for the highly idealized case of a more or less well-ordered society not stirred by deep disputes.

Rawls, however, acknowledges that the inclusive view is better suited to encouraging citizens to honor the ideal of public reason and to securing its social conditions in the longer run in less idealized cases. On that view, citizens are allowed, in some circumstances, "to present what they regard as the basis of political values rooted in their comprehensive doctrine, *provided* they do this in ways that strengthen the ideal of public reason itself" (my emphasis).[31] By way of illustration, Rawls discusses two cases. The first involves a nearly well ordered society in which there is a serious dispute about the application of one of the

---

[27] IPRR, 797.   [28] *PL*, 247.   [29] Ibid. 35.
[30] Ibid. 248.   [31] Ibid. 247.

shared principles of justice. Suppose religious groups dispute about whether the principle of fair equality of opportunity, as applied to education, supports state aid to parochial schools. Rawls imagines that religious leaders might, by introducing portions of their comprehensive doctrines into the public forum, show how those doctrines affirm the values of the shared political conception. If the religious leaders succeeded in doing this, they would, Rawls thinks, strengthen the ideal of public reason and thereby satisfy the proviso of the inclusive view. His second case involves a society that is not well ordered in which there is a profound division about constitutional essentials. He asks us to consider the historical examples of the nineteenth-century abolitionists and the civil rights movement led by Martin Luther King, Jr. His claim is that they did not go against the ideal of public reason, even though they appealed to comprehensive doctrines, "provided they thought; or on reflection would have thought (as they certainly could have thought), that the comprehensive reasons they appealed to were required to give sufficient strength to the political conception to be subsequently realized."[32] Though this remark is a bit cryptic, I take it the idea behind it is that the abolitionists and civil rights leaders would have satisfied the proviso of the inclusive view if they had thought that invoking comprehensive doctrines was the best way, or perhaps the only way, open to them to contribute to bringing about a society in which the ideal of public reason eventually could be honored.

And as we move away from highly idealized cases, it seems that Rawls is willing to relax, to some extent, other constraints such as full satisfaction of the criterion of reciprocity. Ideally, public reason asks that the balance of political values we consider most reasonable is one we sincerely believe others can also see as reasonable, if only barely so. But Rawls allows that the best we can do on some questions may be to strike a balance we think "can be seen as at least not unreasonable in this sense: that those who oppose it can nevertheless understand how reasonable persons can affirm it."[33] The general idea, I presume, is that when, in unfavorable circumstances, full compliance with the ideal of public reason is not feasible, our departures from full compliance should be both reluctant and minimal.

In "The Idea of Public Reason Revisited," Rawls signals a change of mind when he replaces the inclusive view with the wide view of public political culture. Like the inclusive view, the wide view is specified in terms of a proviso, but its proviso is more permissive than that of the inclusive view. According to the wide view, "reasonable comprehensive doctrines, religious or nonreligious, may be introduced in public political discussion at any time, *provided* that in due course proper political reasons—and not reasons given solely by comprehensive doctrines—are presented that are sufficient to support whatever the comprehensive doctrines are said to support" (my emphasis).[34] Rawls is aware that the wide view's new proviso will give rise to questions. When does it need to be satisfied, and who is obliged to satisfy it? However he professes not to be able provide

32 Ibid. 251.   33 Ibid. 253.   34 IPRR, 783–4.

much help in answering such questions. He thinks the details of how to satisfy it "must be worked out in practice and cannot feasibly be governed by a clear family of rules given in advance."[35] An advantage of the wide view is that it enables Rawls to simplify his treatment of the abolitionists and the leaders of the civil rights movement. He no longer needs to speculate about the truth of counterfactuals concerning what they would have thought on reflection. Instead he simply notes that the wide view's proviso "was fulfilled in their cases, however much they emphasized the religious roots of their doctrines, because these doctrines supported basic constitutional values—as they themselves asserted—and so supported reasonable conceptions of political justice."[36] Even if they had not thought that the measures they advocated were supported by a reasonable balance of political values, we see that they are so supported, and on that account the new proviso is satisfied in their cases.

I conjecture that Rawls moved from the inclusive view to the wide view in part because he wanted to address the concerns of some religious citizens that his political liberalism is biased toward the secular and unnecessarily exclusive of the religious. But there is only so far he can move while remaining wedded to the core idea of liberalism. For Rawls, I think, this is its principle of legitimacy. According to that principle, our exercise of coercive political power "is proper and hence justifiable only when it is exercised in accordance with a constitution the essentials of which all citizens may reasonably be expected to endorse in the light of principles and ideals acceptable to them as reasonable and rational."[37] So even when the proviso of the wide view is in place, ultimate political justification must be in terms of a reasonable balance of the values of a political conception of justice and so must be conducted within the limits of public reason. As Rawls puts it, "this justification is still given in terms of a family of reasonable political conceptions of justice."[38] Nor does a core idea of this sort seem to be distinctive of Rawlsian political liberalism. Something similar is at the heart of Charles Larmore's liberalism of equal respect. As Larmore sees it, "To respect another person as an end is to insist that coercive or political principles be as justifiable to that person as they are to us. Equal respect involves treating in this way all persons to which such principles are to apply."[39] The common idea is that liberal justification of at least the fundamental principles of the exercise of coercive political power must be justification to all persons to whom those principles are to be applied.

Rawls is candid about the ways in which the ideal of public reason is supposed to constrain discussion in the public forum. It asks citizens to submit to the discipline of working up and being prepared to defend a political conception of justice. For Rawls, "the point of the ideal of public reason is that citizens are to conduct their fundamental discussions within the framework of what each

---

[35] IPRR, 784. [36] Ibid. 785–6. [37] *PL*, 217. [38] IPRR, 784.
[39] Charles Larmore, *The Morals of Modernity* (Cambridge: Cambridge University Press, 1996), 137.

regards as a political conception of justice based on values that the others can reasonably be expected to endorse and each is, in good faith, prepared to defend that conception so understood."[40] It also asks citizens to submit to the discipline of using their political conceptions as a filter on arguments that makes the route from their comprehensive doctrines to ultimate political justification inevitably indirect. According to Rawls, "What we cannot do in public reason is to proceed directly from our comprehensive doctrine, or a part thereof, to one or several political principles and values, and the particular institutions they support. Instead, we are required first to work to the basic ideas of a complete political conception and from there to elaborate its principles and ideals, and to use the arguments they provide."[41] We must proceed by way of political conceptions because in public reason we aim at justification in terms of values all can reasonably be expected to endorse. And we must proceed by way of complete political conceptions because in public reason we aim at a unified system of answers to the full range of fundamental questions of constitutional essentials and basic justice. Neither of these requests is trivial. Bearing the yoke of the discipline they call for will not be equally easy for all citizens and cannot be expected always to be easy for each citizen.

Is this too much to ask of the religious citizens of a liberal democracy? Nicholas Wolterstorff thinks so. I now turn to an examination of his views.

II. THE RAWLSIAN IDEA CRITICIZED AND DEFENDED

Let me make two preliminary remarks before I begin explaining and criticizing Wolterstorff's arguments. The first is that he himself is committed to some liberal political values; the final paragraph of his book, *John Locke and the Ethics of Belief*, makes this very clear. It says this:

Yet we must live together. It is to politics and not to epistemology that we shall have to look for an answer as to how to do that. "Liberal" politics has fallen on bad days recently. But to its animating vision of a society in which persons of diverse traditions live together in justice and friendship, conversing with each other and slowly altering their traditions in response to their conversation—to that, there is no viable alternative.[42]

So Wolterstorff does not reject liberalism's animating vision; he thinks there is no viable alternative to endeavoring to realize and live in accord with it. His quarrel is with what some liberal theorists tell us about what this project requires of us.

It is also worth noting for the record that the Rawls Wolterstorff attacks is not exactly the same as the Rawls I shall try to defend. The two book chapters in which Wolterstorff criticizes Rawls, both of which were published in 1997,

---

[40] *PL*, 226.   [41] IPRR, 777–8.

[42] Nicholas Wolterstorff, *John Locke and the Ethics of Belief* (Cambridge: Cambridge University Press, 1996), 246.

target the views of *Political Liberalism* and do not take into account the shifts of emphasis, clarifications, elaborations, and even changes of mind contained in "The Idea of Public Reason Revisited," which was also published in 1997. My exposition of Rawls, though it points out some salient differences between the views of *Political Liberalism* and those of "The Idea of Public Reason Revisited," draws freely on both sources. Hence it presents a picture that is not a perfect match with the one likely to emerge from reading *Political Liberalism* on its own. Yet it is this picture I want to defend. And I hope to show that it contains the features of Rawlsian liberal theory that Wolterstorff finds generally and most deeply objectionable.

We can gain entry into the general perspective from which Wolterstorff approaches liberal theorists if we start by considering an image he uses to paint in broad brushstrokes an aspect of their ideas he rejects. He distinguishes between a parliamentary session and a quaker meeting. In a parliamentary session, after appropriate discussion has occurred, a vote is taken, and the will of a suitable majority constitutes the decision of the body. By contrast, in a quaker meeting, as Wolterstorff is conceiving it, a proposal is regarded as adopted by the body only if it is supported by a consensus, where a consensus involves positive agreement by all and not just the mere acquiescence, on the part of some, represented by failure to dissent. Criticizing Robert Audi and other unnamed liberal theorists, Wolterstorff accuses them of seeing "the concept of liberal democracy as incorporating the ideal of all the citizens together constituting a quaker meeting when it comes to the choosing of laws and governmental policies that are in any way coercive."[43] Of course, as Wolterstorff acknowledges, such theorists realize that sometimes, on account of persisting disagreement, the citizens will have no recourse but to constitute themselves as a parliamentary session. But when they do, their society, by falling short of the ideal, either is to that extent not a liberal democracy or is a malformed liberal democracy. Nor is Wolterstorff the first to raise a worry of this sort about Rawlsian liberalism. Writing slightly before *Political Liberalism*'s publication, Robert M. Adams had said that it seemed to him that "Rawls underemphasizes the combative aspects of a democratic polity and tends to overestimate the level of theoretical agreement in political ethics needed for an attainably just society."[44]

Whatever may be the case for Audi and others, it is surely no part of Rawlsian political liberalism to conceive of the citizens of a liberal democracy as ideally constituting a quaker meeting whenever it comes to choosing coercive laws and policies. As we have seen, the ideal of public reason applies only to questions of constitutional essentials and basic justice. It says nothing against adopting coercive laws and policies on other matters in parliamentary session. What is more, even

---

[43] Robert Audi and Nicholas Wolterstorff, *Religion in the Public Square: The Place of Religious Convictions in Political Debate* (Lanham, Md. Rowman and Littlefield, 1997), 152. (Hereafter cited as *RPS*.)

[44] REPS, 112.

in the extremely idealized case of a society more or less well ordered by a single political conception, Rawls recognizes, as his example of a serious dispute over government aid of parochial schools makes clear, that there may be disagreement about the application of shared political values in particular situations. In light of the burdens of judgment, reasonable citizens will acknowledge that public reason does not require of them a resolution of such disputes by unanimous agreement. And in less idealized cases, in which public reason takes on several of its permissible forms and society contains a family of political conceptions, there may be reasonable disagreement in particular instances about exactly which political values are applicable and how the applicable political values are to be ordered or balanced. In short, even when constitutional essentials and matters of basic justice are at stake, Rawls leaves room for many issues that it is beyond the scope of public reason to adjudicate in terms of the unanimous agreement of the model of the quaker meeting.

Wolterstorff's striking image of the liberal polity as a quaker meeting would, then, be misleading if it were applied to Rawlsian political liberalism. Wolterstorff does not explicitly make such an application. However, he does say things about Rawls that strongly suggest an interpretation which distorts in a similar way. He asserts, for example, that Rawls "employs a *consensus populi* strategy."[45] Though he admits that Rawls does not use the words *"consensus populi,"* he takes it that Rawls's "suggestion, at bottom, is that, in a liberal democracy, the *consensus populi* ought to be used to form the political basis of the discussions and decisions of the citizens."[46] Wolterstorff apparently thinks that this is the suggestion because of the way Rawls specifies the second and third features of political conceptions. As previously noted, political conceptions are supposed to be worked up from ideas implicit in the public political culture of a constitutional regime and freestanding in the sense of being able to be presented independently of comprehensive doctrines. Wolterstorff seems to think Rawls wants political conceptions to have these features in order to guarantee or at least make it likely that there will be a *consensus populi* on a single favored political conception. He rightly observes that such an outcome is not likely. As he puts it, "no matter what principles of justice a particular political theorist may propose, the reasonable thing for her to expect, given any plausible understanding whatsoever of 'reasonable and rational,' is *not* that all reasonable and rational citizens would accept those principles, but rather that *not all* of them would do so."[47] But, not only does Rawls not deny this point, he insists that even within the limits of public reason there will be different formulations of the principles of justice. It seems to me Rawls is correct to insist that the content of public reason cannot be fixed in the form of a single liberal political conception of justice; the fundamental ideals

---

[45] Nicholas Wolterstorff, "Why We Should Reject What Liberalism Tells Us," in Paul J. Weithman (ed.), *Religion and Contemporary Liberalism* (Notre Dame: University of Notre Dame Press, 1997), 171. (Hereafter cited as WWSR.)

[46] *RPS*, 92.   [47] Ibid. 99.

of the public political culture from which it derives can reasonably be interpreted in different ways and are likely to continue to permit such diverse interpretations as long as free inquiry endures.

When Wolterstorff notices that Rawls does not think that public reason requires us all to agree on a single political conception of justice, he regards this as remarkable. He takes Rawls to be making, in the interests of realism, the concession that "we do not need, for political life in a liberal democracy, principles endorsed by all reasonable and rational citizens."[48] And he concludes that such unanimous endorsement of principles and so public reason itself must be ideals, the difficulty being that they may never be anything more. Of course, it may be that Rawls thinks that it would be ideal in some sense if we were all to endorse the same principles of justice, but public reason does not demand this of us. And he does subscribe to an ideal of public reason, but it can be satisfied even in the absence of unanimous endorsement of principles of justice. Yet it does not occur to Wolterstorff to reconsider his claim that Rawls employs a *consensus populi* strategy. This is unfortunate. Had he done so, he might have seen that Rawlsian political liberalism does not insist on and, in fact, does not even aspire to *consensus populi* about the content of public reason or at the level of principles of justice.

Perhaps Rawls does indeed aspire to a level of agreement in political morality that is neither feasible nor desirable. But his ideal of public reason does not require anyone to aspire to the level of agreement of Wolterstorff's imaginary quaker meeting. Nor does public reason aim at a *consensus populi* on a single political conception or a single set of principles of justice. On these issues Wolterstorff's critique sees Rawlsian political liberalism through a distorting lens. Rawls simply does not aspire to agreement in political morality to the extent Wolterstorff thinks he does, much less to the level Wolterstorff attributes to Audi and other unnamed liberal theorists.

It seems clear to me, however, that Wolterstorff's main quarrel with Rawls does not lie in the area of how much agreement it is reasonable to expect or aspire to in a liberal society. Even if Wolterstorff were to concede that Rawls, perhaps unlike some other liberal theorists, does not make the unreasonable or unrealistic demands implicit in the quaker meeting image or the *consensus populi* strategy, he would still object to conducting political argument within the limits of Rawlsian public reason because he thinks its limits impose an unfair burden on religious citizens of certain sorts. Where the shoe really pinches, for Wolterstorff, is where it excludes, as he sees it, the reasons of comprehensive religious doctrines from the public forum. I read him as having two arguments for the unfairness of the exclusion. The first focuses on the idea of the free exercise of religion, and so I shall call it the free exercise argument. The second emphasizes the concept of living a religiously integrated existence, and so I shall call it the integrity argument.

[48] *RPS*, 101.

The free exercise argument comes in two versions. The premise of the first concerns the religious convictions of some religious citizens. Wolterstorff says: "It belongs to the *religious convictions* of a good many religious people in our society that *they ought to base* their decisions concerning fundamental issues of justice *on* their religious convictions."[49] The conclusion he draws from this premise is this: "Accordingly, to require of them that they not base their decisions and discussions concerning political issues on their religion is to infringe, inequitably, on the free exercise of their religion."[50] In order to understand the second version of the free exercise argument, we need to grasp what Wolterstorff describes as liberalism's independent-basis principle. It is the principle that citizens of a liberal democracy "are to base their political debate in the public space, and their political decisions, on the principles yielded by some source *independent of* any and all of the religious perspectives to be found in the society."[51] The premise of the second version is closely related to the conclusion of the first. Wolterstorff claims: "Should someone try to stop me from voting, and acting politically, on the basis of my religious convictions, that would violate the free exercise of my religion."[52] From this claim he infers immediately the following conclusion: "Accordingly, if honoring the freedom and equality of citizens did require adherence to the independent-basis principle, then honoring the freedom and equality of citizens would also require non-adherence."[53] What are we to make of this chain of arguments?

I think both of them prove to be, upon examination, bad arguments. Consider the first version. Its premise is undoubtedly true. There are religious citizens whose religious convictions include the belief that they should base their political responses to fundamental questions of justice on their religion. Its conclusion, however, is ambiguous. If there were a legal requirement that they not do so, it would clearly infringe on the free exercise of their religion. But Rawlsian political liberalism proposes no such legal duty. As previously noted, its duty of civility is a moral rather than a legal duty. Rawls is explicit about how this distinction bears on constitutionally protected liberties. He emphasizes that the duty of civility is not a legal duty because "in that case it would be incompatible with freedom of speech."[54] Similarly, the duty of civility would be incompatible with the free exercise of religion if it were a legal duty. So if the conclusion of the argument is to make contact with Rawls, it must be understood to say that morally requiring religious citizens not to base their political activity on their religion is an infringement of the free exercise of their religion. But thus interpreted the conclusion is false, and the argument is unsound. Morally prohibiting religious citizens from basing their political activity on religious convictions would no more infringe on their free exercise of religion than would morally prohibiting them from treating homosexuals with a lack of respect for religious reasons. In

49 Ibid. 105.   50 Ibid. 105.   51 WWSR, 166.
52 Ibid. 176.   53 Ibid. 176.   54 IPRR, 769.

both cases, the free exercise clause constitutionally protects conduct that violates moral requirements, and as long as religious citizens are legally free to violate such requirements there has been no infringement of the free exercise of their religion.

Turn now to the second version. Something closely akin to its premise is true. Someone who tried to stop Wolterstorff from acting politically on the basis of his religious convictions would, at least if the attempt succeeded, violate the free exercise of his religion, assuming of course that his religiously based conduct was not contrary to legitimate law. However, nothing in Rawls's political liberalism justifies anyone in making an attempt of this sort, and so it is not easy to see how this premise is supposed to support a conclusion applicable to his view. Indeed I do not even find it easy to make sense of the conclusion's claim that if honoring the freedom and equality of citizens required adherence to the independent-basis principle, it would also require non-adherence. Evidently Wolterstorff thinks the independent-basis principle is self-undermining or something of that sort, but some work is needed to get at his reasons for thinking so. I presume he thinks Rawls is committed to the conclusion's antecedent. It is plausible to attribute to Rawls the thought that we are morally required to adhere to the principle in order to honor the freedom and equality of our fellow citizens because, if we did not, we would act politically on a basis they could not reasonably endorse consistent with their freedom and equality. So suppose the conclusion's antecedent is true on this interpretation. On this assumption, the conclusion's consequent should be taken to assert that we are also morally required not to adhere to the principle in order to honor the freedom and equality of our fellow citizens. The only reason I can come up with that might be offered in support of this assertion and invokes the free exercise of religion is the claim that we would violate the free exercise of religion by some of our fellow citizens and so fail to honor their freedom and equality if we adhered to the principle. But this claim is false. If we adhered to the principle, we would be committed to thinking that religious citizens who violated it when they exercised their religious freedom were doing something contrary to duty. However we would not be violating their free exercise unless we also went on to prevent them from acting in this way. Hence I can see no good reason deriving from the free exercise of religion that supports the conclusion's consequent. What is more, its consequent is pretty clearly false. We do not violate the religious freedom of fellow citizens and thus fail to honor their freedom and equality when we adhere to a principle according to which some legally permissible exercises of that freedom are contrary to moral duty, and so we are not morally required not to adhere to such a principle in order to honor their freedom and equality. Therefore, on an interpretation of the argument's conclusion which at least has the merit of making the idea of free exercise of religion cited in its premise relevant to the conclusion, the conclusion's antecedent is true while its consequent is false. Thus the conclusion as a whole is false, and the argument is unsound.

The integrity argument is meant by Wolterstorff to challenge a wide range of liberal positions. It is directed against the independent-basis principle as well as against the separation principle, according to which "government is to do nothing to advance or hinder any religion."[55] Because Rawls does endorse a version of the independent-basis principle when he includes the duty of civility within public reason, the argument applies to his view. Wolterstorff sees a common pattern in the liberal's impression that these two principles deal fairly with religion. His argument, which is worth quoting at length, continues as follows:

> That common pattern is this: The liberal assumes that requiring religious persons to debate and act politically for reasons other than religious reasons is not in violation of their *religious* convictions; likewise he assumes that an educational program which makes no reference to religion is not in violation of any parent's religious convictions. He assumes, in other words, that though religious people may not be in the *habit of* dividing their life into a religious component and a nonreligious component, and though some might be *unhappy* doing so, nonetheless, their doing so would not be in violation of anybody's religion. But he's wrong about this. It's when we bring into the picture persons for whom it is a matter of religious conviction that they ought to strive for a religiously integrated existence—it's then, especially, though not only then, that the unfairness of liberalism to religion comes to light.[56]

Wolterstorff is obviously quite fond of this argument. It appears almost word-for-word identically in both the book chapters in which he attacks liberalism![57]

I think Wolterstorff is on to something important when he makes this argument, though it will take some work to get clear about exactly what it is. Wolterstorff seems to believe the argument shows that liberalism is unfair to religion as such or to religious people generally, but it is not strong enough to do that. While there are, to be sure, some religious people for whom it is a matter of religious conviction that they ought to strive for a religiously integrated existence, there are others for whom it is not. Some people who are religiously devout are content to separate their lives into religious and non-religious spheres, acting politically for reasons other than religious reasons does not violate their religious convictions. So even if the argument is successful, its conclusion applies only to some and not to all religious citizens. In addition, there are non-religious people whose comprehensive doctrines make it a matter of conviction for them that they ought to strive for lives integrated by those doctrines. Examples include some secular Millian liberals and Marxist socialists. Hence if the argument succeeds, a parallel argument will show that liberalism is also unfair to non-religious citizens of these kinds. In other words, the question we ought to be asking is not whether liberalism is unfair to religion but whether it is unfair to a group of people, some of whose members are religious while others are not, all of whom as a matter of conviction want to live in ways tightly integrated around their comprehensive doctrines. For the sake of convenience, let us call the members of this group "the integralists."

---

[55] WWSR, 165.   [56] Ibid. 176–7.   [57] Compare *RPS*, 116.

It seems to me appropriate to ask whether Rawlsian political liberalism in particular is unfair to the integralists. As previously noted, public reason asks citizens generally to work up and be prepared to defend a political conception of justice; according to Rawls, "it is central to political liberalism that free and equal citizens affirm both a comprehensive doctrine and a political conception."[58] What is more, it also asks them to argue politically from their political conceptions rather than directly from their comprehensive doctrines. Of course it asks these two things of all free and equal citizens. But compliance is likely to be a heavier burden for the integralists than for others, because they would prefer to argue politically directly from their comprehensive doctrines and so will be skeptical of the value of working up a political conception that is to be interposed, so to speak, between their comprehensive doctrines and the public political forum. They may also fear, with some justification, that people of their sort are bound to decline in numbers and influence in a society in which the ideal of public reason becomes more fully realized over time.

It should be granted to Wolterstorff, then, that political liberalism does impose special burdens on the integralists. It may even in the long run, to the extent that it comes to prevail in a society, doom integralist forms of life, religious and non-religious alike, to extinction. But should it also be granted that Rawlsian political liberalism is, on that account, unfair to the integralists? I think not. Along with Rawls, I endorse Berlin's view that there is no social world without loss. The fact, should it turn out to be a fact, that the integralists cannot, as a matter of social necessity, reproduce themselves over time in a society well ordered by political liberalism would no doubt be cause for regret. However, as Rawls insists, such social necessities "are not to be taken for arbitrary bias or injustice."[59] Even the relatively capacious culture and institutions of liberal democracy are bound to prove uncongenial to some valuable forms of life, and integralism of various stripes may be among them. Obviously we must, with Rawls, reject the notion that "only unworthy forms of life lose out in a just constitutional regime."[60] Once that has been done, there remains no good reason to think that religion as such or integralism in general has been unfairly treated if integralist forms of life, religious and otherwise, fail to pass the historical test of enduring and gaining adherents in a liberal democratic society. So I conclude that Wolterstorff has not shown that Rawlsian political liberalism is unfair to integralist religion, much less to religion as such.

As I see it, therefore, Wolterstorff has established neither that Rawlsian political liberalism demands too much agreement in their views from those who live under a regime ordered by it nor that it is unfair to religious citizens. In other words, he has not shown that it asks too much of the religious citizens of a liberal democracy. But it may ask too much even if he has not proved that it does. Does it? I am on record as having argued that an inclusivist ideal of public political discourse

---

[58] IPRR, 800.   [59] *PL*, 197.   [60] Ibid. 198.

is more attractive, all things considered, than the ideal of public reason proposed by Rawls.[61] In concluding, let me return briefly to this issue.

It must be acknowledged that Rawls's position has become more inclusive as a result of the substitution of the wide view of public political culture for the inclusive view of public reason. Does his ideal remain, by my lights, too restrictive? This is not an easy question to answer. Rawls himself modestly concludes: "I do not know how to prove that public reason is not too restrictive, or whether its forms are properly described. I suspect it cannot be done."[62] He thinks this will not be a serious problem if, as he believes, most cases fit the framework of public reason and those that do not have special features that enable us to understand why they cause difficulty and show us how to cope with them as they arise. And I, of course, do not know how to prove that public reason is too restrictive and suspect that cannot be done either. Nor can I show that we will be unable to deal with the hard cases in the way Rawls hopes we can. It seems clear to me, moreover, that it would be foolish to abandon the ideal of public reason merely because it is restrictive to some extent. It would be highly desirable if exercises of political coercive power on fundamental questions were able to be justified to all reasonable citizens of a polity in terms of a balance of political values they could reasonably endorse as consistent with their freedom and equality even if some citizens regarded other balances of political values as more reasonable to endorse. Surely there will be some restrictions on political discourse and voting whose acceptance would be a price well worth paying in order achieve such a desirable state of affairs.

Perhaps, given prevailing circumstances in the United States here and now, it is unrealistic to expect the ideal of public reason to be attained. It is evidently not always a serious criticism of an ideal that it is unrealistic. However I think it is a serious criticism of an unrealistic ideal that imposes moral duties. Clearly Rawls conceives of his ideal of public reason as imposing a moral duty, the duty of civility. As Paul Weithman has pointed out, we should be puzzled about how moral ideals can impose moral requirements.[63] According to a somewhat different conception of moral ideals, they urge or advise conduct that is morally good but above and beyond the call of duty. On this conception, I am prepared to subscribe to the ideal of public reason, understood as including the wide view of public political culture, despite its restrictions, as a political ideal in our present circumstances. Under different and presently non-actual circumstances, for example, circumstances including the existence of an overlapping consensus on a family of reasonable political conceptions of justice by all the reasonable comprehensive doctrines present in our society, I would be prepared to subscribe

---

61 Philip L. Quinn, "Political Liberalisms and Their Exclusions of the Religious," in Weithman (ed.), *Religion and Contemporary Liberalism*, 156 [Ch. 8, p. 165 in this volume].

62 IPRR, 803.

63 Paul J. Weithman, "Citizenship, Reflective Endorsement and Political Autonomy," *Modern Schoolman*, 78 (2001), 135–49.

to the ideal of public reason conceived in the way Rawls thinks of it, as imposing a duty of civility. I take these two commitments to be a way of subscribing to articles of a liberal political faith. But I am not persuaded that the ideal of public reason, interpreted as adapted to present circumstances in the United States, imposes moral duties such as the duty of civility.

So, to ask the Kantian question implicit in the title of my paper, should religious citizens here and now live within the limits of Rawlsian public reason? I think it would be, morally speaking, very good indeed if they did, and I would encourage them to try to do so. I do not, however, think they presently act contrary to duty or are guilty of wrongdoing if, chafing at even the modest restrictions implied by the wide view, they choose not to live within those limits.

TOPICS IN CHRISTIAN
PHILOSOPHY

10

'In Adam's Fall, We Sinned All'

The great drama of sin and atonement holds a central place in Christian life and thought. It shapes Christian views of history, is recapitulated in the lives of individual Christians, and is reenacted in Christian liturgies. A large part of what is distinctively Christian in Christian theism derives from this drama. Traditionally it has been an important theme in the thought of Christian theologians and philosophers. Among those who have contributed to our store of philosophical reflections on it are Augustine, Anselm, Aquinas, Scotus, Martin Luther, John Calvin, Jonathan Edwards, and Immanuel Kant. In the light of this tradition, it is striking that sin and atonement have not been at center stage in twentieth century analytic philosophy of religion. They have not been among the doctrines that have preoccupied even those philosophers sympathetic or committed to Christianity who employ the analytic style in their work.

There are, of course, features of the philosophical scene that help to explain this neglect. One is the linguistic turn and the positivistic challenge to the meaningfulness of religious language. In response to this challenge, many philosophers of religion turned their attention away from the study of substantive religious doctrines in order to explore the bewildering variety of uses and functions of religious language. Another such feature is the epistemological turn and the skeptical challenge to the rationality of religious belief. In response to this challenge, many philosophers of religion focused their attention on the problem of justifying some sort of generic theism, for instance the claim that there is an omniscient, omnipotent, and omnibenevolent being who created and conserves the universe of contingent things. What got neglected when these two projects were dominating the agenda in philosophy of religion was the enterprise of explicating and clarifying such distinctively Christian doctrines as the Trinity, the Incarnation, Original Sin, and Vicarious Atonement. A common attitude was that such Christian mysteries are entirely outside the scope of philosophical investigation and had best be left to the theologians to ponder. It was even alleged from time to time that such distinctively Christian doctrines are demonstrably

An earlier version of this paper was presented in a symposium at the 1987 APA Pacific Division Meeting. I am grateful to Richard Swinburne for his comments on that occasion. I also wish to thank Karl Ameriks, Robert McKim, and Eleonore Stump for helpful correspondence and Alfred J. Freddoso and Nicholas Wolterstorff for stimulating discussion.

incoherent, though conclusive demonstrations of their incoherence were never produced.

Recently, however, there have been signs of something of a renaissance of interest in distinctively Christian doctrines on the part of philosophers of religion who work in the analytic mode. Sin and atonement have once again become topics that spark lively debate among philosophers of religion. This paper is intended to be a contribution to that debate. In it I examine the theories of original sin propounded by Anselm and Kant. I select those two theories to scrutinize for two reasons. First, they come at the beginning and the end, respectively, of the period in the history of Western philosophy when original sin received its most sustained and serious treatment at the hands of philosophers. So they bracket a line of theoretical development that contains within it the most acute and interesting things philosophers have so far had to say by way of explicating the doctrine of original sin. In the absence of a contemporary research literature that has fully appropriated this historical tradition, we must turn directly to it to discover the resources available to us when we begin to philosophize about original sin. Second, there is a sharp contrast between the two theories. For Anselm, the flaw in us that goes by the name 'original sin' is something we literally inherit from our first parents; for Kant, the flaw in us that goes by the name 'radical evil' is something we literally bring upon ourselves by free acts. Yet both Anselm and Kant claim scriptural warrant of one sort or another for their theories, and this suggests that the full range of options to be considered when we look for the best philosophical interpretation of the doctrine of original sin is very large. Such stark contrasts also indicate that original sin has given rise to some philosophical problems that resist easy solution.

These problems arise, of course, within the larger theological context of attempts to interpret the myth of the fall of Adam and Eve in Genesis 3. In an effort to appropriate that story for Christianity by exhibiting a network of parallel contrasts between Adam and Christ, Paul says:

> To sum up, then: just as a single offense brought condemnation to all men, a single righteous act brought all men acquittal and life. Just as through one man's disobedience all became sinners, so through one man's obedience all shall become just.[1]

Attempting to make sense of the strand of Pauline thought expressed in this and similar passages, Augustine claims:

> God, the Author of all natures but not of their defects, created man good; but man, corrupt by choice and condemned by justice, has produced a progeny that is both corrupt and condemned. For, we all existed in that one man, since, taken together, we were the one man who fell into sin through the woman who was made out of him before sin existed. Although the specific form by which each of us was to live was not yet created and assigned, our nature was already present in the seed from which we were to spring.

---

[1] Romans 5: 18–19. I quote *The New American Bible*.

And because this nature has been soiled by sin and doomed to death and justly condemned, no man was to be born of man in any other condition (my emphasis).[2]

This Augustinian view became dominant in western Christianity. To cite but one example, the ninth of the Thirty-Nine Articles of the Church of England reads in part as follows:

Original sin standeth not in the following of *Adam* (as the *Pelagians* do vainly talk); but it is the fault and corruption of the nature of every man, that naturally is engendered of the offspring of *Adam*; whereby man is very far gone from original righteousness, and of his own nature inclined to evil, so that the flesh lusteth always contrary to the Spirit; and therefore in every person born into this world, it deserveth God's wrath and damnation.[3]

Both Anselm and Kant are firmly ensconced within this Augustinian tradition of attributing depravity meriting condemnation to fallen human nature itself. Anselm represents the first sustained effort during the high middle ages to provide a rigorous theoretical foundation for the Augustinian view, and Kant represents the last serious attempt to defend the moral core of that view within the limits of Enlightenment reason.

The paper is divided into five sections. In the first section, I present a puzzle about original sin whose purpose is to make clear one of the ways in which the doctrine is philosophically problematic. In the next section I present a sketch of the account of original sin found in Anselm's *De Conceptu Virginali et Peccato Originali*. The third section is devoted to a discussion of two objections, one metaphysical and the other moral, to the Anselmian account. I argue that Anselm's theory does not provide an adequate solution to the puzzle with which we began our discussion of original sin. Then, in the fourth section, I present a summary of Kant's theory of radical evil from the *Religion innerhalb der Grenzen der blossen Vernunft* and compare it with Anselm's theory of original sin. I try to show that Kant succeeds where Anselm fails in solving our initial puzzle. In the fifth and final section, I consider the costs of this Kantian success and suggest that they may add up to something traditional Christians should not willingly pay. My conclusion will be that neither Kant nor Anselm gives us a theory of original sin that is wholly satisfactory from both philosophical and theological points of view.

A PUZZLE ABOUT ORIGINAL SIN

What is sin? A conception broad enough to encompass both Anselmian and Kantian views takes sin to be an evil for which a person deserves condemnation by a

---

[2] Augustine, *The City of God*, 13, 14. It is sometimes argued that such claims derive, at least in part, from a misinterpretation of Romans 5: 12. For discussion of the exegetical issues, see Elaine Pagels, *Adam, Eve, and the Serpent* (New York: Random House, 1988), 109 and 143 and the specialist literature cited in the note to the discussion on p. 143.

[3] Quoted in E. J. Bicknell, *A Theological Introduction to the Thirty-Nine Articles of the Church of England*, 3rd edn. (London: Longmans, Green and Co., 1955), 171.

morally perfect judge. The emphasis on desert of condemnation reflects the references to condemnation or damnation in the passages from Paul, Augustine, and the Thirty-Nine Articles quoted above; as we shall see, it also fits nicely with the judicial cast of mind displayed by both Anselm and Kant. Anselm describes sin as failure to render to God the honor due to him, and Kant characterizes sin as transgression of the moral law considered as a divine command.[4] Obviously such failures and transgressions are evils on account of which a person who is guilty of them deserves condemnation by a divine judge. Paradigmatic examples of such evils are morally wicked actions such as brutal murders and spiteful lies. Vicious character traits such as envy, pride, and malice, if acquired in the right way, are other clear cases of such evils. It seems, however, that a person deserves condemnation for an evil by a morally perfect judge only if the person is accountable for the evil. And it also seems that a person is accountable for an evil only if the evil was in some sense avoidable for the person. There are, to be sure, familiar difficulties that arise if the avoidability condition is taken too strictly. We think the drunk driver who kills a small child deserves condemnation for evil doing even if it was not within his power at the time of the accident to avoid hitting the child. But I suppose we also think that there was at some time prior to the accident something within the driver's power to do such that, if he had done it, it would have been within his power to avoid hitting the child at the time of the accident. Similarly, we think the vicious man deserves condemnation for his evil character even though he cannot shed his character like a soiled suit of clothes. But I take it we also assume that the vicious man could have avoided becoming vicious. Let us say that evils of the sort illustrated by the cases of the drunk driver and the vicious man are assumed by common sense morality to be broadly avoidable. On this supposition, we may then say it seems that a person is accountable for an evil only if the evil was broadly avoidable for the person. So, since sin is an evil for which a person deserves condemnation by a morally perfect judge, the sinner is accountable for sin and sin was broadly avoidable for the sinner, if things are as they seem to be.

We get a conception of original sin wide enough to cover both Kantian and Anselmian views if we suppose original sin to be innate sin. Kant tells us that we may call radical evil innate in human nature, and Anselm says that original sin is contracted with human nature in the very origin of the human person (Kant, *Religion*, p. 28; Anselm, *Virgin Conception*, ch. 1, p. 170). But then it becomes clear that things cannot be as they seem to be if we are to have a coherent

---

[4] Anselm of Canterbury, *Why God Became Man and The Virgin Conception and Original Sin*, tr. Joseph M. Colleran (Albany: Magi Books, 1969), 84; Immanuel Kant, *Religion Within the Limits of Reason Alone*, tr. T. M. Greene and H. H. Hudson (New York: Harper and Row, 1960), 37. Anselm gives the description cited in ch. 11 of Bk. I of *Why God Became Man*. Hereafter references to Anselm's *Virgin Conception* and Kant's *Religion* will be made parenthetically in the body of the text, and citations of Anselm's *Virgin Conception* will include chapter references for the convenience of those with editions other than the one I use.

conception of original sin. For it also seems that any evil which is innate in a person is not an evil that was broadly avoidable for the person. And, in the light of our principle linking accountability and avoidability, it further seems that any evil which is innate in a person is not an evil for which the person is accountable. Worse still, because of the connection between desert of condemnation and accountability, it seems that any evil which is innate in a person is not an evil for which the person deserves condemnation by a morally perfect judge. So it appears that, if we take original sin or radical evil to be something that is both innate and sin, it will turn out to be an evil for which its possessor both does and does not deserve condemnation by a morally perfect judge, something for which the sinner both is and is not accountable, and sin that both was and was not broadly avoidable for the sinner. Or, in other words, it will turn out that there can be no such thing as original sin or radical evil.

In order to avoid this unwelcome conclusion, we must deny at least one of the assumptions that lead to it. But all of them are apparently plausible. So which shall we choose? One way of thinking about the contrast between Anselm and Kant focuses on the differences between their theoretical options in response to this problem. Kant attempts to break the tie between innateness and unavoidability. He argues that there is a kind of evil which is properly said to be innate in a person and which is also broadly avoidable for the person. Such radical evil turns out to be something for which its possessor deserves condemnation by a morally perfect judge and is accountable, yet something that is both broadly avoidable for, and innate in, its possessor. By contrast, Anselm tries to sever the connection between accountability and avoidability.[5] He argues that there is a kind of sin for which the sinner is accountable and which is not also broadly avoidable for the sinner. Such originalsin turns out to be something for which the sinner deserves condemnation by a morally perfect judge and is accountable, but something that is innate in, and is not broadly avoidable for, the sinner. Neither of these alternatives has an air of intuitive plausibility about it. But perhaps that is only to be expected. After all, one thing our puzzle seems to show is that any theory according to which original sin is logically possible must be counterintuitive in some ways. So if we are to find one of these positions rationally preferable to

---

[5] One might try to attack the connection between accountability and avoidability by means of Frankfurt–Nozick counterexamples. Since space does not permit full discussion of this issue, I must here confine myself to a brief expression of my doubts about the force of those examples within the kind of ethical framework adopted by Anselm and Kant. Typically, they are cases in which the agent does what he or she wills and so is accountable for the action but in which, if the agent had willed otherwise, some external cause would have so affected the agent's behavior that the result would be the same. Because in such cases one can consistently add the supposition that the agent could have willed otherwise, these examples do not serve to break the connection between accountability and avoidability with respect to states of the will. And since on the intentionalistic views of Anselm and Kant nonderivate moral good and evil reside wholly in the will, it is not at all clear that such examples can get a grip on the connection at the level at which it really matters for Anselm and Kant.

the other, we must look beyond the initial appearance of implausibility they share to discover some other basis for deciding between them. Maybe such a basis will become visible if we scrutinize the larger theoretical contexts in which the two positions are embedded.

The remainder of this paper is devoted to a comparative critical examination of some of the details of the Anselmian and Kantian theories of original sin. I turn first to Anselm.

ORIGINAL SIN

Anselm begins the *De Conceptu Virginali* by drawing a sharp and irreducible contrast between original sin and personal sin. A metaphysical presupposition of this contrast is the distinction between nature and person. Each human being is metaphysically composite and includes both a nature, which makes him or her human like all the rest, and a principle of individuation, which makes him or her a particular person distinct from all the rest. Original sin is sin that one contracts with human nature at the very origin of one's existence as a person; personal sin is sin one commits at some time after one has begun to exist as a person (*Virgin Conception*, ch. 1, p. 170). Being contracted with one's human nature, original sin is inherited like a burden of genetic disease; it is innate and unavoidable. Being committed after one has begun to be an individual person, personal sin is evildoing; it is not innate and is avoidable. The two are as different as chalk and cheese. What, if anything, do they have in common in virtue of which both are kinds of sin?

Anselm's answer is that both are injustice. According to his radically intentionalistic views on ethics, justice is uprightness of the will preserved for its own sake (*Virgin Conception*, ch. 3, p. 173).[6] In a rational creature, the upright orientation of the will consists of the will being subject to the will of God. Since injustice is no positive thing but is instead a mere lack, it must be defined negatively as the absence of due justice. In other words, it is the lack of justice where justice ought to be, namely, in the will. So both justice and injustice reside in the will and there alone (*Virgin Conception*, ch. 3, pp. 172–4). The just will is one in which uprightness is preserved for its own sake; the unjust will is one in which there ought to be but is not uprightness preserved for its own sake. In rational creatures, the just will is one subject to the will of God, and the unjust will is one that ought to be but is not subject to the will of God. Because all sin is injustice, it too resides only in the will. A sinful will is one in which there ought to be but is not an upright orientation preserved for its own sake; it is one which should be but is not subject to the will of God. Since any failure of the will to be duly subject to the will of God is a deviation from the will's proper upright orientation, sin consists of the will being disordered both with respect to its own proper orientation and in relation to God's will.

---

[6] This definition comes from Anselm's *On Truth*.

It is easy enough to see how to apply these considerations to the elucidation of personal sin. To commit a personal sin is to disobey God in deed. The sinner's will, which should have remained subject to God's by obeying his commands, refuses to be subject to God's will when it disobeys his commands. It thereby loses its upright orientation and comes to be characterized by an absence of due uprightness preserved for its own sake. So it becomes unjust. Thus personal sin is injustice. It is more difficult to make sense of the notion that original sin is injustice too. One who suffers from original sin must begin to exist as a person lacking an upright orientation of the will; when such a person contracts human nature, along with it must come a will already not subject to God's will. This may not be too difficult to understand, though we must buy into a sort of Lamarckian view of inheritance if we think of our disoriented wills as inherited from ancestors who acquired disoriented wills by their own actions. Perhaps there is no problem in grasping what it would be like to come to be a person with a will already so damaged and disordered that it lacks upright orientation and is not subject to the will of God. So the mere absence of justice in the will when one begins to be a person need not be a source of fatal perplexity. But more than the mere absence of justice is required for original sin. Original sin is injustice, and justice and injustice are contraries. Injustice is not the mere absence of justice; it is instead the absence of justice where justice ought to be. So we must suppose that one who suffers from original sin begins to exist as a person with a will that ought to possess justice; such a person's will ought to have an upright orientation and be subject to God's will from the very beginning of personal existence. And this is to be supposed despite the fact that the will in question is innately lacking in justice and so does not have an upright orientation at the beginning of personal existence. But maybe even this supposition is not too much to swallow. It may be said that many things which ought to be the case are not the case. The real sticking point comes with the next assumption we must make. For we must further suppose that one who suffers from original sin begins to exist as a person with a will that ought to possess justice in a sense in which that will's lack of the justice it ought to possess makes it sinful and so unjust. To suppose this, however, is to endorse the claim that the lack of uprightness in the will of one who suffers from original sin from the beginning of personal existence is, in spite of being innate and so unavoidable for the sinner, none the less an evil for which the sinner deserves condemnation by a morally perfect judge and is accountable. And this is a very disturbing claim.

Faced with this hard saying, one might well wonder whether Anselm can really mean it. Could it be that he only means to claim that we begin to exist as persons with wills from which uprightness and so justice are absent? Must we read him as asserting also that this absence is sinful and so unjust? I think we must. Anselm explicitly considers the objection that original sin is no more real sin than a painted man is a real man. In response, he notes that, if this were so, an infant who died without Baptism, having no sin but original sin, either would not be condemned or would be condemned without sin. But, says Anselm blandly, we do not accept this consequence (*Virgin Conception*, ch. 3, p. 173). He holds that infants who die without Baptism, having committed no personal sins, are condemned. Since they are condemned by God, who is a morally perfect judge, they are not condemned without sin. Hence, original sin is real sin. It is an evil for which an unbaptized infant deserves condemnation by a morally perfect judge and so is accountable, although it is innate in and unavoidable for the unbaptized infant. Moreover, Anselm denies that an unbaptized infant's inability to possess justice excuses its lack of justice. He claims that the absence of uprightness of the will preserved for its own sake is sinful and so unjust in unbaptized infants because justice is required of infants before Baptism and there is no excuse for its absence in them (*Virgin Conception*, ch. 29, p. 210). Curiously, but not surprisingly, Anselm takes inability to possess justice to be a complete excuse for the absence of uprightness of will in baptized infants, who cannot even understand yet what it is to have an upright will preserved for its own sake. He reasons that the absence of justice in a baptized infant cannot be sinful because in Baptism all the sins that existed in the infant before Baptism are entirely wiped out. So the absence of justice in a baptized infant is not injustice; justice is not even required of baptized infants. This is because what is impossible apart from all fault is not required, and baptized infants who have committed no personal sins are without any fault but unable to have an upright will preserved for its own sake (*Virgin Conception*, ch. 29, p. 211).

But what, then, is the fault in unbaptized infants that precludes their inability to possess justice from serving as an excuse for the lack of uprightness in their wills and allows uprightness of will to be required of them, though it is not required of baptized infants in whom the inability to possess justice serves as an excuse for its absence? And whence comes this terrible fault that is in the unbaptized infant from the beginning of its existence as a person and so is unavoidable for it? In order to get at the answers Anselm returns to these questions, we must next turn our attention to his account of the manner in which that fault is transmitted from our first parents to us.

According to Anselm, the mechanism by which sin passes from Adam and Eve to their descendants is causal, and the causal pathway passes through human nature. Anselm initially puts this point in terms of what we might think of as a two-way transmission principle. What is personal passes over to the nature, and what is natural passes over to the person (*Virgin Conception*, ch. 23, p. 202). Thus, by the first half of this principle, the sin of Adam and Eve passes over to human nature, and, by its second half, the sin of human nature passes over to their descendants. By a two-step process, then, sin is handed on from Adam and Eve to their descendants. But, of course, this initial formulation is too crude. It is apt to mislead us into thinking of sin as a sort of stuff that could literally be transmitted from one person to another like the viral particles that cause a communicable disease. And if we operated under the influence of this picture, we might well be tempted to think that the sin which is in infants from the very moment they begin to exist as persons is numerically identical with, or is a part of, the sin of Adam and Eve. But, if that were so, infants who die unbaptized and are condemned would be condemned for the sin of another or others. This Anselm will not allow, presumably because a morally perfect judge would not condemn one person for the sin of another. He is at pains to insist that the sin of Adam and Eve is discernible from the sins of infants. Adam and Eve were unjust, not because someone else abandoned required justice, but because they themselves did; newly born infants are unjust, not because they abandoned required justice, but because someone else did (*Virgin Conception*, ch. 26, p. 207). Hence the sin of Adam and Eve is distinct from the sins of infants. When an infant is condemned for original sin, Anselm tells us, the infant is not condemned for the sin of Adam and Eve. Instead, the infant is condemned for a sin of its own, for it would not be condemned unless it had sin of its own. What we should say, when speaking strictly, is that the sin of Adam and Eve causes the sin of the infant. Accordingly, a more precise version of Anselm's two-way transmission principle is this: What is personal causes what is natural, and what is natural causes what is personal. Thus the persons Adam and Eve make human nature sinful by the first half of this principle; they do this by deviating from the uprightness of will with which they were created and which they were empowered to preserve by their creator. And sinful human nature in turn makes the descendants of Adam and Eve sinful in their own right, from the very first moment they possess it, by the second half of this principle; it does this by a natural necessity with which the nature's destitution of required justice causes those whom the nature propagates from itself also to be destitute of required justice and so unjust (*Virgin Conception*, ch. 23, pp. 202–3).

But how are we to understand the two links in this causal chain? Consider the first part of the causal story, according to which the sin of Adam and Eve makes human nature itself sinful. How is this possible? For Anselm, all sin is injustice, and injustice, the absence of required justice, can only reside in a will. So sin exists only in the will. It thus appears that nothing can be sinful unless it possesses a will of its own. But how are we to make sense of the notion that human nature has a will of its own? Consider the second part of the causal story, according to which sinful human nature makes the descendants of Adam and Eve sinful by natural necessity. How is this possible? The nature's lack of justice causes the descendants of Adam and Eve to be destitute of justice by natural necessity. Yet justice is required of those descendants, since its absence in them is sinful. It thus appears that something can be required of a person that the person lacks by natural necessity. And this seems to violate the moral ought-implies-can principle because the requirement in question is such that failure to fulfill it merits condemnation by a morally perfect judge. So how are we to make sense of the notion that there is sin which occurs by natural necessity? Grave difficulties lurk in this neighborhood.

We will be able to appreciate the answers Anselm gives to these questions only if we are prepared to enter with some sympathy into a world of thought very different from our own. We tend to take it for granted that a nature is an abstract entity of some sort. We might, for instance, think of human nature as a complex property, perhaps rationality and animality conjoined, such that all humans instantiate it and nothing could be a human without instantiating it. On this view of the matter, it seems absurd to suppose that human nature has a will of its own and is capable of sinning. But this view is not Anselm's. He has a homuncular view of human nature itself; it is, so to speak, an extra actor on the scene. It has its own obligations and commits its own sins. Anselm says:

And because the whole of human nature was in them [Adam and Eve] and there was nothing pertaining to it that was not in them, it was weakened and corrupted in its entirety. There remained in it, therefore, the obligation of being in the state of undiminished justice which it had received free from any injustice, and the obligation of making satisfaction for having abandoned justice, along with the state of corruption which it incurred on account of sin. *Hence, just as, if it had not sinned, it would have been propagated in the same condition in which it had been created by God, so, after sin, it is propagated in the condition in which it put itself by sinning* (my emphasis; *Virgin Conception*, ch. 2, p. 171).

Since this homunculus, human nature, commits its own sin, it must have a will of its own that is capable of deviating from an upright orientation which is required of it. And so we would expect Anselm to explain the causal connection between the sin of Adam and Eve and the sinfulness of human nature in terms of a connection between their sinning and its sinning. This is just what we find Anselm doing. The person made the nature sinful, he tells us, because when Adam and Eve sinned, man sinned (*Virgin Conception*, ch. 23, p. 202). Indeed, Anselm occasionally goes farther and claims that, when any human person at all commits sin, man commits sin, so that human nature is rendered more sinful by each personal sin committed by a human (*Virgin Conception*, ch. 27, p. 208). These are alien ideas indeed.

Moreover, this homuncular view of human nature answers questions in one place only to raise them in others. It might occur to one to ask: How many sinners and how many sins were there in the Garden of Eden? Adam and Eve sinned. They are distinct persons, and they committed distinct personal sins. But human nature sinned when they did. It is distinct from both of them, for it is in their descendants but they are not. And its sin is distinct from theirs, because their sins were personal sins and its sin was not. So there were three sinners and three sins in the Garden. But it seems that this is one sinner and one sin too many! Thus it appears that the homuncular view of human nature gives rise to a slight problem of overpopulation. Furthermore, it does little to cast light on the problem of how the sin of the nature can cause descendants of Adam and Eve who possess that nature to be sinful. On the assumption that human nature sins, we may suppose that it deviates from an uprightness of will it was required to preserve and so becomes unjust. So we may conclude that it deserves condemnation by a morally perfect judge. We may also suppose that lack of justice in the nature brings it about that the descendants of Adam and Eve who possess that nature lack justice by natural necessity. But it does not follow from these suppositions that those descendants are unjust, for it does not follow that justice is required of them. So we may not conclude without further ado that they deserve condemnation by a morally perfect judge. To put it crudely, on this scenario it is the nature that is the sinner and not the descendants of Adam and Eve who possess it. Though they do lack justice, this alone is not enough to make them unjust. In addition, justice would have to be required of them, and it is hard to see how a morally perfect judge could impose such a requirement. After all, their lack of justice was not avoidable for them; justice is absent from their wills by natural necessity. When we consider an unbaptized infant who has committed no personal sins, it still looks as though it is only the nature possessed by the infant, and not the infant itself, from which justice was ever required. Thus, even on the homuncular view of human nature, it continues to seem that the infant is not unjust and hence is no sinner. Though the lack of justice in the infant's will is no doubt a very great evil of some kind, perhaps a misfortune worse than blindness, it appears not to be an evil for which the infant deserves condemnation by a morally perfect judge who also knows that this evil arises from a sin of the nature and not from any personal sin of the infant. Or, at least, so it appears to me. Thus I think the homuncular view of human nature does nothing to help us make sense of the notion that there is sin, as opposed to the mere faultless absence of an upright orientation of the will, that occurs by natural necessity.

In order to complete my account of Anselm's theory of original sin, I need to draw attention to one important way in which what has been said so far must be qualified. It merits some consideration both because Anselm himself devotes a fair amount of space to discussing it and because it is of some independent theological interest. This qualification is required if Anselm's account of original sin is to be rendered consistent with orthodox Christian views about the Incarnation. If sinful human nature were to make all the descendants of Adam and Eve sinful by natural necessity, Christ, who is a fully human descendant of Adam and Eve, would be sinful by natural necessity like the rest of postlapsarian humanity. But Christ, who is also God, is impeccable; he is not one of those in whom there is original sin. So sinful human nature does not make all the human descendants of Adam and Eve sinful. How are we to account for the exception in Christ's case in a way that does not smack of the ad hoc?[7] Anselm's ingenious answer to this question derives from a distinction he draws among three kinds of causation. Everything that occurs, he tells us, occurs either by the will of God

---

[7] Anselm devotes chapters 11–21 of *Virgin Conception* to spelling out his complicated answer to this question. He explicitly denies the doctrine of the Immaculate Conception of Mary in ch. 16 of Bk. II of *Why God Became Man*.

alone, or by nature operating by means of powers bestowed on it by its creator, or by the will of a creature (*Virgin Conception*, ch. 11, p. 187). Sin propagates from Adam and Eve to all and only their descendants generated entirely by the natural power of procreation combined with human volition, and any human produced marvelously by the will of God alone from matter that lacks by itself the natural power to generate humans is without original sin. Adam was produced marvelously by the will of God alone from slime; Eve was produced marvelously by the will of God alone from Adam's rib; and Christ the man was produced marvelously by the will of God alone from a virgin. Slime, ribs, and virgins lack by themselves natural powers to generate humans, and so Adam, Eve, and Christ the man are without original sin. No sin propagates from Adam and Eve to Christ because he is not generated from them entirely by the natural power of procreation coupled with human volition. Christ is an exception to the general rule but not a counterexample to the principle of propagation of sin that Anselm endorses.

We have before us now the outlines of Anselm's account of original sin. It is a clever theoretical construction, but it cries out for philosophical criticism. In the next section I respond to this crying need for criticism.

OBJECTIONS TO ANSELM'S ACCOUNT

The main objections to Anselm's theory of original sin may be grouped under two broad headings, the metaphysical and the moral. Under the metaphysical heading I place those criticisms which allege that Anselm's account of the causal mechanisms by which sin is propagated is in one way or another defective. Moral objections are those according to which Anselm's account has morally repugnant consequences.

According to Anselm, there are three stages in the causal process by which sin propagates from Adam and Eve to their descendants. The first stage is that at which sin originates in the personal sin of Adam and Eve; the second stage is that at which the personal sin of Adam and Eve makes human nature sinful; and the third stage is that at which sinful human nature makes the descendants of Adam and Eve other than Christ sinful from the very outset of their human lives. At least one objection with some persuasive force can be mounted against the Anselmian story of each of these three stages.

Consider first the Anselmian account of the origins of sin. It takes for granted the literal, historical truth of the bulk of the scriptural story of Adam and Eve. Such naive literalism may well have been understandable, and even rational, in a person of Anselm's time and place, but it is doubtful that it is rational for an educated person in our culture. We know too much about literature and history to be persuaded by such scriptural literalism. Thus we properly find the details of the scriptural myth of the origins of sin and of the Anselmian story based on that myth, read literally, lacking in historical plausibility. We should not, therefore, assume with Anselm that the story of Adam and Eve in the Garden of Eden represents sober historical truth about the origins of human sin.

The Anselmian account of the causal link between the personal sin of Adam and Eve and the sinfulness of human nature fares no better as a candidate for sober metaphysical truth. Its infirmities derive chiefly from the fact that it depends on a homuncular conception of human nature. It is simply not to be believed that man sinned when Adam and Eve sinned; the thought that human nature has a will of its own and commits sins is intrinsically incredible. Whatever human nature may be, it surely is not an extra actor on the scene, overpopulating the Garden of Eden. If we go along with Anselm in assuming that all sin is injustice and that injustice, like justice, exists only in the will of a rational being, we should draw the line at attributing sin to human nature. We should not, therefore, agree with Anselm that the personal sin of Adam and Eve makes human nature literally sinful or somehow transmits sin to human nature. Instead we should look for some better way to characterize the damage done to human nature by the sin of Adam and Eve if we continue to insist upon a theory according to which the personal sin of Adam and Eve brings about some harm to human nature itself or corruption of it.

But, as I see it, the most serious defect of the Anselmian account is that it lets us down worst at precisely the point where we most desperately need enlightenment. This is the point at which it must be explained how sinful human nature can make the descendants of Adam and Eve who possess it by virtue of the natural power of procreation coupled with human volition sinful rather than merely unfortunate. On the homuncular hypothesis, human nature is sinful because it has abandoned justice, and so it is unjust because it lacks required justice. This explains why it deserves condemnation by a morally perfect judge. Since it lacks justice itself after the fall of Adam and Eve, all the postlapsarian people other than Christ who possess it will be by nature lacking in justice. Justice will be absent from their wills by natural necessity. But all this is not sufficient to explain why those postlapsarian people are unjust, if indeed they are. Anselm insists that the absence of justice is not injustice except in a being that should have justice, and what has not been explained is why those unfortunate postlapsarian people should have justice. Worse still, since the absence of justice is innate in them, it is unavoidable for them. The lack of justice that is theirs by natural necessity seems to give us good reason to suppose that it is not the case that they should have justice. It seems that they are not accountable for their innate and unavoidable lack of justice, and so it appears that they do not deserve condemnation by a morally perfect judge, apart from any personal sins they may commit. They lack justice because their nature does, and so its sinfulness explains their misfortune. But nothing in the story explains why their misfortune is sinful, and some elements in the story point toward the opposite conclusion. We should not, therefore, succumb to the illusion that Anselm's account would, even if it were in other respects acceptable, provide us with a completely satisfactory explanation of why the descendants of Adam and Eve who are made to lack justice by the nature they possess are thereby made sinful.

In my opinion, these three objections to Anselm's theory of original sin add up to a powerful cumulative case against it. But their force extends only to the particularities of the Anselmian account; they do not as they stand tell against the general project of constructing a causal theory of the propagation of sin from the remote past down to the present. Perhaps there is a better causal story to be told than the one Anselm recounts. His, after all, was only the first in a long line stretching through the Middle Ages. The moral objection I shall consider next is more troublesome. It reaches beyond Anselm's causal story and strikes at the heart of the traditional Augustinian notion of original sin. If it succeeds, it demands a more radical response than tinkering with the details of a causal theory about sin propagation.

Up to this point in the argument I have been silent about what happens to those who are deservedly condemned by a morally perfect judge. In the Anselmian scheme of things, punishment follows upon such a condemnation. Those who are deservedly condemned are excluded from everlasting life in the kingdom of heaven. Following Augustine, Anselm holds that there is no third thing in the afterlife between a life of everlasting happiness in heaven and a life of everlasting misery in hell (*Virgin Conception*, ch. 28, pp. 209–10). So, in the Anselmian scheme of things, those who are deservedly condemned suffer everlasting punishment in hell. The application of this stern doctrine to the particular case of infants who die unbaptized is straightforward and a little terrifying. Every human winds up either saved in heaven or condemned in hell, and no human who dies in a state of sin winds up saved in heaven. Hence, every human who dies in a state of sin winds up condemned in hell. But every infant who dies unbaptized is a human who dies in a state of sin. Therefore, every infant who dies unbaptized winds up condemned in hell. By means of this simple argument Anselm's position leads directly to a morally repugnant conclusion.

It is to the credit of the later medievals that they were unwilling to accept this conclusion and so they claimed that there is a third thing between everlasting happiness in heaven and everlasting misery in hell. In limbo, infants who die unbaptized and are excluded from heaven live everlastingly without any pain of loss, because they have no knowledge of heavenly things. But making room for infants who die unbaptized in limbo instead of placing them in hell is only a palliative measure; it mitigates but does not remove the moral repugnancy. Being excluded from the everlasting happiness of heaven is a terrible deprivation, even if those who suffer it have no knowledge of what they are missing and so suffer no pain of loss. Moreover, though the question of the exact kind of deprivation infants who die unbaptized are to suffer makes the issue of their fate valid, this is not the deepest moral concern their case forces to our attention. The central moral question is whether infants who die unbaptized deserve condemnation by a morally perfect judge at all. If they do not, then their condemnation by one who will determine their place in the afterlife will be morally barbaric, regardless of whether it leads to the more repugnant miseries of hell or to the less repugnant deprivations of limbo.

Anselm's view is that infants who die unbaptized do deserve condemnation by a morally perfect judge because they lack required justice (*Virgin Conception*, ch. 29, p. 211). Because the justice which is absent from them is required of them, they are accountable for this lack; the absence of justice in them is not merely a misfortune for them but is also a fault in them. It is in some sense their fault; they are blameworthy for it. Yet it is a consequence of Anselm's own theory of the causal process by which they come to exist as persons suffering from this absence of justice that their lack of justice is a matter of natural necessity. It is innate in them, and it is unavoidable for them. The two parts of this position will be consistent only if accountability does not entail avoidability. As far as I can tell, Anselm's theory of original sin contains no convincing case for denying that accountability entails avoidability. Absent considerations strong enough to outweigh the intuitions that speak in favor of the entailment, our presumption should be that the entailment holds. We should, therefore, reason in the following manner. Because the lack of justice in infants who die unbaptized is unavoidable for them, they are not accountable for that lack. Justice is not required of them, since they are not accountable for its absence in them. And so they do not deserve condemnation by a morally perfect judge for their lack of justice, though this lack is surely a misfortune, because justice is not required of them and its absence in them does not make them unjust. Given his views about how infants who die unbaptized come to lack justice, Anselm cannot consistently hold that such infants deserve condemnation by a morally perfect judge. And it is, in any case, morally barbarous to maintain that those infants deserve such condemnation if one shares Anselm's other views. I submit that Anselm's theory of original sin comes to grief on the rocks of this moral objection. The shipwreck of the Anselmian theory leaves us stranded unless we can find a replacement for it that does not suffer from its infirmities or their like. Precisely at this point in our search Kant's theory of radical evil has something important to offer us. It promises to show us one way to get around all the objections I have directed against the Anselmian account. I turn now to the task of exploring that promise.

RADICAL EVIL

Like Anselm, Kant supposes we may say that humans are by nature morally evil and so deserve condemnation by a morally perfect judge unless there is atonement for this evil (*Religion*, p. 27). Kant proposes to explain how it is possible for humans to be morally evil by nature, remaining within the limits of reason as these limits are defined in the context of his larger philosophical system. The key to this explanation is his claim that there is in humans a propensity to evil. It is this propensity that plays the role of original sin in Kant's theory; he even calls it *peccatum originarium* (*Religion*, p. 26). So we need to focus our attention on Kant's account of the propensity to evil if we are to understand what is to be made of the doctrine of original sin within the bounds of Kantian reason.

A propensity is one among several ways in which the faculty of desire can be related to its objects. It is, Kant tells us, a predisposition to crave a delight which, when once experienced, arouses in the subject an inclination to it (*Religion*, p. 24). Some children of my acquaintance have propensities to chocolate candy. When they had never tasted chocolate, they had no desire for it, but once they had sampled it, they immediately developed a craving for it. Other children have no propensity to chocolate candy. Even after they have tried chocolate repeatedly, they have no craving for it. Such propensities are innate in those who possess them. Presumably there is a causal explanation in terms of natural laws for their presence in those who possess them and a similar explanation for their absence in those who lack them. Kant describes such propensities as physical because they pertain to their possessors considered as natural things, wholly determined by causal laws (*Religion*, p. 26).

If all propensities were physical propensities, then even if there were a propensity to evil in humans, it would not itself be morally evil and so would not make the humans who possessed it morally evil by nature. According to Kant, whatever results entirely from natural laws is morally indifferent; such things stand in no relation to the moral law and so are neither forbidden nor permitted by it (*Religion*, p. 18). So a physical propensity to evil would be morally indifferent. Not being forbidden by the moral law, it would not be morally evil, and, not being permitted by the moral law, it would not be morally good. Thus if a propensity to evil is to make the humans who possess it morally evil, there must be at least one propensity that is not a physical propensity. Kant describes such nonphysical propensities as moral because they pertain to their possessors considered as moral beings, who freely determine themselves to action. Since nothing is morally evil but free action and what derives from it, a moral propensity to evil that is itself morally evil has to be a product of the exercise of freedom. Though the propensity to evil can be represented as innate, Kant tells us, it should not be represented merely as innate. It should also be represented as brought by humans upon themselves (*Religion*, p. 24). Indeed, it must be represented in this way if it is to be thought of as a moral propensity that makes those who possess it morally evil.

But is this feat of double representation possible? How can a single thing be coherently represented both as innate in its possessors and as brought by them upon themselves? These questions parallel general questions that Kant must answer for all morally significant human actions. Taken as events within the spatial and temporal framework of the phenomenal realm, human actions are causally determined by natural laws. If human actions were no more than such events, they would stand in no relation to the moral law and so would be morally indifferent. Because nothing is morally good or morally evil but free action and what derives from it, human actions that are morally good or evil have to be products of the exercise of freedom. Though they can be represented as causally determined events, they should not be represented merely thus. They should also be represented as products of the exercise of freedom, and, indeed, they must be so represented if they are to be thought of as morally good or morally evil. Here is another problematic task of double representation. How is it possible for a single thing to be coherently represented both as a causally determined event and as a product of the exercise of freedom? Because the problem of double representation in the case of the propensity to evil parallels the problem in the case of morally significant human actions, one might expect Kant to try to reduce the former problem to the latter in order to give a tightly unified solution to both. This is exactly what we find him doing. First he presents an account of free human actions, and then he extends this theory, with minor modifications, to cover the case of the propensity to evil.

In order for a human action to be free in the strong libertarian sense Kant deems necessary for moral significance, there must be something in its generation that is completely subject to the spontaneity of the human agent (*Religion*, p. 19). Kant takes this to be the maxim of the action. A maxim for a particular action specifies a fairly full intentional characterization of the action to be done. This characterization incorporates both a description of what is to be done and a description of the incentives for doing that thing. The adoption of maxims is completely subject to the spontaneity of the human agent; the agent is free in the libertarian sense with respect to adopting maxims for action. Once a maxim has been adopted, the incentives incorporated into that maxim determine the agent's will to action, and the agent endeavors to perform the action specified by the maxim adopted. So, although the will of the human agent is determined to action by incentives, the agent remains free to choose among incentives in virtue of being free with respect to the choice among maxims incorporating different incentives or arrangements of incentives.

What are the incentives for a human will? Some of them, our inclinations or sensuous desires, derive from our sensuous or animal nature. They are, so to speak, implanted in us by nature, and so they are, by themselves, neither morally good nor morally evil (*Religion*, p. 30). If inclinations were the only incentives for a human will, they would automatically determine the will to action, and actions so caused would be neither morally good nor morally evil. But inclinations are not the only incentives for a human will; respect for the moral law is also an incentive for the human will. Therefore the choice among maxims incorporating different incentives or arrangements of incentives involves choice as to whether inclinations alone, or respect for the moral law alone, or some combination of the two is to determine the will to action. And so it appears that Kant's solution to the problem of double representation for particular human actions comes to this.

They can be represented as causally determined events because some incentive determines the will to action when the agent performs them, and they can also be represented as products of the exercise of freedom because the will freely adopts the maxim on which the agent acts and in which is incorporated the incentive or arrangement of incentives that determines the agent's will to action. But if this solution is to work, the will's adoption of a maxim for action cannot itself be an action that is an event in time. For the adoption of a maxim for action would be a causally determined event in the phenomenal realm, and so would not be free, if it were an event in time at all. Thus we must represent the free adoption of maxims as effected by some sort of atemporal act on the part of the agent whose maxims they are.

The important role the incentive of respect for the moral law plays in Kant's account of the human condition warrants special emphasis. One can imagine finite rational beings for whom inclinations are the only incentives; perhaps Hume, when he claims that reason is the slave of the passions, is supposing that we are such beings. Or one can imagine finite rational beings in whom the incentive of respect for the moral law is never sufficient by itself to determine the will to action but always requires the assistance of the incentives of inclination when it contributes to determining the will to action (*Religion*, p. 21). As Kant sees it, actual humans are not of either of the two imagined kinds. In humans, the incentive of respect for the moral law can suffice all by itself to determine the will to action. We are aware that respect for the moral law can be the sole and sufficient determining ground of the will because we recognize that respect for the moral law ought to be by itself a sufficient incentive for our wills. It is this awareness that informs us of the independence of our wills from determination by all other incentives, that is, of our freedom, and at the same time of our accountability for all our morally significant actions (*Religion*, p. 21). So there is in humans a capacity for respect for the moral law to be a sufficient incentive of the will in and of itself.

Kant takes this capacity to be a predisposition that is an original constituent of human nature in the sense that it is bound up with the possibility of human nature (*Religion*, p. 23). He describes it as the predisposition to personality; humans possess it because they are rational and at the same time accountable beings. Like animality and rationality, personality is essential to being a full-fledged human; one could not lack it and be fully human. As Kant puts it, the predisposition to personality is an element in the fixed character and destiny of man (*Religion*, p. 21). Because it is a component in human nature and not a product of the exercise of human freedom, the predisposition to personality is neither morally good nor morally evil. It is a predisposition to moral good because it enables its possessors to act from respect for the moral law and thereby to act for the sake of duty. But it is not a morally good predisposition. It serves as the ground in the moral agent's character of actions done from respect for the moral law. Therefore, it is the subjective ground of the possibility of the adherence of maxims to what the moral law requires.

If human agents endowed with the predisposition to personality exercised the capacity for respect for the moral law to be by itself a sufficient incentive of the will whenever they acted, all their actions in accord with the moral law, that is, their legal actions, would also be morally good. But, it is a sad fact that human agents often do not act with respect for the moral law serving by itself to determine their wills to action. Sometimes, even though their conduct accords with the letter of the moral law, it is not motivated by respect for the law; they do their duty but do not do it for duty's sake. On other occasions, their actions are neither legal nor motivated by respect for the law; they do not do their duty and do not act for the sake of duty. Such conduct is morally evil. And, just as there is, according to Kant, a ground in the moral agent's character of actions done from respect for the moral law, so also considerations of theoretical symmetry demand that there be a ground in the moral agent's character of actions not done solely from respect for the law. So there must also be a subjective ground of the possibility of the deviation of maxims from what the moral law requires. The propensity to evil is precisely this subjective ground (*Religion*, p. 24).

However, there is an important disanalogy between the predisposition to good and the propensity to evil that makes the propensity to evil a subjective ground of a very peculiar sort. Though the predisposition to good is not itself morally good, the propensity to evil is itself morally evil. So the propensity to evil cannot be an original constituent of human nature, bound up with its very possibility; it cannot be an element in the fixed character and destiny of man. Instead, it must be a product of the exercise of freedom because its possessors are morally evil in virtue of having it and so must be accountable for having it. In Kant's account of human free actions, maxims freely adopted were the products of the exercise of freedom. Kant's bold reductive stroke is to extend this idea to the analysis of the propensity to evil. It is the underlying common ground, itself a maxim and so freely adopted, of all particular morally evil maxims (*Religion*, p. 16). This supreme maxim, Kant tells us, is a rule made by the will for the use of its freedom (*Religion*, p. 17). We may think of it as a general policy, freely adopted by one who has it, for adopting maxims of particular actions. It is, as it were, a metamaxim, a maxim of maxims which applies to the whole use of the agent's freedom.

Because the propensity to evil applies to the whole use of the agent's freedom and is the underlying ground of all morally evil maxims of particular actions that are represented as events in time, we cannot represent it as having been acquired by the agent at some time after birth. Since it is taken to be in the agent antecedent to every use of freedom that produces particular actions in the temporal realm of phenomenal experience, it must be represented as innate in the agent and thus conceived of as present in the agent at birth (*Religion*, p. 17). However, it must not be thought of as caused to be in the agent by the event of birth or any other event in time. For if its presence in the agent were determined by any such causal origins, it would be morally indifferent and not morally evil. And, if it were to have such a causal origin in time, it would not be a product of freedom and the agent would not be accountable for possessing it. Moreover, because the propensity to evil is a subjective determining ground of the will that is present in the agent antecedent to all the actions in time which are grounded in it, the act by which the agent brings this propensity upon himself or herself cannot be itself an action in time. So it must be, Kant says, intelligible action, cognizable by pure reason alone, apart from every temporal condition (*Religion*, pp. 26–7). In other words, we must think of the evil supreme maxim that is the propensity to evil as being adopted by the agent whose supreme maxim it is in some sort of atemporal act. But, in this respect, the supreme maxim does not differ from the maxims of particular actions. As was pointed out previously, we must also represent those maxims as being adopted by the agent whose maxims they are in some sort of atemporal act. Only thus can we think of the adoption of any maxim as an exercise of freedom, for only thus can we represent the act of adoption as escaping the causal determinism in terms of natural laws that constitutes the phenomenal realm of events in time.

A double representation of the morally evil propensity to moral evil is thus possible. It can be represented as innate in its possessors because, as the underlying ground of all morally evil actions in time, it is to be thought of as present in its possessors antecedent to all such actions and so as present in them from birth, though we must not lose sight of the fact that this way of thinking does no more than to furnish us with a temporal representation of its priority as ground over the actions in time that it serves to ground. And it can also be represented as brought by its possessors upon themselves because it is a maxim whose adoption is an atemporal free act on the part of its possessors, and so it is something for which they are accountable. Humans are, therefore, by nature morally evil only in the sense that the morally evil propensity to evil is, as far as we can tell on the basis of the empirical evidence available to us, universal among humankind. As Kant puts it, given what we know of humans through experience, we may presuppose moral evil to be subjectively necessary to every human, even to the best of them (*Religion*, p. 27). Humans are not by nature morally evil in the sense that moral evil is a constituent of human nature, bound up with its very possibility, or an element in the fixed character and destiny of man. Thus there could be, even if there happens not to be, a fully human being who is without even a propensity to moral evil.

The contrast between Kant and Anselm on original sin is striking. If we represent Kantian moral law as a divine command, we may think of moral evil, which involves transgression of the moral law, as sin. The morally evil propensity to evil, Kant's *peccatum originarium*, is then literally the result of personal sin on the part of each and every human who has this propensity. No wonder then that all those who have a propensity to evil on that account deserve condemnation by a morally perfect judge. Since the propensity to evil is a product of the exercise of freedom in each of those who possess it, it is something for which each of them is accountable but also something each of them could have, by his or her own powers, avoided having. The propensity to evil is not something built into human nature; nor is it something that any human has as the result of causal determination by natural laws. So no human has a propensity to evil by natural necessity. By contrast, Anselm's original sin is in postlapsarian humans other than Christ by natural necessity. It is not avoidable for those humans and is not a product of the exercise of their freedom. Precisely because it is not the result of personal sin on the part of all the descendants of Adam and Eve who suffer from it, it is hard to see why they deserve condemnation by a morally perfect judge on account of it, for it is difficult to understand how they could be accountable for it.

Kant gives a tightly unified account of moral evil. Both the propensity to evil and particular evil actions in time derive from sources of the same kind; in both cases, the source of moral evil is a free atemporal act of adopting maxims that deviate from the moral law. The Kantian account of moral evil is constructed with a stunning economy of means. It needs no causal story about the propagation of sin from Adam and Eve to their descendants by means of the conjunction of the natural power of procreation and of human volition. Thus it cannot be faulted, as Anselm's account of original sin can be, for relying on a causal story about propagation that is in various ways defective. Better still, the Kantian account of the propensity to evil is immune to the moral difficulties that bedevil the Anselmian theory of original sin. Because the propensity to evil is a product of the exercise of freedom on the part of one who has it, it is clearly a moral evil for which its possessor deserves condemnation by a morally perfect judge. It is imputable to its possessors, and they are accountable for having it. But it is also avoidable for any human since it derives from the libertarian freedom of spontaneity in each human who brings it upon himself or herself. And, though it may be represented as innate in those who possess it since it grounds all their morally evil actions in time, the propensity to evil is not caused to be in them by some defective feature of their human nature, and it does not inhere in them by natural necessity of any kind.

The Kantian theory of radical evil, according to which it is a morally evil propensity to moral evil, thus has philosophical advantages Anselm's account of original sin lacks. Kant benefits by the comparison. But costs usually accompany benefits, and both should be included in our final reckoning. So my next job is to count the costs of the Kantian theory.

COSTS OF KANT'S THEORY

It would be unfair to take seriously the objection that Anselm's account of original sin is flawed because it involves an unbelievable mechanism for the propagation of sin from Adam and Eve to their descendants other than Christ and not at least to entertain a similar objection directed against Kant's theory of radical evil. The problematic feature of the Kantian theory is, of course, its postulation of atemporal free acts. Some philosophers think that no sense can be made of the notion of an atemporal act. Or it may be said that, even if the claim that there are atemporal free acts is intelligible, it is unnecessary to postulate such acts in order to account for ordinary human actions being morally evil. And it may also be alleged that we have absolutely no reason to believe that any human has ever performed an atemporal free act. Let us briefly consider each of these objections.

One who believes, as I do, that it is at least epistemically possible that God is timelessly eternal will not be persuaded by the mere assertion that there is no coherent concept of atemporal free activity. On the view that God is timeless, his acts are both atemporal and free. If we distinguish between God's acts and their consequences, it seems possible to hold both that God's acts are themselves timeless and that some of their consequences at least are events in time. It seems, then, that there is a coherent concept of atemporal free divine activity. And there appears to be no reason why the relation between atemporal free human acts and ordinary human actions in time could not be conceived by analogy with the relation of God's atemporal free acts to their consequences in time. So there is a coherent concept of atemporal free human activity if things are as they appear to be. To be sure, things may not be as they seem. But, if we are to be rationally required to go against the appearances, a persuasive argument that the appearances are misleading is called for. I know of no such argument. Therefore, as far as I can tell, we are rationally permitted to hold that there is a coherent concept of atemporal free human activity.

There is much to be said for the view that it is unnecessary to postulate atemporal free human acts in order to account for the moral good and evil of particular human actions in time. If we suppose that only something free in a way that is incompatible with it also being causally determined could be morally good or morally evil, we will be driven to assume that there is a factor in morally good and morally evil human actions that escapes the net of causal determinism. Kant thought this had to be something atemporal because he supposed that human actions taken merely as events in time were subject to a thoroughgoing causal determinism that is constitutive of the phenomenal realm. Apparently, Kant believed the supposition that the phenomenal realm of events in time is subject to an exceptionless causal determinism to be required by the Newtonian science of his day. But it is tolerably clear that our science demands no such supposition. So it is open to us to hold that human actions considered as events in time are not subject to a thoroughgoing causal determinism. We need not assume that the factor in morally good and morally evil human actions that escapes the meshes of causal determinism is atemporal unless we suppose that the only exceptions to causal determinism allowed by our science have no relevance to human actions considered as events in time.

But this concession to the objection does nothing to undermine Kant's account of the propensity to evil. Even if we need not postulate atemporal free human acts in order to account for the moral good and evil of particular human actions, we may still have to postulate atemporal free human activity to make sense of a propensity to evil that is both innate and itself morally evil if we are unwilling to resort to such desperate expedients as a prenatal Sartrean original choice of character that would function just like an innate propensity. Because the propensity to evil is innate in those who possess it, it must inhere in them antecedent to all of their particular actions in time. And since it is morally evil, it must be a product of the exercise of their freedom and so must derive from free activity on their part for which they are accountable. So because the propensity to evil must derive from free activity on the part of those who possess it but cannot plausibly be supposed to derive from any of their free actions in time, it must derive from some atemporal free act they perform. Thus it seems that it is necessary, after all, to postulate atemporal free human acts in order to account for an innate and morally evil propensity to evil in humans. To be sure, a theory that postulated atemporal free human acts in its account of the propensity to evil but did not postulate them in its account of morally significant actions in time would lack the tight unity of Kant's own theory. But such a lack of unity would not, by itself, suffice to show the theory to be in any way explanatorily inadequate.

The allegation that we have no reason to believe that any human has ever performed an atemporal free act seems to me to be unfounded. Of course, no one has observationally verified the claim that humans perform atemporal free acts, but this is just what is to be expected on Kantian principles. According to Kant, only phenomenal events are observable, and everything phenomenal is temporal. So atemporal free human acts, if there were any, would be in principle unobservable. The move of postulating them would have to be justified by theoretical argument if it were to be warranted at all. Kant is well aware of this. At one point, he tells us that we begin by directing our attention to the moral evil of particular human actions and then proceed to argue to the conditions of its possibility, that is, to what must take place within the will if evil is to be performed (*Religion*, p. 35). In my earlier outline of Kant's theory of radical evil, I have rehearsed some of his arguments for the claim that humans do perform atemporal free acts. Though these arguments may not be conclusive, it seems to me they do provide us with some reason to believe that humans perform atemporal free acts.

These three objections, then, do not suffice to show that Kant erred in postulating atemporal free human acts as part of his account of the propensity to evil. Nevertheless, resorting to atemporal free human acts is a pretty drastic expedient even for a philosopher, and it may appear to be an affront to sober common sense. So I shall interject at this point an observation that may help to mitigate a bit the offense to common sense. As our examination of Anselmian and Kantian theories has shown, the explanandum that the Augustinian tradition proposes for a theory of original sin or radical evil is something very peculiar. The more one thinks about it, the more one is apt to be puzzled about how, or even whether, it is possible for something to be both innate in its possessors and a sin for which they deserve condemnation by a morally perfect judge. Perhaps no theory that does not make at least one assumption which is counterintuitive or contrary to common sense has a hope solving this terribly difficult puzzle. If so, it is not an objection to Kant's theory, or to Anselm's, that they make assumptions which common sense finds outrageous. On the contrary, this may be an indication that they are at least on the right track to the extent of reflecting something like the true dimensions of the explanatory difficulty an adequate theory will have to resolve.

A more troublesome feature of Kant's account of radical evil, when it is viewed from a Christian perspective, is that it may not do full justice to the intention underlying traditional Christian affirmations concerning original sin. This is a rather delicate issue, since Christians have never been and are certainly not today of one mind about exactly what it is that the doctrine of original sin claims. But I suppose that some historical claim is an essential part of the doctrine as it has been understood by most of the Christian tradition. On this view some historical catastrophe played a causal role in generating some of the present evil that inheres in humanity, even if the scriptural description of that catastrophe is not to be considered historically accurate in all its details. The source of concern about Kant's account of radical evil is that it includes no such historical claim.

Kant does say that his account agrees well with the manner in which the origin of evil in the human race is presented in scriptural sources (*Religion*, pp. 36–7). However, this agreement consists in nothing more than the fact that what is primary in the Kantian account, independent of time, namely, man bringing upon himself an evil propensity to evil, is presented in the scriptural narrative as having occurred first in time. Agreement to no more than this extent clearly does not commit the Kantian account to the truth of any historical claims based on the scriptural narrative of the fall of Adam and Eve. When Kant endorses the formula that in Adam all have sinned, he means only to be saying that the narrative of the sin of Adam and Eve provides a kind of mythic representation of something that actually occurs, as far as we can tell, in each human life (*Religion*, p. 37).

It may be worth noting that the Kantian account of radical evil does not actually preclude the truth of the claim that some mysterious catastrophe befell the human race in the remote historical past. Kant himself cautions us not to read his somewhat cursory remarks about the agreement of his theory with the scriptural manner of presentation as scriptural exegesis (*Religion*, p. 39). But scriptural exegesis turns out to be, for Kant, on the far side of the limits of reason. Reason would require us to postulate an historical catastrophe in our account of the origins of human moral evil only if there were something conducive to our moral improvement that could not be derived from that account unless it included such a postulate. According to Kant, there is nothing that will help us to become morally better that cannot be apprehended in the absence of any such historical postulation. Hence, within the limits of Kantian reason alone, we are not required to postulate an historical catastrophe at the origins of human moral evil. Moreover, since such an assumption would be subject to the standard uncertainties that affect claims about the remote historical past, it would be apt to give rise to unedifying quarrels between those who thought it should be made and those who thought it should not. So it is likely that making it would even detract from our prospects for moral improvement, and maybe it is fortunate that it is not needed to help us become morally better. And, in any case, it seems plain to me that it is not an assumption Kant is willing to make as long as he is working within the limits of reason alone, and so it is no part of his theory of radical evil. So there is a traditional Christian perspective on original sin in terms of which Kant's account of radical evil is bound to seem unsatisfactory because it is at best incomplete. Since my sympathies lie with that perspective, I consider this incompleteness a defect in Kant's theory.

I am stuck with the conclusion that neither Anselm nor Kant has given us a fully satisfactory theoretical account of the traditional Christian doctrine of original sin. Their main contribution lies, I think, in the fact that between them they make it easier for us to command a clear view of why it is going to be very difficult, if not impossible, to render an adequate account of that doctrine that preserves most of the traditional Augustinian understanding of it and at the same time does not create a moral scandal. We may think of the Anselmian and Kantian theoretical options as defining opposite ends of what might be a spectrum of alternatives within the Augustinian framework. At the one extreme, there are theories like Anselm's, according to which the evil in us from birth is caused to be there by a chain of propagation which ultimately stretches back into the remote historical past. Such theories make it hard to see how original sin can be something for which its possessors deserve condemnation by a morally perfect judge, because they make it difficult to understand how the evil in us from birth can be moral evil. At the other extreme, there are theories like Kant's, according to which the evil in us from birth is entirely a product of the exercise of our own freedom. Such theories make it hard to see how original sin can be something to which the historical past has any relevance whatsoever, because they make it difficult to understand how anything that took place in the remote past, no matter how catastrophic, could contribute to an evil that is wholly the product of the exercise of our own freedom. One might be tempted to suppose that a satisfactory theoretical position must lie between the two extremes. But is this really a spectrum? What coherent positions, if any, lie between its end points? Or must the Augustinian framework itself be modified in response to difficulties of the sort I have raised? That remains to be seen.

11

Christian Atonement and Kantian Justification

Why did God become man? The soteriological question is distinctively Christian, and answers to it are central to Christian theology. A traditional answer has it that atonement was one thing God accomplished by becoming man; Christ's incarnation, suffering, death, and resurrection are supposed to have effected, or at least to have played an important part in effecting, the reconciliation of sinful humanity with God. But why is vicarious atonement necessary? It may be that God will forgive our sins only if we repent of them; however, it does not seem obvious that divine mercy is so constrained that God can forgive our sins only if Christ's suffering and death substitute for or supplement our own efforts toward reconciliation. And how is vicarious atonement possible? Sin appears to be a personal failure that creates a non-transferable liability, and so it is hard to see how one person's atonement could stand in or go proxy for another's. Theories of vicarious atonement should contain the resources to answer questions like these in a coherent and plausible fashion.

It is noteworthy that Christianity has not been forced by struggles over orthodoxy to give a dogmatic formulation or sharp definition of the idea of vicarious atonement. Such motifs as sacrifice, ransom, and satisfaction coexist within orthodox thought from the patristic period through the Reformation. Yet theologians and philosophers have constructed theories of atonement for the purpose of showing that the doctrine is rationally defensible and explicable. Philosophically speaking, the most interesting of these attempts to rationalize the doctrine of vicarious atonement are the so-called 'satisfaction theories' whose primary explanatory concept is the notion of rendering to God satisfaction for sin. This, of course, is not surprising, since Anselm was the first great satisfaction theorist, and Aquinas, too, though he refined, developed, and clarified Anselm's position, was a satisfaction theorist. Even Kant's theory of the justification of sinners in God's eyes, though it differs radically from medieval satisfaction theories and may

Earlier versions of this paper were read at the 1986 Pacific Regional Meeting of the Society of Christian Philosophers, where Richard Purtill and Charles Taliaferro were my commentators, and at the University of Notre Dame, where David Burrell was my commentator. I am grateful to my commentators and others in the audiences on those occasions for helpful discussion. I am also grateful to Eleonore Stump for detailed written comments.

also depart from Christian orthodoxy, makes essential use of the concept of satisfaction and exhibits important theoretical connections between satisfaction and vicarious atonement.

This paper is devoted to an examination of the theories of atonement of Anselm and Kant. It compares the answers they give to the question of how satisfaction for sins can be rendered to God. The first section gives a brief account of Anselm's satisfaction theory of vicarious atonement in his *Why God Became Man*, and the second section lays out some of the more penetrating among the common objections to that theory. In the third section, I present a somewhat detailed exposition of Kant's theory of justification in his *Religion Within the Limits of Reason Alone*, show how that theory avoids some of the difficulties that confront Anselm's theory, and argue that it contains as an essential part the claim that vicarious atonement is possible. The fourth section explores some serious objections to Kant's theory. In the fifth and final section, I conclude by elaborating the suggestion that these objections reveal something important about how limited the prospects are for rationalizing the doctrine of vicarious atonement.

ANSELMIAN SATISFACTION

According to Anselm, to sin is not to render to God what is due to him. What is due to God from his rational creatures is perfect obedience or subjection to the will of God. Hence, to sin is to fail to obey perfectly God's will. Anselm thinks of such obedience as honor which we owe to God. And so "a person who does not render God this honor due Him, takes from God what is His and dishonors God, and this is to commit sin."[1] Sinners thus have defaulted on a debt they owe to God; they have failed to pay God honor owing to him. By way of restitution for this fault, they owe God recompense. It is as if sinners had stolen something belonging to God; as long as they do not return what was taken away, they remain at fault. Hence, "everyone who sins must pay to God the honor he has taken away, and this is satisfaction, which every sinner must make to God" (I. 11; p. 85). It is a demand of divine justice that satisfaction for sin be made to God.

Anselm holds that punishment must ensue if satisfaction is not made. He says that "it is necessary either that the honor taken away be restored, or that punishment follow" (I. 13; pp. 88–9). *Aut satisfactio aut poena!* For Anselm, punishment is an alternative to satisfaction consistent with divine justice, because

---

[1] Anselm of Canterbury, *Why God Became Man and The Virgin Conception and Original Sin*, translated, with an introduction and notes, by Joseph M. Colleran (Albany: Magi Books, 1969), 84. The quotation is from chapter 11 of Book I of the *Cur Deus Homo*. Henceforth references to book and chapter of this work and to pages of this English translation will be made parenthetically in the body of the paper.

he thinks of suffering punishment as a way in which sinners can pay back, albeit unwillingly, what they have stolen out of what belongs to them. Since happiness belongs to sinners in the sense that they could have possessed it if they had not sinned, sinners are to be thought of as unwillingly making recompense for their faults when they are deprived of happiness by being punished on account of their sins. God, so to speak, vindicates his honor by depriving the sinner of happiness, for "by taking it away, He shows that the sinner and the things that belong to him are subject to Himself" (I. 14; p. 90).

Anselm asks himself whether it would be fitting for God to forgive the debt on which the sinner has defaulted, out of mercy alone, without any repayment. He argues that it would not; his view is that "to deal justly with sin, without satisfaction, is the same as to punish it" (I. 12; p. 85). The injustice involved in not punishing a sinner for whom satisfaction has not been made has two aspects. One has to do with broadly distributive considerations of fairness. If sinners for whom satisfaction has not been made are allowed to go unpunished, those who sin and those who do not will be equally favored in God's eye. But, according to Anselm, it is unseemly if "one who sins and one who does not sin will be in the same position before God" (I. 12; p. 86). A man who had paid a very large debt would seem to have some reason for complaint on grounds of unfairness if another man, who owed a debt of the same size to the same person, were let off scot-free when he defaulted, though equally able to pay. The second aspect has to do with more metaphysical considerations of cosmic order. If sinners for whom satisfaction has not been made are allowed to go unpunished, God will allow something inordinate to pass in his kingdom. But, according to Anselm, it is an intolerable disruption of the proper order of things "for a creature to take away the honor due to the Creator and not make recompense for what he takes away" (I. 13; p. 88). A cosmic polity in which subjects could default on debts owed to their almighty ruler without making recompense or suffering punishment would appear to be a very poorly arranged kingdom. Hence, Anselm concludes, and not without some reason, that punishment is the only alternative to satisfaction consistent with divine justice. And so, God being perfectly just in his dealings with his rational creatures, the sinner's only escape from punishment is if satisfaction is made for his or her sins.

Justice, then, requires that humanity recompense God for the fault of sin, either by making satisfaction to God for the default or by suffering punishment at God's hands. But no mere human can discharge this obligation by making satisfaction. All mere humans owe God perfect obedience; if one who has sinned is subsequently completely obedient to God, such a sinner renders to God no more than what is due to God. Hence, no merely human sinner can, as it were, accumulate the surplus capital or extra merit to pay back to God the debt on which he or she has defaulted by sinning. As Anselm has Boso put it, "if even when I am not in the state of sin, I owe Him myself and whatever I can do, in order to avoid sinning, I have nothing to offer Him in compensation for sin" (I. 20; p. 107). Moreover, recompense is to be made in proportion to the gravity of sin, and even the slightest sin, such as casting a glance in opposition to the will of God, is so grave that Boso is constrained to acknowledge that "I should do nothing against the will of God, to preserve the whole of creation" (I. 21; p. 109). Hence, the burden of even the slightest sin is so great that the proportionate satisfaction owing to God by way of recompense is too large for any mere human to have it within his or her power to make, even if mere humans could, contrary to fact, do anything beyond what is already due to God to gain surplus merit.

Fortunately, the debt of honor on which human sinners have defaulted can be repaid to God by God himself, but only God can make satisfaction for human sinners. Debts of honor like pecuniary debts are transferable, and so one person may make recompense for another's default. Hence, satisfaction can be vicarious; one person can make satisfaction to God for the sins of another. Yet God himself is the only person who is in a position to make satisfaction for human sinners. God does not owe himself obedience to his own will, and so he can have something to give himself that he does not already owe himself because he is not indebted to himself. A sacrifice that God made to himself on behalf of sinful humans would not be payment of a debt, since God owes no debts to himself; nor would such a sacrifice be recompense for a debt on which God had defaulted, since God, being without sin, is without any fault. Hence, such a sacrifice would be supererogatory and could count as making vicarious satisfaction for the faults of human sinners. So God is in a position to make satisfaction on behalf of human sinners. However, on account of the gravity of sin, satisfaction cannot be made "unless there is someone to render to God, for the sin of man, something greater than everything that exists outside of God" (II. 6; p. 124). But only someone who surpassed everything other than God could be able to give God something greater than everything that exists outside of God, and "there is nothing that surpasses everything that is not God but God Himself" (II. 6; p. 124). So only God is in a position to make satisfaction on behalf of human sinners. Hence, if not all human sinners are to be punished for their sins and God is to allow no injustice, God must make satisfaction to God for human sins and thereby atone vicariously for such sins.

So Anselm concludes that, unless satisfaction for human sins is made to God, all human sinners will be punished for their sins with a severity proportionate to the extreme gravity of even the slightest among them. And, since Anselm denies that all human sinners will be so punished, he further concludes that the requisite satisfaction is to be made. But, Anselm supposes, the human default for which satisfaction must be made cannot be transferred outside humanity; a man must make good on the debts humans owe. Thus, "if no one but God can make that satisfaction and no one but man is obliged to make it, then it is necessary that a God-Man make it" (II. 6; p. 124). If the divine decision to spare at least some sinners the punishment that is the only just alternative to satisfaction is gracious rather than logically necessary, then presumably the kind of necessity in question is conditional moral necessity.

Having presented in outline Anselm's by now classic answer to the soteriological question, I next turn my attention to some of the objections that have been raised against it.

DISSATISFACTIONS WITH SATISFACTION

Over the years Anselm's satisfaction theory has been subjected to much criticism from within Christian traditions. Some of this criticism is not very impressive. For example, G. C. Foley alleges that Anselm's picture of a conflict between divine justice and mercy, portraying justice as demanding what mercy does not, amounts to "a practical revival of the Gnosticism of Marcion."[2] Presumably the reference is to Marcion's view that justice and mercy toward sinners are so radically opposed that the being who justly punishes sinners cannot be the same as the being who mercifully forgives them. If so, it is unfair to Anselm to accuse him of reviving such a dualistic view. Anselm's endeavor is to show how it is possible for God to treat sinners with both justice and mercy. To be sure, he thinks divine justice requires recompense from sinners for their faults by way either of punishment or of satisfaction. But he also thinks that divine mercy operates to fulfill the demands of divine justice by graciously making vicarious satisfaction for human sins so that recompense may be made without sinners having to suffer punishment.

However, other objections to Anselm's theory are more serious. Three among them are of particular importance in the context of the present investigation.

The first is a worry about Anselm's view that divine justice does indeed require full payment of the debt of honor on which sinners have defaulted. If we go along with Anselm in conceiving of sin as default on a debt owed to God, then it seems natural to suppose that God has a right to recompense. But it also seems plausible to claim that God could waive that right without doing or permitting any injustice. Since the original debt is owed to God alone, it appears that he could mercifully waive his claim to full recompense without wronging anyone else or violating another person's rights. Hence, it appears that full satisfaction is not the only alternative to punishment consistent with divine justice. Presumably this is why Aquinas holds that God would not be unjust if he forgave the debt without receiving full recompense and that the death of Christ is necessary for our salvation only on the supposition that God requires satisfaction proportionate to the gravity of sin.[3] If God were thus mercifully to waive his right to full recompense

---

[2] George Cadwalader Foley, *Anselm's Theory of the Atonement* (New York: Longman's, Green, and Co., 1909), 173.

[3] Thomas Aquinas, *Summa Theologiae*, III. 46.

for the default of sin, it would not necessarily be the case that one who sins and one who does not are in the same position before God. God might make such an exercise of mercy conditional upon sincere repentance on the part of the sinner, and so require some compensation from one who sins that he does not require from one who does not sin if both are to be saved. Doubtless sincere repentance is a satisfaction less than proportionate to the gravity of sin, but it is nonetheless painful enough to make it difficult for most sinners to manage. And one could respond to Anselm's concern that exercises of saving mercy in the absence of full recompense for the default of sin would introduce something inordinate into God's kingdom by noting that the political analogy is apt to be misleading in the context of discussions of mercy. Christians think of God not only as Sovereign Lord but also as Loving Father, and there seems to be nothing inordinate or improper in a loving parent mercifully forgiving even uncompensated defaults on debts by his or her children. A cosmic family in which parents could forgive their repentant children defaults on debts without having received recompense or inflicting punishment would appear to be a morally admirable arrangement without being unjust.

The second objection to Anselm's satisfaction theory cuts deeper into its foundations, for it challenges the moral appropriateness of conceiving of what we owe God by analogy with pecuniary debts and of sin by analogy with default on a debt. A crude way of putting the objection is that Anselm thinks of making satisfaction as like paying the German *Wergeld*, or blood money, by which the murderer or his representative paid compensation for the crime to the victim's kin. A more refined formulation of the underlying point begins by noting a salient disanalogy between pecuniary and moral debts. It seems that moral debts are not transferable or transmissible in the way that pecuniary debts are. If one person owes another money, the debt can be transferred to and paid by a third party, and if one person defaults on a pecuniary debt to another, recompense can be made to the person to whom the debt is owed by a third party. Hence, it is easy to see how vicarious satisfaction for pecuniary debts can be made. But things are different for other kinds of debts. If one person murders another, we sometimes say that the murderer owes a debt to society which is to be paid by suffering punishment. But this is not a transferable debt that could be paid by the murderer's friends or relatives. Even if the murderer's aged aunt willingly agreed to serve his whole prison term, that would not pay his debt to society. And if the murderer were to default on his debt to society by fleeing into exile before his prison term began, this default could not be compensated for by having his elderly uncle voluntarily serve a prison term in his stead. Hence, it is difficult, if not impossible, to see how vicarious satisfaction for the debt a murderer owes society could be made.

It seems that, even if it is appropriate to think of what we owe God as a debt, the analogy with the case of the debt a murderer owes society under criminal law is better than the analogy with pecuniary debt under civil law. If what we owe

God is to be subsumed under the category of debt at all, some of our debts to God at least appear to be moral debts, and it seems that they are too personal to be transferable. If I owe it to God to love my neighbor, it does not seem that this debt is paid if another loves my neighbor a little extra but I do not love my neighbor at all. Moreover, if sin is to be subsumed under the category of default on debt, some of our defaults on debts to God at least appear to be moral failings for which no one other than we ourselves can make recompense. If I owe it to God to give part of my fortune to feed the hungry and fail to contribute to famine relief, it does not seem that my rich brother could make recompense for my default by donating twice as much of his fortune to famine relief. As G. C. Foley notes, a moral default is "a *personal* failure whose liability cannot be transferred."[4] The moral liability to punishment that comes in the wake of sin does not appear to be transferable, and if recompense for the default of sin can be made so as to justify the remission of punishment, it seems that each sinner must make such recompense for himself or herself. Hence, it is doubtful that, for at least those sins which are moral offenses against God, vicarious satisfaction is possible, even if such sins may be thought of as failures to pay debts we owe to God. And so it is doubtful that Christ's vicarious atonement for our sins can be explained in terms of Christ making vicarious satisfaction for debts on which we sinners have defaulted.

The third objection to Anselm's satisfaction theory amounts to an attack from a slightly different angle on the correctness of conceiving of atonement as satisfaction for debts on which sinners have defaulted. If Christ has made full satisfaction for our sins, he has made full recompense to God by paying not only all the original debts on which we sinners defaulted but also whatever penalties are needed to compensate God for the insult or inconvenience of our defaults. If Christ has made full recompense to God in this way, then the debts in connection with which we have sinned have been fully cleared from our accounts. If those debts have been fully cleared from our accounts, then divine justice is constrained to acknowledge that we are free of those debts. And if divine justice is constrained to acknowledge that we are free of those debts, then we have no need of additional divine mercy to forgive our sins. Hence, if Christ has made full satisfaction for our sins, we have no need of additional divine mercy to forgive our sins. In short, there is no need for God mercifully to forgive us for failing to satisfy a legitimate claim he has on us if Christ has already paid that claim in full by means of his vicarious satisfaction. As Foley quaintly puts it, "there can be no compassion or generosity in foregoing a claim which has been paid to the uttermost farthing."[5] Yet Christians who are quite sure that Christ has atoned for their sins nevertheless think it incumbent on them to pray to God to forgive their sins. If what we owe God has been amply paid, why then do we pray to God to pardon us? Or, as Boso asks Anselm, "Is God unjust, that He demands, a second time, what has already been paid?" (I. 19; p. 105). Moreover, if Christ has in this way made full

---

[4] Foley, *Anselm's Theory*, 155.   [5] Ibid. 164–5.

recompense to God for all human sins, then no one is ever justly punished in hell. This suggests that, whatever may be going on when Christ vicariously atones for our sins through his suffering and death, it is not rendered fully intelligible if thought of in terms of Christ making vicarious satisfaction for our sins by paying our debts together with penalties accrued on account of our defaults.

Though Anselm's theory could be criticized in other ways, perhaps the objections I have raised will suffice to show that it confronts serious difficulties. But what conclusions should we draw from these difficulties? Is Anselm's fatal flaw the excessive legalism of his theory, as some of his critics have charged?[6] Should we abandon the attempt to make sense of the atonement in terms of the categories of debt and default? In trying to answer these questions, we will find it helpful to compare Anselm with Kant. Though their views differ in many ways, Kant and Anselm share the legalistic cast of mind. Kant's text contains two footnote references to Anselm's views. Kant's theory of justification makes use of the concepts of debt and satisfaction and contains a place for vicarious atonement. Yet Kant's theory of justification has within it the resources to give a plausible response to each of the three objections I have directed against Anselm's satisfaction theory. For this reason, it may be thought of as making progress beyond Anselm's theory in some respects, though, as we shall eventually see, it faces some difficulties of its own.

KANTIAN JUSTIFICATION

Kant begins section One of Book Two of *Religion Within the Limits of Reason Alone* by telling us that "it is our universal duty as men to *elevate* ourselves" to the ideal of "*mankind* (rational earthly existence in general) *in its complete moral perfection*."[7] Human moral perfection includes two components. The first is moral goodness of disposition. To attain moral goodness of disposition one must make the moral law the supreme ground of one's maxims, "whereby it is not merely associated with other incentives, and certainly not subordinated to any such (to inclinations) as its conditions, but instead must be adopted, in its entire purity, as an incentive *adequate* in itself for the determination of the will" (p. 42). A person with a morally good disposition is a person of good moral character, that is, "a man endowed with virtue in its intelligible character (*virtus noumenon*) and one who, knowing something to be his duty, requires no incentive other than this representation of duty itself" (pp. 42–3). The second component of human

---

6 An example is Gustaf Aulén, *Christus Victor*, trans. A. G. Herbert with a foreword by Jaroslav Pelikan (Macmillan: New York, 1969), 84–92.

7 Immanuel Kant, *Religion Within the Limits of Reason Alone*, trans. Theodore M. Greene and Hoyt H. Hudson with introductory essays by Theodore M. Greene and John R. Silber (New York: Harper and Row, 1960), 54. Henceforth page references to this work will be made parenthetically in the body of the paper.

moral perfection is moral goodness of deed. Kant tells us that "it would have to consist of a course of life completely and faultlessly harmonious with that perfect disposition" (p. 59). So complete moral perfection is constituted of both a morally good disposition to act purely on the incentives provided by the moral law and a morally good course of life full of deeds in harmony with that disposition.

Kant holds that each of us has a duty to conform to this ideal of moral perfection. And, "we *ought* to conform to it; consequently we must *be able* to do so" (p. 55). So it must be within our power to conform to the ideal of moral perfection. But how is this possible?

After all, if we are honest with ourselves, we must acknowledge that we have performed evil actions which are now past and unalterable. Hence we have already fallen far short of perfection in deed. Worse still, there is in each of us, according to Kant, a morally evil propensity to moral evil, which is "the subjective ground of the possibility of the deviation of the maxims from the moral law" (p. 24). As ground of the possibility of deviation of the maxims of particular actions from the moral law, this propensity must be operative in the agent antecedent to the adoption of the maxims of particular evil actions and so must be represented as innate in the agent. As morally evil, it must be a product of the agent's freedom and so must be represented as brought by the agent upon himself or herself. It can be represented in both these ways if we think of it as "an underlying common ground, itself a maxim, of all particular morally evil maxims" (p. 16), whose free adoption is "intelligible action, cognizable by means of pure reason alone, apart from every temporal condition" (pp. 26–7). Such an evil supreme maxim is, according to Kant, "inextirpable by human powers, since extirpation could occur only through good maxims, and cannot take place when the ultimate subjective ground of all maxims is postulated as corrupt" (p. 32). Since each of us has brought upon himself or herself in this way an inextirpable morally evil disposition, we have also forfeited perfection of disposition. Being by our own choice evil in both disposition and deed, we cannot now elevate ourselves to the ideal of complete moral perfection.

It is, perhaps, a tribute to Kant's moral optimism that he refuses to accept this grim assessment as the whole story about human moral destiny. We can, he thinks, overcome the propensity to moral evil. But, if this overcoming is to transform the moral character from evil to good, it "cannot be brought about through gradual *reformation* so long as the basis of the maxims remains impure, but must be effected through a *revolution* in the man's disposition (a going over to the maxim of holiness of the disposition)" (p. 43). Yet one must wonder whether such a moral revolution in the disposition is even possible if the evil disposition is to be represented as both innate and inextirpable. Kant concedes that it must seem to us that "this restoration through one's own exertions directly contradict[s] the postulate of the innate corruption of man which unfits him for all good" (p. 46). But he thinks there will be such apparent contradictions in all cases in which something "is to be regarded as an event in time (as change), and to that extent as necessary under laws of nature, while at the same time its opposite is to be represented as possible through freedom under moral laws" (p. 46). So Kant is convinced that the contradiction is merely apparent. He thinks we may rest assured that moral revolution is possible, because "duty bids us to do this, and duty demands nothing of us which we cannot do" (p. 43), though we cannot conceive how it is possible. Transformation of the moral disposition, though mysterious, is for Kant no more mysterious than any other genuinely free action.[8]

But a switch of supreme maxims from evil to good is bound to leave a gap between noumenal disposition and phenomenal deeds. Since we begin from evil, the good disposition manifests itself in time as unending progress from bad to better. Hence, "the distance separating the good which we ought to effect in ourselves from the evil whence we advance is infinite, and the act itself, of conforming our course of life to the holiness of the law, is impossible of execution in any given time" (p. 60). So even if an evil person can acquire a morally good disposition by the free exercise of his or her own powers, it looks as if the ideal of complete moral perfection remains elusive for such a person, since such a person will not lead a life completely and faultlessly in harmony with the good disposition he or she has acquired by virtue of carrying out a moral revolution. How, then, are we humans to attain complete moral perfection? Or, as Kant puts it, "How can a disposition count for the act itself, when the act is *always* (not eternally [*überhaupt*], but at each instant of time) defective?" (p. 60). How, in other words, are we to be morally justified in the eyes of God?

The answers Kant gives to these questions make up his theory of atonement. It is a theoretically subtle and complex piece of philosophy, and it merits careful and detailed exegesis.

Kant begins by specifying a sense in which having acquired a good disposition can compensate for defects of conduct. God, who knows the human heart through an atemporal intellectual intuition, will judge the progress derived from the good disposition as a completed whole, though it is temporally unending, and will thus regard the man of good disposition as "being actually a good man (pleasing to Him)" (p. 43). Apparently this is because God's atemporal judgment attends to the man's atemporal moral character which is constituted by the good disposition. From this atemporal perspective, the temporal progress that derives from a good character can correctly be seen as a completed whole. Thus one who has acquired a good disposition that is stable may, despite his unending deficiency in deed, hope "to be *essentially* [*überhaupt*] well-pleasing to God, at whatever instant his existence be terminated" (p. 61). If there is a divine decree justifying those who have acquired a stable good disposition, it will be in accord with God's justice, for it will be "based upon a giving of satisfaction (a satisfaction

---

[8] I have elsewhere argued that such a transformation is not so much mysterious as downright impossible, given certain other Kantian doctrines. See Philip L. Quinn, "Original Sin, Radical Evil and Moral Identity," *Faith and Philosophy*, 1 (1984), 188–202.

which consists for us only in the idea of an improved disposition known only to God)" (p. 70). But this is satisfaction we make out of our own resources by freely acquiring a good disposition. It is not vicarious. Nor does it exhaust the full range of things for which satisfaction must be made. As Kant explicitly tells us, "the disposition, which stands in the place of the totality of this series of approximations carried on without end, makes up for only that failure which is inseparable from the existence of a temporal being as such, the failure, namely, ever wholly to be what we have in mind to become" (p. 61). But this is not our only failure; we have also performed evil actions. And Kant also tells us he does not hold that "the disposition shall serve to *compensate* for failure in allegiance to duty, or consequently, for the actual evil in this endless course of progress" (p. 61). So the good disposition cannot make satisfaction for the evil in our particular actions which are defaults from duty. What, if anything, is to compensate for these evils?

Kant thinks of the evil deeds a man has done and of the propensity to moral evil in which they are rooted as "a debt he can by no possibility wipe out" (p. 66).[9] His reasons for so thinking echo Anselm's. The man cannot reasonably regard future good conduct as making recompense for past evil conduct. He cannot, "through future good conduct, produce a surplus over and above what he is under obligation to perform at every instant, for it is always his duty to do all the good that lies in his power" (p. 66). Moreover, the burden of debt a man acquires in virtue of having done evil is very heavy. Moral evil "brings with it endless violations of the law and so *infinite* guilt" because it "lies in the *disposition* and the maxims in general, in *universal basic principles* rather than in particular transgressions" (p. 66). But Kant also agrees with critics of Anselm who insist that this debt is not transferable. He says that "this is no *transmissible* liability which can be made over to another like a financial indebtedness (where it is all one to the creditor whether the debtor himself pays the debt or whether some one else pays it for him); rather it is *the most personal of all debts*, namely a debt of sins, which only the culprit can bear and which no innocent person can assume even though he be magnanimous enough to wish to take it upon himself for the sake of another" (p. 66). It is worth emphasizing, however, that Kant carefully qualifies this claim about the non-transmissibility of the debt of sin by telling us explicitly that the debt "can never be discharged by another person, so far as we can judge according to the justice of our human reason" (p. 66, my italics). So it would seem that, from the point of view of human reason, all of us who are sinners "must look forward to *endless punishment* and exclusion from the kingdom of God" (p. 66).

As Kant sees it, it is only because the moral revolution, whereby one replaces the propensity to moral evil with the good moral disposition as the highest subjective ground of one's maxims, is a discontinuity in moral character so radical

---

[9] Kant's translators remark in a footnote that *Verschuldung*, which they translate as 'debt,' might as well have been translated by 'offense' or 'guilt.' They consider 'debt' suitable to express Kant's legalistic cast of mind.

that it is tantamount to a lack of moral identity between the pre-revolutionary and post-revolutionary persons that the new moral person who emerges from the revolution may rationally hope to be spared endless punishment for the sins of the old moral person. Suppose the old, pre-revolutionary moral person has not been punished for his sins. Shall such deserved punishments for those sins be inflicted on the new, post-revolutionary moral person? Kant thinks it would not comport well with divine justice to inflict these punishments on the new moral person. After the revolution, "the penalty cannot be considered appropriate to his new quality (of a man well-pleasing to God), for he is now leading a new life and is morally another person" (p. 67). But Kant also thinks divine justice would be flouted if the sins of the old moral person were not punished at all. He insists that "satisfaction must be rendered to Supreme Justice, in whose sight no one who is blameworthy can ever be guiltless" (p. 67).[10] But if punishment has not been inflicted before the revolution, cannot properly be inflicted after the revolution, and yet must be inflicted, the only remaining alternative is to "think of it as carried out *during* the change of heart itself, and adapted thereto" (p. 67). So Kant suggests that we try to find, in the very act of moral revolution itself, "such ills as the new man, whose disposition is now good, may regard as incurred by himself (in another state) and, therefore, as constituting *punishments* whereby satisfaction is rendered to divine justice" (p. 67). Such ills are not hard to find. Carrying out a moral revolution in one's innermost disposition is painfully difficult, and this merely sets one on the path of painful moral struggle upward from bad to better. Hence, "the coming forth from the corrupted into the good disposition is, in itself (as 'the death of the old man,' 'the crucifying of the flesh'), a sacrifice and an entrance upon a long train of life's ills" (p. 68). But the new man voluntarily undertakes to suffer these ills for the sake of the moral good he is engaged in pursuing by means of his struggle, "though really they are due as *punishments* to another, namely to the old man (for the old man is indeed morally another)" (p. 68). And presumably, though Kant is not explicit about this, these ills suffice as punishments for the lapses of the new man in the course of his upward struggle. Since it is the old man's fault that a struggle upward from evil must be undertaken, these lapses too belong to him in some extended sense.

To make sense of all this, we must, I think, appeal to two rather different conceptions of personal identity. On the one hand, there is what Kant thinks of as physical personal identity, which is determined by one's empirical nature as a sentient being. On the other hand, there is what Kant thinks of as moral personal identity, which is determined by one's moral character in accord with the principle that no moral person of an evil disposition is identical with any moral

---

[10] Perhaps the thought would be clearer at this point if we replaced the phrase 'no one who is blameworthy can ever be guiltless' in the standard translation with 'no one who is deserving of punishment may ever go unpunished.' This alternative translation is adopted in Allen W. Wood, *Kant's Moral Religion* (Ithaca: Cornell University Press, 1970), 235.

person of a good disposition. The two identity relations do not coincide. It is one and the same physical person who persists through a moral revolution. As Kant puts it, "the man (regarded from the point of view of his empirical nature as a sentient being) is *physically* the self-same guilty person as before and must be judged as such before a moral tribunal and hence by himself" (p. 68). Satisfaction is rendered to divine justice because the physical person suffers punishment for his sins. But, during a moral revolution, one moral person ceases to be and another begins to be, though both are tied to the same physical person. The new, post-revolutionary man, because of his good disposition, "is (regarded as an intelligible being) *morally* another in the eyes of a divine judge for whom this disposition takes the place of action" (p. 68). The new man suffers a full measure of life's ills for the sake of the good he pursues by his course of arduous upward progress. These sufferings, voluntarily endured, cannot be regarded as punishments for his sins, since his has incurred no penalties, but they may be regarded as making vicarious satisfaction to God for the sins of the old man whom he replaced, or, what amounts to the same thing, vicarious satisfaction to God for the sins of the physical man with whom he is so intimately associated. Kant summarizes the view in this memorable sentence: "And this moral disposition which in all its purity (like unto the purity of the Son of God) the man has made his own—or, (if we personify this idea) this Son of God, Himself—bears as *vicarious substitute* the guilt of sin for him, and indeed for all who believe (practically) in Him; as *savior* He renders satisfaction to supreme justice by His sufferings and death; and as *advocate* He makes it possible for men to hope to appear before their judge as justified" (p. 69). But we must not allow ourselves to be misled by Kant's use of figurative language. It is not that one physical person, say, Christ, makes vicarious satisfaction for the sins of other physical persons; the debt of sin is not transmissible from one physical person to another. Rather, a moral person makes vicarious satisfaction for the physical person to whom he or she is tied, or if literal talk of moral persons strikes one as philosophically disreputable, an acquired characteristic of a physical person, his or her good moral disposition, is taken by God to have rendered satisfaction for the sins of the whole physical person. So Kant's doctrine of atonement is a doctrine of vicarious satisfaction, not in the full-blooded sense in which one person bears as vicarious substitute the burden of sin for another, but only in the somewhat attenuated sense in which one part of a person, as it were, bears the entire burden of the person's sins.

Yet a major puzzle remains. We were assured that it is within our power to carry out a moral revolution in disposition because the moral law requires us to do this. So, though we start from a propensity to moral evil, it is no more than our duty to acquire a good moral disposition. But then it would seem that acquisition of a good disposition could not produce a surplus of good over and above what is morally obligatory sufficient to pay the debt of sin. How is it possible for the good disposition to make satisfaction for sin if in acquiring it one is doing no more than the moral law demands?

Kant's answer to this question must be that the good disposition does not suffice to pay the debt of sin. The debt can literally never be paid in full, since the sinner cannot pay it and no one else can pay it for the sinner. But the debt can mercifully be forgiven provided the sinner does what he can by way of making satisfaction and acquires a good disposition. But what every sinner can and must do is to acquire a good disposition; desert of mercy is conditional upon a moral revolution in the basic disposition. The good disposition can serve as a basis of desert of mercy because it is "something *real* which of itself is well-pleasing to God" (p. 161), but even the good disposition cannot establish a legal claim in strict justice to God's justifying verdict. Only if we had never sinned, either in disposition or in deed, would we have a legal claim based in justice alone to God's justifying decree, for only then would we have satisfied every demand the moral law makes upon us. Given that we have sinned, the good disposition we acquire through moral revolution establishes in us no more than "a *capability of receiving*, which is all that we, for our part, can credit to ourselves" (p. 70). Since "a superior's decree conferring a good for which the subordinate possesses nothing but the (moral) receptivity is called *grace*," God's justifying decree "is always one of grace alone" (p. 70). Hence, the surplus of good needed to pay the debt of sin cannot be something of our own which we have acquired and can credit to ourselves but must be "a profit which is reckoned to us by *grace*" (p. 70). If "what in our earthly life (and possibly at all future times and in all worlds) is ever only a *becoming* (namely, becoming a man well-pleasing to God) should be credited to us exactly as if we were already in full possession of it" (p. 70), this would not be because God owes it to us in justice to credit us with being well-pleasing to him, for we are not well-pleasing to him and he knows it, even if we have acquired a disposition to be well-pleasing to Him, which is itself something well-pleasing to him. Rather, it would be because God mercifully credits to us some moral goodness not our own by forgiving us the debt of our sins and absolving us from guilt in his gracious justifying decree. So Kant must hold that the righteousness imputed to us by the divine justifying decree "will ever remain a righteousness not our own" (p. 59) because we have not earned it by perfect obedience to the moral law, and he must also maintain that "an appropriation of this righteousness for the sake of our own must be possible" (p. 60) if God's justifying decree is not to be based on an inaccurate assessment of our ultimate moral status. In short, we do not even have the capability of receiving this gift of grace unless we have acquired the good disposition, and we must freely accept this grace when it has been offered if there is to be a divine justifying decree. But God does not make us be more righteous than we formerly were; it is open to us to decline rather than to appropriate the alien righteousness we are offered.

But whence comes this surplus goodness, which is a profit reckoned to us by grace, and how can it be imputed to us as our goodness? And how can there be a righteousness not our own that we can appropriate for the sake of our own right-eousness? Moral goodness and righteousness appear to our reason to be every bit as non-transferable as moral debt and guilt. Here we reach the limits of philosoph-ical rationalization, the outer bounds of religion within the limits of reason alone. We confront what Kant calls the mystery of atonement, a mystery "revealed to us through our reason" (p. 133). God, commanding through the moral law, has made it our duty to elevate ourselves to the ideal of complete moral perfection in both disposition and deed in order that we might be members of the kingdom of heaven, and yet we have sinned by disobeying the moral law and made ourselves unworthy to be members of the kingdom of heaven. This is man's moral predic-ament. But "if the goodness of God has called him, as it were, into being, i.e., to exist in a particular manner (as a member of the kingdom of Heaven), He must also have a means of supplementing, out of the fullness of His own holiness, man's lack of requisite qualifications therefore" (p. 134). So God must be able to atone vicariously for man's sins, to make man a gracious gift of a righteousness not man's own. Yet this seems to be quite impossible, for it appears to reason that any moral quality a man may have must be imputable to him and, hence, must arise from some exercise of his own freedom. In other words, it seems that "this contradicts spontaneity (which is assumed in all the moral good or evil which a man can have within himself), according to which such a good cannot come from another but must arise from man himself, if it is to be imputable to him" (p. 134). Hence, as far as reason can see, God cannot atone vicariously for man's sins or bestow upon him a righteousness not his own, for "so far as reason can see, no one can, by virtue of the superabundance of his own good conduct and through his own merit, take another's place" (p. 134). So if we propose to accept vicarious atonement, as Kant pretty clearly does, we must, Kant admonishes us, "*assume it* only from the moral point of view, since for the ratiocination it is an unfathomable mystery" (p. 134). But it is, according to Kant, only a mystery and not an out and out impossibility. Like a moral revolution in the ultimate ground of one's maxims and, indeed, in the last resort, everything connected with the spontaneity of freedom, its impossibility "cannot really be proved, because free-dom itself, though containing nothing supernatural in its conception, remains, as regards its possibility, just as incomprehensible to us as is the supernatural factor which we would like to regard as a supplement to the spontaneous but deficient determination of freedom" (p. 179). And so, Kant seems to be saying, the bottom line is that we may assume from the moral point of view that a righteousness not the product of our own freedom can be transmitted to us, though how this is possible is completely inexplicable to human reason.

By way of summary, then, we may say that Kant's theory of atonement has two main parts. The first has to do with what one must do on one's own to make satisfaction for one's sins. One must carry out a moral revolution in the highest ground of one's maxims and acquire a good disposition in place of the propensity to evil one has brought upon oneself. This is a necessary condition of being justified in the eyes of God. As Kant tells us, "only the supposition of a complete change of heart allows us to think of the absolution, at the bar of heavenly justice, of the man burdened with guilt" (p. 71). But it is not a sufficient condition of being justified in God's eyes; nothing one can do suffices fully to pay the debt of sin. The second part of Kant's theory has to do with what one may hope God will do to supplement one's efforts. One may hope that God will graciously bestow upon one a righteousness not one's own on account of the moral receptivity to grace one has in virtue of having acquired a good disposition. This merciful gift of grace is also a necessary condition of being justified in the eyes of God. The two conditions together are sufficient for being justified in God's eyes. In short, justification in the eyes of God requires the cooperation of freedom and grace.

Among the merits of Kant's theory is its ability to go a long way toward meeting objections to Anselm's theory of the sort I have laid out above. In response to my second objection, Kant would insist, along with Anselm's critics, that moral debts and credits are not transferable, so far as it is permissible to judge of the matter according to our reason. But he goes on to say that it cannot be proved that something like the transmission of moral goodness from one person to another is impossible, though such a transmission is bound always to be an unfathomable mystery for reason. Hence, we may do no more than assume vicarious atonement from the moral point of view, and we may "hope to partake in the appropriation of another's atoning merit, and so of salvation, only by qualifying for it through our own efforts to fulfill every human duty" (p. 108). In response to my third objection, Kant would agree with Anselm's critics that it is a mistake to think of atonement as a satisfaction made to God which pays the debts on which we have defaulted in full, together with accrued penalties, and thereby justifies us in the sight of God. The satisfaction we render to God by acquiring the good disposition through moral revolution and enduring consequent ills as punishments for past particular sins is necessary but insufficient to justify us in God's eyes. We must also appropriate a righteousness not our own, which is offered to us as a gift of grace, if we are to be justified. Although this merciful gift is in accord with divine justice, since we have done what we can to deserve it by making the satisfaction it is within our power to make, it is not a demand of strict justice that we be given this gift, and it is not owed to us by right. Hence, it is appropriate for us to pray for this gift, even after we have rendered to God all the satisfaction we can, in order that we may be fully absolved from our sins and justified in the eyes of God. And finally, in response to my first objection, Kant would agree with Anselm's critics that God can waive his claim to full recompense for sin without doing anything unjust, provided the sinner makes the satisfaction that is within his power by acquiring a good disposition. Since such satisfaction as sinners can make is insufficient to justify them in the sight of God, God's decree of justification is bound to be one of grace and to be based, on God's part, on mercifully waiving the claim to full recompense for sin. Yet such a justifying decree would not place one who sins and one who does not in the same position before God, for one who sins would, as a prerequisite for being justified in the sight of God, have made a satisfaction to God that one who does not would not have made. Nor, Kant thinks, would there be anything inordinate about such a decree, since it would be in accord with divine justice on account of being based upon a giving of satisfaction.

So there are respects in which Kant's theory of atonement is a clear improvement upon Anselm's. But there are also objections to be made to Kant's theory. I next turn to an examination of some of them.

UNJUSTIFIED JUSTIFICATION?

At the heart of Kant's practical philosophy lies the conviction that whatever one may do by way of moral good or moral evil must be imputable to him or her and so must be a product of some exercise of his or her own freedom. The propensity to moral evil, which is a supreme maxim governing the whole use of freedom, is itself morally evil just because it is freely adopted and so imputable to one who has it. The good disposition is itself morally good precisely because one is responsible for having it on account of having freely acquired it. And particular temporal actions are good or evil, morally speaking, just because their maxims are freely adopted. As Kant puts it, "man *himself* must make or have made himself into whatever, in a moral sense, whether good or evil, he is or is to become" (p. 40). It is this conviction that underlies Kant's insistence that, as far as human reason can judge, neither moral merit nor moral demerit is transferable or transmissible. But if Kant is right on this score, then the very possibility of vicarious atonement is precluded, as far as human reason can tell. Even if there were a surplus of goodness in the universe, it could never be reckoned to us as our own moral goodness because it would not be imputable to us. Since it would not be a product of the exercise of our freedom, we would not be responsible for it, and so it would forever remain a goodness that was not our own moral goodness. A righteousness not our own could never become our righteousness, for our righteousness is something we must earn by our own efforts to obey the moral law. And so even if Christ, who is without sin, has accumulated in heaven's treasury a surplus of moral merit by voluntarily submitting to his passion and death, this can be of no help to human sinners, for it must forever remain his moral merit and can never become ours. Or so it must seem to human reason if one shares Kant's conviction about the impossibility of transferring or transmitting moral goodness from one person to another.

And so one objection to Kant is that he misstates the case when he describes vicarious atonement as a mystery revealed to us through our reason. What our reason reveals to us is that there can be no vicarious atonement. Perhaps there is some way in which God can bring sinners to salvation through his mercy. If there is, it will not involve a divine decree justifying sinners in the sight of God.

According to human reason, an omniscient God would not issue such a decree, for he would know that human sinners are not righteous by their own efforts and cannot acquire righteousness by transfer. So sinners must remain unjustified in the eyes of God even if they are also saved by his mercy. Hence, as far as human reason can judge, Kantian justification is not merely mysterious; it is, on Kantian principles, utterly unjustified.

Of course, it is only proper to share Kant's modesty about the powers of human reason in the present context. Despite the difficulties, perhaps there is some way of reconciling vicarious atonement with the non-transferability of moral qualities in the ordinary course of things. But even if there were, Kant's account of the justification of sinners in the sight of God would still be open to two other rather serious objections.

According to the first, even if vicarious atonement were possible and were to occur, it would not suffice to justify sinners in the sight of God and so would not warrant a decree of justification by God. We must, Kant supposes, think of God "(1) as the omnipotent Creator of heaven and earth, i.e., as *holy* Legislator, (2) as Preserver of the human race, its *benevolent* Ruler and moral Guardian, (3) as Administrator of His own holy laws, i.e., as *righteous* Judge" (p. 131). As holy legislator, God is author of the moral law. The moral law commands us to elevate ourselves to the ideal of complete moral perfection. Since it is our duty to do this, we must be able to do it. As righteous judge, God will find us justified in his eyes only if we have done all that it is our duty to do. But complete moral perfection requires both that we acquire a good disposition and that we not bring upon ourselves a morally evil propensity to evil. Yet, though we could have done otherwise, we have brought upon ourselves a morally evil propensity to evil. Thus we have disobeyed the moral law's command concerning our disposition. And complete moral perfection also requires both that we perform morally good deeds in time and that we not perform morally evil deeds in time. Yet, though we could have refrained from doing so, we have done morally evil deeds. Thus we have disobeyed the moral law's command concerning our deeds. Having failed to elevate ourselves to the ideal of complete moral perfection, we have not done all that it is our duty to do, and so God will not find us justified in his eyes. Even if a vicarious atonement should allow us to appropriate a righteousness not our own, this would not undo or wipe out the evils we have done, for the propensity to moral evil is inextirpable by human powers and our evil deeds are past and unalterable. Hence, we would not by such an appropriation elevate ourselves to the ideal of complete moral perfection, since such an elevation consists in achieving a perfect righteousness of our own and not in appropriating some alien righteousness. Therefore, even if a vicarious atonement were to occur, it would not justify us in God's sight; only elevating ourselves to the ideal of complete moral perfection could justify us in God's eyes. God, being omniscient, knows all this as well as we do. As a righteous judge, God will not issue a decree of justification for us, since he knows that we sinners are not justified in his sight, though it was within our power to be so justified and we alone are responsible for not being so justified. Perhaps God will graciously save us, though we remain unjustified in his sight, if we do all we can to make satisfaction for the evils we have done. But if God does this, we do not thereby become justified in God's eyes. In such circumstances, a divine decree of justification would be quite inappropriate, and so Kantian justification is unjustified. Vicarious atonement simply is not good enough to warrant a verdict of justification from a righteous judge; only the individual achievement of complete moral perfection could suffice for that purpose.

The second objection resembles one formulated by John Silber.[11] Even if a righteousness not our own were made available to us by grace and we were able to appropriate it, a decree of justification based on such an appropriation would be a moral outrage. A person who has never disobeyed the moral law has no need of grace in order to be justified in the sight of God; such a person has acquired his or her own righteousness by his or her own efforts and has earned God's justifying decree. The moral law demands that each of us acquire such a perfect righteousness of our own, and so every one of us is able to acquire such righteousness. Hence, anyone who does not acquire such perfect righteousness but instead disobeys the moral law becomes a sinner by free choice. But a sinner by free choice stands condemned in the sight of God and has earned a divine decree of condemnation. Even if such a sinner manages to appropriate an alien righteousness, it remains the case that the sinner has not done what he or she was obliged to do and could have done, and so such a sinner continues to deserve a decree of condemnation rather than a decree of justification from a righteous judge. To issue a decree of justification for such a sinner on account of an appropriated righteousness not his or her own, when what he or she has earned by his or her own efforts and therefore deserves is a decree of condemnation, would be to comprise the strictness of the moral law. Such laxness would be a moral outrage; a righteous judge would never behave in this indulgent fashion. For this reason too, then, Kantian justification is unjustified. Possession of a righteousness not one's own is not so much as relevant to what one deserves at the hands of a righteous moral judge; all that is relevant is whatever righteousness of one's own one has acquired through one's obedience to the moral law.

CONCLUSIONS

Our reflections upon Kant and Anselm point to one major conclusion. It is that any doctrine of vicarious atonement will be difficult, if not impossible, to square

---

[11] John R. Silber, "The Ethical Significance of Kant's *Religion*," in *Religion Within the Limits of Reason Alone* (New York: Harper and Row 1960), pp. cxxxi–cxxxiii. But the objection I state only *resembles* Silber's because Silber's criticism is based on the mistaken assumption that Kant flatly rejects the doctrine of vicarious atonement. Allen Wood challenges Silber's interpretation of Kant on this point (Wood, *Kant's Moral Religion*, 237). Because I side with Wood in this dispute, I have tried to extract from Silber's objection what remains of value after the mistaken assumption is corrected and to reformulate this point in my own words.

with a conviction that is central to the conceptual scheme of common sense morality.

According to common sense moral thinking, moral credits and debits are neither transferable nor transmissible. Kant's doctrine that moral worth, since it must be imputable, has to be the product of an exercise of free will and can only be imputed to the person whose free will produced it goes some way toward explaining this intuitive conviction about morality. Sin, which consists of disobedience to the will of God, is a moral evil. Hence, if sin is a moral debt on which the sinner has defaulted, it is not a transferable debt which another could pay for the sinner, thereby clearing the sinner's accounts with God. Righteousness, which consists of obedience to the will of God, is a moral good. Hence, if anyone can accumulate an excess of righteousness over what morality requires, it is not a transmissible surplus which could be credited to another's account, thereby clearing a sinner's accounts with God. Though I would not presume to claim that these intuitions are cultural invariants, I dare say they are widely shared in our culture. They are my considered opinions. They also underlie some of the more cogent objections to Anselm's and Kant's theories of atonement.

In these theories, it is the element of vicariousness that is the source of difficulties. Anselm requires that Christ vicariously substitute for the sinner in bearing the burden of the debt of sin, and this can be done only if the burden of the debt of sin can be transferred from the sinner to Christ. Kant requires that the sinner vicariously appropriate another's righteousness in order to be justified in the sight of God, and this can be done only if another's righteousness can be transmitted to the sinner. Such transfers or transmissions would be possible only if moral merit and demerit were alienable from those who acquire them through their own efforts. But moral merit and demerit are inalienable. To suppose otherwise is to imagine that they are extrinsic to their possessors. It is to imagine that the moral economy could, as it were, be adequately represented by some sort of system of double-entry bookkeeping which kept track of transfers of moral credits and debits from one person to another. This is the thought that clashes with moral convictions. And so it seems that we are driven to jettison the traditional picture according to which atonement is a matter of the moral arithmetic of exchange.

If we do take the radical step of abandoning this picture, we are not driven to say that God cannot save sinners. Surely we may continue to hold that God's mercy extends to forgiving sins and to remitting the full temporal punishment due for sins, even if we insist that the forgiven sinner continues to lack righteousness and thus to be unjustified in the sight of God. If such an exercise of mercy is also to be just, perhaps we must insist that the sinners have done something by way of repentence in order to deserve mercy. As Kant's theory shows us, the notion of satisfaction might be of some use to us in this connection. Maybe divine justice requires that such an exercise of mercy be conditional upon the repentent sinner having done all that lies within his or her power to make satisfaction to God for sin, both in terms of improving his or her moral character and by way of gladly enduring the ills attendant upon the struggle upward to a better course of life. But such satisfaction would not, as even Kant admits, suffice to justify the sinner in the eyes of God; only a life entirely free from sin would suffice for that purpose. So even a sinner who had made satisfaction would remain unjustified, and a divine decree of condemnation of such a sinner could not be replaced by a decree of justification. But because the sinner had done what was required to become worthy of mercy, God could graciously exercise clemency in remitting some of the punishment he would have inflicted upon the sinner if the sinner had not made satisfaction. And God could reconcile the sinner to himself by forgiving the offense to himself in the sin if the sinner had made satisfaction. Hence, God could grant salvation to the repentant sinner who had made satisfaction to the extent within his or her power without either the sinner's debt having been transferred to and fully paid by another or another's righteousness having been transmitted to and appropriated by the sinner. So it seems that vicarious satisfaction for sins is unnecessary for salvation, which is a good thing if vicarious satisfaction for sins is, as it appears to be, impossible.

But there is a price to be paid for taking this line. If we rule out the possibility of transferring or transmitting to us the merits of Christ's sacrifice for our justification, the merits of Christ's sacrifice cannot be necessary for our salvation. If we can be saved and yet Christ's sacrifice cannot pay in full our debt of sin, then vicarious satisfaction by Christ for us is not, contrary to Anselm, necessary for our salvation and is not, contrary to Aquinas, necessary for our salvation upon the condition that God demands satisfaction proportionate to the gravity of our sins. Indeed, if the merits of Christ's sacrifice are not transferable to us for our justification and God does demand satisfaction proportionate to the gravity of our sins, then we sinners cannot be saved. But if Christ's sacrifice was not even conditionally necessary for our salvation, what then was its purpose? It is sometimes said that Christ's sacrifice, though not necessary for our salvation, was a fitting way of atoning for our sins. However, it would seem that Christ's sacrifice could not even make a contribution to atoning for our sins if the debts of our sins are not transferable to him and the merits of his sacrifice are not transmissible to us. So one is left wondering whether philosophy can make any sense at all of the claim that Christ, by his incarnation, passion, death, and resurrection, atoned for our sins.

If this is the situation in which Christian philosophers find themselves, they should find atonement a problematic and puzzling answer to the original soteriological question. And so we have returned to the point from which we began. The soteriological question has merely become more perplexing under philosophical examination of the traditional answer offered by the doctrine of vicarious atonement. Why, then, did God become man?

12

Kantian Philosophical Ecclesiology

Much recent work in philosophy of religion by Christian philosophers has been done, so to speak, under a banner on which is emblazoned the motto 'Faith Seeking Understanding.' That motto adorns the cover of this journal [*Faith and Philosophy*]. Such philosophy typically operates within a theological circle; it is philosophical theology with philosophy firmly fixed in the adjectival position. It has produced noteworthy explications and defenses of such distinctively Christian doctrines as the Trinity, the Incarnation, and the Atonement.[1] It also stands in sharp contrast to the philosophy of religion more customary in modernity since Hume, which views theological circles from the outside. They are dimensions of human culture that form the subject matter of religious studies, but philosophy, like the other disciplines that constitute religious studies, approaches them with secular methods and assumptions. From this perspective, many distinctively Christian doctrines are highly problematic; being revealed mysteries of faith, they resist philosophical examination and on that account suffer from neglect or perhaps misunderstanding by philosophers.

Yet recent Christian philosophical theology has not been comprehensive in its engagement with theology. It is striking that it does not contain a richly textured discussion of philosophical ecclesiology, a doctrine of the church or churches. I think this is an unfortunate lacuna, and my hope is that this paper will serve as a stimulus to a discussion that begins to fill the gap. In order to be provocative, I focus on the ecclesiology Kant sets forth in *Religion within the Limits of Reason Alone* and *The Conflict of the Faculties*. Some Christians will probably find my choice of a starting point odd if not offensive. As John Hare observes, "especially in America, Christians who know about Kant tend to think of him as the major philosophical source of the rot which has led to the decline of Christianity in the West in the last two hundred years. He is seen as having taken a decisive step, perhaps the decisive step, away from the traditional faith."[2] I disagree with

I am grateful to Karl Ameriks, Richard P. McBrien, and Thomas F. O'Meara, OP, for helpful bibliographical suggestions. A shortened version of this paper was the Konyndyk Memorial Lecture I gave to a session sponsored by the Society of Christian Philosophers at the 2000 APA Central Division Meeting. I dedicate the paper to the memory of Ken Konyndyk.

[1] For some examples, see the essays in Ronald J. Feenstra and Cornelius Plantinga, Jr. (eds.), *Trinity, Incarnation and Atonement* (Notre Dame: University of Notre Dame Press, 1989).

[2] John E. Hare, *The Moral Gap* (Oxford: Clarendon Press, 1996), 35.

this view. Like Hare, I take seriously what he calls the Christian seriousness of Kant. I plan to argue that Kant's ecclesiology contains a lesson that contemporary Christian philosophical theologians would do well to learn.

The paper is divided into four sections. In the first, I give a rough sketch of some of the main themes in Kant's ecclesiology. The second lays out Kant's solutions to two important problems; they concern scriptural interpretation and religious toleration. In the third, I consider a major objection to Kant's views and suggest a modified Kantian ecclesiology that tries to accommodate the aspect of it that I find persuasive. The fourth and final section compares the Roman Catholic ecclesiology of the Second Vatican Council with both Kant's ecclesiology and my modified Kantian ecclesiology. It argues that on some points the ecclesiology of Vatican II represents substantial movement in the direction of Kant's ecclesiology while on other points tension between Kant and Vatican II can be reduced by my modified Kantian ecclesiology.

I. KANT'S ECCLESIOLOGY

In response to doubts about the work's intention, Kant begins the preface to the second edition of *Religion within the Limits of Reason Alone* with an explanation of what he hopes to accomplish in the book. Since a faith that purports to contain historical revelation can include the pure religion of reason while the latter cannot include what is historical in the former, he tells us, we should make the experiment of regarding the two as related like a pair of concentric circles. The pure religion of reason will be contained within the inner circle, and the philosopher, as a teacher of pure reason according to a priori principles alone, will be restricted to the inner circle. If this experiment succeeds, Kant wants us to conduct another. It is to examine alleged revelation, which is to be found in the part of the outer circle not contained in the inner circle, in the light of moral concepts in order to "see whether it does not lead back to the very same pure *rational system* of religion."[3] If it does, Kant thinks, "we shall be able to say that reason can be found to be not only compatible with Scripture but also at one with it, so that he who follows one (under guidance of moral concepts) will not fail to conform to the other" (p. 11). For Kant, much is at stake in the second experiment because he thinks all of us are committed to the pure religion of reason by virtue of our possession of reason. So if the second experiment succeeds, those of us who are also committed to revelation cannot be shown to have inconsistent commitments provided we interpret revelation in the light of moral concepts. If this is not the case, Kant sees only two possibilities for those who are committed to revelation.

[3] Immanuel Kant, *Religion within the Limits of Reason Alone*, trans. Theodore M. Greene and Hoyt H. Hudson (New York: Harper Torchbooks, 1960), 11. Hereafter page references to this work by Kant will be made parenthetically in the body of the text.

Either they will have two religions within them, and the two will be inconsistent. Or they will have within them the pure religion of reason and a conflicting cult of ceremonial worship. However this combination is bound to be unstable because a cult has value only as a means. As Kant puts it, if the religion of reason and a ceremonial cult conflict, then, though shaking them up together might temporarily unite them, "directly, like oil and water, they must needs separate from one another, and the purely moral (the religion of reason) be allowed to float on top" (p. 12). Clearly Kant's project then is to use the pure religion of reason, if it is possible to do so, as a critical control on faith that relies on purported historical revelation.

How does the project provide a way into a discussion of ecclesiology? In Book One of the *Religion*, Kant argues that we all suffer from a propensity to evil which is itself evil because we have brought it upon ourselves and are thus accountable for it. In Book Two, he goes on to contend that each of us can, because he or she ought to do so, carry out a moral revolution, aided by extrahuman assistance we cannot understand if it is needed, that dethrones, though it cannot eradicate, the evil propensity, depriving it of sovereignty over us.[4] But even if each of us overthrows the sovereignty of this evil principle, all of us remain at risk and in danger that its sovereignty will be reestablished because we have not yet removed ourselves from an ethical state of nature, as it were, in which we are apt to corrupt one another. According to Kant, in such a state "despite the good will of each individual, yet because they lack a principle which unites them, they recede, through their dissensions, from the common goal of goodness and, just as though they were *instruments of evil*, expose one another to the risk of falling once again under the sovereignty of the evil principle" (p. 88). Our response to this risk ought to be to bestir ourselves to leave the ethical state of nature in order to become members of an ethical commonwealth. Kant thinks we have a duty to do so.[5]

An ethical commonwealth is to be distinguished from a political state. In a political state, we stand under coercive laws that regulate outer behavior while, in an ethical commonwealth, only non-coercive laws concerning inner morality, laws of virtue alone, unite us. Moreover, unlike moral laws, which concern what we are certain lies within our power, the idea of an ethical commonwealth involves "working toward a whole regarding which we do not know whether, as such, it lies in our power or not" (p. 89). Hence the duty to endeavor to become members of such a social union is, according to Kant, a *sui generis* duty of the human race toward itself. Since public human laws can only regulate outer behavior, we cannot think of ourselves as the legislators of an ethical commonwealth. Nor

---

[4] For critical discussion, see my "Original Sin, Radical Evil and Moral Identity," *Faith and Philosophy*, 1 (1984).

[5] For a more detailed treatment of Kant's conception of the ethical commonwealth or, as he translates the German, ethical community, see Allen Wood, "Religion, Ethical Community and the Struggle Against Evil," *Faith and Philosophy*, 17 (2000).

can we suppose that its laws are statutes enacted merely by the will of a superior being, divine positive laws, for in that case they would not be moral laws and the duty to comply with them would not be the free duty of virtue. Kant concludes that "only he can be thought of as highest law-giver of an ethical commonwealth with respect to whom all *true duties*, hence also the ethical, must be represented as *at the same time* his commands; he must therefore also be 'one who knows the heart,' in order to see into the innermost parts of the disposition of each individual and, as is necessary in every commonwealth, to bring it about that each receives whatever his actions are worth" (pp. 90–1). But the concept of such a highest legislator just is the concept of God as moral ruler of the world. And so an ethical commonwealth must be thought of as "a people under divine commands, i.e., as a people of God, and indeed *under laws of virtue*" (p. 91). Of course, for Kant, a people of God is not a state with a theocratic constitution in which humans are subject to divine statutory laws; the divine legislation of a people of God is reason's moral self-legislation transformed into a public principle of social union. Thus the idea of an ethical commonwealth as a people of God under laws of virtue possesses objective reality in human reason itself, and it fits comfortably within Kant's inner circle, where it contributes, as we shall see, to his account of the pure religion of reason.

Kant considers this idea a sublime ideal, but he is not optimistic about our prospects for realizing it on earth under our own steam. He tells us that it is never wholly attainable and dwindles markedly under human hands; he thinks something about sensuous human nature circumscribes the means at our disposal for embodying it in any human institution. Given the stuff we are made of and the evil propensity we have brought upon ourselves, how, he asks rhetorically, "can one expect something perfectly straight to be framed out of such crooked wood" (p. 92)?[6] He therefore suggests that founding a moral people of God is really a task only God can consummate, but he also insists that we must proceed as if everything depends upon us. What shall we do now to prepare ourselves for the divine completion of our endeavors? Kant's answer to this question is his ecclesiology.

For Kant, an ethical commonwealth under divine moral legislation is a church. Considered merely as an ideal, such an ethical commonwealth may be thought of as the church invisible. An actual social union of humans that harmonizes with this ideal is a visible church, and "the true (visible) church is that which exhibits the (moral) kingdom of God on earth so far as it can be brought to pass by men" (p. 92). The political constitution of the true visible church will be neither that of a monarchy, ruled by a pope or patriarch, nor that of an aristocracy, ruled by bishops and other prelates. It will not be a democracy in which each member is governed by special inspiration or private illumination. Kant

---

[6] Isaiah Berlin was fond of Kant's comparison of humanity to crooked wood; a collection of his essays bears the title *The Crooked Timber of Humanity*.

thinks its constitution is best grasped in terms of a domestic analogy familiar from Christian piety. The true visible church will be like "a household (family) under a common, though invisible, moral Father, whose holy Son, knowing His will and yet standing in blood relation with all members of the household, takes His place in making His will better known to them" (p. 93). So our endeavors are to be directed to doing what we can to bring about the existence of the true visible church and our membership in it.

One might consider it an easy task to bring about the existence of the true visible church. Since its divine legislation is also reason's self-legislation, reason itself tells us what its laws must be. Hence it may seem that pure religious faith, which consists of belief in God together with our belief in morality's laws, suffices to enable us to bring the true visible church into existence. Kant rejects this optimistic view. He insists that "by reason of a peculiar weakness of human nature, pure faith can never be relied on as much as it deserves, that is, a church cannot be established on it alone" (p. 94). As a matter of empirical fact, churches always originate in historical or revealed faiths. But such faiths contain not only moral laws that are universally binding but also specifications of the organizational norms of concrete social unions or congregations. Kant thinks the question of how a church ought to be organized under particular conditions of experience "appears to be unanswerable by reason alone and to require statutory legislation of which we become cognizant only through revelation, *i.e.*, an historical faith which, in contradistinction to pure religious faith, we can call ecclesiastical faith" (p. 96). We have no way of knowing whether or not such organizational statutes are divine statutory law. On the one hand, it would be presumptuous to assume that they are, because doing so might lead us to neglect the task of trying to improve the church's form. On the other, it would be equally presumptuous to deny that they are if they are completely harmonious with morality and, in addition, we cannot account for them in terms of normal processes of cultural development. Because of a weakness in human nature, Kant concludes, "in men's striving toward an ethical commonwealth, ecclesiastical faith thus naturally precedes pure religious faith; *temples* (buildings consecrated to the public worship of God) were before *churches* (meeting-places for the instruction and quickening of moral dispositions), *priests* (consecrated stewards of pious rites) before *divines* (teachers of the purely moral religion)" (p. 97).

Yet, morally speaking, the temporal order of precedence is the reverse of the correct order; pure religious faith morally precedes ecclesiastical faiths. Statutory ecclesiastical faith should be only a vehicle for pure religious faith, and observance of the statutes specified by ecclesiastical faith is only a means to reaching the goal of living as a member of an ethical commonwealth. Nevertheless, Kant supposes the vehicle is important. Its purpose is to preserve pure religious faith and insure its propagation in the same form to various times and places. According to Kant, ecclesiastical faiths founded on scriptures are better suited to serving this purpose than those merely grounded in tradition. History shows, he tells us, that "it has never been possible to destroy a faith grounded in scripture, even with the most devastating revolutions in the state, whereas the faith established upon tradition and ancient public observances has promptly met its downfall when the state was overthrown" (p. 98). Even if one doubts these sweeping historical generalizations, one can easily see the plausibility of the suggestion that scriptural faiths are, other things being equal, better able to preserve and propagate themselves than those that rest entirely on custom and oral tradition.

For Kant, there is only one pure religion of reason, which consists of belief in morality and morality's God. The pure religion of reason can, however, be consistently embedded in more than one ecclesiastical faith, and so many ecclesiastical faiths, all of which are its vehicles, are only to be expected. In terms of Kant's analogy with the pair of concentric circles, the inner circle can be consistently contained in a variety of outer circles. Kant seems willing to allow that several ecclesiastical faiths actually do, or could come to, serve as vehicles for the religion of pure reason. He says: "There is only *one* (true) *religion*; but there can be *faiths* of several kinds. We can say further that even in the various churches, severed from one another by reason of the diversity of their modes of belief, one and the same true religion can yet be found" (p. 98). None of these churches is, as it stands, identical with the true visible church, for all of them lack the universality Kant regards as a mark of the true visible church. All of them, being based on ecclesiastical faiths, contain elements of historical or revealed faith that cannot command, as the pure religion of reason can, universal assent, because, Kant contends, "an historical faith, grounded solely in facts, can extend its influence no further than tidings of it can reach, subject to circumstances of time and place and dependent upon the capacity [of men] to judge the credibility of such tidings" (p. 94). Yet each such church contains within the shell of its ecclesiastical faith, so to speak, a kernel that is the pure religion of reason. Each has within it the potential to grow closer to the true visible church.

According to Kant, it is incumbent on us, in striving toward an ethical commonwealth, to liberate the kernel from the shell to the extent that it is humanly possible for us to do so. How far can we hope to get in this project? On this question, Kant appears to be of two minds. In one passage, he expresses an optimistic moral eschatology. He predicts that "in the end religion will gradually be freed from all empirical determining grounds and from all statutes which rest on history and which through the agency of ecclesiastical faith provisionally unite men for the requirements of the good; and thus *at last* the pure religion of reason will rule over all, 'so that God may be all in all'" (p. 112, my emphasis). But shortly thereafter he cautions us that this divine ethical state on earth "is still infinitely removed from us" (p. 113). And in a less optimistic projection, though he insists that "we ought even now to labor industriously, by way of continuously setting free the pure religion from its present shell, which as yet cannot be spared," he immediately goes on to say of ecclesiastical faith "not that it is to cease (for as a vehicle it may perhaps always be useful and necessary) but that it be able to cease; whereby is indicated merely the inner stability of the pure moral faith" (p. 126). So Kant, in one frame of mind, predicts that the pure religion of reason will eventually become freestanding and the true visible church will be realized on earth. In another, however, he more guardedly claims that, though it could be freestanding, the pure religion of reason may never actually succeed in becoming free of the shell of ecclesiastical faith. Yet, in either case, we ought even now to do what we can, in striving toward an ethical commonwealth, to liberate the pure religion of reason from the shell of ecclesiastical faith and to realize the true visible church on earth.

A famous paragraph in which Kant lays out a taxonomy can be put to work in summing up his ecclesiology. It goes as follows:

Religion is (subjectively regarded) the recognition of all duties as divine commands. That religion in which I must know in advance that something is a divine command in order to recognize it as my duty, is the *revealed* religion (or the one standing in need of a revelation); in contrast, that religion in which I must first know that something is my duty before I can accept it as a divine injunction is the *natural* religion. He who interprets the natural religion alone as morally necessary, *i. e.*, as duty can be called the *rationalist* (in matters of belief); if he denies the reality of all supernatural divine revelation he is called a *naturalist*; if he recognizes revelation, but asserts that to know and accept it as real is not a necessary requisite to religion, he could be named a *pure rationalist*; but if he holds that belief in it is necessary to universal religion, he could be named the pure *supernaturalist* in matters of faith. (pp. 142–3)

Where does Kant himself fit into this set of categories? The question bristles with difficulties.

Kant tells us that his distinction between natural and revealed religion is meant to classify religion with reference to its first origin and inner possibility. In these terms, the pure religion of reason is the natural religion, and various ecclesiastical faiths are forms of the revealed religion. Kant himself is a rationalist of some kind; he thinks our moral duties are exhausted by those prescribed by the pure religion of reason. He is not a naturalist, for he does not deny the reality of supernatural revelation. A rationalist, he tells us, "will never contest either the inner possibility of revelation in general or the necessity of a revelation as a divine means for the introduction of true religion; for these matters no man can determine through reason" (p. 143). Kant contests neither of them. Nor is he a pure supernaturalist. Far from being necessary to universal religion, historical revelation is a formidable if not insurmountable obstacle to universality. Thus the only thing left in Kant's taxonomic scheme for him to be is a pure rationalist. But if he falls into this category, he not only does not deny the possibility of revelation, he affirms its actuality.

But classifying Kant as a pure rationalist by default is problematic. Clearly it is possible to hold that accepting revelation is not necessary for religion and neither to deny the reality of revelation, as the naturalist does, nor to affirm its reality, as the pure rationalist does. In other words, there is logical space in Kant's taxonomy for another category. Since he does not give it a name, I propose to call those who fall into it agnostic rationalists. We can then raise this question: Why should we classify Kant as a pure rationalist rather than as an agnostic rationalist?

The answer, I think, begins to emerge when we note that Kant classifies religion not only with respect to first origin and inner possibility, as noted above, but also with respect to its capacity for being widely shared with others. In terms of the latter classification, we have "either the *natural* religion, of which (once it has arisen) everyone can be convinced through his own reason, or a *learned* religion, of which one can convince others only through the agency of learning (in and through which they must be guided)" (p. 143). According to this classification, the pure religion of reason is natural. Moreover, it seems possible for there to be a religion that is both natural, because everyone can be convinced of it through reason, and revealed in terms of its origin, because its revelation contains nothing incompatible with what reason is capable of discovering. Noting this possibility, Kant says that "such a religion, accordingly, can be *natural*, and at the same time *revealed*, when it is so constituted that men *could and ought to have discovered it* of themselves merely through the use of their reason, although they *would* not have come upon it so early, or over so wide an area, as is required" (pp. 143–4). I consider it characteristic of Enlightenment thought to take this possibility seriously. Kant seems almost to be echoing Lessing, who had earlier said that "revelation gives nothing to the human race which human reason could not arrive at on its own; only it has given, and still gives to it, the most important of these things first."[7] I suggest that Kant takes Christianity, properly interpreted, to be a religion that is both natural and revealed and accepts it thus understood. He therefore recognizes its revelation and is indeed a pure rationalist.[8]

Support for my suggestion can be found in Kant's explicit discussions of Christianity. He first discusses the Christian religion as a natural religion. After summarizing some of the moral doctrines expounded by the figure he describes as the Teacher, Kant delivers the following somewhat convoluted but nevertheless highly favorable verdict: "Here then is a complete religion, which can be presented to all men comprehensibly and convincingly through their own reason; while the possibility and even the necessity of its being an archetype for us to imitate (so far as men are capable of that imitation) have, be it noted, been made evident by means of an example without either the truth of those teachings nor the authority and worth of the Teacher requiring any external certification (for which scholarship or miracles, which are not matters for everyone, would

---

[7] Gotthold Ephraim Lessing, "The Education of the Human Race," in *Lessing's Theological Writings*, trans. Henry Chadwick (Stanford: Stanford University Press, 1957), 83.

[8] I thus side with Hare in a disagreement with Wood. See Hare, *Moral Gap*, 41–5.

be required)" (p. 150). Kant also discusses the Christian religion as a learned religion. If Christianity as a learned religion is not to conflict with the natural religion within it, Kant maintains, "recognition and respect must be accorded, in Christian dogmatic, to universal human reason as the supremely commanding principle in a natural religion, and the revealed doctrine, upon which a church is founded and which stands in need of the learned as interpreters and conservers, must be cherished and cultivated as merely a means, but a most precious means, of making this doctrine comprehensible, even to the ignorant, as well as widely diffused and permanent" (pp. 152–3). It is not obvious which doctrine Kant has in mind when he refers to the project of making a certain doctrine comprehensible, widely diffused, and permanent. However, it makes little sense to suppose that the revealed doctrine is to be cherished as a mere means to making itself comprehensible. So I believe we should understand Kant's thought to be that the revealed doctrine is to be cherished and cultivated as a mere means to making the doctrine of natural religion within Christianity comprehensible, widely diffused, and permanent.[9]

What is the relation, by Kant's lights, between actual Christian churches, founded on the revealed doctrines of Christianity, and his ideal of a true church? Clearly no actual Christian church has yet become the true visible church. But has any of them become a true church in some other sense? Kant's criterion for addressing this question is the following: "When, therefore, (in conformity with the unavoidable limitation of human reason) an historical faith attaches itself to pure religion, as its vehicle, but with the consciousness that it is only a vehicle, and when this faith, having become ecclesiastical, embraces the principle of a continual approach to pure religious faith, in order finally to be able to dispense with the historical vehicle, a church thus characterized can at any time be called the *true* church; but, since conflict over historical dogmas can never be avoided, it can be spoken of only as the church *militant*, though with the prospect of becoming finally the changeless and all-unifying church *triumphant*" (p. 106). I dare say no actual Christian church in Kant's day had either become conscious of the historical or revealed portion of its doctrine as a mere vehicle or embraced the principle of approaching a purely moral religion in order to be able to dispense with that historical vehicle. I also think no actual Christian church in our day has done either of these things. Judged by Kant's standard, no actual Christian church has yet become the true church, not even the true church militant. By his

---

[9] This interpretation is supported by the translation of the *Religion* by di Giovanni in the Cambridge Edition of the Works of Immanuel Kant. See *Religion and Rational Theology*, trans. Allen W. Wood and George di Giovanni (Cambridge: Cambridge University Press, 1996), 186. According to this translation, the doctrine of revelation "must be cherished and cultivated as a mere means, though a most precious one, for giving meaning, diffusion and continuity to *natural religion* even among the ignorant" (my emphasis).

lights, then, the reformation of Christianity, bravely begun by Luther and Calvin, still has a long way to go.[10]

II. TWO IMPLICATIONS OF KANT'S ECCLESIOLOGY

Kant's ecclesiology influences his views on many topics that should be of interest to Christian philosophers. I shall discuss only two of these topics: scriptural interpretation and religious tolerance. Both are of considerable intrinsic importance. However, I focus on Kant's views about them chiefly because his views on these topics provide a basis for my criticism of fundamental features of his ecclesiology.

According to Kant, the pure religion of reason ought to serve as the interpreter of ecclesiastical faiths. If an ecclesiastical faith's revelation is to be united or harmonized with the pure religion of reason and not to separate from it like water from oil, an interpretation of the revelation is required that agrees with the universal moral rules laid down by practical reason. When the revelation is contained in scripture, as Kant thinks it best that it should be, interpretation will consist of textual exegesis. He cautions us that "frequently this interpretation may, in the light of the text (of the revelation), appear forced—it may often really be forced; and yet if the text can possibly support it, it must be preferred to a literal interpretation which either contains nothing at all [helpful] to morality or else actually works counter to moral incentives" (pp. 100–1). In *The Conflict of the Faculties*, Kant proposes a specific principle of scriptural exegesis. It says this: "If a scriptural text contains certain *theoretical* teachings which are proclaimed sacred but which *transcend* all rational concepts (even moral ones), it *may be* interpreted in the interests of practical reason; but if it contains statements that contradict practical reason, it *must* be interpreted in the interests of practical reason."[11] Examples Kant provides can be used to illustrate the two clauses of this principle at work.

Consider first the topic of Christology. According to a high Christology, Christ possesses both a divine nature and a human nature, united in a single person. Kant can find nothing in such a conception that serves the interests of practical reason. As he points out, if we think of Christ "as the Divinity 'dwelling incarnate' in a real man and working as a second nature in him, then we can draw nothing practical from this mystery: since we cannot require ourselves to rival a God, we cannot take

---

[10] After noting that, for Kant, the Christian church was seen as the precursor of a true ethical commonwealth, Keith Ward asks whether a universal moral community is "what Jesus and his community of disciples was [sic] really concerned with." See Keith Ward, *Religion and Community* (Oxford: Clarendon Press, 2000), 303. Almost certainly the answer to this question is negative. But we can also ask ourselves whether a universal moral community is what the Christian church today ought to be really concerned with. This is Kant's question. A negative answer to Ward's question does not entail a negative answer to Kant's question.

[11] Immanuel Kant, *The Conflict of the Faculties*, trans. Mary J. Gregor (Lincoln, Nebr.: University of Nebraska Press, 1992), 65.

him as an example."[12] In addition, we must confront the puzzle of why, if such a union can be brought about in one case, God does not produce it in every human case, thereby making all of us essentially well-pleasing to God. But Kant does find something that serves the interests of practical reason in a Christology which interprets Christ as the personification of the idea of humanity in its complete moral perfection. Hence he considers it permissible for him to employ this idea in interpreting scriptural texts that, if taken more literally, seem to support a high Christology. In a famous passage, he offers such an interpretation of the first verses of the Prologue to John's Gospel. It goes as follows:

Mankind (rational earthly existence in general) *in its complete moral perfection* is that which alone can render a world the object of a divine decree and the end of creation. With such perfection as the prime condition, happiness is the direct consequence, according to the will of the Supreme Being. Man so conceived, alone pleasing to God, "is in Him through eternity"; the idea of him proceeds from God's very being; hence he is no created thing but His only-begotten Son, "the *Word* (the *Fiat!*) through which all other things are, and without which nothing is in existence that is made" (since for him, that is, for rational existence in the world, so far as he may be regarded in the light of his moral destiny, all things were made). (p. 54)

Nicholas Wolterstorff intriguingly likens the sketch of an interpretation in this passage to "Brendel's giving one of his pupils some suggestions for interpreting the *Hammerklavier.*"[13] No doubt some Christian readers of the Prologue to John's Gospel will consider the interpretation Kant sketches arbitrary or capricious; others will view his suggestions as forced or strained. To the charge of arbitrariness, Kant could respond that his interpretation is constrained by the interests of practical reason. Taking Christ to be a personification of the idea of humanity in its complete moral perfection provides us with a vivid paradigm to imitate in our moral striving. As we have seen, Kant would not be bothered by the objection that his interpretation is forced. Even if it is, he would insist, provided the text can support it, if only barely so, it is permissible and, indeed, must be preferred to more literal rivals that do not serve the interests of practical reason.

Consider next the narrative in Genesis 22 of the *akedah*, the binding of Isaac. According to the story, God commands Abraham to sacrifice his beloved son, innocent Isaac, and Abraham consents to do so. If the story is taken to be literally true, Abraham actually is divinely commanded to kill Isaac. For Kant, however, Abraham clearly has a moral duty not to kill Isaac derived from practical reason, and so Abraham must be represented as divinely commanded not to kill Isaac. Hence the story, taken literally, contradicts practical reason in the sense that together they yield the result that Abraham is divinely commanded to perform each member of a pair of contradictory actions. According to the second clause of his principle of scriptural exegesis, Kant must interpret Genesis 22 in the interests

---

[12] Ibid. 67.
[13] Nicholas Wolterstorff, *Divine Discourse* (Cambridge: Cambridge University Press, 1995), 178.

of practical reason. He does so by denying, in effect, that God ever told Abraham to sacrifice Isaac. As Kant sees it, "in some cases man can be sure that the voice he hears is *not* God's; for if the voice commands him to do something contrary to the moral law, then no matter how majestic the apparition may be, and no matter how it may seem to surpass the whole of nature, he must consider it an illusion."[14] And in a footnote Kant goes on to say that "Abraham should have replied to this supposedly divine voice: 'That I ought not to kill my good son is quite certain. But that you, this apparition, are God—of that I am not certain, and never can be, not even if this voice rings down to me from (visible) heaven.'"[15] So Kant defends the interests of practical reason in the case of the story of the *akedah* by insisting that, if Abraham heard a voice commanding him to sacrifice Isaac that seemed to be God's, he could and should have been sure that it was instead the voice of an illusory apparition. He does not suggest that the story provides any positive service to those interests. But I suppose one might read it in a morally edifying way by holding that the point of having the angel in the story allow Abraham to sacrifice a ram rather than Isaac was to teach that God disapproves of human sacrifice.

Since we are two centuries more removed than Kant was from the Wars of Religion, religious toleration is perhaps a less burning issue for us than it was for him. In the West, it is largely taken for granted now, except in peripheral trouble spots such as Beirut, Belfast, and Bosnia. But for most of the common era respectable Christian opinion endorsed the use of the coercive power of the state to persecute religious dissent. From the time of Augustine onward, Luke 14: 23 was often cited as justification in revelation for such an endorsement. In that verse, which is contained in the Parable of the Great Dinner, the master says to the slave, "Go out into the roads and lanes, and compel people to come in, so that my house may be filled." Advocates of religious toleration before Kant, for instance Pierre Bayle in his *Philosophical Commentary on the Words of the Gospel, "Compel them to come in,"* had grappled with this text.[16] Kant alludes to it in a brief treatment of toleration.

Kant's discussion of toleration is set in the context of an exposition of his doctrine of conscience. He defines conscience as "a state of consciousness which in itself is duty" (p. 173). Opposing the probabilist principle that the opinion that an action may well be right is sufficient to justify performing it, he insists that I must be sure that any action I propose to perform is right. In other words, I have a duty to be conscious that any action I intend to perform is right. Kant illustrates how the duty of conscience works with the case of an inquisitor who is called upon to pass judgment on someone charged with heresy but otherwise a good citizen. Is it morally permissible for the inquisitor to condemn the accused person

---

[14] Kant, *The Conflict of the Faculties*, 115.

[15] Ibid. 115. I have silently corrected a typo in the quotation.

[16] For interesting discussion of Bayle's views on toleration, see John Kilcullen, *Sincerity and Truth* (Oxford: Clarendon Press, 1988).

to death? In a sentence that alludes to the famous verse from Luke's Gospel, Kant asks us to suppose that the inquisitor "was firm in the belief that a supernaturally revealed Divine Will (perhaps in accord with the saying, *compellite intrare*) permitted him, if it did not actually impose it as duty, to extirpate presumptive disbelief together with the disbelievers" (pp. 174–5). But does the inquisitor's belief, firm though we suppose it to be, have a high enough epistemic status that the inquisitor can in good conscience intend to act on it? In a familiar passage in which he alludes to the *akedah*, Kant returns a negative answer to this question. It goes as follows:

That it is wrong to deprive a man of his life because of his religious faith is certain, unless (to allow for the most remote possibility) a Divine Will, made known in extraordinary fashion, has ordered it otherwise. But that God has ever uttered this terrible injunction can be asserted only on the basis of historical documents and is never apodictically certain. After all, the revelation has reached the inquisitor only through men and has been interpreted by men, and even did it appear to have come to him from God Himself (like the command delivered to Abraham to slaughter his own son like a sheep) it is at least possible that in this instance a mistake has prevailed. But if this is so, the inquisitor would risk the danger of doing what would be wrong in the highest degree; and in this very act he is behaving unconscientiously. (p. 175)

According to Kant, then, the inquisitor's situation is to be analyzed in epistemic terms along these lines. The duty not to kill people on account of their religious faith is part of the pure religion of reason and lies within the inner circle. The claim that it binds the inquisitor has a very high epistemic status. By contrast, the claim that killing heretics is morally permissible, or even required, belongs to the historical or revealed part of an ecclesiastical faith and lies in that portion of the outer circle not also contained within the inner circle. It has a lower epistemic status. And even if killing heretics were apparently directly commanded by God, the claim that killing heretics is not wrong would not acquire an epistemic status exceeding that of the claim that killing heretics is wrong. Hence the inquisitor can never be sure that killing a heretic is morally right. The inquisitor would therefore act unconscientiously and thereby violate a duty by condemning a heretic, who is otherwise a good citizen, to death. Kant generalizes from the example to other cases in which following an injunction rooted in the historical or revealed part of an ecclesiastical faith carries with it "the danger of disobedience to a human duty which is certain in and of itself" (p. 175). And presumably the generalization is meant by Kant to cover not only extreme cases such as killing heretics but also other uses of coercive measures by church or state to suppress dissent from a particular ecclesiastical faith.

What is more, Kant extends the argument to acts allowable in themselves and taken by the revealed part of an ecclesiastical faith to be divinely commanded such as worshipping in public on a certain day of the week or professing firm belief in doctrines whose sole source is historical revelation. He asks whether ecclesiastical authorities may or should impose what they hold to be such positive revealed law on the laity as an article of faith they must subscribe to on pain of forfeiting their status in their empirical church. The fault he finds with such an imposition is that "the clergyman would be requiring the people at least inwardly to confess something to be as true as is their belief in God, *i. e.*, to confess, as though in the presence of God, something which they do not know with certainty" (p. 175). In doing this the clergyman would, Kant thinks, be acting in an unconscientious manner. He "would himself go counter to conscience in forcing others to believe that of which he himself can never be wholly convinced; he should therefore in justice consider well what he does, for he must answer for all abuse arising out of such a compulsory faith" (p. 176). If we take Kant's reference to being wholly convinced to concern complete psychological conviction, we will probably think he underestimates the extent to which the clergy can acquire convictions whose psychological certitude outstrips their epistemic certainty. So we would probably do better to attribute to him the thought that it is unconscientious and so contrary to duty to force others to believe anything one cannot be, and so is not, epistemically certain of oneself. On this interpretation, the duty of conscientiousness supports, as Kant sees it, not only mutual toleration among diverse ecclesiastical faiths but also free faith, that is, faith freely assented to by all, within each of them.

III. KANT'S ECCLESIOLOGY CRITICIZED AND REVISED

Christians may well wish to quarrel with Kant's ecclesiology on numerous points of detail. It might be argued, for example, that the text of the Prologue to John's Gospel cannot support the interpretation of it Kant sketches. Or, it might be claimed that Kant's understanding of the case of the inquisitor and of the *akedah* is incorrect. He allows, after all, for the remote possibility that the inquisitor has been ordered by God to kill heretics by means of a divine command made known in extraordinary fashion. And clearly it is within God's power, though it would indeed be extraordinary, to provide evidence that would make the claim that such a command had been given maximally certain. To be sure, as Kant notes, even if God did this and the inquisitor took the command to have come from God, it would remain possible that a mistake had prevailed. However, one might disagree with the Kantian view according to which it is maximally certain that it is always wrong to deprive someone of life for heresy. It is also possible that there are exceptions to this moral principle. So it seems at least possible for it to be more certain that God has commanded an inquisitor to kill a heretic than that it is wrong for the inquisitor to do so. Similarly, it seems at least possible for it to be more certain that Abraham has been commanded by God to sacrifice Isaac than that it is wrong for Abraham to sacrifice Isaac. Hence it seems at least possible for there to be a conscientious inquisitor who condemns a heretic to death and an Abraham who conscientiously consents to sacrifice Isaac.

But, for present purposes, I think it would not be useful to linger too long over points of detail. I propose instead to proceed directly to what I take to be the deepest objection to Kant's ecclesiology, which is a challenge to its basic structure. The objection is that practical reason is just not up to the task Kant assigns it in his ecclesiology. In order to present the objection, let me draw attention to a feature of Kant's image of the concentric circles I have heretofore not mentioned. Kant needs the circumference of the inner circle to mark two distinct boundaries. On the one hand, within it lies the pure religion of reason, which consists of Kantian morality and its postulated God, while outside it lie other historical and revealed doctrines of ecclesiastical faiths. On the other hand, within it lie propositions with some very high epistemic status such as being certain in and of themselves while outside are to be found only propositions with one or another lower epistemic status. Kant supposes that these two distinctions, one based on kinds of doctrine and the other epistemologically based, coincide in extension and so determine a single boundary. As I see it, this supposition is the ground of his confidence that the pure religion of reason ought to serve as the interpreter of ecclesiastical faiths and that, when conflict arises, scripture must be interpreted in the interests of practical reason. It is also what lies behind his view that the moral deliverances of practical reason are fit to serve as an Archimedean fixed point from which ecclesiastical faiths, relegated to role of mere vehicles, can be subjected to critique, purification, reformation, and perhaps even elimination. Yet there are, in my opinion, two good reasons for us to doubt Kant's powerful supposition.

One stems from the historical fate of Kant's own moral theory. In the course of the more than two centuries during which it has been debated, it has not become the focus of a consensus on the part of all reasonable moral inquirers who have considered it. Many reasonable people reject the conclusions Kant draws about the famous four examples of the *Groundwork*. Of course there are strategies for salvaging parts of Kantian moral theory. It can be argued, for instance, that Kant himself misunderstood his own theory in some respects and thus made mistakes in applying it to one or more of the four examples. The predictable result of such salvage operations, however, seems to me to be the plurality of reasonable views found on the contemporary philosophical scene that are more or less Kantian in spirit. And other modern moral theories have suffered similar fates. I think Robert M. Adams has made the correct pessimistic induction. He says: "Nothing in the history of modern secular ethical theory gives reason to expect that general agreement on a single comprehensive ethical theory will ever be achieved—or that, if achieved, it would long endure in a climate of free inquiry."[17] Like rock and roll, reasonable pluralism in moral theory is here to stay. From the fact of

[17] Robert Merrihew Adams, "Religious Ethics in a Pluralistic Society," in Gene Outka and John P. Reeder, Jr. (eds.), *Prospects for a Common Morality* (Princeton: Princeton University Press, 1993), 97.

reasonable pluralism in moral theory, I draw the conclusion that it is utopian to hope that, under conditions of free inquiry, any moral theory will, in its entirety, ever acquire the high epistemic status for all of us needed to fit it for the role Kant wanted his moral theory to play in the universally shared pure religion of reason.

A second reason for skepticism about Kant's powerful supposition can be generated from the method of reflective equilibrium that has received a good deal of attention in recent discussion of the methodology of moral theorizing.[18] According to that method, roughly described, one is to seek coherence in one's views, starting from one's considered judgments, by proceeding first to a narrow equilibrium in ethics between judgments about principles and judgments about particular cases and then to a wide equilibrium between ethical judgments and judgments about other matters such as the nature of human persons. In the course of employing the procedure, when conflicts in judgment come up and must be resolved in the interest of achieving coherence, one is to stick with the judgment that seems to one more likely to be correct and reject or revise the other judgment. If the procedure is successful, its output will be a large and coherent body of judgments, some ethical and some not. Suppose that one belief seeming more likely than another to be correct is both a contributor to and an indicator of the former having a higher epistemic status than the latter. Consider people who have religious beliefs and treat them as inputs to the process of seeking wide reflective equilibrium. Is it likely that at wide reflective equilibrium their beliefs will be structured in a way that is aptly represented by Kant's concentric circles? I think not.

Think first about what is likely to happen when the people under consideration proceed to narrow reflective equilibrium. Their method does not guarantee convergence in judgment. I imagine it is possible that they converge on a single set of moral judgments that coincides everywhere with Kant's morality. But if they are even moderately diverse in cultural background and personal experience, then, though some overlap in moral judgment at narrow reflective equilibrium would not be surprising, it is highly unlikely that there will be complete agreement on Kant's morality. Think next about the move from narrow reflective equilibrium of moral beliefs to wide reflective equilibrium of moral beliefs with theological beliefs from historical sources or revelation. Again, I imagine it is possible that, whenever conflict between moral beliefs and theological beliefs arises, all the people being considered always resolve it by sticking with the moral beliefs and revising or reinterpreting the theological beliefs. But this too is vastly unlikely. It is much more likely that many of them will sometimes resolve conflict in favor of moral beliefs and sometimes in favor of theological beliefs. Finally, think about the people in question after they have reached theo-ethical coherence

[18] See John Rawls, *A Theory of Justice* (Cambridge, Mass.: Harvard University Press, 1971), 19–21 and 48–51, and Norman Daniels, "Wide Reflective Equilibrium and Theory Acceptance in Ethics," *Journal of Philosophy*, 76 (1979).

at wide reflective equilibrium; consider what would be the result of trying to isolate for each of them an inner kernel of beliefs with maximal certainty or some comparable high epistemic status by drawing a circle around exactly those beliefs. Would this inner core consist in all cases of Kant's pure religion of reason? I grant that this is possible, but, once more, I consider it extremely unlikely. It is very likely that there would be no universally shared inner core at all. It is also very likely that for many of the people under consideration the inner core, if there were one, would contain a mixture of moral and theological beliefs rather than consisting entirely of belief in Kant's morality and its deity.

I believe the method of wide reflective equilibrium is a useful method in ethics. In the present context, however, it serves for me mainly as a device for representing what is likely to happen in conditions of moderate cultural and experiential diversity under the free play of human reason. My conclusion is that reason is unlikely to yield a comprehensive moral doctrine capable of functioning as Kant expects his morality operate. It is highly improbable that reason will carve out for all who employ it conscientiously anything like Kant's pure religion of reason that can both be universally shared and serve as a fixed point in a critique of the revelations of various ecclesiastical faiths. From an epistemological point of view, Kant's ecclesiology is therefore excessively ambitious.

But it is important not to throw the baby out with the bath water. If we look at things less systematically and more on a piecemeal basis, I dare say most of us will discover cases in which we have moral convictions we rightly consider more likely to be correct than competing convictions whose source is the historical part of an ecclesiastical faith. So I see promise in a chastened Kantianism that proceeds on a case by case basis to deploy moral beliefs of high epistemic status as levers, as it were, to move churches and their members in the direction of reforming ecclesiastical arrangements and reinterpreting scriptures. It may be that such a critical stance toward ecclesiastical faiths is only feasible in a culture in which there are accessible moral sources independent of ecclesiastical faith. If so, chastened Kantian ecclesiology will be as much a product of modernity as Kant's own more ambitious systematic project of ecclesiological critique was.

Something like a chastened Kantianism seems to be at work in a recent discussion of the *akedah* by Robert M. Adams. In his *Finite and Infinite Goods*, there is a chapter devoted to Abraham's dilemma, though the Abraham of whom Adams speaks is not exactly the Abraham of the Hebrew Bible. Adams operates with a methodology that allows for ethical sources independent of theology to exert critical leverage on theological ethics; he tells us that "we simply will not and should not accept a theological ethics that ascribes to God a set of commands that is *too much* at variance with the ethical outlook that we bring to our theological thinking."[19] He cites the passage from *The Conflict of the Faculties*, quoted above,

---

[19] Robert Merrihew Adams, *Finite and Infinite Goods* (New York and Oxford: Oxford University Press, 1999), 256.

in which Kant provides Abraham with a reply to the supposedly divine voice, and he goes on to say that it is not easy to reject Kant's verdict on the case. Like Kant, Adams concentrates on the epistemological aspects of the situation. He comes down on Kant's side of the epistemological issue. Reflecting on the possibility of divinely commanded but otherwise unnecessary human sacrifices, he observes that "a situation in which I would find it reasonable to believe that a good God had given such an abhorrent command seems to me so unimaginable, however, that I think it is at best a waste of spiritual energy to try to decide what one should do in that case."[20] And in the same vein, he concludes the chapter with the remark that "the question whether God commands such a thing should stay off our epistemological agenda as long as it possibly can, which I expect will be forever."[21] Yet Adams does not rule out altogether the possibility that he might believe a divine command to sacrifice an innocent person had been issued. He considers the story, told in Shalom Spiegel's *The Last Trial*, of a Rabbi Samuel and his son Yehiel, also a rabbi, who were confronted with the alternatives of death and forced conversion to Christianity.[22] In the story, Yehiel offers himself to be sacrificed, and Samuel kills him. Commenting on it, Adams states that "if they claimed that God told them to do what they did, I would not say that no such command could come from God."[23] It is in the spirit of the chastened Kantianism I find promising to conduct discussion of the issue of divinely commanded human sacrifice on a case by case basis, as Adams does. It is also consonant with its spirit to expect some reasonable disagreement between him and others about either the case of Abraham and Isaac or the case of Samuel and Yehiel or about both cases.

But what, if anything, does Kantian ecclesiology, chastened or not, have to do with actual Christian churches and the ecclesiologies their theologians provide for them? In conclusion, I address this question with reference to the Roman Catholic ecclesiology of the Second Vatican Council.

IV. CHASTENED KANTIAN ECCLESIOLOGY AND ROMAN CATHOLIC ECCLESIOLOGY

No doubt there are contemporary religious movements that have gone a long way toward the Kantian ideal of a largely moral core embedded in an historical vehicle that minimizes commitment to revealed doctrine. Subject to correction by those who view them from the inside, I would say that Unitarian Universalism is one example rooted in Christianity and Reform Judaism is another. But the idea that the ecclesiology of the Roman Catholic Church has moved in a Kantian direction may initially seem quite surprising. I propose to explore this idea

---

[20] Robert Merrihew Adams, *Finite and Infinite Goods*, 290.   [21] Ibid. 291.

[22] Shalom Spiegel, *The Last Trial*, trans. Judah Goldin (Woodstock: Jewish Lights, 1993), 22–3.

[23] Adams, *Finite and Infinite Goods*, 286.

briefly with reference to the ecclesiology of Vatican II, basing my discussion on the summary of that ecclesiology found in Richard P. McBrien's magisterial *Catholicism*. It would, of course, not be plausible to claim that Kant directly influenced the ecclesiology of Vatican II. A standard history of the Catholic Church, written by the theologian McBrien praises as the most important ecclesiologist of the twentieth century, does not even mention Kant in its brief treatment of the *Aufklärung*.[24] However, I think it is plausible to view Kant as having articulated in a particularly forceful and radical way thoughts that have become increasingly influential in recent Catholic ecclesiology.

McBrien sums up the ecclesiology of Vatican II in ten points and spells out how each of them represents a change in Catholic thought. After reporting what he says, I shall in each case add my own comparisons with Kantian ecclesiology.

First, the church is, first and foremost, a mystery or sacrament. According to McBrien, this principle "supplants the pre-Vatican II emphasis on the Church as a *means* of salvation."[25] In Kant's ecclesiology, mystery and sacrament lie outside the inner circle that circumscribes the pure religion of reason and belong to the part of ecclesiastical faith that is not included in this religion. Yet the philosopher has no reason to deny them provided they do not conflict with morality. They must, however, be regarded as means, not of salvation but of strengthening human efforts to create an ethical commonwealth. In my chastened Kantian ecclesiology, it is not impossible in principle for claims about sacramentality to achieve high epistemic status at wide reflective equilibrium. But there remains a large gap between Kant's vision of the core of the church as nothing but a moral community and the view of Vatican II that it is a mystery.

Second, the church is the whole people of God. McBrien takes this principle to have "replaced the pre-Vatican II emphasis on the Church as hierarchical institution, which tended to make the study of the Church more akin to 'hierarchology' than to 'eccesiology' " (p. 684). This principle is consonant with Kant's ecclesiology in two ways. The ethical commonwealth, which is the *telos* of empirical churches, is to be represented as a people of God, potentially universal in scope, under laws of virtue. And the principle's opposition to hierarchy matches Kant's insistence that the true visible church will be neither a monarchy nor an aristocracy. The chastened Kantian ecclesiology I favor can endorse these two points of agreement between Kant and Vatican II.

Third, the whole people of God—laity, religious, and clergy alike—is called to participate in the mission of Christ as Prophet, Priest, and King. McBrien thinks this principle "replaces the pre-Vatican II notion of 'Catholic Action,' wherein the laity participates only in the mission of the hierarchy" (p. 684). To

[24] Yves Congar, *L'Église: De saint Augustin à l'époque moderne* (Paris: Éditions du Cerf, 1970), 409–12.

[25] Richard P. McBrien, *Catholicism*, vol. ii (Minneapolis: Winston Press, 1980), 684. Hereafter page references to this volume will be made parenthetically in the body of the text.

the extent that the thrust of this principle is against hierarchy it is harmonious with Kant's ecclesiology. However, there is tension between its conception of the mission of Christ and Kant's christology. For Kant, Christ functions as the exemplar of humanity in its complete moral perfection and as the Teacher of the morality of the Gospels. Within the limits of reason, Christ serves only moral purposes, though reason is not in a position to deny flatly other christological mysteries. Kant could, I think, find no moral use for Christ as a king. He could allow there to be a role for Christ as a prophet if we think of prophets chiefly as preachers of moral reform. And he could even make room for a priestly function for Christ provided it placed the emphasis on his work as what Kant describes as a divine, that is, a teacher of moral religion, rather than as what Kant thinks of as a priest, a steward of pious rites. So there is partial overlap rather than complete coincidence between this principle of Vatican II and Kant's ecclesiology. My more latitudianarian chastened Kantianism leaves open the possibility of greater overlap with the principle at wide reflective equilibrium.

Fourth, the mission of the people of God includes service to human needs in the social, political, and economic orders as well as the preaching of the Word and the celebration of the sacraments. McBrien argues that this principle "supplants the pre-Vatican II notion of 'pre-evangelization,' wherein such service is, or may be, a necessary preparation for the preaching of the Gospel (evangelization) but is not itself essential to the Church's mission in the same way as the preaching or the celebration of the sacraments" (p. 684). By promoting service to human needs from the status of a means to evangelization to that of a central part of the mission in its own right, this principle takes a step in the direction of the Kantian view that morality must be at the core of any church with prospects for becoming a true church. Kant's own ecclesiology, however, would assign sacramentality to the part of ecclesiastical faith that belongs to the shell rather than the kernel of pure moral religion. As previously noted, a chastened Kantian ecclesiology does not guarantee that graduations in epistemic status will enforce an invidious distinction of this sort.

Fifth, the church is realized and expressed at the local as well as the universal level; it is a communion of churches. McBrien's view is that this principle "supplants the common pre-Vatican II notion that the Church is, for all practical purposes, always understood as the Church universal, centralized in the Vatican under the supreme authority of the pope, with each diocese considered only as an administrative division of the Church universal, and each parish, in turn, an administrative subdivision of the diocese" (p. 685). Kant's ecclesiology does not go into detail about how to set up the administration of a large empirical church. But it does not aspire to the kind of universality that depends on securing agreement by submission to a centralized authority. Instead it looks for spontaneous agreement in morality that derives from the self-legislation of practical reason in each of us. So Kant's ecclesiology is consistent with the full realization of the moral core of the pure religion of reason in local churches. Chastened

Kantianism's more modest expectation is that there will be a reasonable pluralism of moral views both within and among local churches; it also supports the conclusion that a central authority's attempts to impose agreement in moral belief are unlikely to succeed under conditions of free inquiry.

Sixth, the church embraces more than the Roman Catholic Church; it is the whole Body of Christ: Catholics, Orthodox, Anglicans, and Protestants alike. McBrien holds that this principle "sets aside the pre-Vatican II concept that the Roman Catholic Church alone is the one, true Church, and that the other Christian communities (never called 'churches' before Vatican II) are somehow 'related' to the Church but are not real members of it" (p. 685). Like this principle, Kant's view rejects Roman Catholic ecclesiological exclusivism. By Kant's lights, however, no actual Christian church is, as we have seen, the true church, not even the true church militant. Yet, like this principle, his ecclesiology does allow that true religion can be found in various Christian churches despite the diversity of their modes of belief. A chastened Kantian ecclesiology will, of course, also allow that various Christian churches can achieve epistemic parity. Lacking Kant's pure religion of reason in its unadorned form to serve as a *telos* for ecclesiastical development, chastened Kantianism cannot appeal to it as a benchmark by which to judge that any actual Christian church falls short of being a true church.

Seventh, the mission of the whole church is (a) one of proclamation of the Gospel that is always subordinate to the Word of God; (b) one of celebration of the sacraments in a way that engages the intelligent participation of worshippers; (c) one of witnessing to the Gospel through a life-style that is marked by humility, compassion, respect for human rights, etc.; and (d) one of service to those in need, both inside and outside the Church. McBrien believes this principle "expands upon a narrower view of mission in pre-Vatican II ecclesiology, namely, one that tended to restrict the mission to the preaching of the Word and the celebration of the sacraments, and one which perhaps paid too little attention to the missionary responsibility of corporate witnessing to the Gospel" (pp. 685–6). To the extent that this expansion's third and fourth points stress the importance of morality by adding weight to the tasks of witnessing through virtuous living and serving those in need, they represent movement in the direction of Kant's ecclesiology and are compatible with chastened Kantianism. But, as we saw in the discussion above of the fourth principle, the second point's emphasis on sacramentality gives it a role somewhat at odds with Kant's view that sacramentality is to be relegated to the empirical vehicle from which pure moral religion should strive to free itself. And if the ranking referred to in the first point involves subordinating the morality of the Gospels to revealed doctrine, Kant would surely insist that the proper order of subordination is the reverse. A chastened Kantianism will not necessarily be in tension with the ecclesiology of Vatican II on these two points.

Eighth, all authority in the church is to be exercised as a service and in a collegial mode. McBrien maintains that this principle "is intended to transform the exercise of authority from one of domination and unilateral decision-making, as prevailed in the pre-Vatican II period" (p. 686). Since Kant says repeatedly that the ministers of a church should be servants of its invisible head and not high officials who exercise domination over its members, he would undoubtedly approve of the intention to work such a transformation in the exercise of ecclesiastical authority. Chastened Kantianism too permits and can endorse change along these lines.

Ninth, religious truth is to be found outside the Body of Christ and should be respected wherever it is found; in no case is anyone to be coerced to embrace Christianity or Catholicism. In McBrien's opinion, this principle "replaces a too-exclusive understanding of revelation as 'Christian revelation,' as well as the formula 'Error has no rights' " (p. 686). By means of this principle, Vatican II joins Kant in supporting religious freedom and religious toleration, and these values have become sufficiently robust under democratic regimes that most chastened Kantians who have the good fortune to live under such regimes would also support them at wide reflective equilibrium. And both Kant's ecclesiology and its chastened kin lack the resources to establish the claim that revelation cannot occur outside of Christianity.

Tenth, the nature and mission of the church are to be understood in relationship and in subordination to the Kingdom of God. McBrien supposes that this principle "replaces what was perhaps the most serious pre-Vatican II ecclesiological misunderstanding, namely, that the Church is identical with the Kingdom of God" (p. 686). If this were so, he adds, the church would be beyond all need for institutional reform. No doubt there are eschatological differences between Kant and Vatican II. Kant thinks that the gradual transition from ecclesiastical faith to the exclusive sovereignty of pure moral faith is the coming of the Kingdom of God. He tells us: "We have good reason to say, however, that 'the Kingdom of God is come unto us' once the principle of the gradual transition of ecclesiastical faith to the universal religion of reason, and so to a (divine) ethical state on earth, has become general and has also gained somewhere a *public* foothold, even though the actual establishment of this state is still infinitely removed from us" (p. 113). But even when the Kingdom has come in principle, there will remain, before it is established, an interval of time that may never end or may end only in a divinely produced consummation. Throughout that interval, critique and reform of ecclesiastical institutions will continue to be needed. Though the picture Vatican II presents of what the Kingdom of God will look like when it is fully realized may differ substantially from Kant's vision, the gap between the church of the present and the foreseeable future and the Kingdom of the *eschaton* leaves similar space for institutional critique and reform. It is likely that a gap of this kind will also exist at wide reflective equilibrium in chastened Kantianism.

In order to paint a balanced and comprehensive picture of both convergences and divergences of the ecclesiologies of Kant and Vatican II, I have covered all ten of the points under which McBrien organizes his treatment of the ecclesiology of Vatican II. It is obvious that my discussion of that ecclesiology does not delve deeply into it and is far from exhaustive. It does, however, allow us to discern a pattern. By comparison with pre-Vatican II Catholic views, the ecclesiology of Vatican II represents movement in a Kantian direction on several moral and political issues. They include opposition to hierarchical domination in the church, recognition of the centrality in the church's mission of moral service to those in need, acceptance of reasonable ecclesiastical pluralism within Christianity, support for religious freedom and religious toleration, and, most important of all, acknowledgement of the continuing legitimacy of institutional critique and reform. But sources of tension remain, the most salient of which is the emphasis in the ecclesiology of Vatican II on sacramentality as a crucial part of the definition of the church and its mission. For Kant, a doctrine of sacramentality would belong to the part of ecclesiastical faith that is not also a part of the pure religion of reason. Though he would allow that reason is not competent to deny such a doctrine provided it does not conflict with morality, he would locate it, along with other historical or revealed doctrines, in the vehicle of moral religion, which can be dispensed with in principle, and deny it the importance it has in the ecclesiology of Vatican II. I have argued that a chastened Kantianism, which is more realistic about the limits of reason as we have come to understand them since the time of Kant, would serve to reduce if not eliminate tension of this kind.

In ecclesiology, Kant may properly be conceived, in my opinion, as continuing and radicalizing the tradition of the Reformation.[26] Its slogan, 'Always Reforming,' signals a recognition that, all things human being susceptible to corruption, the work of reformation is never done. By analogical extension, we may think of idolatry of a certain sort as the danger against which ongoing reform is to help safeguard us. According to Robert M. Adams, this sort of idolatry "happens when one fails to distinguish devotion to God or the good from devotion to one's own religion or one's own idea of God or the good."[27] One's church too can become an idol in this sense. The ecclesiology of Vatican II insists that the Catholic Church is not identical with the Kingdom of God; in so doing it

---

[26] While I was working on this paper, I learned that my project, announced above in my introduction, of trying to provoke Christian philosophers to discuss ecclesiology has very recently been in part preempted by two papers on Kierkegaard's ecclesiology, Michael Plekon's "Kierkegaard at the End: His 'Last' Sermon, Eschatology and the Attack on the Church" and Bruce H. Kirmmse's "The Thunderstorm: Kierkegaard's Ecclesiology," both published in *Faith and Philosophy* 17/1 (2000). Despite large differences in their interpretations of Kierkegaard's view of the church, both Plekon and Kirmmse portray him as further radicalizing, in ways that I would say go well beyond Kant, the Reformation's tradition of critique of ecclesiastical institutions.

[27] Adams, *Finite and Infinite Goods*, 210.

opens a possibility for ecclesiastical reform that counteracts the human tendency toward this form of idolatry. In a more radical way, Kant had earlier made room for a similar possibility by distinguishing between the empirical churches of the ecclesiastical faiths and the true church of pure moral faith, which has not yet been realized on earth and may never be fully realized unless God intervenes. I think a less radical chastened Kantianism should not lose sight of this possibility. Its ecclesiology should share with those of Kant and Vatican II openness, stretching indefinitely into the future, to critique and reform of ecclesiastical institutions. This is an important lesson Christian philosophers can and should discover in Kantian philosophical ecclesiology.

RELIGIOUS DIVERSITY

13

Towards Thinner Theologies: *Hick and Alston on Religious Diversity*

Western Christianity has never been ignorant of religious diversity. Early Christianity had to make its way in the religiously pluralistic environment of late antiquity. During the medieval period, Islam put cultural and military pressure on European Christendom. And religious diversity has often been seen by Christians as an intellectual challenge to which a response must be made. Origen wrote *contra Celsum* to defend Christianity against pagan critique. Thomas Aquinas wrote *contra gentiles* to make the case for the rationality of Christian belief. So Western Christianity has never been without a philosophical problem of religious diversity of some sort.

But there seems to me to be something special about the form the problem of diversity assumes for Christians today. Frequently in the past the problem has been taken to be vindicating Christian exclusivism about doctrinal truth or access to salvation by writing polemics against the beliefs and practices of other religions. However many Christians have lost confidence in exclusivism, and even among the remaining exclusivists there are few with a taste for polemical warfare with other religions. Though armchair theorizing is no substitute for empirical research, I think it would not be excessively speculative to number among the causes of this change in attitude better acquaintance with religions other than Christianity and increased acknowledgement of evils associated with Christian exclusivism. Those Christians who live in pluralistic democracies have numerous opportunities to develop first-hand familiarity with religions other than their own. Modern scholarship has produced good translations of powerful texts from religious traditions other than Christianity, and cultural anthropologists have provided fascinating thick descriptions of the practices of such traditions. Educated Christians find it increasingly easy to discover much to admire in religions other than their own and hard to hang on to negative stereotypes of such religions. When religions are considered as social movements, they must, of course, be assigned a share of the responsibility for various social evils. But Christianity

An earlier version of the second part of this paper was presented at an Author Meets Critic Season on Alston's *Perceiving God* at the 1993 APA Pacific Division Meeting. I am grateful to Bill Alston for a response to my criticism that helped me in making revisions.

is no exception. Many Christians are now prepared to acknowledge that attitudes and practices informed by Christian exclusivism have contributed to evils derived from colonialism and antisemitism. The upshot is an attitude toward religions other than Christianity that is more respectful, less inclined to denigrate them, and less concerned to engage them in intellectual combat. Needless to say, there have been similar developments in other religious traditions. As a result exciting new possibilities for conversations among the world religions have opened up, and the philosophical discussion of religious diversity now takes place in a transformed intellectual climate.

Two of the best recent treatments of religious diversity by analytic philosophers of religion occur within this new climate. In his Gifford Lectures, published as *An Interpretation of Religion*, John Hick shows his respect for all the world religions by proposing a pluralistic hypothesis according to which there is parity among their truth claims. In his *Perceiving God*, William P. Alston shows his respect by proposing an account of mystical doxastic practices according to which the mystical practices of other religions are not precluded from achieving epistemic parity with the Christian practice. I think there is much to be learned, as well as something to criticize, in each of these discussions. In this paper I try to spell out one of the lessons to be drawn from them. I argue that movement in the direction of a refined version of Hick's position, which amounts to movement towards thinner theologies, is a rational course of action within the framework of Alston's doxastic practice approach to religious epistemology.

The paper is divided into two parts. The first is devoted to Hick, and the second focuses on Alston.

1. HICK'S RELIGIOUS PLURALISM

According to Hick, what the great religious traditions have in common is that each offers a path to salvation, which involves a transformation of human existence from self-centeredness to reality-centeredness. As far as we can tell, all of these traditions are of roughly equal effectiveness in producing this transformation. This suggests to Hick that a single ultimate reality is being differently conceived, experienced, and responded to from within different religious traditions. He develops this suggestion with the assistance of terminology and ideas borrowed from Kant. Like Kant, he distinguishes between the phenomenal and the noumenal. Using this distinction, he proposes that "the noumenal Real is experienced and thought by different human mentalities, forming and formed by different religious traditions, as the range of gods and absolutes which the phenomenology of religion reports."[1]

[1] John Hick, *An Interpretation of Religion* (New Haven and London: Yale University Press, 1989), 242. Hereafter references to this book will be made parenthetically in the body of my text. Hick also discusses religious diversity in "Religious Pluralism and Salvation," *Faith and Philosophy*,

These gods and absolutes, these divine *personae* and metaphysical *impersonae*, are phenomenal, and so they "are not illusory but are empirically, that is experientially, real as authentic manifestations of the Real" (p. 242). On a naturalistic interpretation of religion, according to which there is no noumenal Real, the various divine *personae* and metaphysical *impersonae* are illusory because they reduce to purely human projections. As Hick sees it, his is a religious interpretation of religion precisely because it postulates the noumenal Real.

Hick is not a slavish disciple of Kant; he himself draws attention to some of the ways in which their views differ. Thus, for example, Kant was driven to postulate God in response to moral demands, but Hick postulates the noumenal Real to explain the apparently equal salvific efficacy of the great religious traditions. Yet there is a difficulty in interpreting Hick's use of the distinction between the noumenal and the phenomenal that neatly parallels a difficulty Kant scholars find in interpreting his use of that distinction.

According to what is sometimes called the "double aspect" interpretation of Kant, his distinction between the phenomenal and the noumenal is not a distinction between two kinds of objects, appearances and things in themselves.[2] An analogy proposed by George Mavrodes can be used to illustrate the point.[3] Suppose a prince wants to get an undistorted idea of what the lives of his people are like and so decides to travel among them in disguise. In one village he appears and is experienced as an itinerant monk; in another he appears and is experienced as a journeyman stone-mason. One and the same prince visits both villages, but he appears and is experienced in different ways in the two villages.

When this disguise model is applied to Hick's appropriation of the Kantian distinction, Hick's pluralistic hypothesis is to be understood as postulating a single noumenal Real and diverse ways in which *it* appears and is experienced in different religious traditions. Some of the things Hick says when he introduces his pluralistic hypothesis call for this interpretation. Thus he tells us that Kant distinguished "between a *Ding an sich* and *that thing as it appears* to human consciousness" and that, for Kant, "the noumenal world exists independently of our perception of it and the phenomenal world is *that same world as it appears* to our human consciousness" (p. 241, my emphasis). And, speaking for himself, he claims that, though the noumenal Real is not directly known as such, "when human beings relate themselves to it in the mode of I–Thou encounter they *experience it as* personal" but "when human beings relate themselves to the Real in the mode of non-personal awareness they *experience it* as non-personal" (p. 245,

5 (1988), 365–77, and in *Disputed Questions in Theology and the Philosophy of Religion* (New Haven: Yale University Press, 1993), pt. IV.

  [2] Karl Ameriks, "Recent Work on Kant's Theoretical Philosophy," *American Philosophical Quarterly*, 19 (1982), 1–24. This interpretation might also aptly be described as the one world view.
  [3] George I. Mavrodes, "Polytheism," in Thomas D. Senor (ed.), *The Rationality of Belief and the Plurality of Faith* (Ithaca: Cornell University Press, 1995), 261–86.

my emphasis). On this interpretation, the noumenal Real itself is experienced, but it is experienced as personal in some religious traditions and is experienced as non-personal in others.

According to what is sometimes called the "two object" interpretation of Kant, his distinction between the phenomenal and the noumenal is a distinction between two kinds of objects.[4] Mavrodes provides us with another helpful analogy.[5] Imagine that two artists, who work in different non-representational styles, sit side by side, looking back and forth from a common landscape to their easels, and paint. When their paintings are finished, we find that they do not resemble one another and neither resembles the common landscape. Nonetheless both artists are confident that, had the landscape been significantly different, their paintings would have been noticeably different. The landscape furnished real input to the paintings, and they depend on it in some way. But of course they also depend on artistic decisions made by the painters. They are human constructs. And the two paintings are diverse from one another and from the landscape.

When this construct model is applied to Hick's appropriation of the Kantian distinction, Hick's pluralistic hypothesis is to be understood as postulating not only a single noumenal Real but also many phenomenal Reals that are joint products of the interaction of the noumenal Real and various human religious traditions. Some of the things Hick says when he proposes the pluralistic hypothesis call for this interpretation. Acknowledging that the noumenal provides informational input to human experience, he cautions us that "all that we are entitled to say about the noumenal source of this information is that it is the reality whose influence *produces*, in collaboration with the human mind, the phenomenal world of our experience" (p. 243, my emphasis). On this interpretation, the noumenal Real itself cannot be experienced, but it contributes to producing phenomenal objects, the divine *personae* and metaphysical *impersonae* of the religious traditions, that are experienced.[6]

Having distinguished the single noumenal Real, on the one hand, from either the many ways in which it is experienced in various religious traditions or the many phenomenal Reals it contributes to producing in collaboration with various religious traditions, on the other, Hick proceeds to make claims about the conclusions that can be drawn from his distinction. He says:

It follows from this distinction between the Real as it is in itself and as it is thought and experienced through our religious concepts that we cannot apply to the Real *an sich* the characteristics encountered in its *personae* and *impersonae*. Thus it cannot be said

[4] Ameriks, 'Recent Work'. This interpretation might also aptly be described as the two worlds view.

[5] Mavrodes, 'Polytheism'.

[6] This explains why Hick is included in the treatment of polytheism by Mavrodes. Within the construct model, the divine *personae* are distinct objects, and so Hick is a polytheist at the phenomenal level and not a theist at all at the noumenal level.

to be one or many, person or thing, substance or process, good or evil, purposive or non-purposive. None of the concrete descriptions that apply within the realm of human experience can apply literally to the unexperiencable ground of that realm (p. 246).

In this passage Hick's use of both the disguise model and the construct model leads him into inconsistency. In its first sentence he says that the noumenal Real is experienced, albeit through our concepts. This claim holds within the disguise model. And in its third sentence he implies that the noumenal Real is not experienced, because it belongs to a world that is the unexperiencable ground of the realm of human experience. This claim holds within the construct model. Hence it seems that Hick will be forced to choose between the two models in order to achieve consistency at this point. But no matter how he chooses, these conclusions do not in fact follow from his distinction unless he makes at least one additional assumption.

Consider first the disguise model. A prince can appear as and be experienced as a prince, clad in royal robes and seated on a throne. In order to exclude this possibility from the model, we must assume that every guise in which something can appear is a disguise. Less picturesquely but more accurately, Hick must assume that the noumenal Real cannot appear as or be experienced as it is in itself. Otherwise put, he must make the strong negative assumption that none of the ways in which the noumenal Real appears can be ways it is in itself. Exclusivists from all religious traditions will, of course, reject this assumption. They will insist that at least some of the ways in which the noumenal Real appears in their tradition are, or at least are closely analogous to, ways it is in itself. In short, Hick must not only distinguish between the phenomenal and the noumenal; he must also make a strong negative assumption about how they are related in order to get to the conclusion that we cannot apply to the Real *an sich* the characteristics encountered in its *personae* and *impersonae*.

Consider next the construct model. Artists who work in a representational style can paint landscapes. In order to exclude this possibility from the model, we must assume that there can be no representational landscape paintings. More accurately, Hick must assume that the noumenal Real cannot possess any positive attribute that is also possessed by the phenomenal Real of any of the great religious traditions. Otherwise put, he must make the strong negative assumption that no positive attribute of any of the phenomenal Reals of the great religious traditions can be an attribute of the noumenal Real. Exclusivists from all the traditions will also reject this assumption. They will insist that at least some of the positive attributes of the phenomenal Real of their own tradition, or at least closely analogous attributes, are also attributes of the noumenal Real. In sum, Hick must not only distinguish between the phenomenal and the noumenal; he must also make a strong negative assumption about how the various phenomenal Reals are related to the one noumenal Real in order to get to the conclusion that none of the concrete descriptions that apply within the realm of human experience can apply literally to the unexperiencable ground of that realm.

Hick does not argue directly for such strong negative assumptions. He certainly does not prove that those who reject them are mistaken. But if we grant such assumptions, it is easy to see how they can be used to establish parity among the truth claims of the great religious traditions.

In the disguise model, apparently conflicting claims about ultimate reality will be construed as truths about how the noumenal Real appears to various groups but falsehoods about how it is in itself. There is nothing contradictory in supposing that the noumenal Real appears as and is experienced as personal by Christians, and appears as and is experienced as impersonal by advaitic Hindus, but is in itself neither personal nor impersonal.[7] So all the great religious traditions will be on a par in two senses: they are all equally correct if their claims are taken to be about the ways in which the noumenal Real appears to them, and they are all equally mistaken if their claims are taken to be about the ways in which it is in itself. Similarly, in the construct model, apparently conflicting claims about ultimate reality will be construed as truths about the positive attributes of the diverse phenomenal Reals of the various religious traditions but falsehoods about the positive attributes of the noumenal Real. Neither is there anything contradictory in supposing that the phenomenal Real of Christianity is personal, the distinct phenomenal Real of advaitic Hinduism is impersonal, but the noumenal Real, which is yet a third thing, is neither personal nor impersonal. So, once again, all the great religious traditions will be on a par in two ways: they are all equally correct if their claims are taken to be about the positive attributes of their diverse phenomenal Reals, and they are all equally mistaken if their claims are taken to be about the positive attributes of the noumenal Real.

Honesty demands the admission that Hick's pluralistic hypothesis purchases such parity at a very high price. It must be viewed as an alternative and rival to the main lines of self-understanding within the great religious traditions. As one perceptive commentator notes, it proposes "a revisionist conception of religions and religious diversity."[8] A great many of the members of the great religious traditions would reject the claim that their religious beliefs are true only of the ways in which the ultimate religious reality appears to them, or only of phenomenal objects it contributes to producing, and not true of that reality as it is in itself. For example, an ordinary Christian theist who grasped the distinction between the phenomenal and the noumenal would be likely to insist that the noumenal Real

---

[7] At least this is so if we construe being personal and being impersonal as *contrary* properties. A charitable reading demands that we construe as contraries, not contradictories, all the pairs of attributes both of whose members Hick denies are possessed by the noumenal Real. This works well enough for such pairs as substance and process or good and evil, but I do not see that it so much as makes sense for such pairs as one and many or purposive and non-purposive. But let that pass.

[8] Sumner B. Twiss, "The Philosophy of Religious Pluralism: A Critical Appraisal of Hick and His Critics," *Journal of Religion*, 70 (1990), 543.

itself, and not just its way of appearing in Christian experience or a phenomenal object partly derived from it, is personal or, at least, that the noumenal Real itself is closely analogous to one or more human persons. Hick does what he can to accommodate such views, but the logic of his position does not permit him to do much. He recognizes that literal and analogical language about objects of religious worship or meditation always intends to be about the noumenal Real itself, but he holds that such language actually functions mythologically with respect to the noumenal Real. As he sees it, "we speak mythologically about the noumenal Real by speaking literally or analogously about its phenomenal manifestations" (p. 351). But, according to the definition he proposes, "a statement or set of statements about X is mythologically true if it is not literally true but nevertheless tends to evoke an appropriate dispositional attitude to X" (p. 348). All that Hick can concede to the ordinary Christian theist is that it is mythologically but not literally true that the noumenal Real is personal. However, such Christians typically believe or have beliefs which imply that it is literally true that the noumenal Real is personal. Similarly, all that he can concede to the ordinary advaitic Hindu is that it is mythologically but not literally true that the noumenal Real is impersonal. But such Hindus typically believe or have beliefs which imply that it is literally true that the noumenal Real is impersonal. So Hick's pluralistic hypothesis attributes large errors to a great many members of these two traditions. I doubt that such people would be consoled by the thought that it also attributes equally large errors to a great many members of all the other great religious traditions.

But perhaps there is massive error in the great religious traditions. The fact that Hick's pluralistic hypothesis is revisionary is, by itself, no proof of its falsehood. So it at least merits further consideration. Such consideration quickly reveals a problem with the formulation of the hypothesis.

According to the pluralistic hypothesis, the noumenal Real, the Real *an sich*, "cannot be said to be one or many, person or thing, conscious or unconscious, purposive or nonpurposive, substance or process, good or evil, loving or hating" (p. 350). To say such things of the noumenal Real is to say things that are not literally true of it. Yet Hick realizes that he is committed to some claims that have to be taken as literal truths about the noumenal Real if the pluralistic hypothesis is to make sense. Thus he supposes we can, presumably with literal truth, "say of the postulated Real *an sich* that it is the noumenal ground of the encountered gods and experienced absolutes witnessed to by the religious traditions" (p. 246). And the question is how the claims that are literally true of the noumenal Real are to be demarcated from those that are not. Hick tries to demarcate in terms of a distinction between concepts and statements that are purely formal and those that are not. He is aware that some such distinction is needed if his view is to escape self-refutation. Thus, for example, if the noumenal Real does not fall under any concepts that are not purely formal, then it must fall under the purely formal concept of being such that it is beyond the scope of other than purely formal concepts. Unfortunately, however, Hick does not provide a definition of purely formal concepts or statements, and so we are left to gather as best we can the distinction he has in mind from the examples he presents. Hence, we must conjecture about how he demarcates the claims he takes to be literally true of the noumenal Real from those he considers not literally true of it, and in framing such conjectures we have only his examples to go on. But the examples create difficulties.

At one point Hick asks why pluralism postulates a single noumenal Real. He concedes that there is "no reason, *a priori*, why the closest approximation that there is to a truly ultimate reality may not consist in either an orderly federation or a feuding multitude or an unrelated plurality" (p. 248). Indeed, Hick's explanandum, the roughly equal salvific efficacy of the great religious traditions, could be accounted for by postulating that each tradition is in contact with a distinct religious reality, each of which is roughly as it is experienced and conceived in its tradition and all of which are roughly equal in salvific power. Hick appeals to the theoretical virtue of simplicity to justify postulating a unique noumenal Real; he regards the issue as finding "the simplest hypothesis to account for the plurality of forms of religious experience and thought" (p. 248). But the appeal to theoretical simplicity in this context is problematic in several ways. One might deny, as some philosophers of science do, that theoretical simplicity is indicative of truth, viewing it instead as a merely pragmatic virtue. More importantly, Hick's claim that the Real *an sich* cannot be said to be one or many seems to be inconsistent with his insistence that we can, for reasons of simplicity, say that it is not a plurality, whether orderly, feuding, or unrelated. In addition, the claim that the Real *an sich* is a single thing and not a plurality, a one and not a many, appears to be not a purely formal statement. And, finally, if theoretical considerations can justify a substantive claim about the noumenal realm in this instance, what if anything is to prevent them from doing so in other cases?

Recall, too, that Hick claims that the Real *an sich* provides informational input into the human mind and that we are entitled to say about the noumenal source of this information that its influence produces, in collaboration with the human mind, the phenomenal world of human experience. Presumably the pluralistic hypothesis, when understood in terms of the construct model, requires that these be claims to literal truth. But they entail claims about the causal powers of the noumenal Real, its powers to transmit information to the human mind and to contribute to the production of experience in it, and such claims must also be claims to literal truth. But they are substantive claims, albeit fairly abstract ones, and hence the statements making them appear to be not purely formal. It may be that the statement that the postulated Real *an sich* is the ground of the divine *personae* and metaphysical *impersonae* of the religious traditions is purely formal in some sense. But even if that is so, the statement that it performs this grounding function by transmitting information to the human mind and collaborating with it in the production of religious experience makes a substantive causal claim.

There is also something to worry about in one of Hick's most prominent examples of a purely formal statement we can make. He says that

The most famous instance in western religious discourse of such a formal statement is Anselm's definition of God as that than which no greater can be conceived. This formula refers to the ultimate divine reality without attributing to it any concrete characteristics. (p. 246)

But maximal conceivable greatness may well entail other divine attributes. Anselm himself argued that it does, and several contemporary philosophers of religion follow in his footsteps. For example, Alvin Plantinga, in his well-known ontological argument for God's existence, appeals to the property of having maximal greatness. According to Plantinga, the property of having maximal greatness entails the property of having maximal excellence in every possible world and the property of having maximal excellence entails the properties of omniscience, omnipotence, and moral perfection.[9] Moreover, the property of being morally perfect entails the property of being personal. Hence, the property of having maximal greatness entails the property of being personal. Similar lines of argument are contained in work by George Schlesinger and Thomas Morris.[10] Even if it is epistemically possible that such authors are mistaken about the entailment relations in question, it is far from clear that they have in fact fallen into error on this point. And if they have not, Hick's position is in trouble. According to Hick, the statement attributing maximal greatness to the noumenal Real is purely formal, and so it is an instance of those statements we can make about the postulated Real *an sich*, presumably with a claim to literal truth. But it entails and thus logically commits us to a statement, presumably with the same claim to literal truth, attributing personhood to the noumenal Real, which commitment is not consistent with Hick's claim that the noumenal Real cannot be said to be person or thing and, hence, that personhood cannot literally be one of its attributes. What is more, things would not be any better for Hick's position if being maximally great did not entail being personal but instead entailed being impersonal.

So Hick's attempt to formulate the pluralistic hypothesis in a way that defines clearly what is literally true of the postulated noumenal Real runs into trouble. As I see, the best way to respond to the difficulties I have pointed out is to refine the hypothesis rather than to abandon it. Since it is his hypothesis, Hick will to some extent be authoritative about how to resolve problems in formulating it with clarity and precision. But I would like to propose a strategy for making refinements that I take to be in the spirit of Hick's thought, as I understand it.

---

[9] Alvin Plantinga, *The Nature of Necessity* (Oxford: Clarendon Press, 1974), 214.
[10] George N. Schlesinger, *New Perspectives on Old-Time Religion* (Oxford: Clarendon Press, 1988), ch. 1; Thomas V. Morris, *Anselmian Explorations* (Notre Dame: University of Notre Dame Press, 1987), 433–48.

At bottom, Hick finds religious diversity problematic because the great religious traditions attribute contrary properties to the religious ultimate.[11] Advaitic Hindus say it is impersonal; Sunni Muslims say it is personal. The members of a pair of properties are contraries if, as a matter of logic, nothing can have but something can lack both members of the pair. Hick's basic move is to deny that the religious ultimate really has either member of any such contrary pair. So the first steps in constructing a pluralistic hypothesis are these. Fix the religious traditions that are to fall within the scope of the hypothesis and determine what properties they attribute to the religious ultimate. Next check these properties for pairwise contrariety. Then postulate a common religious ultimate that has no property which entails either member of any contrary pair. Once you have gotten this far, there are a couple of explanatory options. Following the disguise model, you can explain apparent contrariety in terms of diverse ways in which the common ultimate appears in different traditions. Or, following the construct model, you can explain apparent contrariety by postulating different objects for different traditions to bear the members of contrary pairs. And you may then flesh out the hypothesis by attributing further properties, formal or substantive, to the common religious ultimate, as theoretical considerations dictate, provided you refrain from attributing to it any property that entails either member of any of the contrary pairs previously enumerated. I suggest that this recipe will allow you to construct coherent pluralistic hypotheses if such constructions are possible.

Of course this strategy will not yield interpretations of religion that would be acceptable to most current members of the great religious traditions. But those traditions have undergone development in the past, and no doubt they will continue to change in the future. Hence it is worth asking whether the belief systems of the great religious traditions ought to be altered to bring them into conformity with the truth of the matter as it is understood by some refined pluralistic hypothesis. Would it be rational for members of such a tradition to endeavor to change its belief system in the direction of such conformity? I address this question by means of a discussion of William P. Alston's treatment of the problem of religious diversity.

2. ALSTON ON RELIGIOUS DIVERSITY

It is only in the penultimate chapter of his book, *Perceiving God*, that Alston addresses what he takes to be "the most difficult problem for my position."[12] It

---

[11] See n. 7, above.

[12] William P. Alston, *Perceiving God: The Epistemology of Religious Experience* (Ithaca and London: Cornell University Press, 1991), p. 255. Hereafter references to this book will be made parenthetically in the body of my text. Alston also discusses religious diversity in "Religious Diversity and Perceptual Knowledge of God," *Faith and Philosophy*, 5 (1988), 433–48.

is a problem posed by religious diversity. What is it? How does Alston propose to solve it within the framework of his religious epistemology?

The notion of a doxastic practice is central to Alston's general epistemology. He thinks of a doxastic practice as a way of forming beliefs and evaluating them epistemically in terms of a background system of beliefs that furnish potential defeaters or overriders. He argues that it is practically rational to engage in socially established doxastic practices that are not demonstrably unreliable or otherwise disqualified for rational acceptance. In the religious sphere, Alston thinks of mystical perception as religious experience in which a presentation or appearance to the subject of something the subject identifies as the Ultimate occurs. When the notion of a doxastic practice is applied to mystical perception, Alston urges us to acknowledge that there are different socially established mystical practices in diverse religious traditions because there are substantial differences in their overrider systems of background beliefs. One such practice is Christian mystical practice (CMP). Alston argues at length that it is not demonstrably unreliable. It does not display massive and persistent internal inconsistency in its outputs; nor does it display persistent and unresolvable conflict with more basic secular doxastic practices. However, both the outputs of CMP and its overrider system appear to be massively inconsistent with their counterparts in the mystical practices of other religious traditions. Does this disqualify CMP and its equally well established rivals in other traditions from being rationally engaged in? Considerations that count in favor of a positive answer to this question give rise to Alston's problem of religious diversity. What are these considerations?

It is a presupposition of the claim that religious diversity renders the rationality of engaging in any mystical perceptual practice problematic that the belief systems of the great religious traditions are massively incompatible. On the face of it, they seem to be, but attempts have been made to construe them as mutually compatible, appearances to the contrary notwithstanding. Alston considers two such attempts. One might, he notes, "trim each system of its 'exclusivist' claims, so that it presents only one possible way to salvation, only one part of the story as to what the Ultimate is like and how we are and should be related to it" (p. 263). Though he expresses skepticism about whether the strategy of abandoning exclusivist claims would succeed in resolving all doxastic conflict among the great religious traditions, he declines to follow this path for another reason. His project is the epistemic evaluation of doxastic practices that are socially established and widely engaged in, and there are no mystical perceptual practices of a nonexclusivist sort that are actually engaged in by any significant community. Though it might be nice if there were such practices, evaluating merely hypothetical practices of this kind is not part of Alston's enterprise.

Another attempt to resolve doxastic conflict among the great religious traditions involves reinterpretation of what is going on in actually existing religious doxastic practices. Alston takes Hick's religious pluralism to be the most prominent representative of this position on the current scene because he construes

Hick as holding that the apparently incompatible beliefs associated with various mystical perceptual practices are not really incompatible, since they are not about the one noumenal Real but are instead about the many phenomenal Reals of diverse religious traditions. Thus construed, Hick's position encounters a difficulty mentioned previously. As Alston puts it, Hick's proposed interpretation of religion is not faithful to the self-understandings embedded in existing religious doxastic practices because "most practitioners of one or another religion are pre-Kantian in their realist understanding of their beliefs" (p. 265). In other words, on Hick's view, most such practitioners misunderstand what is going on in their own religious doxastic practices, for they take their beliefs to embody true accounts of the noumenal Real and its relations to them. For the sake of fidelity to their self-understandings, Alston proposes to take the great religious traditions to be making noumenal truth claims that are logically incompatible with one another and to assess the implications of this assumption for his view that it is nonetheless practically rational to continue engaging in CMP.

But how, exactly, does the incompatibility of various forms of mystical perceptual practice threaten the rationality of engaging in any of them? After canvassing several defective ways of posing the problem, Alston settles on the following formulation. On account of the incompatibility, at most one form of mystical practice can be a sufficiently reliable way of forming beliefs about the Ultimate to be rationally engaged in. But why should one suppose that CMP in particular is the one that is reliable if any is? To be sure, CMP can come up with internal reasons for supposing that it is more reliable than its rivals. However, each of its rivals can do the same. Hence, according to the objection, "if it is to be rational for me to take CMP to be reliable, I will have to have sufficient *independent* reasons for supposing that CMP is reliable, or more reliable or more likely to be reliable, than its alternatives" (p. 269). But no such independent reasons are forthcoming. Thus it is not rational to engage in CMP. And, by parity of reasoning, it is also not rational to engage in any other particular form of mystical perceptual practice.

A slightly different way of expressing what is essentially the same point goes as follows. All the competing mystical practices are equally well socially established; none of them has greater prima facie credibility than its rivals on grounds of deeper social entrenchment. So each of the competing practices is confronted with a plurality of uneliminated alternatives. According to the objection, the following conclusions are to be drawn in these circumstances: "Thus, in the absence of some sufficient independent reason, no one is justified in supposing her own practice to be superior in epistemic status to those with which it is in competition. And hence, in this situation no one is being rational in proceeding to employ that practice to form beliefs and to regard beliefs so formed as ipso facto justified" (p. 270).

As Alston notes, this line of argument takes it for granted that there are no independent reasons for an epistemic preference of one form of mystical practice over its rivals, and this assumption can be challenged. But successfully mounting such a challenge on behalf of CMP would involve telling a very long story about evidences for Christianity, and Alston chooses not to undertake this project except in a sketchy form in his final chapter. Instead he proceeds at this point in accord with a worst-case scenario in which it is just assumed that there are no independent reasons for preferring CMP to its rivals. He seeks to show that, even on this assumption, the justificatory efficacy of CMP is by no means dissipated, though it is significantly weakened. Of course, if the assumption is false and there are such independent reasons for the reliability of CMP but none for the reliability of its rivals, things are all the better for CMP and all the worse for its rivals.

But just how bad are things for CMP in Alston's worst-case scenario? How much is its justificatory efficacy actually weakened in those circumstances? In discussing the genuine epistemic consequences of religious diversity, Alston invites us to look at the matter this way. Suppose our sole respectable basis for a positive epistemic evaluation of CMP were the fact that it is a socially established doxastic practice that has not been shown to be unreliable. On that assumption, Alston admits, religious diversity would reduce its epistemic status to an alarming degree. Given the equal social establishment of several mutually incompatible mystical practices, he thinks that "it is at least arguable that the most reasonable view, even for a hitherto committed participant of one of the practices, would be that the social establishment in each case reflects a culturally generated way of reinforcing socially desirable attitudes and practices, reinforcing these by inculcating a sense of the presence of Supreme Reality and a way of thinking about it" (p. 276). And that in turn, he allows, would imply that the justificatory efficacy of all of these practices had been altogether dissipated.

It is worth noting that Alston does not explicitly endorse the claim that he says is at least arguable. But he does not dispute it. Instead he observes that so far the whole story has not yet been told. We must also take into account the significant self-support CMP derives from the way in which promises it represents God as making are fulfilled in the spiritual lives of its practitioners, fulfilled in growth in sanctity, joy, love, and other fruits of the spirit. As Alston sees it, "in the face of this self-support it is no longer the case that the most reasonable hypothesis is that none of the competing practices provide an effective cognitive access to the Ultimate" (p. 276). Hence, "one may quite reasonably continue to hold that CMP does serve as a genuine cognitive access to Ultimate Reality, and as a trustworthy guide to that Reality's relations to ourselves" (p. 276). And, again by parity of reasoning, a similar conclusion may be drawn for any of the alternative mystical practices that enjoy comparable self-support.

I concur with Alston in thinking that self-support counts, epistemically speaking, in favor of the rationality of engaging in a doxastic practice. So I agree that things are not as bad for CMP in his worst-case scenario as they would be in the absence of self-support. Just how bad are they? In the absence of self-support, the justificatory efficacy of CMP arguably would be altogether dissipated. So, in the presence of self-support, the justificatory efficacy of CMP is, at the very least, not altogether dissipated. Of course, this conclusion is consistent with Alston's claim that, given the self-support CMP enjoys, it is no longer the case that the most reasonable hypothesis is that none of the competing mystical practices provides an effective cognitive access to the Ultimate. But it is also consistent with the claim that, despite the self-support CMP enjoys, it remains the case that the most reasonable hypothesis is that none of these practices provides such access. For all that has been shown thus far, then, it may be that, though CMP has some justificatory efficacy because of the self-support it enjoys, it does not have enough to make it reasonable to hold that it serves to yield genuine access to the Ultimate.

Hence, as I see it, the difficulty religious diversity generates for Alston's position may be summarized in this way. The fact that CMP is a socially established doxastic practice that has not been shown to be unreliable counts in favor of the rationality of engaging in it. It derives therefrom a certain amount of justificatory efficacy. In the context of the worst-case scenario, there being equally well established rival practices that also have not been shown to be unreliable weakens its justificatory efficacy, but its significant self-support strengthens its justificatory efficacy. Either it enjoys enough self-support to make engaging in it rational despite the weakening effect of there being uneliminated rivals, or the self-support it enjoys falls short of what is required to make engaging in it rational in the face of that effect. What reasons are there for preferring one of these alternatives to the other?

Alston offers reasons of two sorts for preferring the first alternative. I next examine the arguments in which he sets them forth.

His first argument plays off of a disanalogy between conflict within a single doxastic practice and conflict among diverse doxastic practices. Consider alternative methods of predicting the weather such as scientific meteorology, going by the aches in one's joints, and observing groundhogs. Since these competitors confront one another within sensory perceptual practice, it is clear what would constitute noncircular grounds for supposing one of them to be superior to the others, even if we do not have such grounds. Observed predictive success provides neutral grounds for choosing among methods of weather forecasting, and the lack of such grounds has negative epistemic consequences for the competing methods. Indeed, according to Alston, "it is because the absence of such reasons is the absence of something there is a live possibility of one's having, and that one knows how to go about getting, that this lack so clearly has negative epistemic consequences" (p. 271). But in the case of conflict among mystical perceptual practices the competitors lack the kind of common procedure for settling disputes that is available to the participants in a shared practice, and so participants in rival mystical practices do not lack something they know how to get. Hence, as Alston sees it, we may conclude: "The lack does not have the deleterious consequences found in the intrapractice cases. Or, at the very least, it is not clear that it has those consequences" (p. 272).

Alston's conclusion must not be interpreted as the claim that religious diversity has no bad epistemic consequences. He explicitly acknowledges that "it can hardly be denied that the fact of religious diversity reduces the rationality of engaging in CMP (for one who is aware of the diversity) below what it would be if this problem did not exist" (p. 275). Rather his claim is that this bad consequence is not, or at least is not clearly, the same as the deleterious consequences found in the intrapractice cases, and surely he is right about at least this much. In the intrapractice cases, something we know how to get by way of justification for beliefs or methods is lacking. It is because of the presence of this feature in the cases that there are those deleterious consequences. How bad are they? At worst, according to Alston, they amount to nullification of one's justification or elimination of one's basis for a belief or practice. This feature is absent in the case of conflict of mystical practices. In this interpractice case, what is lacking, for example, a proof of the reliability of CMP, is not something we know how to get. Of course, it does not follow from the absence of the feature in question that nullification or elimination does not occur in our interpractice case. What follows is only that nullification or elimination does not occur because of the presence of that feature. If it occurs in the case of conflict of mystical practices, it occurs for some other reason. But it is not clear that there is any such reason, and so it is not clear that nullification or elimination occurs. What might such a reason be? Since I have none to propose, I am prepared to grant for the sake of argument that nullification or elimination does not occur in our interpractice case.

But this is not the end of the story. The bad consequences of religious diversity amount to a reduction that falls short of nullification of one's justification for engaging in CMP; they involve a weakening of its justificatory efficacy. What is the extent of this reduction or weakening? It is probably impossible to answer this question with quantitative precision, but two possibilities remain open. One is that it is small enough that engaging in CMP remains rational, and the other is that it is large enough that engaging in CMP is not rational. The absence of the crucial feature of the intrapractice cases is, in effect, the absence of a reason for thinking that the latter possibility is realized. By itself, however, this absence does not furnish a reason for thinking that the former possibility is realized. In other words, the disanalogy between the intrapractice cases and our interpractice case undercuts a reason that might be offered for thinking that it is not rational to engage in CMP but does not provide a reason for thinking that it is rational to engage in CMP. Thus Alston's first argument does not show that it is rational to engage in CMP. As he is well aware, it serves only to block one path to the conclusion that it is not rational to engage in CMP.

But I think Alston's second argument is meant to yield the conclusion that engaging in CMP is rational. It proceeds by way of an analogy between the actual diversity of mystical perceptual practices and a merely hypothetical diversity of sensory perceptual practices. We are to imagine there being a plurality of sense perceptual doxastic practices as diverse as forms of mystical practice are in fact. As Alston fleshes out the story, "suppose that in certain cultures there were a well established 'Cartesian' practice of seeing what is visually perceived as an indefinitely extended medium that is more or less concentrated at various points, rather than, as in our 'Aristotelian' practice, as made up of more or less discrete objects scattered about in space" (p. 273). We are to imagine in other cultures an established Whiteheadian practice in which the visual field is seen as made up of momentary events growing out of each other in a continuous process. Further suppose that all these practices are equal in terms of the fruits they produce; each serves its practitioners well in their dealings with the environment and has associated with it a developed physical science. Imagine also that in this situation we are as firmly wedded to our Aristotelian practice as we are in fact yet can find no neutral grounds on which to argue effectively that it yields more accurate beliefs than the alternatives. It seems clear to Alston that "in the absence of an external reason for supposing that one of the competing practices is more accurate than my own, *the only rational course* for me is to sit tight with the practice of which I am a master and which serves me so well in guiding my activity in the world" (p. 274, my emphasis). But this imagined situation is precisely parallel to our actual situation with respect to CMP. Hence, by parity of reasoning, the only rational thing for a practitioner of CMP to do is to stick with it and, more generally, to continue to accept and operate in accordance with the system of Christian belief.

Beyond saying that it seems clear to him, Alston gives no reasons for supposing that, in the imagined situation, the only rational course is to sit tight with the sensory practice of which one is a master. But there is a line of argument that can be deployed to support this supposition. Declining to engage in any sensory perceptual practice is presumably not a live option for me. Hence it seems that my options are restricted to sitting tight with my Aristotelian practice and switching to one of its established rivals. However switching would carry with it very large costs in terms of resocialization. I would have to spend a lot of time and energy getting trained to see things in new ways. And even if I could be successfully trained, what assured benefits would accrue to me as a result? By hypothesis, I would not be better off in terms of fruits; I would not be better at coping with my environment or have access to a more advanced physical science. Of course, it could be that I would be swapping inaccurate beliefs for accurate beliefs and thereby getting closer to my epistemic goal. But again, by hypothesis, I have no neutral ground on which to base an argument that this would be the outcome. And switching would be risky because it could equally well be that I would be swapping accurate beliefs for inaccurate beliefs. I also have no neutral ground on which to base an argument that this would not be the outcome. Hence cost–benefit considerations, which surely count for a lot in deliberations about practical rationality, weigh very strongly in favor of sitting tight with my Aristotelian practice.

In my view, this argument is flawed because, appearances to the contrary notwithstanding, I do not have to obey the injunction to sit tight or switch. There is another live option that ought to be considered. I also have the choice of revising my Aristotelian practice from within and working toward a situation in which my revised practice becomes socially established. A precedent for making revisions in one's sensory perceptual practice is to be found in the way people respond to learning that such things as phenomenal colors are not mind-independent. Revisions of my sensory practice might proceed in a Kantian direction. Suppose it occurs to me that a plausible explanation of the success of the diverse sensory practices in the imagined situation is the hypothesis that each of the established practices is reliable with respect to the appearances things present to its practitioners but none is reliable with respect to how things are in themselves. Motivated by this consideration, I decide to modify the functions of my sensory practice so that they map sensory inputs onto doxastic outputs about the appearances things present to me but not about how things really are independent of me. I also do what I can to see to it that my revised sensory practice gradually becomes socially established.

Transforming my Aristotelian practice into a Kantian practice would in some ways be like switching to a Cartesian or Whiteheadian practice. I see no reason to suppose I would be worse off in terms of fruits as a result. I would not lose the ability to deal well with my environment; nor would I lose access to a developed physical science, though some reinterpretation of its metaphysical import would probably be required. In addition, I would lack neutral grounds on which to base an argument that my revisions are going to get me closer to my epistemic goal by improving the reliability of my sensory practice. But there are salient differences too. Instead of having to be trained to acquire substantially different inputs to my sensory practice, I would only have to make the slight modifications in its functions needed to produce slight alterations in its doxastic outputs. Because I think this change would not require costly resocialization, I do not think cost–benefit considerations count strongly against revising my Aristotelian practice in a Kantian direction.

It is doubtful that the costs and benefits of sitting tight with Aristotelian practice and those of transforming it into a Kantian practice can be quantified precisely enough to allow us to say with much confidence which of the two is the more rational course. So I do not wish to conclude that it is irrational to sit tight with Aristotelian practice. But I submit that we can conclude that it is not the only rational thing to do. In our imagined situation, then, it would be rational to stick with our Aristotelian practice but it would also be rational to transform it into a Kantian practice. Each of these courses of action would be rationally permitted; neither of them would be rationally required.

And, of course, our imagined situation is, in the relevant respects, parallel to the actual situation in regard to competing mystical practices.[13] Hence, by parity of reasoning, though it is rational for practitioners of CMP to continue to engage in it, it is not *the only* rational thing for them to do, there being more than one thing it is rational to do in the face of competing mystical practices. Another thing it is rational for them to do is to revise CMP from within in ways that would improve its reliability if some refined pluralistic hypothesis were true. Each of these courses of action is rationally permissible in the light of religious diversity. Neither of them is irrational, but neither is rationally required. And absent any relevant dissimilarities, the same goes for those engaged in other socially established mystical practices with significant self-support.

Alston's views do not rule out the possibility of the great religious traditions evolving in such a way that they converge on consensus about a self-understanding in the neighborhood of a refined pluralistic hypothesis. He explicitly notes that "the system of Christian belief has undergone a great deal of change in its history, and we cannot be sure that it will not continue to do so; the same holds for other major religions" (p. 278). And he allows that future developments in the great religious traditions might be in the direction of greater consensus. But he does not explicitly acknowledge the rationality of trying to bring such consensus about by revising the belief systems and doxastic practices of the presently existing world religions, including Christianity, so that they are no longer pre-Kantian in their understandings of their beliefs. Thus his advice to the knowledgeable and reflective Christian is that "she should do whatever seems feasible to search for common ground on which to adjudicate the crucial differences between the world religions, seeking a way to show in a non-circular way which of the contenders is correct" (p. 278). I do not think it would be irrational to follow this advice. However I also think it should not be taken for granted that any of the contenders in its present form is correct. Hence I think it would be rational for a knowledgeable and reflective Christian to revise CMP from within in ways that are designed to bring it into line with a Kantian understanding of Christian belief of the sort expressed by some refined pluralistic hypothesis and to try to get CMP thus revised socially established.

If I am right about this, Alston's second argument gives him what he needs to solve the problem of religious diversity he has posed. It builds a good analogical

---

[13] A disanalogy is worth mentioning. Since mystical practice is not universal, ceasing to engage in any mystical practice is a live option in at least some cases. Limitations of space preclude a thorough discussion of the costs and benefits of this course of action, and so I shall confine myself to remarking that it should not be assumed that in all cases exercising this option would result in the uncompensated loss of benefits of spiritual fruits. Religious life is often very hard. If we attend only to what can be observed in this life, it is easy to imagine cases in which opting out of mystical practices would be tantamount to shedding a burden rather than forgoing a benefit.

case for the conclusion that it is rational for practitioners of CMP to continue engaging in it despite the fact of religious diversity. And, as Alston notes, this conclusion holds, *pari passu*, for practitioners of other established and internally validated forms of mystical perceptual practice. But the argument does not establish the stronger claim that is its stated conclusion, for it is not a good analogical argument to the effect that this is the only thing it is rational for practitioners of CMP to do. Thus it does not impugn the rationality of those Christians whose response to religious diversity is to seek a more inclusivist or pluralist understanding of their own faith and who are, accordingly, interested in altering CMP in order to bring the beliefs that are its outputs into line with such an understanding. In particular, it does not impugn the rationality of those Christians who are prepared to move in the direction of thicker phenomenologies and thinner theologies, even if they are not yet ready to go all the way to the Hickian view that it is nothing but phenomenology almost all the way down. And I would say this too holds, *pari passu*, for practitioners of other established and internally validated forms of mystical perceptual practice.

14

On Religious Diversity & Tolerance

Since September 11, 2001, the fragility of tolerance has become a source of acute anxiety in scholarly reflection on religion—as shown by some of the contributions to the Summer 2003 issue of *Dædalus* on secularism and religion. In that context, James Carroll asked how it was possible for people committed to democracy to embrace religious creeds that underwrite intolerance. Daniel C. Tosteson identified conflicting religious beliefs as a particularly serious cause of the plague of war.

Such anxieties are reasonable. After all, Osama bin Laden professes to fight in the name of Islam. And in the aftermath of 9/11, the United States has experienced a significant rise in reported incidents of intolerant behavior directed at Muslims.

Moreover, tolerance has long been under assault in more limited conflicts fueled in part by religious differences. Religious disagreement has been a cause of violence in Belfast, Beirut, and Bosnia during recent decades. The terrorism of Al Qaeda threatens to project the religious strife involved in such localized clashes onto a global stage. In short, early in the twenty-first century, the practice of tolerance is in peril, and religious diversity is a major source of the danger.

During the past two decades, diversity has also been a topic of lively discussion among philosophers and theologians. What philosophers have found especially challenging about religious diversity is an epistemological problem it poses. Here the philosophical debates have focused primarily on the so-called world religions—Hinduism, Buddhism, Judaism, Christianity, and Islam. Though most of the philosophers involved in these debates have not addressed the topic of tolerance directly, there is a clear connection between the epistemological problems posed by religious belief and the political problems posed by religious diversity.

Take the case of Christianity. One way to justify a Christian's belief in God is the arguments offered by natural theologians for the existence of God. Another source of justification is distinctively Christian religious experiences, including both the spectacular experiences reported by mystical virtuosi and the more mundane experiences that pervade the lives of many ordinary Christians. A third source is the divine revelation Christians purport to find in canonical scripture.

This is the last work Professor Quinn completed before his death on November 15, 2004.

And, for many Christians, a fourth source is the authoritative teaching of a church believed to be guided by the Holy Spirit. When combined, such sources constitute a cumulative case for the rationality of the belief in God professed by most Christians.

Let us suppose, if only for the sake of argument, that these sources provide sufficient justification to ensure the rational acceptability of the Christian belief system. But this will be so only if there are no countervailing considerations or sources that present conflicting evidence. Before we can render a final verdict on the rational acceptability of that belief system, challenges to the Christian worldview must be taken into account. One of the most famous challenges is, of course, the existence of evil. The sheer diversity of religions and religious beliefs presents an equally vexing challenge. And the growth of religiously pluralistic societies, global media, and transportation channels has rendered this challenge increasingly salient in recent times.

A Christian today who is sufficiently aware of religious diversity will realize that other world religions also have impressive sources of justification: They too can mobilize powerful philosophical arguments for the fundamental doctrines of their worldviews. They are supported by rich experiential traditions. They also contain both texts and authoritative individuals or institutions that profess to teach deep lessons about paths to salvation or liberation from the ills of the human condition.

Yet quite a few of the distinctive claims of the Christian belief system, understood in traditional ways, conflict with central doctrines of other world religions. Though each world religion derives justification from its own sources, at most one of them can be completely true. Each religion is therefore an unvanquished rival of all the rest.

To be sure, Christian sources yield reasons to believe that the Christian worldview is closer to the truth than its rivals. But many of these reasons are internal to the Christian perspective. Each of the other competitors can derive from its sources internal reasons for thinking it has the best access to truth. Adjudication of the competition without begging the question would require reasons independent of the rival perspectives. It seems that agreement on independent reasons sufficient to adjudicate the rivalry is currently well beyond our grasp.

It is clear that this unresolved conflict will have a negative impact on the level of justification Christian belief derives from its sources. In his magisterial book *Perceiving God* (1991), William Alston investigated the matter of justification for the Christian practice of forming beliefs about God's manifestations to believers. He argued persuasively that the unresolved conflict does not drop the level of justification for beliefs resulting from this practice below the threshold minimally sufficient for rational acceptability. He acknowledged, however, that the level of justification for such Christian beliefs is considerably lowered by the conflict, and that similar conclusions hold, *mutatis mutandis*, for analogous experiential practices in other world religions.

A generalization from the special case seems to be in order. For those Christians who are sufficiently aware of religious diversity, the justification that the distinctively Christian worldview receives from all its sources is a good deal less than would be the case were there no such diversity, even if the level of justification for the Christian belief system were not on that account reduced below the threshold for rational acceptability. And, other things being equal, the same goes for other world religions. This reduction of justification across the board can contribute to a philosophical strategy for defending religious toleration.

The basic idea is not new. The strategy is implicitly at work in a famous example discussed by Immanuel Kant in his *Religion within the Boundaries of Mere Reason* (1793). Kant asks the reader to consider an inquisitor who must judge someone, otherwise a good citizen, charged with heresy. The inquisitor thinks a supernaturally revealed divine command permits him to extirpate "unbelief together with the unbelievers." Kant suggests that the inquisitor might take such a command to be revealed in the parable of the great feast in Luke's Gospel. According to the parable, when invited guests fail to show up for the feast and poor folk brought in from the neighborhood do not fill the empty places, the angry host orders a servant to go out into the roads and lanes and compel people to come in (Luke 14: 23). Kant wonders whether it is rationally acceptable for the inquisitor to conclude, on grounds such as this, that it is permissible for him to condemn the heretic to death.

Kant holds that it is not. As he sees it, it is certainly wrong to take a person's life on account of her religious faith, unless the divine will, revealed in some extraordinary fashion, has decreed otherwise. But it cannot be certain that such a revelation has occurred. If the inquisitor relies on sources such as the parable, uncertainty arises from the possibility that error may have crept into the human transmission or interpretation of the story. Moreover, even if it were to seem that such a revelation came directly from God, as in the story told in Genesis 22 of God's command to Abraham to kill Isaac, the inquisitor still could not be certain that the source of the command really was God.

For Kant, certainty is an epistemic concept. It is a matter of having a very high degree of justification, not a question of psychological strength of belief. Thus his argumentative strategy may be rendered explicit in the following way: All of us, even the inquisitor, have a very high degree of justification for the moral principle that it is generally wrong to kill people because of their religious beliefs. Our justification for this principle vastly exceeds the threshold for rational acceptability. It may be conceded to religious believers that there would be an exception to this general rule if there were divine command to the contrary. However, none of us, not even the inquisitor, can have enough justification for the claim that God has issued such a command to elevate that claim above the threshold for rational acceptability. Hence it is not rationally acceptable for the inquisitor to conclude that condemning a heretic to death is morally permissible.

No doubt, almost all of us will recoil with horror from the extreme form of persecution involved in Kant's famous example. Other cases may not elicit the same kind of easy agreement.

Suppose the leaders of the established church of a certain nation insist that God wills that all children who reside within the nation's borders are to receive education in that orthodox faith. No other form of public religious education is to be tolerated. These leaders are not so naive as to imagine that the policy of mandatory religious education they propose will completely eradicate heresy. But they argue that its enactment is likely to lower the numbers of those who fall away from orthodoxy and, hence, to reduce the risk of the faithful being seduced into heresy. And they go on to contend that the costs associated with their policy are worth paying, since what is at stake is nothing less than the eternal salvation of the nation's people.

The claim that God has commanded mandatory education in orthodoxy might, it seems, derive a good deal of justification from sources recognized by members of the established church. It is the sort of thing a good God, deeply concerned about the salvation of human beings, might favor. Perhaps the parable about compelling people to come in could, with some plausibility, be interpreted as an expression of such a command. So if the challenge of religious diversity were not taken into consideration, the claim that God commands mandatory education in orthodoxy might derive enough justification from various sources to put it above the threshold for rational acceptability for members of the established church. But the factoring in of religious diversity may be enough to lower the claim's justification below that threshold, thereby rendering it rationally unacceptable even for members of the church who are sufficiently aware of such diversity. And an appeal to the epistemological consequences of religious diversity may be the only factor capable of performing this function in numerous instances. Thus such an appeal may be an essential component of a successful strategy for arguing against forms of intolerance less atrocious than extirpating "unbelief together with the unbelievers."

Of course, the strategy being suggested here is no panacea. It is not guaranteed to vindicate the full range of tolerant practices found in contemporary liberal democracies; it may fail to show that the religious claims on which citizens ground opposition to tolerant practices fall short of rational acceptability by their own best lights. This is because the strategy must be employed on a case-by-case basis. However, such a piecemeal strategy has some advantages. It does not impose on defenders of tolerance the apparently impossible task of showing that the whole belief system of any world religion falls short of rational acceptability according to standards to which the adherents of that religion are committed. It targets for criticism only individual claims made within particular religions, claims that are often sharply disputed in those religions by believers themselves.

Nor can this strategy be expected to convert all religious zealots to tolerant modes of behavior. All too often religious zealots turn out to be fanatics who will not be moved by any appeal to reason. But in any event, the strategy should not be faulted because it cannot do something that no philosophical argument for tolerance, or for any other practice, could possibly do.

Religious diversity must be counted among the causes of the great ills of intolerance. It also happily shows some promise of contributing to a remedy for the very malady it has helped to create.

Bibliography of the Writings of Philip L. Quinn

Note: This bibliography excludes encyclopedia entries and book reviews in philosophy journals. Quinn also published 193 short reviews in the journal *Mathematical Reviews*.

BOOK

Divine Commands and Moral Requirements (Oxford: Clarendon Press, 1978).

EDITED VOLUMES

Companion to the Philosophy of Religion, with Charles Taliaferro (Oxford: Blackwell, 1997).

The Philosophical Challenge of Religious Diversity, with Kevin Meeker (Oxford: Oxford University Press, 2000).

ARTICLES (IN CHRONOLOGICAL ORDER)

"The Instability of Negative Differential Resistance" (with P. O. Massicot), *Physica Status Solidi*, 13 (1966).

"Inhomogeneous Field Distribution in Homogeneous Semiconductors Having an N-Shaped Negative Differential Conductivity" (with K. W. Boer), *Physica Status Solidi*, 17 (1966).

"The Status of the D-Thesis," *Philosophy of Science*, 36 (1969).

"Methodological Appraisal and Heuristic Advice," *Studies in the History and Philosophy of Science*, 3 (1972).

"On Science: Reflections for its Cultured Despisers," *Issues: The Brown Review*, 1 (1972).

"Three Anti-Scientific Arguments," *Proceedings of the XVth World Congress of Philosophy* (1973).

"The Transitivity of Non-Standard Synchronisms," *British Journal for the Philosophy of Science*, 25 (1974).

"What Duhem Really Meant," *Boston Studies in the Philosophy of Science*, 14 (1974).

"Some Epistemic Implications of 'Crucial Experiments'," *Studies in the History and Philosophy of Science*, 5 (1974).

"Religious Obedience and Moral Autonomy," *Religious Studies* 11 (1975). Repr. in P. Helm (ed.), *Divine Commands and Morality* (Oxford: Oxford University Press, 1981).

"A Pseudosolution to the Problem of Evil," *Zygon*, 10 (1975).

"Intrinsic Metrics on Continuous Spatial Manifolds," *Philosophy of Science*, 43 (1976).

"Abstract of 'Divine Commands and the Logic of Requirement'," *Journal of Philosophy*, 73 (1976).

"Who Can Be Taught and Who Should Teach?", *Issues: The Brown Review*, 7 (1977).

"Improved Foundations for a Logic of Intrinsic Value," *Philosophical Studies*, 32 (1977).

"Personal Identity, Bodily Continuity and Resurrection," *International Journal for the Philosophy of Religion*, 9 (1978).

"Rejoinder to Tuana," *Philosophy of Science*, 45 (1978).

"Some Problems about Resurrection," *Religious Studies*, 14 (1978).

"Divine Foreknowledge and Divine Freedom," *International Journal for the Philosophy of Religion*, 9 (1978).

"Existence Throughout an Interval of Time, and Existence at an Instant of Time," *Ratio*, 21 (1979). Trans. as "Dasein wahrend eines Zeitintervalls und Dasein zu einem Zeitpunkt" in the German *Ratio*.

"Divine Conservation and Spinozistic Pantheism," *Religious Studies*, 15 (1979).

"Divine Command Ethics: A Causal Theory," in J. M. Idziak (ed.), *Divine Command Morality: Historical and Contemporary Readings* (New York and Toronto: Edwin Mellen Press, 1980).

"God, Moral Perfection, and Possible Worlds," in F. Sontag and M. D. Bryant (eds.), *God: The Contemporary Discussion* (Rose of Sharon Press, 1982). Repr. in M. L. Peterson (ed.), *The Problem of Evil* (Notre Dame: University of Notre Dame Press, 1992).

"Metaphysical Necessity and Modal Logics," *Monist*, 65 (1982).

"The Mystery of Anna Brito," *Gavea-Brown*, 2 (1982).

"Does Philosophy Have Method?" *Brown Daily Herald* (January 20, 1983).

"Grunbaum on Determinism and the Moral Life," in R. S. Cohen and L. Laudan (eds.), *Physics, Philosophy and Psychoanalysis* (Dordrecht: D. Reidel, 1983).

"Divine Conservation, Continuous Creation, and Human Action," in A. J. Freddoso (ed.), *The Nature and Existence of God* (Notre Dame: University of Notre Dame Press, 1983).

"Original Sin, Radical Evil and Moral Identity," *Faith and Philosophy*, 1 (1984).

"The Philosopher of Science as Expert Witness," in J. T. Cushing, C. F. Delaney, and G. M. Gutting (eds.), *Science and Reality* (Notre Dame: University of Notre Dame Press, 1984). Repr. in M. Ruse (ed.), *But Is It Science?* (Buffalo: Prometheus, 1988).

"Plantinga on Foreknowledge and Freedom," in J. E. Tomberlin and P. van Inwagen (eds.), *Alvin Plantinga* (Dordrecht: D. Reidel, 1985).

"In Search of the Foundations of Theism," *Faith and Philosophy*, 2 (1985). Repr. in L. P. Pojman (ed.), *Philosophy of Religion* (Belmont, Calif.: Wadsworth, 1986). Repr. in D. Kolak and R. Martin (eds.), *Self, Cosmos, God* (New York: Harcourt Brace Jovanovich, 1993). Repr. in M. Y. Stewart (ed.), *Philosophy of Religion* (Boston: Jones and Bartlett, 1996). Trans. as "Auf der Suche nach den Fundamentan des Theismus" and repr. in C. Jäger (ed.), *Analytische Religionsphilosophie* (Paderborn: Schöningh, 1998). Repr. in K. J. Clark (ed.), *Readings in the Philosophy of Religion* (Peterborough: Broadview, 2000). Repr. in R. Gale and A. R. Pruss (eds.), *The Existence of God* (Aldershot: Ashgate Publishing, 2001).

"Moral Obligation, Religious Demand, and Practical Conflict," in R. Audi and W. J. Wainwright (eds.), *Rationality, Religious Belief, and Moral Commitment* (Ithaca: Cornell University Press, 1986).

"A Trend Toward Temporary Jobs?" *Proceedings and Addresses of the American Philosophical Association*, 59 (1986).

"Christian Atonement and Kantian Justification," *Faith and Philosophy*, 3 (1986). Repr. in P. Athay, P. Grim, and M. A. Simon (eds.), *The Philosopher's Annual*, vol. ix (Atascadero: Ridgeview, 1988).

"Comments on Laudan's 'Methodology: Its Prospects'," in A. Fine and P. Machamer (eds.), *PSA 1986*, vol. ii (Philosophy of Science Association, 1987).

"Remarks on the Sociology of Philosophy," *Proceedings and Addresses of the American Philosophical Association*, suppl. to 61/1 (1987).

"Abstract of 'Divine Conservation, Secondary Causes, and Occasionalism'," *Proceedings and Addresses of the American Philosophical Association*, 61/2 (1987).

"Creationism, Methodology and Politics," in M. Ruse (ed.), *But Is It Science?* (Buffalo: Prometheus, 1988).

"Divine Conservation, Secondary Causes, and Occasionalism," in T. V. Morris (ed.), *Divine and Human Action* (Ithaca: Cornell University Press, 1988).

" 'In Adam's Fall, We Sinned All'," *Philosophical Topics*, 16/2 (1988).

"Tragic Dilemmas, Suffering Love, and Christian Life," *Journal of Religious Ethics*, 17 (1989).

"Aquinas on Atonement," in R. Feenstra and C. Plantinga (eds.), *Trinity, Incarnation, and Atonement* (Notre Dame: University of Notre Dame Press, 1990). Abbreviated version repr. in M. Peterson, W. Hasker, B. Reichenbach, and D. Basinger (eds.), *Philosophy of Religion* (Oxford: Oxford University Press, 1996).

"A Response to Hauerwas: Is Athens Revived Jerusalem Denied?" *Asbury Theological Journal*, 45 (1990).

"Does Anxiety Explain Original Sin?" *Noûs*, 24 (1990).

"Duhem in Different Contexts: Comments on Brenner and Martin," *Synthese*, 83 (1990).

"An Argument for Divine Command Ethics," in M. D. Beaty (ed.), *Christian Theism and the Problems of Philosophy* (Notre Dame: University of Notre Dame Press, 1990).

"Agamemnon and Abraham: The Tragic Dilemma of Kierkegaard's Knight of Faith," *Journal of Literature and Theology*, 4/2 (1990).

"Saving Faith from Kant's Remarkable Antinomy," *Faith and Philosophy*, 7 (1990).

"The Recent Revival of Divine Command Ethics," *Philosophy and Phenomenological Research*, 50 (1990).

"Epistemic Parity and Religious Argument," in J. E. Tomberlin (ed.), *Philosophical Perspectives, v. Philosophy of Religion* (Atascadero: Ridgeview, 1991).

"Hell in Amsterdam: Reflections on Camus's *The Fall*," in P. A. French, T. E. Uehling, and H. K. Wettstein (eds.), *Midwest Studies in Philosophy, 16. Philosophy and the Arts* (Notre Dame: University of Notre Dame, 1991).

"On Demythologizing Evil," in F. Reynolds and D. Tracy (eds.), *Discourse and Practice* (Albany, NY: SUNY Press, 1992).

"On the Mereology of Boethian Eternity," *International Journal for Philosophy of Religion*, 32 (1992).

"The Primacy of God's Will in Christian Ethics," in J. E. Tomberlin (ed.), *Philosophical Perspectives, vi. Ethics* (Atascadero: Ridgeview, 1992). Repr. in M. Beaty, C. Fisher, and M. Nelson (eds.), *Christian Theism and Moral Philosophy* (Macon: Mercer University Press, 1998).

"The Foundations of Theism Again: A Rejoinder to Plantinga," in L. Zagzebski (ed.), *Rational Faith* (Notre Dame: University of Notre Dame Press, 1993). Repr. in part in W. L. Craig (ed.), *Philosophy of Religion: A Contemporary Reader and Guide* (New Brunswick: Rutgers University Press, 2002).

"Social Evil: A Reply to Adams," *Philosophical Studies*, 69 (1993).

"Abelard on Atonement: 'Nothing Unintelligible, Arbitrary, Illogical or Immoral about It'," in E. Stump (ed.), *Reasoned Faith* (Ithaca: Cornell University Press, 1993).

"Affirmative Action and the Multicultural Ideal," in S. Cahn (ed.), *Affirmative Action and the University* (Philadelphia: Temple University Press, 1993).

"Creation, Conservation and the Big Bang," in J. Earman, A. I. Janis, G. J. Massey, and N. Rescher (eds.), *Philosophical Problems of the Internal and External Worlds* (Pittsburgh: University of Pittsburgh Press, 1993).

"Moral Objections to Pascalian Wagering," in J. Jordan (ed.), *Gambling on God* (Totowa: Rowman and Littlefield, 1994).

"Swinburne on Guilt, Atonement and Christian Redemption," in A. Padgett (ed.), *Reason and the Christian Religion* (Oxford: Oxford University Press, 1994).

"Ecclesioethics: Theologically Neutral But Morally Toothless," *Professional Ethics*, 3 (1994).

"Religious Pluralism and Religious Relativism," *Scottish Journal of Religious Studies* (1994). Repr. in C. M. Lewis (ed.), *Relativism and Religion* (New York: Macmillan, 1995).

"Cosmopolitanism and Christianity," *Boston Review* 20/1 (1995).

"Political Liberalisms and Their Exclusions of the Religious," *Proceedings and Addresses of the American Philosophical Association*, 69/2 (1995). Repr. in P. Weithman (ed.), *Religion and Contemporary Liberalism* (Notre Dame: University of Notre Dame Press, 1997).

"When May Liberty Be Constrained," *Boston Review*, 20/4 (1995).

"Comments," in C. M. Lewis (ed.), *Relativism and Religion* (New York: Macmillan, 1995).

"Challenges to Philosophy and Its Organizations," *Proceedings and Addresses of the American Philosophical Association*, 69/2 (1995).

"Toward Thinner Theologies: Hick and Alston on Religious Diversity," *International Journal for Philosophy of Religion*, 38 (1995). Repr. in E. T. Long (ed.), *God, Reason and Religions* (Dordrecht: Kluwer, 1995). Repr. in P. Quinn and K. Meeker (eds.), *The Philosophical Challenge of Religious Diversity* (Oxford: Oxford University Press, 2000).

"Relativism about Torture: Religious and Secular Responses," in D. Z. Phillips (ed.), *Religion and Morality* (New York: St Martin's, 1996).

"The Divine Command Ethics in Kierkegaard's *Works of Love*," in J. Jordan and D. Howard-Snyder (eds.), *Faith, Freedom, and Rationality* (Totowa: Rowman and Littlefield, 1996).

"Some Puzzles about Moser's Conditional Ontological Agnosticism," *Philosophy and Phenomenological Research*, 56 (1996).

"Pluralism in Philosophy Departments," *Proceedings and Addresses of the American Philosophical Association*, 70/2 (1996).

"The Cultural Anthropology of Philosophy of Religion," in W. J. Wainwright (ed.), *God, Philosophy, and Academic Culture* (Scholars Press, 1996).

"Memorial for Jean E. Hampton," *Society of Christian Philosophers Newsletter* (1997).

"Sin and Original Sin," in P. Quinn and C. Taliaferro (eds.), *A Companion to Philosophy of Religion* (Oxford: Blackwell, 1997).

"Introduction" (with C. Taliaferro), in P. Quinn and C. Taliaferro (eds.), *A Companion to Philosophy of Religion* (Oxford: Blackwell, 1997).

"Resources for Further Study" (with C. Taliaferro), in P. Quinn and C. Taliaferro (eds.), *A Companion to Philosophy of Religion* (Oxford: Blackwell, 1997).

"Religious Ethics After *Ethics After Babel*: MacIntyre's Tradition vs Stout's *Bricolage*," in S. T. Davis (ed.), *Philosophy and Theological Discourse* (New York: Macmillan, 1997).

"Tiny Selves: Chisholm on the Simplicity of the Soul," in L. E. Hahn (ed.), *Roderick M. Chisholm*, Library of Living Philosophers (La Salle: Open Court, 1997).

"Religious Awe, Aesthetic Awe," in P. French, T. Uehling, and H. Wettstein (eds.), *Midwest Studies in Philosophy*, 21 (Notre Dame: University of Notre Dame Press, 1997).

"Evaluation of the Søren Kierkegaard Research Centre," *Hvordan er det gået*, Danmarks Grundforskniningsfond (1997).

"Kierkegaard's Christian Ethics," in A. Hannay and G. Marino (eds.), *Cambridge Companion to Kierkegaard* (Cambridge: Cambridge University Press, 1998).

"Augustinian Learning," in A. O. Rorty (ed.), *Philosophers on Education* (London: Routledge, 1998).

"The Virtue of Obedience," *Faith and Philosophy*, 15 (1998).

"Disputing the Augustinian Legacy: John Locke and Jonathan Edwards on Romans 5: 12–19," in G. B. Matthews (ed.), *The Augustinian Tradition* (Berkeley and Los Angeles: University of California Press, 1999).

"Yandell on Religious Experience," *International Journal for Philosophy of Religion*, 46 (1999).

"Epistemological Problems of Religious Pluralism," in K. L. Stoehr (ed.), *Proceedings of the Twentieth World Congress of Philosophy*, iv (Philosophy Documentation Center, 1999).

"How Christianity Secures Life's Meanings," in N. Martin and J. Runzo (eds.), *The Meaning of Life in the World Religions* (Oxford: Oneworld Publications–Penguin, 1999).

"Divine Command Theory," in H. LaFollette (ed.), *The Blackwell Guide to Ethical Theory* (Oxford: Blackwell, 1999).

"The Meaning of Life According to Christianity," in E. D. Klemke (ed.), *The Meaning of Life*, second edition (Oxford: Oxford University Press, 2000).

"Introduction" (with K. Meeker), in P. Quinn and K. Meeker (eds.), *The Philosophical Challenge of Religious Diversity* (Oxford: Oxford University Press, 2000).

"Divine Command Ethics," in A. Hastings (ed.), *The Oxford Companion to Christian Thought* (Oxford: Oxford University Press, 2000).

"Theories of Atonement," in A. Hastings (ed.), *The Oxford Companion to Christian Thought* (Oxford: Oxford University Press, 2000).

"Kantian Philosophical Ecclesiology," *Faith and Philosophy* (2000).

"Religious Citizens within the Limits of Public Reason," *Modern Schoolman* (2001).

"Can God Speak? Does God Speak?" *Religious Studies* (2001).

"Religious Diversity and Religious Toleration," *International Journal for Philosophy of Religion*, 50 (2001). Repr. in E. T. Long (ed.), *Issues in Contemporary Philosophy of Religion* (Dordrecht: Kluwer, 2001).

"Unity and Disunity, Harmony and Discord: A Response to Lillegard and Davenport," in J. Davenport and A. Rudd (eds.), *Kierkegaard After MacIntyre* (La Salle: Open Court, 2001).

"God and Morality," in J. Feinberg and R. Shafer-Landau (eds.), *Reason and Responsibility*, 11th edn. (Belmont, Calif.: Wadsworth, 2002).

"Obligation, Divine Commands and Abraham's Dilemma," *Philosophy and Phenomenological Research* (2002).

"Epistemology in Philosophy of Religion," in P. K. Moser (ed.), *The Oxford Handbook of Epistemology* (Oxford: Oxford University Press, 2002).

"Honoring Jonathan Edwards," *Journal of Religious Ethics* (2003).

"On Religious Diversity & Tolerance," *Daedalus* (2005).

"Religious Diversity: Familiar Problems, Novel Opportunities," in W. J. Wainwright (ed.), *The Oxford Handbook of Philosophy of Religion* (Oxford: Oxford University Press, 2005).

"Theological Voluntarism," in D. Copp (ed.), *The Oxford Handbook of Ethics* (Oxford: Oxford University Press, 2006).

"Christian Ethics and Human Rights," in N. Martin and J. Runzo (eds.), *Human Rights in the World Religions* (Oxford: Oneworld Publications, forthcoming).

"The Master Argument of *The Nature of True Virtue*," in P. Helm and O. Crisp (eds.), *Jonathan Edwards: Philosophical Theologian* (Aldershot: Ashgate Publishing, forthcoming).

"Religion and Politics," in W. Mann (ed.), *The Blackwell Guide to Philosophy of Religion* (Oxford: Blackwell, forthcoming).

"Religion and Politics, Fear and Duty," in J. Wallulis and J. Hackett (eds.), *Philosophy of Religion for a New Century: Essays in Honor of Eugene Thomas Long* (Dordrecht: Kluwer, forthcoming).

"Can Good Christians Be Good Liberals? On the Ambivalent Answer of Nicholas Wolterstorff," in A. Chignell and A. Dole (eds.), *God and the Ethics of Belief: New Essays in Philosophy of Religion* (Cambridge: Cambridge University Press, forthcoming).

"Critical Study of *Papers in Ethics and Social Philosophy* by D. Lewis," *Noûs* (forthcoming).

"Cosmological Contingeny and Theistic Explanation," *Faith and Philosophy* (forthcoming).

"Gale on a Pragmatic Argument for Religious Belief," *Philo* (forthcoming).

"Donagan on the Prospects for a Common Morality," final draft.

"Can the Christian God Be Both My Foundation and My Beloved?" final draft.

"Schleiermacher and the Problem of Religious Diversity," final draft.

Index